Macroeconomics without the Errors of Keynes

Modern macroeconomics is in a stalemate, with seven schools of thought attempting to explain the workings of a monetary economy and to derive policies that promote economic growth with price-level stability.

This book pinpoints as the source of this confusion errors made by Keynes in his reading of classical macroeconomics, in particular the classical Quantity Theory and the meaning of saving. It argues that if these misunderstandings are resolved, it will lead to economic policies consistent with promoting the employment and economic growth that Keynes was seeking.

The book will be crucial reading for all scholars with an interest in the foundations of Keynes's theories, and anyone seeking to understand current debates regarding macroeconomic policy-making.

James C. W. Ahiakpor is Professor Emeritus, Department of Economics, California State University, East Bay, USA.

Routledge Studies in the History of Economics

Business Cycles and Economic Crises
A Bibliometric and Economic History
Niels Geiger and Vadim Kufenko

A Contemporary Historiography of Economics
Edited by Till Düppe and Roy E. Weintraub

Money, Finance and Crises in Economic History
The Long-Term Impact of Economic Ideas
Edited by Annalisa Rosselli, Nerio Naldi and Eleonora Sanfilippo

Macroeconomic Theory and the Eurozone Crisis
Edited by Alain Alcouffe, Maurice Baslé and Monika Poettinger

The Economic Thought of Friedrich List
Edited by Harald Hagemann, Stephan Seiter and Eugen Wendler

Economic Crisis and Economic Thought
Alternative Theoretical Perspectives on the Economic Crisis
Edited by Tommaso Gabellini, Simone Gasperin and Alessio Moneta

Schumpeter's Capitalism, Socialism and Democracy
A Twenty-First-Century Agenda
Edited by Leonardo Burlamaqui and Rainer Kattel

Divine Providence in Early Modern Economic Thought
Joost Hengstmengel

Macroeconomics without the Errors of Keynes
The Quantity Theory of Money, Saving, and Policy
James C. W. Ahiakpor

For more information about this series, please visit www.routledge.com/series/ SE0341

Macroeconomics without the Errors of Keynes

The Quantity Theory of Money, Saving, and Policy

James C. W. Ahiakpor

LONDON AND NEW YORK

First published 2019 by Routledge

2 Park Square, Milton Park, Abingdon, Oxon, OX14 4RN
605 Third Avenue, New York, NY 10017

Routledge is an imprint of the Taylor & Francis Group, an informa business

First issued in paperback 2020

British Library Cataloguing-in-Publication Data
A catalogue record for this book is available from the British Library

Library of Congress Cataloging-in-Publication Data
A catalog record for this book has been requested

ISBN: 978-1-138-65856-1 (hbk)
ISBN: 978-0-367-72776-5 (pbk)

Typeset in Times New Roman
by Apex CoVantage, LLC

To all those working to restore macroeconomics to its classical roots from John Maynard Keynes's distortions

Contents

Figures

Tables

Preface

This book continues with my efforts to explain the extent of John Maynard Keynes's misrepresentations of classical macroeconomics to the detriment of finding resolution to the persistent disputes in modern macroeconomics. My earlier attempts are collected in the edited volume, *Keynes and the Classics Reconsidered* (1998a), and *Classical Macroeconomics: Some Modern Variations and Distortions* (2003). Some journal referees' encouraging comments before and since the publication of these books and my experiences with several reviewers for journals who have held staunchly onto Keynes's ideas have also motivated me to write this book. Letters from John Hicks in 1989 and Paul Samuelson in 1994, responding to my queries about their endorsement of Keynes's interest theory, as well as several communications with post-Keynesians have impressed on me the possibility of resolving the interminable disputes in modern macroeconomics by clarifying Keynes's misrepresentations of classical economic concepts.

Hicks did not defend Keynes's interest theory but referred me to his 1989 book in which he finally conceded the correctness of Alfred Marshall's restatement of the classical theory of interest. Samuelson instead declared Keynes not to have understood "his own system." However, Samuelson did not appreciate the significance of Keynes's misinterpreting "capital" in the classical theory of interest. Most of the post-Keynesians ultimately just gave up defending Keynes's arguments when presented with the writings of Marshall and classical economists.

Among the encouraging referees' comments is a 1988 report for the *History of Political Economy* on Keynes's misinterpretation of "capital" in the classical theory of interest. The report begins:

> This is an excellent paper which I read with very considerable enjoyment. It is an excellent counter to the absurd tradition, endlessly reiterated by writers like Joan Robinson, that Marshall had no theory of interest. Keynes's disgraceful misrepresentation of Marshall – when in truth much of Keynes's own treatment of money comes <u>from</u> Marshall – is the source of this. In a sense it is sad that this paper should be necessary at all but people will continue to take Keynes at his word.

There are so many good points in this paper that it is quite unnecessary to pick out the high points although I particularly liked pp. . . . . The point about the role of the Austrian approach to capital is particularly well-taken.

(underline original)

The article was published in 1990, but hardly has any serious Keynes scholar, including Milton Friedman (in Snowdon and Vane 1997a), David Laidler (1999, 2006), Robert Skidelsky (2016), Roger Backhouse (2006), Roger Backhouse and Bradley Bateman (2006, 2011), Mark Blaug (1995), or Axel Leijonhufvud (2006) paid any attention to it. Keynes's interest theory, out of which he derived the possibility of a liquidity trap, still dominates modern macroeconomic analysis.

However, H. H. Binhammer, author of a Canadian money and banking textbook, wrote in November 1990:

Thank you very much for sending along your two articles which I believe neatly put to rest the confusion between Keynes and the Classical economists over the determination of the rate of interest. I have always felt uncomfortable over the distinction which is made by most of us to this day. Old habits are not readily shed, and if one is not an authority over the history of economic thought one is reluctant to question the accepted gospel. You are to be congratulated for opening the book again on this shibboleth in such a well researched and expository manner.

An author of a Canadian macroeconomics textbook also wrote in November 1990, "Thank you for sending me your paper on Keynes' misinterpretation of capital. I enjoyed reading it. I think it may be a little esoteric for my intermediate principles book but you certainly make a convincing case. With best wishes."

To recommend acceptance of my manuscript explaining the error of Keynes's "paradox of thrift" for the *Southern Economic Journal*, a referee in 1994 began her/his report with: "This is an interesting, well researched and generally well written paper. It merits publication with only minor revisions. I judge it to be an above average work." The referee continues:

REPORT: The author effectively documents that Keynes altered the classicals' definition of the term "saving," and that as a result to him their theory of economic growth no longer appeared to be valid (*except* in conditions of full employment.) In addition, the author demonstrates that Keynes's invalid proposition about saving is still imposed upon undergraduates today. Moreover, many professional economists – including some of today's better known theorists – are themselves confused about why the algebra works out so neatly, while empirically the proposition itself is so clearly wrong. Finally, the author illustrates how subjectively (and down-right poorly) the job of reviewing is often done. (The author *must* leave in endnote #9!) [My endnote 9 reads: An anonymous reader of an earlier version of this article fails to find citations of "saving" in the index of "either the Wealth of Nations or Ricardo's

Principles," and concludes that "'saving' did not figure as a technical term in the discourse of the early classical writers," hence Keynes could not have misinterpreted them. But quotations from the classics equating saving with "capital" in this article, and which exclude hoarding, show otherwise.]

After the referee's suggested revisions, the report ends with: "COMMUNICA-TION TO AUTHOR: Thanks for persevering. In 16 years of reviewing for the SEJ this is one of only four papers for which the effort of reading brought its own reward. Remember Walras, and don't let the bastards grind you down!"

The article was published in 1995. Still, most macroeconomists, especially the neoclassical Keynesians, new Keynesians, and post-Keynesians, continue to treat saving as a withdrawal from the expenditure stream rather than being the source of investment funds – acquisition of fixed and circulating capital, the latter including the wages fund and cash-on-hand. The Keynesian interpretation of saving mars their analysis, as several chapters in this book will explain. The Austrian economists appear to be the exception; even as they may not all interpret saving exactly as in classical macroeconomics.

The latest very encouraging referee's report, for the *History of Economic Ideas* regarding my explaining the error of Keynes's liquidity-trap proposition (Ahiakpor 2018a), opens with:

This is what I am saying to the editor and so I will say it to you as well:

This is an extraordinarily good paper that must be published. It is comprehensive, thorough, convincing and important. It provides a deconstruction of Keynes's liquidity trap from a classical perspective that is long overdue. Papers such as this is what the history of economic thought is for.

The second referee's report starts with:

This is an interesting paper, well written, well researched, provocative, novel and enlightening from a classical perspective. It is thus worthy of publication, though my own view is that the author's strong endorsement of the classical analysis is itself more open to challenge than he concedes or acknowledges. Of course, Keynes himself challenged the classicals, and the author explains why he did so, without accepting Keynes's case.

Several other journals previously had rejected the manuscript mainly because it does not include the latest macro models. Thus, an editor's rejection letter for the *Journal of Money, Credit, and Banking* explains: "macro and monetary economics has moved away from the original Keynesian model"; the journal is rather interested in "stochastic dynamic general equilibrium models." Similarly, an editor for the *Journal of Macroeconomics* based his desk rejection on the ground that the manuscript does not have testable models! But mathematical economic models that are founded on the wrong conceptual foundations hardly yield meaningful conclusions. The failure of several highly regarded macroeconomists, including Milton Friedman (in Snowdon and Vane 1997a), David Laidler (1993b, 2004), and Paul Krugman (1998, 2013), to have recognized the fundamental errors of Keynes's liquidity-trap proposition, well illustrates the point.

I have had a similar experience with attempting to publish my explanation of David Ricardo's contemporaneous equivalence between debt and tax finance of government spending as his relevant argument rather than the intertemporal equivalence argued by Robert Barro (1976, 1989) and endorsed by James Buchanan (1976). The article was finally published in the *Journal of the History of Economic Thought* (2013). The journals whose editors summarily rejected the manuscript include *Journal of Political Economy*, *Economic Journal*, and *Journal of Public Economics*. Their principal reason was that my paper was not testing the Ricardian equivalence theorem with data. But nearly two decades of data testing of Barro's proposition yielded no firm conclusions because Barro's formulation relies on Keynes's definition of saving as non-spending, which is incorrect. Also, it is nearly impossible to collect data on individuals' reasons for saving in the form of acquiring government bonds or some other financial assets.

The chapters in this book explain the alternative conclusions that derive from interpreting such important macroeconomic concepts as money, saving, "capital," and investment in the classical tradition rather than in Keynes's understanding and not attributing to classical macroeconomics the assumption that full employment of labor always exists. It will be shown that Milton Friedman's (1968b) concession, "We are all Keynesians now. . . . We all use Keynes's language and apparatus," has not served macro and monetary analysis well. Correcting Keynes's errors of interpreting classical economic concepts also has the potential of facilitating a greater degree of consensus in economic policy formulation.

James C. W. Ahiakpor
November 2018

Acknowledgments

Writing this book has benefitted from the helpful comments of my colleagues at California State University, East Bay, on various papers that form the chapters. Notable among them are Charles Baird, Greg Christainsen, Shyam Kamath, and Steve Shmanske. Comments I received at the various conferences at which I discussed the papers have been helpful as well. I would like to recognize especially those by John Berdell, Patrick Deutscher, Bruce Littleboy, Don Matthews, Roger Sandilands, and George Tavlas. However, none of them is responsible for any remaining errors of my arguments. Those are mine.

It has been very helpful to have received travel support from the College of Business and Economics (CBE) to present my papers at conferences. Having the often skeptical reactions from conference participants to my arguments critical of Keynes's distortion of the language of macroeconomics has been very stimulating. I am therefore very grateful to CBE for the travel support.

I have benefitted from anonymous referees too. The dissenters among them have shown me the forms in which I better may clarify my arguments, although not all of them have been helpful. I have cited some of them in the chapters to illustrate their unhelpfulness. The supportive referees have sustained my hope that it is possible to rescue modern macroeconomics from its stalemate, owing mainly to its adoption of Keynes's "language and apparatus," as Milton Friedman (1968b) has acknowledged. Both the Preface and some chapters include examples of the supportive comments.

Finally, I would like to thank the editorial team at Routledge, beginning with Ms. Emily Kindleysides. She was my first contact, who processed the initial submission, including finding reviewers. She also helped with framing the final title of the book. Ms. Laura Johnson and Ms. Natalie Tomlinson have taken turns answering my queries. Their suggestions have been helpful. They also are absolved from any defects of argument in my book.

1 Introduction

The sorry, puzzling state of macroeconomics after Keynes's *General Theory*

That modern macroeconomics is currently in a sorry and puzzling state may be gauged by its including at least seven schools of thought, six of whose members have been awarded the Nobel Prize in economic science. The schools include (i) Neoclassical Keynesians, (ii) New Keynesians, (iii) post-Keynesians, (iv) Monetarists, (v) New Classicals, (vi) Real Business Cycle Theorists, and (vii) Austrians.[1] The post-Keynesians have yet to earn the Nobel Prize. Each school claims to present the best explanation of the workings of the macroeconomy: determination of output, employment, the level of prices, inflation, the level of interest rates, variations in exchange rates, and the appropriate fiscal and monetary policies. In a sense, the multiplicity of schools is an indication of the inadequacies of the explanations each school has given, in spite of the massive amounts of statistical verifications of their explanations. Hardly is any other social science plagued with so many competing claims for relevance.

My book offers an explanation for this sorry and puzzling state of macroeconomics since the publication of John Maynard Keynes's *General Theory* (1936), mainly in terms of the failure of macroeconomists to address Keynes's changed meaning of economic concepts in "classical" macroeconomics, including saving, capital, investment, and money. Several reviewers of Keynes's book in 1936 and 1937, including A. C. Pigou (1936), Dennis Robertson (1936), Jacob Viner (1936), and Frank Knight (1937), pointed out his having misrepresented classical economic concepts. Thus Viner (1936; italics added) notes:

> The book . . . breaks with traditional modes of approach to . . . problems . . . and no old term for an old concept is used when a new one can be coined, and if old terms are used new meanings are generally attached to them. . . . The old-fashioned economist must, therefore, struggle not only with new ideas and new methods of manipulating them, but also with a *new language*.

Knight (1937) observes: "familiar terms and modes of expression seem to be shunned on principle in this book" (108), while Pigou (1936) refers to Keynes's use of terms as "loose and inconsistent" (119–20); Ahiakpor (1998a: Ch. 2) elaborates. Some reviewers also noted Keynes's having attributed to classical analysis assumptions they do not hold, including there always being the full employment of labor and a rapid or instantaneous adjustment of market prices.

Paul Samuelson, easily the most effective disseminator of Keynes's economics at the undergraduate level around the world, reflects the power of Keynes's misattribution of the assumptions of full employment and all markets continually clearing to classical macroeconomics. He studied economics for his first degree at the University of Chicago (1932–35), taking courses from the likes of Aron Director, Lloyd Mints, and Henry Simons, and "from 1932 to 1936 I was besotted on Frank Knight" (Colander and Landreth 1996: 148). He claims initially to have "resisted" Keynes's arguments in the *General Theory* (Colander and Landreth 1996: 159) but finally "succumbed" to them during his graduate studies at Harvard (1936–40) because the world around him in the 1930s did not fit the Walrasian assumptions being taught (Samuelson 1985: 11; Colander and Landreth 1996: 153, 160, 163).[2] Mostly, Samuelson just stopped pursuing the puzzlements he initially found in the *General Theory*, rather feeling "like a tuna: the Keynesian system had to land me, and I was fighting every inch of the line" (ibid.: 159, 161).

But Frank Taussig's (1921) copious descriptions of the nature and causes of economic recessions and depressions, accompanied by increased unemployment in the US (besides England and continental Europe) as well as the possible cures in Volume 1, Chapter 28, "Crises," and Chapter 29, "Financial Panics," leave little justification for Samuelson's "succumbing" excuse. Regarding financial panics, Taussig concludes:

> In the main, oscillations of industry must be accepted as inevitable concomitants of the regime of private property. They may be mitigated, but they are not likely to cease. . . . Helpless embarrassment, halting production, hardship and *suffering* for the *unemployed laborers* – these are held up by the socialist critics, not without show of reason, as damning facts.
>
> (1921, 1: 413–4; italics added)

J.-B. Say's *Treatise* (1821a: 142) also lists among the "greatest obstructions" to production, resulting in increased unemployment, "wars, embargoes, oppressive duties," as well as "times of alarm and uncertainty . . . and speculation." Samuelson could have related some of Say's causes to the banking crises of the early 1930s, resulting in the significant contraction of savings and investment along with the disappearance of nine thousand banks in the US, besides the 1930 Smoot-Hawley Tariff Act, rather than to have accepted Keynes's "demand deficiency" explanation of the depression.[3] But to correctly employ the classical arguments, Samuelson needed to interpret saving, capital, investment, and money as they, not Keynes (1936), did. He instead gave macroeconomics the Keynesian cross and balanced-budget multiplier arguments (Colander and Landreth 1996: 166).[4]

J. R. Hicks (1937) papers over criticisms of Keynes's book by creating his now familiar IS-LM (originally IS-LL) model as a vehicle to sort out disagreements between Keynes and his critics – the early, most effective propagator of Keynes's ideas. Subsequent protestations against the model's mischaracterization of classical arguments, including the existence always of full employment by Pigou (1941), left little mark on the Keynes-versus-the-classics debate. Rather, the position of full employment of labor has become depicted as an economy's long-run equilibrium position towards which the classical theorists claimed a monetary economy automatically returns on its own, if only the government simply stays out of the way. Mark Blaug (1996: 641–2) restates the mischaracterization:

> The idea that the competitive process continually drives the economy back towards a steady state of full employment whenever it falls below the full-capacity utilization of the capital stock permeated all macroeconomic thinking before Keynes. Indeed, it was so widely held that it was frequently implied rather than argued explicitly. If there is anything profoundly new in Keynes it is this deliberate assault on the faith in the inherent recuperative powers of the market mechanism.

But the claim confuses the argument that free-market enterprise or capitalism is more conducive to the most wealth creation and employment opportunities for labor with a claim that government has no positive role in an economy (see Adam Smith's [1776] "legitimate functions" of government). Classical laissez-faire capitalism is not anarcho-libertarianism. Money and public confidence, the two important variables in short supply during the Great Depression, do not automatically create themselves in classical analysis; Chapter 5 elaborates on this point.

Keynes (1924: 88; italics original) earlier had ridiculed classical long-run analysis with the quip: "this *long run* is a misleading guide to current affairs. *In the long run* we are all dead." In fact, in the monetary long run, the population is greater than in the short run. Keynes (1935: xxiii) also explains that the "composition of this book has been for the author a long struggle of escape . . . from habitual modes of thought and expression." In his September 1936 preface to the German edition, Keynes (1936: xxv) adds that he had been "brought up" in the Ricardian economics tradition of Alfred Marshall's *Principles*: "I taught these theories myself and it is only within the last decades that I have been conscious of their insufficiency." Thus, without a clear explanation of Keynes's misrepresentations of classical concepts, not much of which was forthcoming from R. G. Hawtrey, Pigou, and Robertson (Keynes's undergraduate student), his arguments appeared persuasive (see also Robert Leeson 1998).

From the IS-LM model, it is not clear that

i   saving means acquiring interest- and/or dividend-earning financial assets by households in classical economics (Smith *WN*, 1: 358; Marshall 1920: 191–6, 443–4, 482–4) whereas saving and cash hoarding are indistinguishable in their effects on the economy, according to Keynes's (1936: 167) definition;

ii   savings are spent by borrowers in classical economics (Smith *WN*, 1: 359; Marshall and Marshall 1879: 34, cited in Keynes 1936: 19) whereas savings are a withdrawal from the expenditure stream in Keynes's (1936: 210) definition;

iii   capital means loanable funds or savings by households that are employed in production as fixed and circulating capital, including the wages fund and cash-on-hand, in classical economics (Smith *WN*, 1: 294–9; Marshall 1920: 60–3), but capital means only capital goods in Keynes's (1936: 62) definition;

iv   investment means purchasing interest- and/or dividend-earning assets by income earners in classical economics (Smith *WN*, 1: 358–60; Marshall 1923: 46) or employing funds in the sphere of production as in (iii) above versus the purchase or production of capital goods only in Keynes's (1930: 2, 207; 1936: 62) definition; and

v   money means only cash (specie or a central bank's fiat notes) in classical economics (Smith *WN*, 1: 308–10; Marshall 1923: 39; Pigou 1917) versus money variously defined as central bank money only in some contexts (Keynes 1936: 174) and central bank money plus commercial bank deposits and such financial assets as government treasury bills in some others (ibid.: 167, n. 1).

But it is Keynes's definitions and the assumptions that he attributed to the classics that Hicks and subsequent analysts have employed in the development of post-1936 macroeconomics. As Milton Friedman (1968b:15) declares: "We are all Keynesians now. . . . We all use the Keynesian language and apparatus." Friedman (1970a: 133) also calls the *General Theory* "a great book."

The IS-LM model has little room, as in Say's Law, for the equilibrating process of a monetary economy whereby variations in the relative prices of goods and services, changes in the value of money, and variations in interest rates necessarily cause changes in the production of goods and services, money (in a commodity money system), and savings by households that fund investment spending. The model excludes the insights of Say's Law because Keynes (1936: 25, 26) misrepresents it as having claimed, "Supply creates its own Demand,"[5] and "there is no obstacle to full employment." In fact, the law applies only to produced commodities, whose quantities in the marketplace vary depending upon the profitability of their sale: "*productions can only be purchased by productions*" (Say 1821b: 13; italics original). Say's primary statement of his law, "the mere circumstance of the creation of one product immediately opens a vent for other products" (1821a: 134–5), also shows its distortion by Keynes.

Yet David Laidler (1999: 3; italics added) contends that

> there was no overthrow of an old economic orthodoxy after 1936. What happened was altogether more mundane, though perhaps a good deal *more useful*: economics acquired a new formal model, around which there would, in due course, develop an orthodox body of analysis called macroeconomics.

He argues: "IS-LM was coherent and easily taught and grasped, and it provided a logical basis for policy conclusions that already had widespread support" (1999: 320). However, Laidler, like most other Keynes adherents, does not address any of the above problems with Keynes's changed meaning of classical economic concepts (see also Laidler 2006).[6] In his extensive study of the development of modern macroeconomics since Keynes, Michel de Vroey (2016) also ignores the conceptual confusions introduced by Keynes through his changed definitions. In fact, macroeconomists concerned about the truthfulness of what they teach, should present the IS-LM model as mostly reflecting Keynes's thought rather than as accurately representing the workings of a monetary economy.

Until Hicks (1980/81) declared his dissatisfaction with the IS-LM model, he defended the model's realism and argued the lack of consistency in classical arguments with a monetary economy.[7] Don Patinkin, particularly his *Money, Interest, and Prices* (1965 [1956]), has served further to distill Keynes's economics for many graduate students. The text has also been very effective in communicating Keynes's arguments since it surveys classical and early neoclassical writers' analyses of which Keynes was critical. But Patinkin's conclusions invariably favor Keynes's arguments. Friedman sought to defend the classical Quantity Theory against Keynes's (1936) criticism as being irrelevant to an economy in depression. But, beginning with his 1956 "restatement" of the Quantity Theory, Friedman's work has undermined that theory.

First, Friedman declares the theory not to be about the level of prices, but about the demand for "money." Secondly, Friedman adopts Keynes's broad definition of money (M1 and M2). Worse yet, Friedman (2008: 803) declares: "Keynes did not deny the validity of the quantity theory, in any of its forms – after all, he had been a major contributor to the quantity theory." Indeed, most of Friedman's monetarism is merely an extension of Keynes's monetary analysis to encompass more assets than do Keynesians (see Friedman 1970a: 28–9; 1970b: 25). Friedman (2008: 806) explains:

> The difference between the quantity theorists [monetarists] and the Keynesians is less in the nature of the process [of adjustment] than in the range of assets considered. The Keynesians tend to concentrate on a narrow range of marketable assets and recorded interest rates. The quantity theorists insist that a far wider range of assets and interest rates must be taken into account – such assets as durable and semi-durable consumer goods, structures, and other real property.

Much of modern macro and monetary analysis has proceeded following Friedman's lead (e.g., Laidler 1969, 1993b). Such treatment of the Quantity Theory has inhibited a clear understanding of the proper role of a central bank, which is to stabilize the level of prices or target a zero inflation rate rather than attempt to control the growth of M1 or M2. It has also inhibited recognition of the impossibility of Keynes's liquidity trap proposition at a theoretical level, let alone in practice: income earners have better things to do than to hoard all their incomes in cash simply because interest rates have fallen to some low level (Ahiakpor 2018a). Remarkably, Friedman also granted the theoretical possibility of the liquidity trap (see Snowdon and Vane 1997a: 196).

Joseph Schumpeter's *Ten Great Economists: From Marx to Keynes* (1951) and *History of Economic Analysis* (1954) both praise Keynes's contributions to macroeconomic analysis, without pointing out his misrepresentations of classical concepts. The first book includes Schumpeter's 1946 memoriam in the *American Economic Review*, whose praise of Keynes's arguments against classical analysis creates difficulties for easy recognition of Keynes's errors. Rather than noting the problems with Keynes's changed meaning of economic concepts, including saving not to mean the purchase of interest- and/or dividend-earning assets, Schumpeter thinks "Distinctive terminology helps to drive home the points an author wishes to make and to focus his reader's attention" (1946: 510, n. 25). He argues: "every economist *should* have known that the Turgot-Smith-J. S. Mill theory of the saving and investment mechanism was inadequate and that, in particular, saving and investment decisions were linked together too closely" (513; italics original); "the theory, according to which the investment demand for savings and the supply of savings that is governed by time-preference . . . is equated by the rate of interest[,] breaks down" (514); "the decision to save does not *necessarily* imply a decision to invest; we must also take account of the possibility that the latter does not follow or not follow promptly" (ibid.; italics original); and "many more of us will now listen to the proposition that interest is a purely monetary phenomenon than were ready to listen 35 years ago" (ibid.). Schumpeter here reflects his own "Austrian" economics background that is hostile to the classical "capital" supply and demand theory of interest (Ahiakpor 1997b). Schumpeter writes: "I wish however to welcome [Keynes's] purely monetary theory of interest which is, as far as I can see, the first to follow upon my own" (1936: 795).[8] Schumpeter also does not acknowledge that savings are borrowed to be spent quickly (see also Schumpeter [1954] 1994: 323–5).[9]

Schumpeter (1946) reports having received a note from a "prominent American economist" remarking the "salutary effects of a fresh breeze" that was Keynes's *General Theory*. The note adds: "It did, and does, have something which supplements what our thinking and methods of analysis would otherwise have been. It does not make us Keynesians, it makes us better economists" (1946: 517). Schumpeter cites the message as "express[ing] the essential point about Keynes's achievement extremely well" (ibid.), rather than the author's failure to appreciate the extent of Keynes's misrepresentations of classical economic analysis. An alternative assessment by Henry Simons (1936) is that Keynes's "attacks, not [on] the bad applications of traditional theory, but [on] the theory itself . . . will impress only the incompetent" (cited in Roger Backhouse 1999: 68).

However, other than having endorsed Keynes's interest theory, Schumpeter's (1936) review of Keynes's *General Theory* mostly criticizes his arguments, including Keynes's having employed the "technique of skirting problems by *artificial definitions* which, tied up with highly specialized assumptions, produce paradoxical-looking tautologies, and of constructing special cases which in the author's mind and in his exposition are invested with a treacherous generality" (1936: 702; italics added). He also criticizes Keynes's presumption of a constant labor-output coefficient in production, that is, that Keynes's "reasoning on the assumption that variations in output are uniquely related to variations in employment imposes the further assumption that all production functions remain invariant" (1936: 704).

Schumpeter's *History of Economic Analysis* served for a long time as a standard reference in the history of economic analysis or thought, particularly at the graduate level. In that text, Schumpeter ([1954] 1994: 1171) argues, "Keynes was Ricardo's peer in the highest sense of the phrase," and Keynes's return to the pre-classical (mercantilist) money supply and demand theory of interest, "from the standpoint of theoretical analysis alone, [was] perhaps the most important contribution of the *General Theory*" (1178, n. 16).

Subsequent texts in the history of economic thought, including Mark Blaug (1996) and Robert Ekelund, Jr. and Robert Hébert (2014), similarly praise Keynes's contributions to modern macroeconomics without reference to his misrepresentations of classical economic concepts. Blaug finds nothing wrong with Keynes's "entirely new suggestion that it is variations in output or income rather than variations in the rate of interest that work to equate saving with investment. With it came the equally novel idea that it is investment and not saving that sparks off changes in income" (1996: 641). He does not address the question of how anyone could invest without employing borrowed funds or their own savings. Blaug also adopts Keynes's misrepresentation of classical economics, arguing: "orthodox economics . . . undoubtedly included the faith that competitive forces are capable of driving the economy towards a steady state of full employment without the assistance of governments" (1996: 675). He ignores Pigou's (1913) recommending counter-cyclical government spending, for example. John Stuart Mill's (*Works*, 3: 516, 574) explanation of a commercial crisis generating an excess demand for money, causing rising interest rates, and falling prices all around, for as long as the supply of money has not adequately responded or the public's shaken confidence been restored, also contradicts Blaug's repetition of Keynes's claim. Such was the case during the Great Depression that Keynes cited as invalidating the relevance of classical economics outside of full employment.[10] But from his incomplete representation of classical analysis, Blaug (1996) concludes: "the Keynesian Revolution marked the true end of the 'doctrine of laissez faire'" (642); moreover, "Keynes had one critical advantage over his orthodox contemporaries: he was right!" (675).

Ekelund and Hébert (2014) consider Keynes "a superb historian of [economic] thought" (532, n. 4) and "a first rate theorist" (551). They also do not address Keynes's changed meaning of economic terms. Thus, they employ Keynes's definitions of saving and investment to fault the meaningfulness of Say's Law: "The classics reasoned that at interest rate r_0 savings equaled investment, which meant that what is not spent on consumption goods (saved) was invested (spent on capital goods). A flexible interest rate mechanism guaranteed this result" (2014: 533). But, according to classical theory, saving is purchasing interest- and/or dividend-earning assets supplied by borrowers or depository institutions, while investment means more than spending the borrowed funds on capital goods only.

Axel Leijonhufvud (1981: 132–3) similarly claims the interest rate mechanism could fail to coordinate savings and investment decisions as the classics presumed and create economic dislocation exactly as Keynes (1936) alleges – Leijonhufvud's so-called "coordination failures" hypothesis. But Leijonhufvud does not recognize that it is the supply and demand for loanable funds that the rate of interest coordinates instead of savings and the demand for *capital goods*. Such has been the evolution of modern macroeconomics that it employs Keynes's changed language or definitions that fail to describe correctly the workings of a monetary macroeconomy.

Confronted with Keynes's misrepresentations of classical macroeconomics, most Keynes adherents tend to shrug them off. They would rather we focused on Keynes's main goal of finding solutions to the problem of unemployment, not whether he understood correctly what he read in "classical" economics. "Keynes saved capitalism for the world with his policy prescriptions; so what if he did not correctly understand what classical economics says?" seems to be their inclination. It is with such inclination that Terrence Hutchison (1981) also fails to recognize Keynes's distortions of classical economic concepts and focuses mainly on assessing how consistent Keynes's young followers, particularly Joan Robinson, Richard Kahn, and Nicholas Kaldor, were in their policy recommendations in the 1950s and 1960s with Keynes's own ideas. He disagrees with "the views of Professors Hayek and Johnson that Keynes's doctrines were fatally erroneous *from the start*" (1981: 111; italics original; see also Backhouse and Bateman 2011). Thus, a commentator on the Post-Keynesian Thought debating forum in November 1995 reacted to my explaining Keynes's changed meaning of economic terms with the declaration: "I have plenty of arguments with Keynes and his followers, but next to him we're scribes and pipsqueaks. As I think Lou Reed once said, his day beat our week. I don't give a damn how much he did or didn't know about Marshall or Pigou or anyone. . . . as Harold Bloom said of poets, all original minds misinterpret their predecessors, often quite heroically."

The comment is similar to a surprising 4 February 1992 response I received from Paul Samuelson to my 1990 *HOPE* article documenting Keynes's misinterpretation of "capital" in the classical theory of interest and that being his primary reason for failing to recognize the validity of that theory in Marshall's *Principles*. Samuelson writes:

> On reflection I have some doubts as to whether a closer reading by [Keynes] of S-R-M(ill), B-B, Irving Fisher, or Marshall would have made much difference. Nor would it perhaps have mattered much if he had read Marshall and Pigou more carefully or if Marshall had been more optimally unfuzzy in his textbook expositions. (For a scholar with keen insights at bottom, Marshall is amazingly slippery in his wordages on so many subjects!)

More surprising is Samuelson's view that Keynes did not understand "his own system" regarding the theory of interest:

> But Keynes never (or often fails to) understands his own system. In the (1937?) Fisher *Festschrift* he writes stupidly: "Here is a test to separate classical fools from wise disciples of mine. Increase technical potentialities of capital and investment while holding M constant. If you think that raises r,

you are a classical fool." (I write from imperfect memory and use *my* words.) Actually, a rise in the marginal efficiency schedule will, in Keynes's own simple system, raise r! [It leads to more I, more nominal Y, more need for transaction M_1, so that reduced $M_2 = M - M_1$ will raise r on the liquidity preference schedule. The loanable funds zealots can work out their Esperanto version of the same substance.]

On my substantive point about Keynes's misinterpretation of "capital" in the classical theory of interest, Samuelson showed no recognition:

The fol-der-rol about "funds," " advances," "circulating" vs "fixed capital," which is so garbled among the classicals, and JSM, Thornton, Taussig, and others, really has nothing to do with what is wrong and what is right about 1936 Model T Keynesianism, in the short and long run and as compared with say 1950, 1992, or other times. Keynes for much of his lifetime was fuzzy on simultaneous equation equilibrium. M can affect r in a L-P $M + L(Y,r)$ function and still r can be affected by a rise in the parameter a in the marg-efficiency function $I = a + F(r, Y; k, \ldots)$.

Samuelson could have benefited from a more careful reading of the classics and the early neoclassicals to appreciate the significance of the meanings of capital involved in their disputes.[11] That appears still to be a problem with most modern macroeconomists.

In response to my 1989 letter asking why J. R. Hicks did not recognize Keynes's misinterpretation of "capital" in Marshall's statement of the classical theory of interest, he also gave no direct answer. Instead, Hicks writes (2 May 1989):

I am sorry to have to inform you that there is a chapter in my forthcoming book *A Market Theory of Money* . . . which contains a careful statement of my present views on the dispute on interest theory. I know that what I have said in this place has the approval of Prof. S. C. Tsiang, who always thought that what I said in V&C [Value and Capital] was wrong. So I fear that there will be more to be said before you can go into press. . . .

There was practically no professional teaching in Oxford until the year when I took my degree (1925). In that year Harrod was appointed at Christ Church. I learned my economics, from 1926 onwards while I was supposed to be teaching at LSE. See the autobiographical papers in my *Collected Essays*.

My letter was attached to a paper in which I disputed a referee's claim that Hicks had sorted out Keynes's confusion over the theory of interest long before my 1990 *HOPE* article. Hicks (1989: 78) indeed grants Marshall victory over Keynes on the theory of interest, but not from having clarified Keynes's misinterpretation of "capital." Thus, Keynes's liquidity-preference theory of interest still dominates modern macroeconomics.

N. Gregory Mankiw (1992) also well illustrates some analysts' attitude towards explaining Keynes's misrepresentations of classical macro-monetary analysis. He considers the first among his six "dubious Keynesian propositions" the need to understand what Keynes himself wrote: "Moreover, after fifty years of additional progress in economic science, the *General Theory* is an outdated book. The rigor with which we develop economic theories and the data and statistical techniques with which we test out theories were unknown half a century ago. We are in a much better position than Keynes was to figure out how the economy works" (cited in Snowdon and Vane 1997b: 446–7). But applying powerful statistical techniques to the wrong data because of the wrong definition of variables could hardly yield the correct conclusions. For example, defining investment as only the purchase of capital goods rather than the employment of borrowed or one's own savings in the sphere of production must find a rather weak or non-existent causal relation between savings and investment, as Keynesian economics argues, at least for the short run; Robert Solow's (1956) growth model argues otherwise for the long run. Also, defining money, not as central bank currency, but inclusive of the public's bank deposits, has led to fruitless attempts to test for the existence of Keynes's alleged liquidity trap (Laidler 1993b: 152).

Thus, the neoclassical Keynesians focus on government's aggregate demand management policies to deal with unemployment and economic recessions, just as Keynes (1936: Ch. 24) argues: "The central controls necessary to ensure full employment will, of course, involve a large extension of the traditional functions of government" (379). Snowdon and Vane (1997b: 6) summarize their view as arguing that "the classical model recognizes only the supply constrained regime, whereas Keynes and Keynesians believe that the economy is capable, at different times, of being in either [the supply or demand constrained] regime." The neoclassical Keynesians appear to ignore the fact that, except for borrowing from a central bank or foreigners, governments cannot spend without first taking the funds from the public through taxation or borrowing (Ahiakpor 2013) and that there is no positive government expenditure multiplier effect (Ahiakpor 2001).[12] J. S. Mill (1874) well explains the error of the Keynesian positive view of government spending in his day, still relevant now:

> The utility of a large government expenditure, for the purpose of encouraging industry, is no longer maintained. Taxes are not now esteemed to be "like the dews of heaven which return again in prolific showers." It is no longer supposed that you benefit the producer by taking his money, provided you give it to him again in exchange for his goods. There is nothing which impresses a person of reflection with a stronger sense of the shallowness of the political reasonings of the last two centuries, than the general reception so long given to a doctrine which, if it proves anything, proves that the more you take from the pockets of the people to spend on your own pleasures, the richer they grow.
>
> (47–8)

The new Keynesians correct some of the assumptions underlying neoclassical Keynesianism, including their acknowledging rigidity in the prices of goods and labor. They nevertheless proceed as if government spending is not at the expense of private sector spending or that a positive government expenditure multiplier effect exists (see, e.g., Mankiw 1992). Some among the new Keynesians also believe in the ability of a central bank to control real interest rates (Romer 2000), which is impossible. A central bank controls only its own rate of currency creation, which in the short run may influence the level of nominal interest rates and the rate of inflation. But a central bank cannot control the level of equilibrium nominal interest rates – the price-level and expectations effects counter the liquidity effect of currency creation – and thus it cannot control the level of real interest rates. I elaborate further on this subject in Chapter 9.

The post-Keynesians appear to have no use for equilibrating market models, such as the IS-LM, or wage rate determination in the labor market (see, e.g., Galbraith and Darity 1994). Their focus, however, is on designing policies to promote increased employment through income redistribution from the rich to the poor, because the latter have a higher marginal propensity to consume (see Dow 2017 for a recent example). The view derives mostly from Keynes's representing saving as a withdrawal from the expenditure stream, whereas the state of employment is determined by "aggregated demand," and Keynes's denial that savings supply most of the loanable funds or credit for investment (1937c: 668–9). The post-Keynesians' concern over income inequality thus becomes a hindrance to their accepting the validity of classical economics since the latter emphasizes the importance of savings, rather than consumption, to promote economic growth and employment.

Besides, savings are spent by borrowers and consumed reproductively: "What is annually saved is as regularly consumed as what is annually spent, and nearly in the same time too; but it is consumed by a different set of people" (Smith *WN*, 1: 359). Moreover, Smith argues the protection of private property and easy taxes as prerequisites for promoting the prosperity of nations: "Little else is requisite to carry a state to the highest degree of opulence from the lowest barbarism but peace, easy taxes, and a tolerable administration of justice: all the rest being brought about by the natural course of things."[13]

Some post-Keynesians also attempt to explain inflation as resulting from a struggle between profits and wage rates (see, e.g., Kregel 1989) rather than from the excessive growth of money's supply relative to the growth of its demand. They have no use for the classical Quantity Theory as an explanation of the level of prices, emphasizing instead the possible use of mark-up pricing above wage costs by firms. They seem to ignore the fact that, if mark-up pricing really were always operational, no firms would ever make losses. Besides, an economy is not one giant factory whose managers could implement the mark-up pricing technique to determine commodity prices. The post-Keynesians also appear unique among the competing schools of thought in emphasizing the endogeneity of money (M1 or M2), which thus cannot be controlled by a central bank. However, they fail to recognize that the modern equivalent of classical money is not M1 or M2, but central bank money (H) only, whose quantity is determined only by a central bank (Pigou 1917).

But all the above three schools of thought in the Keynesian tradition believe in the power of activist government spending to promote economic prosperity. Remarkably, some post-Keynesians also deny the meaningfulness of analyzing an aggregate labor market (Galbraith and Darity 1994: 393), the very point Pigou (1933: 63) makes, but which Keynes ignored: "a general demand function for labour cannot be obtained by adding together the different demand functions for different sets of [employment] centres." Such is the irony of some post-Keynesians in citing "classical" arguments in defense of their adherence to Keynes's criticisms of "classical" macroeconomic analysis. However, in illustrating Keynes's discussion of involuntary unemployment as having nothing to do with the labor market clearing, William Darity, Jr. and Arthur Goldsmith (1995) still use the aggregate labor demand and supply curves.

The other four schools of macroeconomic thought are skeptical of, or reject, the possible beneficial effects of government spending policies beyond some minimal level. Monetarism emphasizes inflation and deflation as both monetary phenomena: inflation arising from the excessive creation of money, and deflation from an inadequate creation of money (e.g., Friedman 1970a). To argue the efficacy of free markets and the propensity for government intervention to be more of a hindrance to the efficiency of markets, Friedman, the leader of that school, cites the Great Depression as proof. He indicts the US Federal Reserve System for having failed to prevent a one-third monetary contraction (M1 and M2) and thus to have caused the catastrophe, when, in fact, the Fed did expand the high-powered money (H), the only magnitude it can control, by more than 20 percent over the period. Rather, the Fed's actions had been frustrated by gold exports and the domestic hoarding of both gold and currency by the public (see Chapter 5 below for an elaboration on this point).

The new classicals take Friedman's monetary analysis and free-market prescriptions a step further by introducing the possibility of rational expectations on the part of the public (Lucas and Sargent 1978). Thus, they tend to deny the short-run positive effect of monetary growth on output and employment that monetarism allows, except for unanticipated changes in monetary policy. If the public fully expects a central bank's increased rate of money creation, the new classicals argue that the public would immediately reduce their rate of saving and neutralize the liquidity effect of money's increase. Wage contracts may also be designed such that nominal wage rates would immediately rise in anticipation of the increased money supply's effect on prices, thus assuring no reductions in real wage rates. The short-run non-neutrality of money that generates the downward-sloping Phillips curve would then turn into a vertical Phillips curve. But the unreality of the public's inability to anticipate fully a central bank's actions has left the new classical proposition in the realm of theoretical speculation, with very few adherents (Clower and Howitt 1998).[14]

The real business cycle theorists find little basis for recognizing the ability of a central bank to affect the growth of output and employment with changes in the rate of money creation (Nelson and Plosser 1982; Kydland and Prescott 1982). They argue that real economic shocks, such as technological innovations, are the drivers of economic or business cycles to which a central bank's money creation merely responds. They claim support for their view from econometric estimates of total factor productivity changes in various countries. But evidence of real economic disturbances related to central banks' monetary policies or the effects of financial market disturbances around the world undermine much adherence to their view. Temin 2008 is an effective critique of their work.

Finally, the Austrian economists argue against belief in the efficacy of government intervention in the economy. The modern Austrians draw most of their theoretical insights from the works of Carl Menger and Eugen Böhm-Bawerk, who were critical of classical economic analysis (Ahiakpor 1997b). They reject the classical "capital" supply and demand theory of interest and argue their combination of time-preference and capital productivity theory. They fail to recognize the fact that the classical theory of interest already embodies the role of time preference: consumption decisions affect the savings rate or supply of "capital" or loanable funds. The modern Austrians also reject the classical Quantity Theory as a theory of inflation, preferring to analyze prices in individual markets. They apparently have paid little attention to Hume's (1752, "Of Money") explanation of the level of prices from individual commodity markets, an argument J. S. Mill (*Works*, 3: 509, 515) elaborates on, rather than Keynes's supply and demand for "output as a whole" determining the "price level" (see Chapter 3 below for further explanation on this subject).

Some Austrians also advocate free banking, that is, the freedom of commercial banks to issue their own notes in place of a central bank's monopoly of note issue, as the most efficient monetary system (see Chapter 6 below for a critique of their argument). Others prescribe, along with some monetarists (e.g., Friedman 1960), 100 percent reserve banking as a means of preserving financial stability. They appear to ignore the economy's huge opportunity cost in terms of the tremendous growth of output and employment that fractional-reserve banking promotes (see Smith *WN*, 1: 340–1).

Since the 1970s, the Austrians have recovered some of the following in economics that they lost during the 1930s, from their advocacy of no central bank response to price deflation during the Great Depression. They had argued that economic recessions are the natural outcome of an earlier excessive credit (money) creation by a central bank. Thus, letting a recession or depression run its course is the most efficient corrective (see, e.g., Gottfried Haberler 1932; see also Hayek 1935; Robbins 1934). However, the modern Austrians' positions on the theory of interest, inflation, and banking still leave them on the fringe of mainstream macroeconomic analysis.

The modern Austrians, nevertheless, share monetarists' rejection of government interventionism as the cure for economic malaise. Individuals are better at evaluating their own economic advantages and acting upon them than government bureaucrats. Smith argues the same view in his *The Theory of Moral Sentiments* (1759) and his policy prescriptions in the *Wealth of Nations* (1776). But none of the four schools – monetarists, new classicals, real business theorists, and Austrians – employs consistently classical monetary or macroeconomic analysis, mainly because they all tend to use Keynes's definitions of saving, capital, investment, and money.

The rest of the book explains how the persistent differences in modern macro-economics, other than for philosophical dispositions between being socialist or free-market (liberty) oriented, can be resolved with careful attention to the forms in which macroeconomists' adherence to the Keynesian "language and apparatus" has preserved the divisions. It may well be that the post-Keynesians cannot be per-suaded to follow Keynes's own view about classical economics. In his concluding chapter, Keynes (1936) argues: "Our criticism of the accepted classical theory of economics has consisted not so much in finding logical flaws in its analysis as in pointing out that its tacit assumptions are seldom or never satisfied, with the result that it cannot solve the economic problems of the actual world" (378). But it was mainly because Keynes mistakenly believed that classical economic principles, including the theories of interest, the level of prices and inflation, forced saving, and Say's Law, are founded upon there always being full employment of labor, that he faulted them as irrelevant to an economy in less than full employment (Ahiakpor 1997a, 2003a). Keynes's claim that the classics assumed that people form expecations about the future with certainty or 100% probability, but which no one actually does (1936: 24, n. 3; 1937a: 222) or that "the Classical Theory has been accustomed to rest the supposedly self-adjusting character of the economic system on an assumed fluidity of money-wages" (1936: 237) also are not true.

Keynes (1936) immediately follows the above claims in the final chapter about classical "tacit assumptions" by arguing the reverse process by which an economy would attain the level of output when classical theory becomes relevant. Now, clas-sical theory, particularly in Smith, J.-B. Say, and David Ricardo, explains how the pursuit of self-interest by sellers and buyers in the marketplace leads the economy by an invisible hand to create the most output attainable. Instead, Keynes's (1936: 378–9) faith is in extensive government management of the economy until full employment.

Keynes's argument ignores Smith's warning against the "folly and presump-tion" of those who would attempt to "direct private people in what manner they ought to employ their capitals" (*WN*, 1: 478). Having appropriately warned about the hazards of guessing the future, Keynes's urging the state "to take hold of the central controls and to govern them with *deliberate foresight* and thus modify and condition the environment within which the individual freely operates with and against other individuals" ([1932] 1982: 88; italics added) appears self-contradictory. Keynes (1936: 379) also acknowledges, "There are, of course, errors of foresight." Marshall (1920: 289) similarly observes, "We cannot foresee the future perfectly." Taussig (1921) employs the uncertainty "of what the future will bring" to explain the halting behavior during an economic crisis of dealers and middlemen who "curtail purchases [causing] the manufacturing employers to cut down produc-tion," leading to "workmen [being] thrown out of employment, and [who] in turn do not buy of the retailers" (1: 394).

The Great Depression may have given Keynes the grounds for claiming that private enterprise is incapable of promoting or sustaining economic prosperity (Chapter 5 below explains otherwise). Also, instead of recognizing the beneficence of the pursuit of self-interest by sellers and buyers as Smith explains in the *Wealth of Nations*, Keynes conditions the virtues of self-interest on "individualism [being] purged of its defects and its abuses" (1936: 380). But Smith argues the state's role of providing "a tolerable administration of justice" in order to protect the property rights of individuals and to promote the growth of savings, investment, output, and employment.

Keynes also subsequently disavowed some arguments being made by his young followers, notably Joan Robinson, Richard Kahn, and Nicholas Kaldor (see Hutchison 1981: 119–35). Keynes reported to Austin Robinson in 1944 at breakfast that at dinner the previous evening in Washington, DC, among Keynesians, "I was the only non-Keynesian there" (Hutchison 1977: 58). He is also reported to have declared, "I am not a Keynesian" (Hutchison 1981: 123). In his June 1946 (posthumous) article on the balance of payments of the United States, Keynes writes, "I find myself, not for the first time, to remind contemporary economists that the *classical teaching* embodied some *permanent truths* of great significance, which we are liable to-day to overlook because we associate them with other doctrines which we cannot now accept without much qualification" (185; italics added). He believed he had drawn upon such classical truths in advancing "thoroughgoing proposals . . . on behalf of the United States, expressly directed towards creating a system which allows the *classical medicine* to do its work" (186; italics added). Moreover, Keynes believed his work "shows how much modernist stuff, gone wrong and turned sour and silly, is circulating in our system" (ibid.). He also quotes in the article what he had said in the House of Lords: "Here is an attempt to use what we have learnt from modern experience and modern analysis, not to defeat, but to implement the *wisdom of Adam Smith*" (ibid.; italics added).

Joan Robinson, indeed, believed Keynes's argument in the last chapter of the *General Theory* regarding the usefulness of classical economics after full employment has been established to be "retrograde, both intellectually and politically. It might be excused because in the 'long struggle to escape' from orthodox ideas Keynes simply had not time to escape from all of them" (1975: 130). And on Keynes's 1946 article, Richard Kahn has explained that "the trustees had a long and serious debate about whether to publish it. They thought that Keynes had written it while he was ill, that he had not really meant what he had written" (quoted in Hutchison 1981: 145, n. 19). But the point is that Keynes's policy views evolved over time; while some are self-contradictory, the latter derive from Keynes's misinterpretations of some classical analyses. It is quite unhelpful, therefore, for economic policymaking not to examine carefully his criticisms of classical macroeconomics for their validity.

We may summarize the classical macroeconomic principles Keynes misrepresented thus:

1   Interest rates are determined mostly by the supply and demand for savings, not money; a central bank's money creation may influence the level of

interest rates in the short run, but the price-level and expectation effects of money's increase will soon reverse the short-term (liquidity) effect; the opposite effects occur from a monetary contraction;

2   Savings supply most of the funds for investment spending; thus increased savings, not consumption spending, drive an economy's growth;

3   The level of prices is determined by a central bank's money supply relative to money's demand, and inflation by the growth of that money's supply relative to the growth of the demand;

4   A central bank's matching the growth of its money supply to the growth of the demand is necessary for maintaining the value of money or the average level of prices; rising prices may produce a temporary increase of real output and employment until wage contracts are revised accordingly, and falling prices depress business profits and decrease output and employment in the short run until nominal wage rates have adjusted accordingly;

5   The requisite functions of government for promoting economic prosperity include (i) provision of national defense, (ii) administration of justice through the legislature, the police, and the courts, and (iii) provision of public goods – goods and services necessary for the efficient workings of the private economy, but which private enterprise would not adequately provide on its own – beyond which government spending, financed by taxation and borrowing, exactly substitutes for the more efficient private spending (Ricardo's contemporaneous equivalence theorem, see Ahiakpor 2013);

6   Protective tariffs and monopoly privileges to businesses restrain economic growth; and

7   Say's Law explains that producing a commodity creates demand for other produced commodities; the variations in relative commodity prices, interest rates, and the value of money thus coordinate production and savings decisions in a market economy. The law does not apply directly to labor, which has to compete with equipment, machinery, and land in the production process; there are no fixed labor-output coefficients in production. Say's Law is not what Keynes misinterpreted it to mean: "supply creates its own demand" (Keynes 1936: 18).

The classical views may be hard to fit into a single diagram like the IS-LM model. But greater realism in our representation of the economy is more helpful for policy formulation than the ease by which a model may be taught, which is among the virtues some claim for the IS-LM model, (see, e.g., Laidler 1999: 320; or the IS-MP model by David Romer [2000, 2013]). Chapter 9 below explains their weaknesses.

The classical arguments were mainly in contradiction to mercantilist propositions about how governments could promote economic prosperity through exporting subsidized manufactured goods while restraining manufactured goods imports. The mercantilists also believed that retaining specie in the domestic economy or increasing its inflow in exchange for exports would lower domestic interest rates. David Hume's 1752 *Political Discourses*, particularly those on money, interest, international trade, and taxation refuted these claims and laid the basis for subsequent elaborations, mostly by Smith, Ricardo, and J. S. Mill on down to Marshall.

Keynes (1939, Preface to the French edition) explains that he was returning to the mercantilist doctrines, mainly regarding the determination of interest rates and the role of money in an economy, because he had failed to recognize a valid theory of interest in classical analysis:[15]

> In recent times it has been held by economists that the rate of current saving determined the supply of free capital, that the rate of current investment governed the demand for it, and that the rate of interest was, so to speak, the equilibrating price-factor determined by the point of intersection of supply curve of savings and the demand curve for investment. But if aggregate saving is necessarily and in all circumstances exactly equal to all investment, it is evident that this explanation collapses. We have to search elsewhere for the solution. I find it in the idea that it is the function of the rate of interest to preserve equilibrium, not between the supply and demand for capital goods, but between the supply and demand for money, that is to say between the demand for *liquidity* [cash] and the means for satisfying this demand.
>
> (1974: xxxiii–iv; italics original)

It is clear in the above that, by mistakenly substituting capital goods for "capital" in the classical theory of interest, Keynes thought he had found a fundamental defect in that theory. Also, saving and investment mean different things to Keynes than they do in classical analysis. It was requisite for Keynes to try to understand the concepts deriving from Hume and Smith rather than insist on his own meanings of them. However, both mainstream and other economists have resisted recognizing this problem with Keynes's criticism of classical interest theory.

One of Mankiw's (1992) arguments for being a new Keynesian well illustrates the value of correcting Keynes's changed definitions in economics. Mankiw's third among his six "dubious Keynesian propositions" is about the possibility of "excessive saving, which would lead to secular stagnation" (Snowdon and Vane 1997b: 447). He counters the fear with the observation, "almost all economists now believe that additional saving will, *in the long run*, lead to additional investment rather than inadequate aggregate demand" (Snowdon and Vane 1997b: 448; italics added). Now consider that saving in classical economics is the purchase of interest- and/or dividend-earning assets, and that those who acquire the borrowed funds quickly spend them. Then the increased saving must be beneficial to investment both in the short run and in the long run. Thus, shifting the IS or aggregate demand (AD) curve to the left because of increased saving is incorrect.

Mankiw also accepts the long-run neutrality of money, referring to David Hume's argument. He believes a commitment to a monetary policy rule to avoid inflation is preferable to the sixth of the dubious Keynesian propositions, which recommends discretionary policy. He also thinks teaching students the quantity theory of money is better than teaching the Keynesian cross. Furthermore, "With new Keynesians looking so much like old classicals, perhaps we should conclude that the term 'Keynesian' has out-lived its usefulness." But, as explained above, much more needs to be shed out of Keynesian macroeconomics before we arrive back at classical macroeconomics.

Subsequent chapters will illustrate the benefits for macroeconomic analysis of correcting Keynes's errors of interpreting classical economics. They include:

i   recognizing the superiority of the Quantity Theory's explanation of the level of prices versus Keynes's aggregate supply-aggregate demand analysis;
ii recognizing price-level stability or zero inflation targeting as the appropriate monetary policy;
iii appreciating the validity of the classical savings supply and demand theory of interest rates;
iv recognizing the irremediable flaws of the IS-LM or IS-MP model;
v   recognizing the validity of Say's Law;
vi appreciating the redundancy of free banking advocacy in place of central banking; and
vii interpreting the Great Depression consistently with classical macro-monetary analysis, not Friedman and Schwartz's (1963).

It typically has taken more than two years and several rejections to publish my previous explanations of Keynes's distortions of classical macroeconomics in journals. I have included comments from some dissenting referees who relied on their incomplete reading of the classical literature for rejecting some of the manuscripts included in this book as illustration.

A referee for this book's proposal also exhibits the attitude of some dissenting journal referees. The referee's mistaken claims include: (1) I am only advancing Austrian economics arguments; (2) I am criticizing "old fashion Keynesianism, which faded away this 30–40 years ago"; (3) I am saying nothing that has not been disposed of 30–40 years ago – "Some Keynesian economists did, at that time, misunderstand the classical 'quantity theory' and 'Saving/loanable funds,' which among other [sic] Friedman emphasized over and over again"; (4) my project is incomplete: "to criticize Keynes without mentioning the concept of *Uncertainty*, is like Hamlet without the Prince. If anything the new interpretation of Keynes's economics is so much centred on how to handle 'uncertainty' analytically, cf. Skidelsky's biography among many others"; and (5) "If the author wants to take issue with 'Keynes follies' [my proposed book title], he has to face the Keynes-research represented by among other [sic] 'post-Keynesians'. A good starting point is John King 'The history of Post-Keynesian economics' & Skidelsky (1983, 1992 and 2001) and many more."

Yet my proposal included a chapter, "Saving and the Loanable-Funds Theory of Interest," explaining Jörg Bibow's (2000) erroneous defense of Keynes's critique of the classical loanable-funds theory of interest from a post-Keynesian perspective (Chapter 8 below). The proposal also included updated versions of my 2004, 2009, 2010, and 2013 articles and a 2015 draft of my liquidity trap article (Ahiakpor 2018a), all now excluded because of space limitations. The referee is also quite oblivious of how Keynes's changed meanings of economic concepts have sustained the endless quarrels in modern macroeconomics. Furthermore, the referee is unaware of Keynes's error in attributing to the classics, including Marshall, the presumption of certainty about the future (see, e.g., J. S. Mill *Works*, 2: 165, 402–3, 1874: 107–15; Marshall 1920: 277–81; Ahiakpor 2018b). I wrote an eleven-and-one-quarter-page rebuttal of the referee's arguments, also noting some of Friedman's unhelpful contributions (see Chapters 5 and 6 below). Some referees' biases are just incredible. However, a second referee recognized the validity and positive contributions of my proposed manuscript: "My overall impression is rather positive: the author is qualified for the project, and is recognised as such by his peers."

Notes

1 Marxists are devoted to eliminating private property rather than advancing macroeconomic analysis. For more elaborate descriptions of the modern schools, see Chapter 1 in Brian Snowdon and Howard Vane (1997b: 1–26), Olivier Blanchard and David Johnson (2013: Ch. 25), and Michel De Vroey (2016). However, readers of De Vroey (2016) should read carefully Marshall's *Principles* themselves to correct several misattributions to him, including (a) "Marshall assumed that all agents have a perfect knowledge of market conditions" (10); (b) Marshall employed a "classical dichotomy," including "value theory, dominated by equilibrium principles, where market clearing always obtains" (12); (c) "in Marshall's Principles, the labor market is regarded as working like the fish market" (12); (d) "The standard Marshallian theoretical apparatus is unable to tackle unemployment of any kind, safe for one trivial possibility. This possibility consists in assuming the presence of a price or wage floor, set exogenously" (12–3), rather than wage rates being determined by labor's supply and demand; (e) Marshall employed a model that "implies that firms have perfect foresight" of market conditions (17, 22). These attributions are the opposite of Marshall's own analysis (see, e.g., Marshall [1920] 1990: 277–81, 287–9, 420–1, 442, 448–9, 572, 590–2). Marshall (1920) writes: "we cannot foresee the future perfectly" (289) and "we do not assume that competition is perfect. Perfect competition requires a perfect knowledge of the state of the market" (448), must not be burdened with the assumption of "perfect foresight," for example.

2 Samuelson could have verified from works by J.-B. Say, Ricardo, J. S. Mill, Marshall, Irving Fisher, and Frank Taussig that classical economics, including Say's Law, is consistent with unemployment (Ahiakpor 2003a, 2018b).

3 Samuelson and Nordhaus (1998: 622) still do not interpret Say's Law correctly: "These [classical] economists knew about business cycles, but they viewed them as temporary and self-correcting aberrations. . . . Classical macroeconomists conclude that the economy operates at full employment or at its potential output." David Laidler (2006: 39) also repeats, without contradiction, Keynes's mischaracterization of Say's Law as arguing that "an economy-wide excess supply of output, and *therefore of labour*, was a logical impossibility, and that it was incapable of explaining economy-wide unemployment" (italics added).

4 Both models crumble upon defining saving as purchasing interest- and/or dividend-earning assets; see Ahiakpor (1995, 2001).

5 Leijonhufvud (2006: 65) observes that "Keynes firmly denied the proposition 'Supply creates its own Demand'," but without noting Keynes's misinterpretation of Say's Law thereby. Rather than recognizing Keynes's misinterpretation of "capital" in the classical theory of interest as the source of his confusion, Leijonhufvud also argues,

"Central bank policy or market expectations about the long-term rate of interest may prevent the interest rate from equating saving and investment at full employment" (71). Savers interested in investing long-term purchase long-dated financial assets whiles those interested in short-term investments do the opposite. Thus, interest rates never fail to coordinate savings and investment demands, contrary to Leijonhufvud's (1981) "coordination failures" hypothesis.

6 Kevin Hoover (2006: 89) claims Keynes was "unusually attentive to definitions," but he does not recognize Keynes's changed meaning of economic terms. Hoover also repeats, without contradiction, Keynes's criticism of the classical theory of interest as "maintaining simultaneously two different" versions: one in which interest rates are determined by savings and investment-demand and the other "dealing with the theory of money" (90). But Keynes's confusion derives from his misinterpretation of "capital" in the classical theory of interest (Ahiakpor 1990).

7 Patinkin (1990), nevertheless, defends the IS-LM model, arguing that he saw "Hicks less as a critic of IS-LM, than as an advocate of the general need for greater rigor in the analysis of time in economics" (124). He pays no attention to the fundamental conceptual problems with the model's construction, especially the meaning of saving, investment, and money, and the process of interest rate determination.

8 Keynes (1936: 340–5) elaborates on his following the mercantilist money supply and demand theory of interest rates. Keynes (1939: xxxiv–v) also explains that he was merely returning to the pre-classical liquidity-preference theory of interest, but without acknowledging Hume's (1752) "Of Interest" explaining its error. I have searched unsuccessfully for evidence of Keynes's reference to Hume's essay on interest rate determination.

9 Schumpeter, in fact, bemoans the classical argument that savings supply "capital": "What a mass of confused, futile, and downright silly controversies it would have saved us, if economists had had the sense to stick to those monetary and accounting meanings of the term [capital] instead of trying to 'deepen' them" ([1954] 1994: 323). He could have benefitted from J. S. Mill's (*Works*, 2: 70–2) "third fundamental theorem regarding Capital," for example.

10 See Ahiakpor (2010) and J. Ronnie Davis (1971) for arguments in favor of Federal Reserve monetary expansion, including its financing of deficit spending, to deal with the depression by the likes of Irving Fisher, Ralph Hawtrey, Jacob Viner and eleven other Chicago economists, as well as some economists from other US universities.

11 I was similarly unable to persuade Milton Friedman of Keynes's misinterpretation of "capital" in the classical theory of interest in Marshall's *Principles*. On returning from the Western Economic Association International Meetings in Vancouver in July 1994, I gave Milton Friedman an offprint of my 1990 article on the airplane. Upon landing in San Francisco, he returned the article, unconvinced by my explanation of Keynes's problem.

12 Indeed, the contraction in spending during the Great Depression that Keynes (1936) cites as refuting classical analysis more consistently can be explained by the extreme contraction in savings as the public in the US rushed to redeem their bank deposits into cash or gold, thus reflecting an excess demand for money.

13 The Adam Smith Institute credits Dugald Stewart as having cited the quotation from a 1755 lecture. Also see Smith *WN*, 2: 232, 236.

14 Development of the so-called Dynamic Stochastic General Equilibrium models appears to preserve elements of the new classical macroeconomics, but it still lacks realism. See, for instance, Gordon 2012: 565–6.

15 Keynes (1937a: 210) also asks Dennis Robertson "for at least one reference to where [the] common-sense" classical supply and demand for "capital" or loanable funds theory that he was defending could be found. Proof that Keynes could not recognize that explanation lies in the Marshall quotation he (Keynes 1936: 186–7) cited for criticism.

2   A classical alternative to the AS-AD model of the price level

Introduction[1]

In his 1939 preface to the French edition of the *General Theory*, John Maynard Keynes urges economists to discard the Quantity Theory as the explanation of the level of prices because he "regard[s] the price level as a whole as being determined in precisely the same way as individual prices; that is to say, under the influence of supply and demand" (xxxiv). Rather, the Quantity Theory, Keynes argues, should explain the level of interest rates and thus output as a whole:

> The quantity of money determines the supply of liquid resources, and hence the rate of interest, and in conjunction with other factors (particularly that of confidence) the inducement to invest, which in turn fixes the equilibrium level of incomes, output and employment and (at each stage in conjunction with other factors) the price level as a whole through the influences of supply and demand thus established.
>
> (xxxv)[2]

Keynes arrives at these conclusions from (a) setting aside the application of the classical theory of value to money to explain the level of prices in the Quantity Theory of money (see esp. Chapter 21 of the *General Theory*) and (b) having failed to recognize a valid theory of interest in classical analysis. In his 1912 and 1913 lecture notes on "The Theory of Money," Keynes adopts the application of value theory to money to explain money's value – the level of prices – also declaring the Quantity Theory *"absolutely valid"* (1983: 695; italics original).[3] The latter problem for Keynes appears to have derived mainly from the classical theory of interest being couched in the language of the supply and demand for "capital" rather than for money (see Keynes's criticism of Marshall's restatement of the classical theory of interest in the appendix to Chapter 14 of the *General Theory*, pages 186–90).

Modern macroeconomics has mostly followed Keynes's (1936, 1939) suggestion and attempts to explain the level of prices with aggregate supply (AS) and aggregate demand (AD) curves. Michael Parkin (2000: 86) finds that in "Fifteen texts, used by two-thirds of [introductory level] students . . . the AS-AD model is the workhorse." The AS-AD model also features prominently in many intermediate-level textbooks.[4] Parkin believes some of these texts "present the AD-AS model clearly, accurately, . . . and they use it not as an exclusively short-run model, but as a comprehensive macro model that is useful for understanding the business cycle, inflation, and growth, as well as fiscal and monetary policy and the policy debates" (87). Among recent texts employing the AS-AD model to explain the level of prices, at the introductory level, are Roger Arnold (2008), William Baumol and Alan Blinder (2008), Lee Coppock and Dirk Mateer (2014), Robert Frank and Ben Bernanke (2011), James Gwartney, Richard Stroup, Russell Sobel, and David Macpherson (2018), Robert Hall and Marc Lieberman (2008), R. Glenn Hubbard and Anthony Patrick O'Brien (2014), Peter Kennedy (2010), Paul Krugman and Robin Wells (2009), N. Gregory Mankiw (2015), Campbell McConnell, Stanley Brue, and Sean Flynn (2018), Roger LeRoy Miller (2012), Michael Parkin (2010), and Timothy Taylor (2008). Andrew Abel, Ben Bernanke, and Dean Croushore (2014), Richard Froyen (2013), Olivier Blanchard and David Johnson (2013), Rudiger Dornbusch, Stanley Fischer, and Richard Startz (2008), Robert Gordon (2012), and N. Gregory Mankiw (2013) are among the intermediate-level texts employing the AS-AD model.

Some analysts dispute the legitimacy of attributing the AS-AD model of the textbooks to Keynes's influence. David Colander (1995: 178), for example, argues, "The standard AS/AD analysis emasculates both Keynes and common sense." A reader of my 2009 paper also points to Chapter 4 of the *General Theory*, where Keynes disputes the legitimacy of aggregating "the community's output of goods and services [that] is a non-homogeneous complex which cannot be measured, strictly speaking, except in certain special cases, as for example when all the items of one output are included in the same proportion in another output" (1936: 37–8), as a reason for not attributing the AS-AD model to Keynes. But Keynes's statements in the 1939 Preface to the French edition appear clear enough to suggest the influence he has had in the development of the AS-AD model of the "price level." Amitava Dutt (2002) also argues that the "AD-AS framework continues to be a useful tool," employing "not only standard monetarist/new classical and new Keynesian models, but also those that incorporate imperfect competition, income distributional issues, and the [Keynes alleged] adverse effects of wage reductions stressed by post-Keynesian economists and other more mainstream Keynesians" (358). He thinks the framework is "a more useful device for teaching macroeconomics than alternative presentations such as the income-expenditure and IS-LM models, which do not explicitly incorporate the aggregate supply side" (ibid.).

Ad hoc explanations often tend to be given for employing either a vertical or a horizontal AS curve, even as the analysts do not suggest the existence of similar curves in individual product markets or industries in which production functions exhibit diminishing marginal returns, hence, rising marginal costs. Indeed, the horizontal AS curve, as well as the vertical AS curve, appears to follow from Keynes's (1936: 295) argument that, under some simplifying conditions, "an increase in the quantity of money will have no effect whatever on prices, so long as there is any unemployment, and that employment will increase in exact proportion to any increase in the quantity of money;[5] whilst as soon as full employment is reached, it will thenceforward be the wage-unit and prices which will increase in exact proportion to the increase in effective demand." Absent the simplifying assumptions, Keynes's argument is consistent with a rising short-run AS curve: "instead of constant prices in conditions of unemployment, and of prices rising in proportion to the quantity of money in conditions of full employment, we have in fact a condition of prices rising gradually as employment increases" (296). Confronted with theoretical difficulties of constructing, interpreting, and shifting a downward-sloping AD curve, most macroeconomists, especially the textbook authors, have resorted to the IS-LM model as a foundation for deriving the curve. However, the IS-LM model does not provide a reliable basis for constructing and shifting a downward-sloping AD curve (Chapter 9 below elaborates on this point).

My criticisms of the AS-AD model of the price level go beyond those of Colander (1995) or Colander and Gamber (2002: 304). Without considering the supply and demand for money (currency), the AS-AD model predicts the opposite of its intended results for a closed economy: the level of prices declines when the AD curve shifts to the right, and prices rise when the AD curve shifts to the left. Replacing the level of prices with the rate of inflation in an AS-AD diagram, as some recent analysts, such as David Romer (2000) and John Taylor (2000), have suggested merely skirts the need for a consistent explanation of the level of prices (see also Colander and Gamber 2002: 336–9).

Keynes's problems with the classical theories of interest and the level of prices that led to his suggesting the AS-AD model can be resolved by clarifying the classical concept of "capital" that he misinterpreted. Restoring the determination of the level of prices to the classical Quantity Theory of money has the added advantage of being able to employ Say's Law of markets in modern macroeconomics to discuss the process of economic adjustments, including the Great Depression, contrary to Keynes's view.

Indeed, the "price level," being the weighted average of prices of final goods and services, cannot meaningfully be explained in the context of a non-existent aggregate products market. Rather, it should be explained from changes in the prices of goods and services resulting from changes in the demand for, or the supply of, money (cash), as in classical monetary analysis. Restoring the determination of interest rates to the supply and demand for "capital" or credit, inclusive of the rate of a central bank's money creation, also has the advantage of reconciling some modern analyses with their classical roots, besides guiding the conduct of appropriate monetary policy.

The AS-AD model of the "price level"

Modern (Keynesian) macroeconomics attempts to determine the "price level" from the intersection of the AS and AD curves. The price level is supposed to rise when either the AD curve shifts to the right, while an upward-sloping or vertical AS curve stays in place, or the AS shifts to the left, while the AD stays in place. A simultaneous rightward shift of the AD curve and a leftward shift of the AS curve also would cause the price level to rise, according to the argument. But supply and demand curves and their shifts are legitimate in explaining prices in individual product markets. The typical market demand curve for a product slopes downwards because there are substitutes for it; without substitutes for a product, its demand curve would be vertical. If sellers of a good charged a higher price than those charged for substitute goods, fewer quantities would be demanded. Similarly, greater quantities of a good would be demanded if its producers lowered their price relative to the prices of substitutes. The same reasoning does not apply to the demand for commodities as a whole for a closed economy.

Besides, the assumed downward-sloping AD curve is not independent of production (income) or supply in the aggregate (AS). For a closed economy,[6] the demand for goods and services may increase because of three principal factors: (a) an increase in production or income, (b) a decrease in the demand for money (cash or high-powered money, H) to hold,[7] or (c) an increase in the supply of money. Thus, the "price level" may not change from an increase in aggregate demand (AD) if that increase exactly matches a prior increase in production (income) or aggregate supply (AS). However, given that the demand for money is a function of income and the income elasticity of demand for money is less than unity (see, e.g., Baumol 1952), the rightward shift of the AD curve would be less than the rightward shift of the AS curve. Therefore, an increase in production, while the supply of money (cash) remains constant, would lead to a decrease in the price level even as the AD curve shifts to the right (see Figure 2.1a). That is contrary to what the standard AS-AD diagram is supposed to show. On the other hand, an increase in the supply of money (cash), given its demand, would raise the public's real cash-income ratio above its desired level at existing prices ($k_1 = H_1/P_0 y > k_0 = H_0/P_0 y$, where P = the price level, and y = real income). In the public's attempt to restore the ratio (k) to its desired level, the additional money would be spent on goods and services and raise their prices, $P_1 > P_0$.

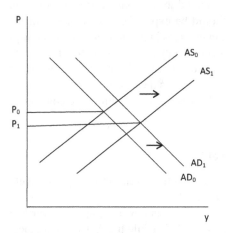

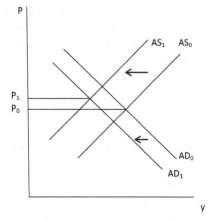

Figure 2.1a Price level falls as AD rises. $P_1 < P_0$

Figure 2.1b Price level rises as AD falls. $P_1 > P_0$

The above three principal factors working in the reverse would account for a decrease in demand for output in the aggregate (AD): (a) a decrease in production or real income, (b) an increase in the demand for money to hold, or (c) a decrease in the supply of money. Thus, to explain a leftward shift of the AD curve requires first a leftward shift of the AS curve. Given the less than unitary income elasticity of demand for money, a reduction in production and real income would be matched by a less than equivalent reduction in AD. Therefore, with both the AS and AD curves shifting to the left, the price level would rise, yielding the opposite of the standard AS-AD model's prediction (Figure 2.1b). The result makes intuitive sense too: we should expect the level of prices to rise from a reduced rate of production, given an unchanged quantity of money, and a reduced level of prices when the rate of production has increased while the quantity of money in circulation remains constant.

An increase in the demand for money (cash) to hold would be reflected in a decrease in spending in order to conserve cash balances. The resulting fall in the level of prices would then raise the public's real cash-income ratio to its desired level. A reduction in the supply of money also reduces the public's real cash-income ratio below its desired level. In their attempt to restore that ratio to the desired level, the public again would curb spending and conserve cash, causing prices to fall.

Thus, rather than shifts of the AD curve yielding the anticipated changes in the price level (P), it is changes in the excess demand for, or the excess supply of, money (H) that reliably produce the expected results. An increase in the excess demand for money raises the value of money ($V_m = 1/P = ky/H$; level of prices falls) while a decrease in the excess demand for money lowers money's value (level of prices rises), exactly as is derived from the (Cambridge) quantity theory equation ($H = kPy = kY$). Similarly, an increase in the excess supply of money lowers the value of money while a decrease in the excess supply of money raises the value of money. Indeed, the aggregate demand (AD) for a closed economy needs to be recognized as constituted by more than consumption (C), investment (I), and government (G) spending. It includes the change in the excess demand for money, $\Delta(H^d - H^s)$, that is, $AD = C + I + G - \Delta(H^d - H^s)$.

Deriving the AD curve from the IS-LM model

In an effort to provide legitimacy for the AD curve, the IS-LM model has been employed to explain it (see, e.g., Froyen 2013: Ch. 8). The explanation is that the intersection of the IS and LM curves is consistent with a point on an existing AD curve. Thus, a fall in the price level (without explaining what makes the price level fall) causes the LM curve to shift to the right and intersect with a downward-sloping IS curve at a higher income level. Connecting the resulting points of higher income and lower price level with the previous lower income and higher price level thus establishes a downward-sloping AD curve, according to the argument. Furthermore, the higher real money (cash) balances cause the public to purchase more financial assets, producing a fall in interest rates. The lower interest rates cause more investment spending, hence increased real income. For an open economy, the fallen price level would cause exports to increase while imports decrease, further reinforcing the increased spending on domestic goods and services along the downward-sloping AD curve. A rightward shift of the AD curve is derived from an increase in government or investment spending while a leftward shift is derived from a decreased government or investment spending.

However, the above attempts at rescuing the logic of an AD curve appear implausible. First, there is no explanation for the price level's decline (or increase) that is associated with an increased (or decreased) level of income. There must be a resort to production or supply in the aggregate or a change in the excess supply of money in order to explain a change in the level of prices. Indeed, the price level (the GDP deflator or the CPI) is a weighted average of the prices of all final goods and services, determined in their respective markets by supply and demand (see, e.g., J. S. Mill *Works*, 3: 509). There is no one market on which AS and AD curves determine the price level independently of those determined on individual markets. Thus, the objections of some analysts to calling the AD curve, derived from the IS-LM model, a "demand curve" appear well founded. For instance, Colander and Gamber (2002: 304) write: "The aggregate demand (AD) curve shows the combinations of price levels and income levels at which both the goods market and the money market are in equilibrium. It really isn't an aggregate demand curve at all – it's a goods market/money market equilibrium curve."[8]

Furthermore, the definition of money employed in modern macroeconomics to derive the LM curve, such as M1 or M2, includes the public's savings. Thus, the LM curve may shift to the right because of increased savings – increased acquisition of bank financial assets, such as savings deposits, time deposits, money market deposit accounts, and money market mutual fund shares – by the public, without a fall in the level of commodity prices. Unless banks increased their rate of cash hoarding or their excess reserves-deposit ratio, increased savings does not change total spending or the level of prices in the short run; borrowers from banks spend the loaned-out savings.[9]

Also, the rightward shift of the IS curve inferred from increased government or private investment spending in the Keynesian cross model ($Y = E = C + I + G$) for a closed economy is inaccurate. The model assumes that government spending and parts of private investment and consumption spending are autonomous; that is, they do not depend upon current income. Thus, the argument goes, increased government spending increases total spending. But government spending must be financed either through taxes and/or borrowing ($G = tY + \Delta B_g$, where B_g = government bonds) – assuming no borrowing from the central bank. Taxes are paid out of current income and government bonds are purchased out of current savings ($S = Y(1 - t) - C - \Delta H_h = \Delta FA^d$, where H_h = households' cash holding and FA = financial assets). Therefore, increased government spending, unless financed by borrowing from a central bank or from abroad, merely displaces private sector spending on consumption or on purchasing interest- and/or dividend-earning assets – a complete "crowding out" (see Ahiakpor 2013). The increased supply of government bonds may lower bond prices and raise interest rates. If, besides reducing consumption spending in order to purchase government bonds, the public also reduces its demand for money (cash) to hold in response to the rise in interest rates, total spending may increase. But here again, it is the reduction in the demand for money (relative to the supply) that increases total spending rather than merely the increase in government spending.

Belief in the expansionary effect of increased government spending is also founded on the view that savings are a withdrawal from the expenditure stream, the meaning of saving Keynes employs to derive his negative views of saving (see, e.g., Keynes 1930: 1, 172; 1936: 210), as well as his expenditure multiplier effect.[10] But, as Thomas Malthus, whom Keynes admired most among the classical writers, points out, "No political economist of the present day can by saving mean mere hoarding" (quoted in Blaug 1996: 161). Smith (*WN*, 1: 359) earlier explains, "What is annually saved is as regularly consumed [or used up] as what is annually spent, and nearly at the same time too; but it is consumed by a different set of people." J. S. Mill emphasizes that: "The word saving does not imply that what is saved is not consumed, nor even necessarily that its consumption is deferred; but only that, if consumed immediately, it is not consumed by the person who saves it. If merely laid by for future use, it is said to be hoarded; and while hoarded, is not consumed at all" (*Works*, 2: 70).[11] Marshall (1923: 46) reiterates the classical definition of saving to mean purchasing financial assets: "in 'Western' countries even peasants, if well to do, incline to invest the greater part of their savings in Government or other familiar stock exchange securities, or to commit them to the charge of a bank." Marshall also explains,

> It is a familiar economic axiom that a man purchases labour and commodities with that portion of his income he saves just as much as he does with that he is said to spend. He is said to spend when he seeks to obtain present enjoyment from the services and commodities which he purchases. He is said to save when he causes the labour and the commodities which he purchases to be devoted to the production of wealth from which he expects to derive the means of enjoyment in the future.
>
> (Quoted in Keynes 1936: 19)

When we correct for the absence of autonomous expenditures and the fact that savings are not a withdrawal from the expenditure stream, the expenditure multiplier effect that drives shifts of the AD curve disappears (Ahiakpor 2001).

Similarly, private investment spending is financed with borrowed (or one's own) savings: $(I = \Delta FA^s = \Delta FA^d = \theta Y(1 - t))$. Banks depend upon the public's deposits (savings) to lend. There would be no need for banks to borrow from each other or a central bank if they could generate their own loanable funds or credit. Purchases of stocks and corporate bonds are also financed by the publics' savings. Thus, increased investment spending, unless financed by borrowing from a central bank or from abroad, constitutes a substitution of business spending for households' spending. An increase in interest rates, resulting from an increased demand for investment funds, would reduce consumption spending in order for savers to meet that increased demand. Total spending on goods and services would remain unchanged unless the increase in interest rates also decreases the demand for money to hold. Also, a decrease in investment demand would lower interest rates but increase consumption spending and thus keep total spending unchanged, if the demand for money is unchanged. If the fall in interest rates increases the demand for money to hold, total spending on commodities would fall.

Thus, the IS curve may not shift to the right because of an increased investment spending or to the left because of a decreased investment spending (or increased saving). Once again, we find that an increase in central bank money used to finance either government or private investment spending or the public's decreased demand for money to hold may increase total spending that a rightward shift of the AD curve is intended to illustrate. Conversely, an increase in the demand for money to hold or a decrease in central bank money supply would decrease the total spending that a leftward shift of the AD curve is supposed to illustrate. The above criticisms of the IS-LM model go beyond such reservations as "there is by now a strong professional consensus that the once-reliable LM curve fell prey years ago to ferocious instabilities in both money demand and money supply. . . . Hence the LM curve no longer plays any role in serious policy analysis" and "key aspects of the IS curve are still in dispute" (Blinder 1997: 240, 241).[12]

It also follows that the level of prices does not rise merely from the increase in government or private investment spending, unless either of such increases occasions a decrease in the demand for money to hold or causes an increase in the supply of money (cash) by the central bank. If the price of investment goods rises because of increased investment spending, the price of consumer goods would fall as consumers reduce their own spending in order to supply the investment funds (capital), given the central bank's quantity of money. The price level, being the weighted average of all final goods[13] and services, would thus not change. Similarly, the price level may not fall merely because of decreased government or private investment spending. Rather, total spending and the level of prices would fall either from a decrease in the supply of money (currency) or an increase in the demand for money.

The classical alternative to the AS-AD price-level determination

The classical Quantity Theory of money employs the same explanation of prices in a typical market from supply and demand – the theory of value – to explain the value of money, $V_m = 1/P$, where $P = \sum w_i p_i$, is a weighted average of all final goods and services, in the case of the GDP deflator, or a weighted average of consumer goods and services, in the case of the consumer price index (CPI).[14] As J. S. Mill (*Works*, 3: 506–7) succinctly explains, "The introduction of money does not interfere with the operation of any of the Laws of Value. . . . Money is a commodity, and its value is determined like that of other commodities, temporarily by demand and supply, permanently and on the average by cost of production." J. S. Mill here restates the classical Quantity Theory of money, dating back to David Hume, who explains:

It seems a maxim almost self-evident, that the prices of everything depend on the proportion between commodities and money, and that any considerable alteration on either has the same effect, either of heightening or lowering the price. Encrease the commodities, they become cheaper; encrease the money, they rise in their value. As on the other hand, a diminution of the former, and that of the latter, have contrary tendencies.

$$(1752: 41-2)$$

Note that the supply of commodities constitutes demand for money in exchange (for similar restatements of the determination of the value of money or the level of prices, see also Smith *WN*, 1: 345, 378, 457; Henry Thornton 1802: 194, 197; J.-B. Say 1821a: 220, 272–3; Ricardo *Works*, 1: 104, 3: 90, 193; J. S. Mill *Works*, 3: 509; Frank Taussig 1921: 1, 232–5; Marshall 1923: 45).

Keynes taught the above principle in his 1912 lecture on "The Theory of Money," for which he lists Frank Taussig's *Principles of Economics*, Book III, as one of the references. Keynes's notes include: "The value of money depends, like anything else, upon the interaction of supply and demand, and can be treated, therefore, as a special case of the general theory of value. But the theory of the value of money is worth treating separately because it is conditioned by certain special simplifying circumstances – on account of which the theory of value as applied to money is sometimes crudely described as the 'Quantity Theory of Money'" (1983: 693). Keynes also credited Marshall's evidence before the Gold and Silver Commission of 1886 and the Indian Currency Committee of 1899 as the "best and clearest statements of the theory" (ibid.).[15]

Money was specie in classical economics, the modern equivalent of which is cash or central bank currency. Since a modern central bank determines the quantity of currency (H), money's supply curve is vertical (Pigou 1917: 55).[16] The classical definition of money has the distinct advantage of enabling the explanation of interest rate determination from the supply and demand for credit or savings without necessarily involving a central bank's money creation or contraction.

The public's demand for currency is a certain proportion (k)[17] of their income (Y) that they wish to hold in readiness to purchase some real volume of goods and services ($H^d = kY = kPy$; see Marshall 1923: 44–7). Therefore, the nominal quantity of money demanded by the public increases when prices rise or the value (purchasing power) of a unit of money falls ($V_m = 1/P$). Fewer quantities of money are demanded when prices fall or the value of money rises. Thus, the money demand curve takes the shape of a rectangular hyperbola, where $V_m.H = (1/P).H$ is constant for a given level of income (Taussig 1921: 1, 234; Marshall 1923: 282–3; Pigou 1917: 42).[18] That is, money's elasticity of demand with respect to variations in its purchasing power is unity (-1); Taussig states: "the elasticity of demand for money is unity" (1921: 1, 234). Keynes (1933: 229, n. 2) also recognizes J. S. Mill's (*Works*, 3: 509–12) discussing "the unitary elasticity of demand for money."

Following Patinkin (1965 [1956]), Blaug (1996: 153–5) deviates from the unitary elasticity of money's demand function in classical analysis and employs a Keynesian money demand function "which is necessarily steeper than a rectangular hyperbola" (153). Also, note that the rectangular hyperbola money demand curve is not the same unitary elasticity AD curve some analysts attribute to classical macroeconomics (e.g., Richard Froyen 2013: 50, 51, 171; N. Gregory Mankiw 2013: 286).[19] A unitary elasticity AD curve presumes nominal income ($Py = Y$) necessarily remains constant at various prices, following changes in aggregate supply (AS). But that argument is inconsistent with classical analysis or reality.

Unlike the AD curve that is not independent of the AS curve, the classical money demand curve (H^d) is independent of the money supply (H^s) curve. The intersection of the money supply and demand curves determines the value of money: $V_m = 1/P = ky/H$ or $P = H/ky$.[20] Thus, given the quantity of money, an increase in its demand ($k_1 > k_0$) causes the public to reduce spending on commodities in order to conserve cash or to increase their supplies of goods and services in exchange for more money. Either of these actions will reduce prices and raise the value of money balances to meet the increased desired real cash-income ratio (see Figure 2.2).[21] Because of wage, interest, and rental contracts, the falling prices would reduce profits and cause a reduction in production and national income. The fall in income would then reduce the demand for money and attenuate the fall of prices – money's demand curve retracts but not to its original position.

On the other hand, a decrease in the demand for money to hold ($k_1 < k_0$) or an increase in money's velocity of circulation leads to increased spending on commodities in order to reduce the excess real cash-income ratio. That would raise prices (reverse of the direction of the money demand curve in Figure 2.2). If the increased spending includes purchasing financial assets, that causes their prices to rise or interest rates to fall. The fall in interest rates further encourages increased consumption and investment spending, putting more pressure on commodity prices to rise and the real cash-income ratio further to fall. However, the rising prices may reduce real wage, interest, and rental rates, and increase profits and production – the classical forced-saving mechanism (see, e.g., Thornton 1802: 239;

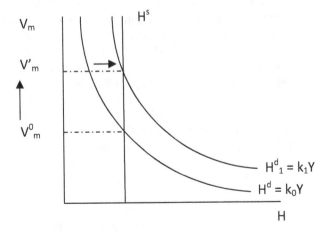

Figure 2.2 Increased demand for money raises the value of money (1/P); price level falls.

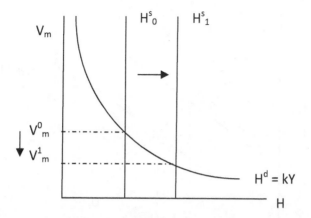

Figure 2.3 Increased supply of money lowers the value of money (1/P); price level rises.

Ricardo *Works*, 3: 318–19, 6: 233). If so, the resulting increase in incomes would be associated with a less than proportionate increase in the demand for money, which would attenuate the effect of the initial decrease in money's demand.

An increase in the quantity of money in excess of its demand by the public ($k_0 < H_1/P_0y_0$) causes increased spending and thus a rise of prices. The rise of prices reduces the value of each unit of money and thus increases the quantity of money demanded in a new equilibrium – assuming no changes in real output or income – in order to purchase the same real volume of goods and services ($H_1/P_1y_0 = k = H_0/P_0y_0$; $H_1 > H_0$ and $P_1 > P_0$) (see Figure 2.3). With wage, interest, and rental rates lagging behind the rise of prices in the short run, real output and employment may increase from the increased supply of money and thereby increase the demand for money somewhat, thereby attenuating the rise of prices. But only the price level rises in full equilibrium when real wage rates, real interest rates, and real rental rates are restored and the rate of output and employment return to their original levels. This is the classical forced-saving mechanism, similar to the modern Phillips Curve analysis (Ahiakpor 2009).

If the increased quantity of money was effected through open market purchases, the price of securities would rise and their yield (interest) fall – the familiar "liquidity effect" of an increase in the quantity of money in the short run (see also William Gibson 1970; Milton Friedman 1972). The fall in interest rates is consistent with an increase in the supply of credit (see Figure 2.4), which hitherto derived only from the increased supply of savings or "capital":[22] $S_{cr} = S_c + \Delta H$; savings being the residual of disposable income over consumption and cash hoarding. Also, if the increased spending of the new money by the public extends to other financial assets, that will extend the interest rate lowering effect further. At lower interest rates, the incentive to increase consumption and investment spending would rise, putting further pressure on prices to rise. The rise of prices will cause an increase

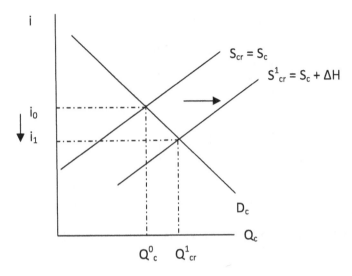

Figure 2.4 Increased supply of money increases the supply of credit and lowers the rate of interest: The liquidity effect.

in the demand for credit and a restoration of the level of interest rates – the "income or price-level effect."[23]

On the other hand, a decreased supply of money ($H_1 < H_0$) through the sale of securities by the central bank would reduce the public's real cash-income ratio below its desired level ($k_0 > H_1/P_0y_0$) and cause a reduction in the public's spending in order to conserve cash. The reduction in spending lowers prices, raises the value of money, and reduces the quantity of money demanded in a new equilibrium. The sale of securities by the central bank also lowers their prices and causes the level of interest rates to rise, further putting pressure on consumption and investment spending to decrease. The rise in interest rates is consistent with a decrease in the supply of credit below the flow of savings or "capital": $S_{cr} = S_c - \Delta H$ (see Figure 5). The public also may wish to increase their sale of goods and services in order to acquire more cash, further putting pressure on commodity prices to fall.

In the presence of wage, interest, and rental contracts, the fall of prices raises real wage, interest, and rental rates and decreases production and employment. The resulting fall in incomes would reduce the demand for money and attenuate the downward pressure on prices. The fall in the level of prices would also reduce business profits (or cause business losses) and decrease the demand for credit or loanable funds, causing the level of interest rates to fall back to their initial level. Thus, the liquidity- and price-level effects of the decrease in the quantity of money on the level of interest rates work in the opposite direction from the increase in the quantity of money explained above: first, an increase in interest rates, and then a fall back of interest rates. Should the public expect the declining level of prices to continue, the rate of savings may increase or the demand

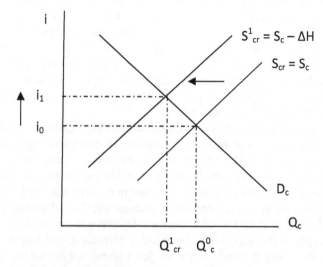

Figure 2.5 Decreased supply of money decreases the supply of credit and raises the rate of interest: The liquidity effect

for credit fall further, causing interest rates to fall below their original level – the "expectations effect."

Most of the above changes in the level of prices or the "price level," due to changes in the demand and supply of money without necessarily the interest rate effects, are the conclusions that the AS-AD model seeks to illustrate. But the arguments employed with that model do not appear well founded or complete. Besides, the determination of the level of prices in classical analysis does not presume its taking place on an aggregate goods and services market but rather through individual markets. As Hume (1752: 37–8) explains,

> Though the high price of commodities be a necessary consequence of the increase of gold and silver, yet it follows not immediately upon that increase; but some time is required before the money circulates through the whole state, and makes its effect be felt on all ranks of people. At first, no alteration is perceived; by degrees the price rises, first of one commodity, then of another; till the whole at last reaches a just proportion with the new quantity of specie which is in the kingdom.[24]

Also, bank deposits and other interest-earning financial assets are alternatives to holding money (cash) in readiness to make purchases. Thus, changes in the benefits of holding assets that serve as alternatives to money, particularly the rate of interest, shift the money demand curve (not a movement along the money demand curve as is typically shown in most macroeconomics texts). The higher the rate of interest, the lower the demand for money to hold, and vice versa. A rise in interest rates may occur because of an increase in the demand for loanable funds or "capital," reflected in an increased supply of financial assets (IOUs) and a fall in their prices. The fallen price of financial assets may cause income earners to economize on both their cash holding and consumption spending in order to increase their purchases of financial assets. The classical analysis thus allows a separation of the supply and demand for credit (or the demand and supply of financial assets) to determine interest rates and the supply and demand for money (cash) to determine the value of money or the level of prices.

Furthermore, other than from its borrowing, money (cash) is acquired with earned income. Thus, an increase in real income (production) shifts the demand for money curve to the right without shifting the money supply curve and raises the value of money or lowers the level of prices. The rate of interest does not rise because of an increase in real income, as argued in the derivation of the LM curve. Indeed, an increase in real income would increase the flow of savings (purchase of financial assets or IOUs) and thus decrease interest rates, given the demand for savings (supply of IOUs). On the other hand, a decrease in real income (production) shifts the money demand curve to the left without shifting the money supply curve and lowers the value of money or raises the price level, $P = H/ky$. Interest rates may rise because of the decrease in income, and hence a decreased supply of savings, if the demand for credit or savings remains unchanged.

Some advantages of the classical alternative to the AS-AD model

Recognizing that the level of prices is derived from individual commodity prices, determined from the demand and supply of goods and services in different individual markets, yields the added advantage of appreciating the logic of Say's Law of markets, with which Keynes had great difficulty. The law explains the interconnection between the markets for various goods and services – "the creation of one product immediately opens a vent for other products" and "the success of one branch of commerce supplies more ample means of purchase, and consequently opens a market for the products of all other branches" (Say 1821a: 135) – such that variations in relative prices motivate producers to adjust their supplies to meet the demands. Fundamental also to the law is the fact that "*productions can only be purchased by productions*" (Say 1821b: 15; italics original), and that money serves mainly as a means of payment. Should production in one market increase relative to its demand, prices in that market would fall. But prices in other markets where commodities were supplied less than the demand likely would rise, reflecting the fact that it is the weighted average of the prices of produced goods and services that measures the value of money. Thus, Say explains, "It is observable . . . that precisely at the same time that one commodity makes a loss, another commodity is making excessive profit" (1821a: 135).

We can explain the fall in the level of commodity prices by an increased demand for money relative to the quantity supplied, as in the case of shaken confidence in the financial markets or banking institutions. The US experience during the Great

Depression, when commodity prices fell while the quantity of Federal Reserve money increased by more than twenty percent, well illustrates the point. As J. S. Mill (*Works*, 3: 574) explains,

> At such times there is really an excess of all commodities above the money demand: in other words, there is an under-supply of money. From the sudden annihilation of a great mass of credit, every one dislikes to part with ready money, and many are anxious to procure it at any sacrifice. Almost everybody therefore is a seller, and there are scarcely any buyers: so that there may really be, though only while the crisis lasts, an extreme depression of general prices, from what may be indiscriminately called a glut of commodities or a dearth of money.

And while nominal wage, interest, and rental rates are yet to fall, businesses would make losses and react by laying off some workers. Furthermore, the distress of business would last for as long as the excess demand for money persists (J. S. Mill *Works*, 3: 516). Marshall (1920: 591–2) repeats the point.

Thus, the law of markets is not what Keynes (1936: 18, 21, 26) popularized it be, including its alleged claims that (a) "supply creates its own demand," (b) all markets clear instantaneously, (c) there is never an excess demand for money (cash), and (d) there is always full employment of labor – "there is no such thing as involuntary unemployment in the strict sense," and "there is no obstacle to full employment." Indeed, J. S. Mill's point about the need for producers to target production to suit the tastes and preferences in different markets in order to avoid the glut of some commodities shows the error of Keynes's rendition of Say's Law as "supply creates its own demand." J. S. Mill explains, "Nothing is more true than that it is produce which constitutes the market for produce, and that every increase of production, *if distributed without miscalculation* among all kinds of produce in the proportion which private interest would dictate, creates, or rather constitutes, its own demand" (1874: 73, italics added).[25]

Another advantage of explaining the level of prices by the supply and demand for money rather than aggregate supply relative to aggregate demand is that we can derive an equation for inflation directly. From $P = H/ky$, we can obtain from the time derivative of the natural log, $(dP/dt)(1/P) = (dH/dt)(1/H) - (dk/dt)(1/k) - (dy/dt)(1/y)$ or $\%\Delta P = \%\Delta H - \%\Delta k - \%\Delta y$. That is, the rate of inflation is determined by the excess creation of money over the growth of money's demand – both from changes in the desired cash-income ratio (k) and the growth in real income (y).[26] No such inflation equation derives from equating the AS and AD curves. The Quantity Theory equation for inflation also helps to guide the conduct of non-inflationary monetary policy: targeting the growth of money's (cash) demand with its supply in order to sustain the level of prices rather than targeting interest rates as some builders of the alternative AS-AD model argue (e.g., Taylor 2000). Interest rates are subject to price-level and expectations effects that counter the initial (liquidity) effects of changes in the supply of money (Chapter 9 below elaborates on this point).

Resolving Keynes's difficulties with classical monetary analysis

Keynes searched for a theory of interest but could not recognize a valid version in classical analysis, particularly in Marshall's *Principles*. The principal hindrance to Keynes's recognition appears to have been the theory's being stated in terms of the supply and demand for "capital," the term "capital" referring to savings or loanable funds. Thus, Keynes objects to Marshall's statement of the theory of interest as, "Interest, being the price paid for the use of capital in any market, tends towards an equilibrium level such that the aggregate demand for capital in that market, at that rate of interest, is equal to the aggregate stock forthcoming there at that rate" (quoted in Keynes 1936: 186). Keynes (1936: 186 n.; italics original) argues:

> It is to be noted that Marshall uses the word "capital" not "money" and the word "stock" not "loans"; yet interest is a payment for borrowing *money*, and "demand for capital" in this context should mean "demand for loans of money for the purpose of buying a stock of capital-goods". But the equality between the stock of capital-goods offered and the stock demanded will be brought about by the *prices* of capital-goods, not by the rate of interest. It is equality between the demand and supply of loans of money, i.e. of debts, which is brought about by the rate of interest.

Now replace "capital" with "loanable funds" or "trade capital" as Marshall (1920: 60) urges economists to do, consistent with "the language of the market-place," just as he urges economists to follow such usage by Smith. We then find that there should have been no need for Keynes's objection to Marshall's restatement of the classical theory of interest.[27]

Keynes's other major problem with classical monetary analysis was its employing the Quantity Theory to explain the level of prices rather than interest rates. Since Hume's (1752) essay, "Of Interest," classical economists have emphasized that although variations in the supply of money may affect interest rates in the short run, interest rates are determined in the long run only by the supply and demand for savings or "capital." In the short run, Hume explains, the "encrease of lenders above the borrowers sinks the interest; and so much the faster, if those, who have acquired those large sums, find no industry or commerce in the state, and no method of employing their money but by lending it at interest" (58). But sooner or later prices rise, from the increased quantity of money, causing borrowers to increase their demand for loanable funds and higher interest rates to return:

> After this new mass of gold and silver [money] has been digested, and has circulated through the whole state, affairs will soon return to their former situations. . . . The whole money may still be in the state, and make itself felt by the encrease of prices. But not being now collected into any large masses or stocks, the disproportion between borrowers and lenders is the same as formerly, and consequently the high interest returns.
>
> (Hume 1752: 58)[28]

Keynes (1936: 190) quotes Ricardo's restatement of the classical principle but fails to interpret it correctly. Instead of recognizing the short- and long-run aspects of Ricardo's explanation of the effect of changes in the quantity of money on interest rates, Keynes focuses on the long-run and misinterprets Ricardo as having assumed "there is always full employment" (1936: 191); Ahiakpor (1997a) explains the error of Keynes's full-employment attribution to classical analysis.

Keynes also wanted to find a means of promoting investment and employment growth other than through increased savings, as classical analysis argues. But believing that, by saving, the classicals meant or included the hoarding of cash, it was logical for Keynes not to accept their analysis. Besides, Keynes could not derive from the classical analysis a consistent interpretation of the forced-saving doctrine, by which increases in the quantity of money may promote output and employment growth in the short run because of the lagged adjustment of contracted wage, interest, and rental rates behind the rise of prices, but no lasting output and employment growth in the long run. He thought the doctrine assumes full employment, that it is not meaningful because no one is forced to hold money against their will (1936: 80, 328), and that only "German writers" employed the doctrine (1930: 1, 171 n). But Keynes was mistaken.[29] Keynes's (1936: 257, 275–8) incorrect attribution of a fully flexible or instantaneous adjustment of wage rates – the "fluidity of money wages" – to classical economics also stood in his way of recognizing the classical forced-saving analysis that was current in his time.

Such were Keynes's problems with interpreting classical monetary analysis. He sought to do more with money than the classical Quantity Theory would suggest, namely, explaining mainly the level of prices. Modern macroeconomics need not follow Keynes's attempting to explain the price level from AS and AD curves or the supply and demand for output as a whole. Following Keynes's suggestion to turn monetary theory into a theory of interest rates and thus output and employment has led to attempts at promoting economic growth with excessive increases in the quantity of money. That has led mostly to disappointment: higher rates of inflation, higher nominal interest rates, and hardly any real output and employment growth.

Conclusion

In the preface to the 1939 French edition of the *General Theory*, Keynes explains that the analysis that led to his proposing the determination of the level of prices by the supply and demand for output as a whole registered his "final escape from the confusions of the Quantity Theory, which once entangled" him (1974: xxxiv). But, as explained above, Keynes's confusions can be resolved with a careful reading of classical monetary analysis. Applying the classical theory of value to money (currency), the value of money can readily be determined by money's supply and demand. Prices are the rates of exchange between money and units of commodities. It therefore makes sense to explain that the greater abundance of money relative to commodities, the higher commodity prices will be: "money is nothing but the representation of labour and commodities, and serves only as a method of rating or estimating them. Where coin is in greater plenty . . . a greater quantity of it is required to represent the same quantity of goods" (Hume 1752, "Of Money": 37). The same application of value theory to "capital" (savings) or loanable funds explains the determination of interest rates in various credit or capital markets. A central bank's introduction of additional credit, as it increases the supply of money, may lower interest rates in the short run (and vice versa), but not in the long run. Thus, the only source of permanently lowering interest rates in order to increase investment and output growth is increased savings.

Recognizing the sources of Keynes's difficulties with classical macroeconomic or monetary analysis should encourage modern macroeconomists to abandon his suggestion that we explain the "price level" by the supply and demand for output as a whole. The difficulties of justifying a downward-sloping AD curve for a closed economy have been well noted in the literature. Giving up on the AS-AD model also has other advantages, including enabling economists to employ Say's Law of markets meaningfully to explain the interconnectedness of markets for goods, services, and credit or "capital," which, in turn, readily explains the principal source of inflation, and to device appropriate, non-inflationary monetary policy.

Notes

1 This chapter is based on my unpublished paper, "Giving up on Keynes's Prescription: A Classical Alternative to AS-AD Curves Analysis" discussed at the History of Economics Society Annual Meetings at the University of Colorado, Denver, June 26–29, 2009. It covers some explanations of the classical theory of the level of prices in Ahiakpor 2003b: Ch. 4.
2 In Chapter 21 of the *General Theory*, Keynes elaborates his criticisms of the Quantity Theory and his suggestions for determining the price level.
3 Finding statistical confirmation of the quantity theory, Keynes in December1908 wrote to Duncan Grant that the results threw him into a "tremendous state of excitement. Here are my theories – will the statistics bear them out? Nothing except copulation is so enthralling and the figures are coming out so much better than anyone could possibly have expected that everybody will believe I have cooked them" (quoted in Skidelsky 1983: 220).
4 Parkin (2000: 87) also finds that in twenty-four textbooks the "most heavily cited economist remains John Maynard Keynes (170), who is followed by Smith (124) and Milton Friedman (102)."
5 Robert Clower (1994: 382) calls Alvin Hansen's restatement of this argument, "Hansen's Law."
6 For an open economy, demand in the aggregate may shift because of changes in net exports: an increase in aggregate demand when net exports increase and a decrease otherwise.
7 The expectation of higher future prices causes an increased current demand for commodities, but that leads to a decrease in the demand for money to hold.
8 The criticism summarizes Colander's (1995) earlier detailed argument. These criticisms notwithstanding, Colander (1995: esp. 184–6) and Colander and Gamber (2002: Ch. 11) still derive price-level changes from variations in AS and AD curves.
9 In the long run, given the quantity of money, the increased savings may reduce the level of prices because of an increased rate of production, made possible by the increased investment of borrowed funds.
10 Keynes's view of saving as being the same thing as, or including, cash hoarding appears in his criticism of the classical explanation of interest being a reward for waiting or

abstinence. He argues: "the rate of interest cannot be a return to saving or waiting as such. For if a man hoards his savings in cash, he earns no interest, though *he saves* just as much as before" (1936: 166–7; italics added). Keynes also thinks the error of classical interest theory "originates from [its] regarding interest as the reward for waiting as such, instead of as the reward for not-hoarding" (182). But his criticism is incorrect since saving, by the classical definition, is purchasing of interest- and/or dividend-earning assets by households, not cash hoarding (see, e.g., Smith *WN*, 1: 358; Senior 1836: 59; J. S. Mill *Works*, 3: 737). Furthermore, the purchase of financial assets imposes waiting-to-consume upon savers. As Marshall (1920: 69) explains, "the *supply* of capital [savings or loanable funds] is controlled by the fact that, in order to accumulate it, men must act purposefully: they must 'wait' and 'save,' they must sacrifice the present to the future" (italics original).

11 Note that "to consume" in the English language does not only mean "to eat." It also means to "use up." J. S. Mill's explanation appears easier to understand when "consumed" is interpreted as "used up." Thus, when savings are borrowed by businesspeople, they are "all consumed; though not by the capitalist. Part is exchanged for tools or machinery, which are worn out by use; part for seed or materials, which are destroyed as such by being sown or wrought up, and destroyed altogether by the consumption of the ultimate product. The remainder is paid in wages to productive labourers, who consume it for their daily wants; or if they in their turn save any part, this also is not, generally speaking, hoarded, but (through savings banks, benefit clubs, or some channel) re-employed as capital, and consumed" (J. S. Mill *Works*, 2: 70).

12 David Romer (2000) dispenses with the LM curve altogether even as he still derives a downward-sloping AD curve, but in respect of inflation. Chapter 9 below explains why Romer's model is worse than the IS-LM model.

13 Note that equipment and machinery, not raw materials, are final goods.

14 The price of money itself is always equal to 1 since a dollar merely exchanges for another dollar – $p_m = 1 = \$1/\$1$, and $V_m = p_m/P = 1/P$.

15 Yet Keynes subsequently accuses classical economics of having adopted a false dichotomy between "the Theory of Value and Distribution on the one hand and the Theory of Money on the other hand" and he therefore seeks to "bring the theory of prices as a whole back to close contact with the theory of value" (1936: 293). Keynes's charge forms the basis of the alleged classical dichotomy that Parkin (2000: 85) finds to be among the "four propositions on which macroeconomists agree." Chapter 3 below clarifies the error of Keynes's charge of a classical dichotomization of prices.

16 On the contrary, the supply curve for modern money, M1 or M2, should be upward-sloping, if drawn with the rate of interest on the Y-axis. The money supply multiplier for M1, $m_1 = (cu + 1)/(cu + r_d + r_e)$, where cu = public's currency-deposit ratio, r_d = required reserve-deposit ratio, and r_e = excess reserves-deposit ratio, increases when interest rates rise and banks economize on their excess or economic reserves in order to extend more loans and the general public reduces its currency-deposit ratio.

17 Note that k is not a constant but depends upon several factors, including the level of interest rates, the availability of credit or the use of other money substitutes in purchases, and the expectation of inflation (see Marshall 1923: Ch. 4).

18 Don Patinkin (1965) employs the rectangular hyperbola money demand curve to illustrate classical monetary analysis, besides reviewing its use by Marshall, Pigou, and Frank Taussig (see particularly pp. 605–8). However, he switches to deriving a "market-equilibrium curve" that is a rectangular hyperbola from conducting a "conceptual market experiment" (48–50). Patinkin even claims that Marshall's money demand curve "depends on the *supply* of money," whose interdependence he recognizes as "so unusual for Marshall" (607; italics original). But this is rather Patinkin's incorrect inference.

19 James Edwards (1991) more consistently represents the classical analysis of the price level, even as he seeks accommodation for the Keynesian AS-AD analysis, supported by the IS-LM model.

20 Robert Barro (2008: Ch. 10) determines the price level from the supply and demand for money (currency) but he does not employ the rectangular hyperbola money demand curve. Rather, his linear money demand curve slopes upwards; the curve rotates upwards to indicate a decrease in money demand and downwards to indicate an increase.

21 An increased demand for cash also results in a reduced circulation or the velocity of money (V). Thus, from the familiar equation of exchange (HV = PT), $P_1 = H_0 V_1/T < P_0 = H_0 V_0/T$, where $V_1 < V_0$. For explanations of changes in the level of prices from variations in money's circulation, see Hume (1752: 42–3), Thornton (1802: 196), Ricardo (*Works*, 3: 90), J. S. Mill (*Works*, 3: 512–13), and Marshall (1923: 43–8). Indeed, Fisher (1922: Ch. 2) draws mainly on analyses by Ricardo and J. S. Mill to derive the equation of exchange, noting that "Ricardo probably deserves chief credit for launching the theory" (26 n).

22 Indeed, the classical theory of interest is an application of the theory of value to "capital" or credit (e.g., Taussig 1921: 2, 27–32).

23 Statements of these effects by the classics include Hume 1752, "Of Interest," Ricardo *Works*, 1: 363–4; 3: 91–2; and J. S. Mill *Works*, 3: 655–6. See Ahiakpor 2003b: 63 for a graphical illustration. J. S. Mill's account also includes what is now called the inflation "expectations effect" on interest rates (e.g., Gibson 1970; Friedman 1972).

24 Ludwig von Mises (1934: 140) appears to have been oblivious of this account in Hume's essay, "Of Money." Instead, he criticizes Hume for his thought experiment in which money is "multiplied fivefold in a night" (1752: 63) and all prices immediately adjust by the same proportion.

25 For a further explanation of the law of markets, including its defense by James Mill and Marshall, in contrast to Keynes's interpretation, see Ahiakpor 2003a.

26 From the equation of exchange, HV = PT, the equation of inflation is, $(dP/dt)(1/P) = (dH/dt)(1/H) + (dV/dt)(1/V) - (dT/dt)(1/T)$.

27 Other relevant pages in Marshall's *Principles* regarding "capital" to mean loanable funds include 61–2, 66 and 647. For similar usage of the term "capital" to refer to loanable funds or savings, see also Smith *WN*, 1: 294; Ricardo *Works*, 1: 363, 3: 89–94; and J. S. Mill *Works*, 3: 647–59. For an elaboration of Keynes's misinterpretation of the classical theory of interest mainly from his having misinterpreted "capital," see Ahiakpor 1990.

28 Ricardo (*Works*, 3: 91) and J. S. Mill (*Works*, 3: 648, 655–7) make the same point, repeated by Marshall (1923: 257). The explanation is similar to the "cumulative process" argument typically ascribed to Knut Wicksell (see, e.g., Patinkin 1965: 239, 368–9). Indeed, Wicksell (1935: 79–80) himself acknowledges Ricardo's analysis.

29 Believing that the classics did not recognize the short-run positive impact of money on output and employment as argued by Hume, Keynes (1936: 343, n. 3) considers Hume to have "had a foot and a half in the classical world"; and "he was still enough of a mercantilist not to overlook the fact that it is in the transition [when the real effects occur] that we actually have our being." But the major classical monetary analysts, including Smith, Henry Thornton, Ricardo, and J. S. Mill, followed mostly after Hume's monetary analysis, particularly in "Of Money" and "Of Interest."

3 Keynes's mistaken charge of a classical dichotomy regarding the Quantity Theory of money

Introduction[1]

Among John Maynard Keynes's enduring influences in modern macroeconomics is his indictment of classical economics as having argued a dichotomy in the explanation of prices: commodity prices by their supply and demand in individual markets, and the "price level"[2] by money's supply and demand with the Quantity Theory of money. In Keynes's view, money's supply and demand should explain interest rates – his (cash) liquidity-preference theory of interest – while the price level should be explained by the supply and demand for "output as a whole" (1974: xxxv). Money's role in interest rate determination, according to Keynes, is to facilitate entrepreneurs' borrowing for production by purchasing capital goods and hiring workers (ibid.). Don Patinkin (1965 [1956]) affirms Keynes's indictment of classical monetary analysis as valid, and several textbook authors continue to repeat the charge. Mark Blaug (1996) disputes Keynes's indictment and its repetition by Patinkin but fully absolves only the neoclassical monetary analysis of Irving Fisher and Knut Wicksell because they appear not to insist on money's long-run neutrality with respect to output and employment. But Blaug (1995: 43) earlier also claims, "even they [Fisher and Wicksell] 'dichotomised the pricing process' as Patinkin (1965 [1956]: 171–86) put it." Blaug partly absolves classical monetary analysis by "generously" interpreting Henry Thornton's "doctrine of the two rates [natural and market rates of interest]" that "emphasizes the connection between money and commodity markets" (1996: 156), even though that analysis belongs with Smith and Ricardo too (see J. S. Mill *Works*, 3: 648). Robert Skidelsky (1983: 214), Roger Backhouse (1985: 342), and David Laidler (1991: 123) are among those who have repeated Keynes's charge without correction.

In fact, determining the value of money from the classical Quantity Theory of money is a direct application of the classical theory of value to money (currency), but through individual commodity markets, as in David Hume's 1752 essay, "Of Money," and argued by subsequent classical writers who followed him. The analysis arises from the use of money both as a unit of account (standard of value), by which individual commodity market prices represent the exchange ratios of money to units of commodities, and as a means of payment. Indeed, the "price level" is a weighted average of individual commodity prices, and there is no single market on which it is determined by money's supply and demand or by the supply and demand for output as a whole. The supply of money may derive from a single source, such as the mint or a central bank (fiat money). But the quantity that is relevant for determining money's value is the amount offered in exchange for commodities in various product markets. Similarly, money's demand derives from the quantity of commodities offered in exchange for it in various markets.

Furthermore, contrary to Keynes (1936), the Quantity Theory explains that variations in the quantity of money affect relative product prices, interest rates, output, and employment in the short run. Keynes earlier had understood this from Marshall's statements in evidence before the 1887 Gold and Silver Commission and the 1899 Indian Currency Committee (collected in Marshall 1926; see also Marshall 1923), and Keynes between 1912 and 1914 taught his undergraduate students the same (Keynes 1983: 693–4, 776–83). That explanation mostly constitutes the classical forced-saving doctrine, which, however, Keynes (1936: 79–81) does not find meaningful after having changed the definition of money to include bank deposits instead of cash only (Keynes 1930, 1936). The classics also argued against the mercantilist belief in the growth of money's supply being the source of long-term economic growth since money is not a factor of production, which formed the basis of money's long-run neutrality proposition with respect to output and employment – a proposition to be distinguished from Keynes's alleged classical dichotomization between individual prices and the level of their average.

Keynes could have found the classical explanation of the level of prices well illustrated in Hume, Smith, Ricardo, J. S. Mill, and Frank Taussig's *Principles*, besides Marshall's Commission and Committee testimonies upon which he earlier relied in his teaching. Marshall's explanations also are made in terms of money as currency only. Asked whether his definition of money used in explaining the Quantity Theory included checks, Marshall replied, "No, because a cheque requires the receiver to have formed some opinion for himself as to the individual from whom he receives it" (Marshall 1926: 35; see also Marshall 1923: 13, 15). In explaining the determination of money's purchasing power with the Quantity Theory, Irving Fisher (1922: 11; italics original) also notes, "But while a bank deposit transferable by check is included as circulating medium, it is not money. A bank *note*, on the other hand, is both circulating medium and money"; Fisher (1913: 148) repeats the point. Keynes (1911) reviewed the first edition of Fisher's, *The Purchasing Power of Money* (1911), for the *Economic Journal* in which he queries Fisher for not having explained the process through which an increased quantity of money (gold) affects commodity prices. Fisher (1922: xiii) subsequently responds by pointing to pages 242–7 in his *Elementary Principles of Economics* (1913) where he gives the detailed explanation. Keynes's review also cites Marshall's explanation in testimonies as "the most important contribution to monetary theory published in England since the time of Ricardo" (Keynes 1911: 395, n. 1).

Keynes's indictment is thus a misrepresentation of the classical Quantity Theory, apparently to suit his pursuit of turning the Quantity Theory into a theory of "output as a whole" through its being a theory of interest rates instead. Acceptance of Keynes's indictment of classical monetary analysis appears unduly to have rendered it largely irrelevant to understanding the determination of the level of prices in the short run and devising appropriate monetary policy. Many macroeconomics textbook authors, noted below, have treated the classical Quantity Theory just as Keynes mistakenly rendered it. This chapter elaborates.

Keynes's indictment of classical monetary analysis

Keynes (1936) disputes the classical Quantity Theory of money as an application of theory of value – determination of commodity prices by their supply and demand – to money, which was specie in classical times and is central bank currency in a modern regime of fiat, paper money.[3] Thus, he begins his indictment of the classicals for having argued separate theories in two volumes. In volume I, relating to individual commodity markets, Keynes argues, the classicals "have been accustomed to teach that prices are governed by the conditions of supply and demand; and, in particular, changes in marginal cost and the elasticity of short-period supply have a prominent part" (1936: 292). "But when they pass in volume II, or more often in a separate treatise, to the Theory of Money and Prices," Keynes continues,

> we hear no more of these homely but intelligible concepts and move into a world where prices are governed by the quantity of money, by its income-elasticity, by the velocity of circulation relative to the volume of transactions, by hoarding, by forced saving, by inflation and deflation *et hoc genus omne*; and little or no attempt is made to relate these vaguer phrases to our former notions of the elasticities of supply and demand.
>
> (Ibid.)

We may recognize in Keynes's complaint, money's supply in "the quantity of money," and money's demand related to "income elasticity," "velocity of circulation" and "hoarding." We also may recognize the short-run consequences of changes in money's quantity relative to its demand in terms of "forced saving," "inflation," and "deflation." Nevertheless, Keynes continues with his indictment: "If we reflect on what we are being taught and try to rationalise it, in the simpler discussions it seems that the elasticity of supply must have become zero and demand proportional to the quantity of money; whilst in the more sophisticated we are lost in a haze where nothing is clear and everything is possible" (1936: 292).

Keynes therefore urges that we "bring the theory of prices as a whole back to close contact with the theory of value" (1936: 293), but a close contact, which the classical Quantity Theory already explains and which Keynes previously taught, including deriving "prices as a whole" from individual commodity markets (e.g., Keynes 1983: 778–81). However, in his new belief that classical analysis involves two separate theories, Keynes (1936) argues, "The division of Economics between the Theory of Value and Distribution on the one hand and the Theory of Money on the other hand is, I think, a false division" (292). He adds, "The right dichotomy is, I suggest, between the Theory of the Individual Industry or Firm and of the rewards and the distribution between different uses of a given quantity of resources on the one hand, and the Theory of Output and Employment *as a whole* on the other hand" (293; italics original).

In any industry, Keynes continues, "its particular price-level depends partly on the rate of remuneration of the factors of production which enter into its marginal cost, and partly on the scale of output" (1936: 294). In the aggregate, the "general price-level depends partly on the rate of remuneration of the factors of production which enter into marginal cost and partly on the scale of output as a whole, i.e. (taking equipment and technique as given) on the volume of employment" (ibid.).[4] Keynes completes his analogy between price-level determination in individual markets and the price level for output as a whole by linking changes in the quantity of money – "gold and silver and legal tender instruments" (294) – directly with changes in "effective demand":

> Thus if there is perfectly elastic [output] supply so long as there is unemployment, and perfectly inelastic supply so soon as full employment is reached, and if effective demand changes in the same proportion as the quantity of money, the Quantity Theory of Money can be enunciated as follows: "So long as there is unemployment, *employment* will change in the same proportion as the quantity of money; and when there is full employment, *prices* will change in the same proportion as the quantity of money."
>
> (1936: 295–6; italics original)

Keynes subsequently relaxes the simplifying assumptions that led him to the above conclusions regarding the determination of the "price level" for output as a whole, including whether (a) there is unemployment or full employment, (b) effective demand changes in exact proportion to the quantity of money, (c) resources are homogeneous, and (d) remuneration of the factors of production entering into the marginal cost will all change in the same proportion. In the end, Keynes concludes that both output (along with employment) and prices will rise as the quantity of money increases, and vice versa. By this argument, Keynes dispenses with the classical explanation of the average level of prices by the Quantity Theory as an application of the theory of value to money that does not depend upon the condition of employment, whether full or less than full. Rather, variations in the supply of money relative to its demand, according to Keynes, should explain the level of interest rates, which should precede the determination of output as a whole. Keynes repeats the argument in his 1939 preface to the French edition of the *General Theory*,

> I regard the price level as a whole as being determined in precisely the same way as individual prices; that is to say, under the influence of supply and demand. . . . prices – both individual prices and the price-level – emerge as the resultant of [the supply and demand] factors. Money, and the quantity of money, are not direct influences at this stage of the proceedings. They have done their work at an earlier stage of the analysis. The quantity of money

determines the supply of liquid resources, and hence the rate of interest, and in conjunction with other factors (particularly that of confidence) the inducement to invest, which in turn fixes the equilibrium level of incomes, output and employment.

([1936] 1974: xxxiv–v)

The modern attempt to determine the "price level" with the aggregate supply (AS)-aggregate demand (AD) diagram (see Chapter 2 above), rather than directly from money's supply and demand, derives from Keynes's argument.

Several macroeconomics textbooks repeat Keynes's charge of a dichotomization between the determination of commodity prices and the level of prices in classical analysis. They appear to follow the charge's elaboration as the "dichotomization of the pricing process" by Patinkin (1965 [1956]). Patinkin's book, which has been rather influential with many macro and monetary analysts, identifies among evidence of a "valid dichotomy" in classical monetary analysis the following:

a   "the classical proposition that a change in the quantity of money merely causes an equiproportionate change in equilibrium money prices" (172);[5]
b   the argument that a change in the quantity of money "has no effect on the equilibrium values of relative prices, the rate of interest, and the real quantity of money" (173); and
c   a classical distinction exits between "monetary theory, on the one hand, and value theory, on the other" (174).

Thus, Patinkin summarizes Keynes's charge of a classical dichotomy: "The dichotomy . . . begins by dividing the economy into two sectors: a real sector, described by the excess-demand functions for commodities, and a monetary sector, described by the excess-demand function for money. The former functions are assumed to depend only on relative prices; the latter, on these variables and the absolute price level as well" (174).[6]

Blaug's (1996) qualified critique of Keynes's charge and its elaboration by Patinkin includes his noting,

Every classical economist conceded that money was nonneutral in the short run, and since the label "classical economist" is frequently misused, I mean Malthus, Thornton, Bentham, McCulloch, John Stuart Mill and Torrens. Only Ricardo and James Mill insisted on the proportionality theorem in both the long run and the short run and admitted nonneutrality in the short run grudgingly when forced, so to speak, in to a corner.

(616)[7]

However, Blaug distinguishes the classical from the neoclassical quantity theory, as argued by Irving Fisher and Knut Wicksell,[8] by the disappearance from the latter of "the proportionality theorem, the strict long-run neutrality of money" (1996: 616). And, very much following Keynes's explanation of the "price level" by the supply and demand for output as a whole, Blaug concludes: "The quantity theory of money in its heyday [neoclassical period, between 1870 and 1930] was no longer what it had once been – a theory of the main causes of changes in the value or purchasing power of money – rather a theory of how M influenced the *aggregate* demand for goods and services MV, and via MV, the level of prices P and the level of output T" (616; italics original).

Blaug does not fully recount the classicals' explaining the level of prices or "mass of prices" (Ricardo *Works*, 3: 299, 301, 311) or "general prices" (J. S. Mill *Works*, 3: 508, 511), which Marshall (1923: 50) calls "the average level of prices, as evidenced by a trustworthy index number" or "general prices," and Pigou (1927: 157) calls "the general level of prices,"[9] as deriving from money's use both as a unit of account and as a means of payment in individual commodity markets. The explanation entails no dichotomy between the determination of commodity prices and their average level. But Blaug refers to Thornton's analysis of the deviation of the market interest rate from the natural rate of interest, owing to an injection of paper credit, that emphasizes the connection between money and commodity markets, and argues that the "classical theory *generously interpreted*, does not dichotomise the pricing process" (1996: 156; italics added). Below, I draw mainly on the monetary analyses of Smith, Ricardo, J. S. Mill, and Marshall to more fully absolve the classics of Keynes's charge of a dichotomization between determining commodity prices and their average level.

The value of money, relative prices, and the quantity theory of money

Since David Hume's (1752) essay, "Of Money," the classical economists have explained the determination of the value of money (inverse of the level of prices: $V_m = 1/P$) as an application of the theory of (exchange) value to money (specie), of which modern fiat money or currency is the equivalent.[10] As J. S. Mill (*Works*, 3: 506–7) argues, the "introduction of money does not interfere with the operation of any of the Laws of Value. . . . Money is a commodity, and its value is determined like that of other commodities, temporarily by demand and supply, permanently and on the average by cost of production." This is the exact opposite of what some modern textbook authors, such as Jansen, Delorme, and Ekelund (1994: 86), claim: "we have found that Classical economists separate monetary theory from value theory (sometimes called 'Classical Dichotomy'). Value theory is known today as microeconomics or price theory."

In the classical commodity money system, money's supply was determined by its cost of production or by its inflow from foreign countries in payments for exports. Money's supply thus was responsive to variations in its value: an upward-sloping supply curve. Lower domestic prices attracted more foreign purchases of domestic goods, in return for which more money flowed into the economy. Otherwise, owners of domestic gold or silver mines found it more profitable to increase the rate of producing the metals for coining into money. An increased value of money also encouraged conversion of non-monetary gold and silver into money. An increased level of domestic prices (fall of the value of money), on the other hand, increased the demand for imports, in payment for which the quantity of domestic money decreased. The elasticity of money's supply with respect to its value was therefore not zero. However, the quantity of fiat money, by itself, does not adjust to variations in its value; the quantity being determined solely by the monetary authorities, as, for instance, asserted by Pigou (1917: 53): money's "supply curve . . . is obviously a vertical line fixed in whatever position the government may choose." Fiat money's supply curve thus has zero elasticity with respect to its own value. But Keynes's (1936: 292) reading of a zero elasticity of money's supply is with respect to the rate of interest, not money's value (1/P), as in classical monetary analysis.

The community's demand for money, whether of specie or fiat money, on the other hand, is for an asset to hold in readiness to make future purchases rather than to endure the inconvenience of barter exchanges. As Smith (*WN*, 1: 26–7), explains:

> In order to avoid the inconveniency of [barter] every prudent man in every period of society, [endeavors] to manage his affairs in such a manner, as to have at all times by him, besides the peculiar produce of his own industry, a certain quantity of some one commodity or other, such as he imagined few people would be likely to refuse in exchange for the produce of their industry.[11]

Thus, given the level of income, more money is demanded at a higher average level of prices (lower value of money) while less money is demanded at a lower average level of prices (higher value of money). Marshall (1923: 45) similarly explains:

> . . . whatever the state of society, there is a certain volume of their resources which people of different classes, taken one with another, care to keep in the form of currency; and, if everything else remains the same, then there is this direct relation between the volume of currency and the level of prices, that, if one is increased by ten per cent, the other also will be increased by ten per cent. Of course, the less the proportion of their resources which people care to keep in the form of currency, the lower will be the aggregate value of the currency, that is, the higher will prices be with a given volume of currency.

That is, the community's demand curve for money has a unitary elasticity with respect to its value: a rectangular hyperbola (Taussig 1921: 1, 234; Marshall 1923: 282–3; Pigou 1917: 42).[12] Note also that the "proportion," inverse of money's velocity, is not assumed to be constant.

Equating money's supply (in demand for commodities) to its demand (supply of commodities) determines money's value. Thus, Hume (1752: 37) argues: "the greater abundance of coin . . . in the kingdom . . . [heightens] the price of commodities, and [obliges] every one to pay a greater number of these little yellow or white pieces for every thing he purchases" (see also Hume 1752: 41–2). Smith's version of the same is, "Any increase in the quantity of commodities annually circulated within the country, while that of the money which circulated them remained the same, would . . . produce many other important effects, besides that of raising the value of money" (*WN*, 1: 378). Ricardo repeats the argument: "Commodities measure the value of money in the same manner as money measures the value of commodities" (*Works*, 3: 104), and "That commodities would rise or fall in price, in proportion to the increase or diminution of money, I assume as a fact which is incontrovertible" (*Works*, 3: 193n).

However, rather than having argued the determination of the average of commodity prices independently of those in individual commodity markets, Hume explains the necessity of money coming into contact with commodities in their various markets to determine their prices. The explanation underlies the role of money's circulation or velocity in determining the level of average prices, which undermines Keynes's charge of a dichotomization in the explanation of individual prices and their average. Hume argues:

> It is also evident, that the prices do not so much depend on the absolute quantity of commodities and that of money, which are in a nation, as on that of *the commodities*, which come or may *come to market*, and of the money which *circulates*. If the coin be locked up in chests, it is the same thing with regard to prices, as if it were annihilated; if the commodities be hoarded in magazines and granaries, a like effect follows. As the money and commodities, in these cases, never meet, they cannot affect each other.
>
> (1752: 42; italics added)

Henry Thornton (1802) makes Hume's point well with respect to paper money:

> The principle which has been laid down as governing the price of goods, must be considered as also regulating that of the paper [money] for which they are sold; for it may as properly be said, on the occasion of a sale of goods, that *paper is sold for goods*, as that *goods are sold for paper*: thus the sale of a single commodity, as it is called, is a twofold transaction, though not commonly understood to be so: I mean, that the price at which the exchange (or sale) takes place depends on two facts; on the proportion between the supply of the particular commodity and the demand for it, which is one question; and on the proportion, also, between the state of the general supply of the circulating medium and that of the demand for it, which is another.
>
> (194; italics added)

J. S. Mill repeats the point: "The supply of money . . . is the quantity of it which people are wanting to lay out; that is, all the money they have in their possession, except what they are hoarding, or at least keeping by them as a reserve for future contingencies. The supply of money, in short, is all the money in *circulation* at the time" (*Works*, 3: 509; italics original). Therefore, "Money kept in reserve by individuals to meet contingencies which do not occur, does not act on prices. The money in the coffers of the Bank [of England], or retained as a reserve by private bankers, does not act on prices until drawn out, nor even then unless drawn out to be expended in commodities" (*Works*, 3: 515). Regarding money's demand, "money is bought and sold like other things, whenever other things are bought and sold *for* money. Whoever sells corn, or tallow, or cotton, buys money" (*Works*, 3: 509; italics original). Similarly, Taussig (1921: 1, 234) argues, the "demand for [money] – what is offered in exchange for it – consists of the commodities on sale."

Hume's explanation of money's effect on prices recognizes the process through different markets:

> Though the high price of commodities be a necessary consequence of the encrease of gold and silver [money], yet it follows not immediately upon that encrease; but some time is required before the money circulates through the whole state, and makes its effect be felt on all ranks of people. At first, no alteration is perceived; by degrees the price rises, first of one commodity, then of another; till the whole reaches a just proportion with the new quantity of specie which is in the kingdom.
>
> (1752: 37–8)

Similarly, Thornton argues: "paper credit . . . enhances the prices not of that single spot in which it passes, but of the adjoining places, and of the world" (1802: 270).

Thus, relative prices change during the adjustment process. Besides, Hume does not argue that relative prices are necessarily restored at the end of the adjustment process. Whether they change depends upon various factors, including the distribution of the new money among different recipients, differential rates of production of commodities in response to changes in their demand (elasticities of supply), and the nature of the tax system. Indeed, Ricardo (*Works*, 6: 36 n. 1) argues that a rise in the level of prices, following an increased quantity of money, may be "accompanied with a fall in the price of some few commodities." Similarly, J. S. Mill (*Works*, 3: 511) argues: "some things would rise in price more than others, while some perhaps would not rise at all."

Ricardo explains the phenomenon by the different distribution of the new money (or credit) and the differential effect of rising prices on different income earners, who necessarily do not have the same taste and preferences: "By altering the distribution of property thus, an alteration would be made in the demand for some commodities, there would be a deficiency of supply to the new taste which came to market, with the increase of property: and there would be too much for the taste whose resources had fallen" (*Works*, 5: 107–8; see also *Works*, 1: 89–90). Ricardo also explains that the existence of absolute and proportional taxes alters the rates of taxation between different commodities as the average level of prices rises, owing to an increase in the money supply. This is a point Ricardo (*Works*, 1: 208) notes as "never [having] been averted to," and "account[s] for the different effects, which it was remarked were produced on prices of commodities, from the altered value of money during the Bank restriction" (*Works*, 1: 209). It thus misrepresents classical monetary analysis to argue that it claims relative commodity prices are left unchanged following variations in the quantity of money, whether in the short or the long run, as claimed by adherents of the dichotomization charge.

The quantity of money, interest rates, and the level of prices

As noted in Chapter 2 above, Keynes's displeasure with the Quantity Theory's explanation of the level of prices by money's supply and demand appears to have been motivated mainly by his intent to explain the determination of interest rates by money's supply and demand instead – Keynes's liquidity-preference theory of interest rates. According to Keynes, the rate of interest, rather than being the price of borrowed "capital" or savings, is "the 'price' which equilibrates the desire to hold wealth in the form of cash with the available quantity of cash" (1936: 167). He did not recognize a valid theory of interest rates in classical economics and credited the pre-classical writers, including Montesquieu, with the insight for his money (cash) supply and demand theory of interest. Keynes also ignored the fact that the pre-classical writers defined money as only specie, not inclusive of bank deposits as in Keynes (1930, 1936). Subsequently, he argues, the "rate of interest is determined by the total demand and supply of cash or liquid resources" (1938: 319). He repeats the claim in the 1939 preface to the French edition of the *General Theory*:

> It is the function of the rate of interest to preserve equilibrium, not between the demand and the supply of new capital goods, but between the demand and the supply of money, that is to say between the demand for *liquidity* and the means of satisfying this demand. I am here returning to the doctrine of the older, pre-nineteenth century economists. Montesquieu, for example, saw this truth with considerable clarity.
>
> (1974: xxxiv; italics original)

Keynes thus believed he was supplying a theory of interest rates that was missing in classical analysis. But it is clear from his treatment of the classical "capital" supply and demand theory of interest in Chapter 14 of the *General Theory* that his mistaken belief arose mainly from his having misinterpreted "capital" to mean capital goods rather than savings or loanable funds (Ahiakpor 1990). Recognition of this fatal misinterpretation by Keynes has been missed by such notable Keynes scholars as J. R. Hicks, Don Patinkin, Paul Samuelson, David Laidler, and Axel Leijonhufvud. In restating Keynes's theory of interest, Michael Lawlor (1997) also fails to recognize this aspect of Keynes's dispute with Marshall's treatment of the theory of interest. Lawlor (1997) even eliminates Keynes's appendix to Chapter 14 in which Keynes's confusion is most clearly revealed.

However, since Hume's (1752) essay, "Of Interest," the classics have explained the short-term effect of variations in the quantity of money on interest rates, as well as commodity prices; Keynes (1983: 782–3) taught Marshall's version of the same explanation in his early lectures too. The classics explained that interest is the cost of credit or borrowed savings. Thus, when credit is extended in the form of money,

money is merely the means of conveying the amount of savings being loaned out (see, e.g., Smith *WN*, 1: 374; Ricardo *Works*, 1: 363–5; 3: 91–2; J. S. Mill *Works*, 3: 508). Furthermore, sellers of debt instruments acquire the funds quickly to spend on other commodities rather than holding on to the money for any considerable amount of time. Herein lies the intimate connection between saving and investment that Keynes missed and that his interpreters, including Schumpeter ([1954] 1994: 513–4), Patinkin (1965 [1956]: 367),[13] and Laidler (2006: 44, 50), continue to repeat with the claim that savers and investors are different agents whose activities are not coordinated by the rate of interest. The spending by borrowers replaces the withholding of spending on commodities by the savers (lenders), thus there is little pressure on prices to rise.[14] But if new money is injected into the economy through the credit market, it adds to the volume of credit beyond the volume of savings, which lowers interest rates and increases the level of total spending in the short run. The increased spending raises commodity prices just as if money's suppliers had spent the increased quantity directly on commodities instead of on debt instruments.

The subsequent rise of commodity prices as a result of the increased spending of borrowed money further increases the demand for credit, which restores interest rates to their previous level. As Hume (1752) explains,

> After a sudden acquisition of money. . . . [t]he encrease of lenders above the borrowers sinks the interest. . . . But after this new mass of gold and silver has been digested, and has circulated through the whole state, affairs will soon return to their former situation. . . . The whole money may still be in the state, and make itself felt by the encrease of prices: But not being now collected into any large masses or stocks, the disproportion between the borrowers and lenders is the same as formerly, and consequently the high interest returns.
>
> (57–8)

Ricardo (*Works*, 3: 91) and J. S. Mill (*Works*, 3: 512, 656–7) repeat the argument. Marshall's version of the same argument is:

> Looking at the special case of the effect of an increase in currency on the rate of discount in the western world, the cycle seems to be this. The new currency, or increase of currency, goes, not to private persons, but to the banking centres; and, therefore, it increases the willingness of lenders to lend in the first instance, and lowers the rate of discount. But it afterwards raises prices. This latter movement is cumulative.
>
> (1923: 257)

Hume thus argues that the quantity of money is irrelevant to the level of interest rates in the long run:

> High interest arises from *three* circumstances: A great demand for borrowing; little riches to supply that demand; and great profits arising from commerce: And these circumstances are a clear proof of the small advance of commerce

and industry, not of the scarcity of gold and silver [money]. Low interest, on the other hand, proceeds from the three opposite circumstances: A small demand for borrowing; great riches to supply that demand; and small profits arising from commerce: And these circumstances are all connected together, and proceed from the encrease of industry and commerce, not of gold and silver.

(1752: 49; italics original)

Indeed, with the same quantity of money (cash) in an economy, interest rates may rise because of an increased demand for savings or loanable funds, and interest rates may fall from an increased supply of savings, with money serving merely as the instrument of conveying savers' funds to borrowers.

As J. S. Mill (*Works*, 3: 655) also argues, the "rate of interest bears no necessary relation to the quantity or value of money in circulation. The permanent amount of the circulating medium, whether great or small affects only prices; not the rate of interest." Marshall's (1923: 73) version of the same argument is:

As a general rule, interest rises in consequence of a greater willingness of borrowers to borrow, or of a greater unwillingness of lenders to lend: the first generally indicates increased confidence, and perhaps increased prosperity; the latter generally indicates the opposite. . . . Thus, a fall in the purchasing power of money tends, after a while, to raise the rate of interest on investments, whether for long periods, or short.

In spite of the above classical explanations, Keynes (1936: 182–3) accuses the classics of having separated the theory of value from the theory of interest: "the classical school have had quite a different theory of the rate of interest in Volume I. dealing with the theory of value from what they have had in Volume II. dealing with the theory of money. They have seemed undisturbed by the conflict and have made no attempt, as far as I know, to build a bridge between the two theories." Samuel Hollander (1987: 275), citing J. S. Mill (*Works*, 3: 648), appropriately dismisses Keynes's charge as "completely misplaced."

Furthermore, Hume (1752) acknowledges a positive impact of an increased inflow of money on output and employment in the short run:

All augmentation [of money] has no other effect than to heighten the price of labour [wage rate] and commodities; and even this variation is little more than that of name. In the *progress towards these changes*, the augmentation may have some influence, by *exciting industry*; but after the prices are settled, suitably to the new abundance of gold and silver, it has no manner of influence.

(48; italics added)

Hume thus cautions against belief in the increased rate of money's inflow being the source of long-term economic growth. Such belief mistakes "a collateral effect for a cause" (1752: 41), Hume argues. Rather, growth arises from the improved "manners and customs" as well as the industry of a people. The more industrious a people, the more money would flow into the economy in payment for exports as the domestic prices fall. Smith (*WN*, 1: 313) appears clearer about the need for increased savings to fund investment spending and economic growth, noting that money is not "capital":

> When we compute the quantity of industry which the circulating capital of any society can employ, we must always have regard to those parts of it only, which consist in provisions, materials, and finished work: the other, which consists of money, and *which serves only to circulate* these three, must always be deducted. . . . Money is neither a material to work upon, tools to work with; and though the wages of the workman are commonly paid to him in money, his real revenue, like that of all other men, consists, not in the money, but in the money's worth; not in the metal pieces, but in what can be got for them.
>
> (*WN*, 1: 313; italics added)

Ricardo (*Works*, 3: 92–3) and J. S. Mill (*Works*, 2: 55) make a similar point. This is the essence of the classicals' position on the increased quantity of money not being a determinant of long-term economic growth.

The short-term excitement of industry may occur when recipients of new money are enabled to hire more workers (at existing contracted wage rates) to increase the rate of production. When commodity prices rise, workers demand higher wage rates as wage contracts expire. The rise in nominal wage rates restores the real wage rate, reduces profits, and leads to the laying-off of some workers and to the return of the rate of production to the pre-monetary increase's level. Contrary to Keynes (1936: 80–1), subsequent classical writers accepted Hume's analysis, without assuming its occurrence only under full employment of labor. Keynes bases that insistence on Hayek's (1932: 125) partial citation of Jeremy Bentham's account of the forced-saving mechanism: "all hands being employed and employed in the most advantageous manner." But Bentham (*Economic Writings*, 1: 170) also explains, "If any [labor] were unemployed, not fully employed, [the increased quantity of money] might encrease industry *pro tanto.*" The classics also acknowledged Hume's precedence in the analysis that Bentham calls "forced frugality" (*Economic Writings*, 3: 349); Henry Thornton calls the resulting capital accumulation "forced" (1802: 239); Ricardo refers to it as "a violent and unjust transfer of property" (*Works*, 3: 93); Thomas Malthus describes it as "unjust [transfer] of property" (1811: 97); and J. S. Mill describes it as "a forced accumulation" (1874: 118).

It is well known in modern macroeconomics that wage contracts delay the adjustment of wage rates to variations in commodity prices, as in the Phillips curve analysis. Classical monetary analysis argues the same (see, e.g., Ahiakpor 2009). As Smith (*WN*, 1: 74) explains, "What are the common wages of labour, depends every where upon the contract usually made between [the] two parties, whose interests are by no means the same. The workmen desire to get as much, the masters to give as little as possible. The former are disposed to combine in order to raise, the latter to lower the wages of labour." Also, Smith observes, the "money price of labour . . . does not fluctuate from year to year with the money price of corn, but seems to be every where accommodated, not to the temporary or occasional, but to the average or ordinary price of that necessary of life" (*WN*, 1: 40–1).

Ricardo's acknowledgment of the short-term effect of an increased quantity of money on output and employment includes:

> There is but one way in which an increase of money no matter how it be introduced into the society, can augment riches, viz. at the *expense of wages of labour*; till the wages of labour have found their level with the increased prices which the commodities will have experienced, there will be so much additional revenue to the manufacturer and farmer they will obtain an increased price for their commodities, and can whilst wages do no increase employ an additional number of hands, so that the real riches of the country will be somewhat augmented. A productive labourer will produce something more than before relatively to his consumption, but this can be only of momentary duration.
>
> (*Works*, 3: 318–9; italics added)

The forced-saving phenomenon, which Keynes (1936: 292) fails appreciate, thus illustrates the nexus between variations in the quantity of money, credit, interest rates, and commodity prices in the short run.

The classical argument was adopted in early neoclassical monetary analysis by writers such as Marshall and Marshall (1879: 156–7), Marshall (1920: 493–4), and Fisher (1926). A version of Pigou's restatement is:

> currency inflation, by conferring a continuing bounty upon business men at the expense of rentiers and wage-earners, can keep an industrial boom alive long after, in the ordinary course, reaction would have set in; and . . . currency deflation can render an industrial depression much deeper in extent and much more prolonged than it would have been if deflation had not been attempted.
>
> (1927: 238)

This is the opposite of Keynes's argument, which claims, the "view that *any* increase in the quantity of money is inflationary (unless we mean by *inflationary* merely that prices are rising) is bound up with the underlying assumption of the classical theory that we are *always* in a condition where a reduction in the real rewards of the factors of production will lead to a curtailment in their supply" (1936: 304; italics original). The classics did not argue that workers would curtail their labor services while commodity prices are rising in the short run. And, by inflation, the classics meant "prices are rising."

Textbook repetitions of Keynes's alleged classical dichotomy

N. Gregory Mankiw appears to have been the most elaborate among textbook authors repeating Keynes's charge of a classical dichotomy. However, rather than

Keynes's own version of the alleged dichotomy, Mankiw follows Patinkin's (1965 [1956]: 172–4) characterization of the alleged dichotomy as the division of an economy strictly between the real and monetary sectors. In his *Principles of Macroeconomics* (2015; boldface in the original), Mankiw argues:

> Hume and his contemporaries suggested that economic variables should be divided into two groups. The first group consists of **nominal variables** – variables in monetary units. The second group consists of **real variables** – variables measured in physical units. . . . The separation of real and nominal variables is now called the classical dichotomy. . . . According to classical analysis, nominal variables are influenced by developments in the economy's monetary system, whereas money is largely irrelevant for explaining real variables.
>
> (251)

Mankiw further equates the alleged classical dichotomy with money's neutrality:

> Changes in the supply of money, according to classical analysis, affect nominal variables but not real ones. When the central bank doubles the money supply, the price level doubles, the dollar wage doubles, and all other dollar values double. . . . Real variables, such as production, employment, real wages, and real interest rates, are unchanged. The irrelevance of monetary changes for real variables is called **monetary neutrality**.
>
> (2015: 252; bolding original)

Mankiw also contrasts the alleged classical dichotomy with the more realistic modern view: "most economists today believe that over short periods of time – within the span of a year or two – monetary changes affect real variables. Hume himself also doubted that monetary neutrality would apply in the short run" (2015: 252). He misattributes to Ricardo the view that "when a central bank doubles the money supply, all prices double, and the value of the unit of account falls by half" (352), without qualifying the argument as Ricardo's long-run proposition.

In Mankiw's (2013: 127) intermediate *Macroeconomics* text, he repeats the characterization of a classical dichotomy as the "theoretical separation of real and nominal variables." He also equates the alleged classical dichotomy with money's neutrality, arguing, "For many purposes – in particular for studying long-run issues – monetary neutrality is approximately correct. Yet monetary neutrality does not fully describe the world in which we live" (ibid.). He underscores the latter view with the observation that "during the time horizon over which prices are sticky, the classical dichotomy no longer holds: nominal variables can influence real variables, and the economy can deviate from the equilibrium predicted by the classical model" (282). Mankiw does not mention the classical forced-saving phenomenon whereby increases in the quantity of money increase commodity prices, real output, and employment in the short run until wage, interest, and rental rates, hitherto restrained by contracts, have adjusted to the monetary increase in the long run.

Other textbook authors who have followed Patinkin's rendition of the alleged classical dichotomy as the separation of the real from the monetary sectors of an economy include Andrew Abel, Ben Bernanke, and Dean Croushore (2014: 398), J. Bradford DeLong and Martha Olney (2006: 227),[15] R. Glenn Hubbard, Anthony O'Brien, and Matthew Rafferty (2014: 217), Frederic Mishkin (2015: 111, 222),[16] and Stephen Williamson (2014: 455). Like Mankiw, these authors also tend to equate the alleged classical dichotomy with money's long-run neutrality with respect to output and employment in classical monetary analysis. Thus, Abel, Bernanke, and Croushore assert, "Although monetary neutrality holds in the long run in the Keynesian model, it holds *immediately* in the basic classical model. So, in the basic classical model, *monetary policy* changes have *no effect* on real exchange rates or trade flows; they affect only the price level" (2014: 509; italics added). DeLong and Olney claim, "Economists also speak of [the classical dichotomy] as the property whereby money is neutral or is a veil, a covering that does not affect the shape of the face underneath" (2006: 227). Hubbard, Anthony O'Brien, and Matthew Rafferty argue, "One implication of the classical dichotomy is *money neutrality*, or the assertion that in the long run, changes in the money supply have no effect on real variables" (2014: 217; italics original). Mishkin claims, "Furthermore, a central bank's work in adjusting the money supply changes only the price level and has no impact on real variables, an implication economists refer to as the neutrality of money. However . . . many economists reject the neutrality of money in the short run" (2015: 111–2).

Equating the two arguments – dichotomy of prices and money's long-run neutrality – is incorrect. One, the alleged dichotomy, does not belong in classical monetary analysis, while the other, money's long-run neutrality with respect to output and employment, is founded on a fundamental understanding: only savings to fund investment make increased production and employment possible in the long run. Were money the "capital" needed for production and hiring labor, no nation would be poor.

Conclusion

Keynes searched for policies that would help solve the problem of unemployment. He found the classical Quantity Theory's conclusion that, in the long run, the level of prices in an economy reflects only the proportion of money to commodities a hindrance to his advocacy of increasing money's quantity as an employment-promotion policy. He considered Hume's explanation that increasing quantities of money may promote output and employment growth only in the short run until all prices, including wage rates, have fully adjusted to the increased quantity to be unhelpful. He believed Hume had missed the fact that it is in the intermediate, short period that we live, whereas the long-run equilibrium period hardly is ever reached: "it is in the transition that we actually have our being" (Keynes 1936: 343, n. 3). Believing he had turned the Quantity Theory into a theory of output as a whole, Keynes felt justified in arguing that it is from the supply and demand of that output that the "price level" is determined.

Money's supply relative to its demand rather should determine the level of interest rates, Keynes argued. But the indictment stems from his misinterpretation of the classical Quantity Theory.

First, the nature of money's supply curve is discernible from classical and neoclassical monetary analysis. So is the nature of money's demand curve that should be a rectangular hyperbola: a unitary elasticity of money's demand with respect to variations in money's value – inverse of the level of prices. By serving both as a unit of account and a means of payment in commodity markets, money features intimately in the determination of commodity prices. Only after commodity prices have been determined can "the mass of prices" (Ricardo *Works*, 3: 299) or "the average level of prices" (Marshall 1923: 50) be determined.

Several repetitions of Keynes's alleged classical dichotomy misstate the charge, following Patinkin's version, as a separation of the monetary from the real sectors of an economy in classical monetary analysis. Some textbook authors also incorrectly have equated the alleged classical dichotomy with the classicals' proposition of money's long-run neutrality with respect to output and employment growth. Both Keynes's (1936) original charge and the modern versions distort classical monetary analysis, and in the process obscure the relevant classical insight about the proper role of monetary policy. That policy is to sustain the level of prices through variations in the supply of money to meet the growth of its demand, not to attempt to manipulate the level of interest rates. Rather, policies to encourage increased savings to supply the funds for investment should be pursued because money is not "capital." Keynes, on the other hand, mistook saving to be the equivalent of, or include, cash hoarding and thus logically imputed a negative effect of increased savings on output and employment growth.

The attempt in many countries to promote economic growth and increased employment with increasing quantities of money has instead mostly resulted in inflation and higher rates of interest when the increased quantities of money have been exchanged for commodities in the marketplace, just as the classics argued. Keynes's misinterpretation of the classical Quantity Theory has been a great source of confusion in modern macroeconomics.

Notes

1 This chapter is based on my paper, "A Classical Dichotomy or Keynes's Misinterpretation of the Classical Quantity Theory of Money?" presented at the History of Economics Society Annual Meetings, Duke University, Durham, NC, June 17–20, 2016.

2 Keynes uses "the price level" but the classics used variously "the average level of prices," "the level of prices," "general prices," "the price of commodities," or "the mass of prices" that immediately communicates its determination by prices in various commodity markets. Modern macroeconomics appears to have settled on using Keynes's "price level" to mean the average level of prices.

3 As noted in Chapter 2 above, Keynes taught the same principle in his first lecture on the theory of money in 1912: "The value of money depends, like anything else, upon the interaction of supply and demand, and can be treated, therefore, as a special case of the general theory of value . . . the theory of value as applied to money is sometimes crudely described as the 'Quantity Theory of Money'." (Keynes 1983: 693).

4 Note that Keynes's argument makes it difficult to explain variations in the level of prices from changes in the demand for money that do not arise from changes in the level of output. The classical Quantity Theory does not entail that difficulty. Increased demand for money at the expense of purchasing commodities, but not financial assets, lowers the level of commodity prices without immediately affecting interest rates, according to classical analysis.

5 Patinkin here appears to have accepted as valid Keynes's (1936: 305) derivation of a "proportionate change in prices in response to a change in the quantity of money, [which] can be regarded as a generalized statement of the Quantity Theory of Money."

6 This form of Keynes's charge of a classical dichotomy has been most influential with many textbook writers, including Abel, Bernanke, and Croushore (2014), DeLong and Olney (2006), Hubbard, O'Brien, and Rafferty (2014), Mankiw (2013, 2015), and Williamson (2014). Patinkin (1965) also discusses the "valid classical dichotomy" on pages 180, 251 n, 297–8, and 306–7.

7 Blaug (1996: 147) also acknowledges that, in classical monetary analysis, "Changes in absolute prices are almost always associated with alterations in relative prices." On Ricardo's analysis of money's non-neutrality in both the short run and long run – with respect to relative prices, see Ahiakpor 1985.

8 David Laidler (1991) appears to side with Blaug's more favorable treatment of the neoclassicals over the classicals regarding the alleged dichotomy. Laidler argues: "Wicksell understood far more clearly than had Mill (1844), and indeed just as clearly as Patinkin (1965 [1956]), that the 'classical dichotomy' between theories of relative prices and the general price level could not be generally valid, and had to be abandoned if the causative mechanisms bringing about price level variations were to be analysed" (1991: 123).

9 Keynes (1936: 3n) includes among the classical economists, Ricardo, J. S. Mill, Marshall, and A. C. Pigou.

10 Similarly, the classical theory of interest is an application of the theory of value to "capital" or savings (see, e.g., Hume 1752, "Of Interest"; Smith *WN*, 1: 99–100, 358, 374; Ricardo *Works*, 1: 363–4, 2: 331, 3: 88–9, 143; J. S. Mill *Works*, 3: 647, 655; Marshall 1920: 443–4, and Bk 6, Ch. 6, "Interest of Capital"). Dennis Robertson (1940: 12) also restates the classical theory of interest as "the interaction of schedules of supply and demand [for] free or floating capital," which "recent writers seem to have settled down to calling 'loanable' or 'investible fund'," referring to the theory's explanation in Marshall's *Principles*.

11 Smith's explanation of the demand for money is similar to Carl Menger's (1892) explanation of a commodity's "saleableness" being the key characteristic for its becoming the common medium of exchange. Menger himself however claims originality of the idea: "Nor do even the theorists above mentioned [including Adam Smith] honestly face the problem that is to be solved, to wit, the explaining how it has come to pass that certain commodities (the precious metals at certain stages of culture) should be promoted amongst the mass of all other commodities, and accepted as the generally acknowledged media of exchange" (241).

12 Note again that the unitary elasticity of classical money's demand curve is not with respect to the rate of interest, as Keynes (1936: Chs. 13 and 17) conceives of money's demand curve.

13 Patinkin even incorrectly claims that "there was no precise attempt in the classical literature to distinguish between savings and the supply of loans, on the one hand, and between investment and the demand for loans, on the other" (1965 [1956]: 367). But by purchasing financial assets, savers supply the loanable funds demanded by the suppliers of the financial assets: $S = \Delta FA^d = \Delta FA^s = I$; the acquired funds are employed in the form of fixed and circulating capital in the sphere of production.

14 Prices may rise if banks reduce their excess reserve-deposit ratios to increase their rate of lending. Such increased rate of credit extension amounts to a reduction in the banks' demand for money to hold, which increases money's velocity or "rapidity of circulation" (see, e.g., J. S. Mill *Works*, 3: 512–3).

15 DeLong and Olney also argue that the "power to analyze real variables without referring to the price level is a special feature of the flexible-price full-employment model of the economy. Economists call it the **classical dichotomy**: Real Variables (such as real GDP, real investment spending, or the real exchange rate) can be analyzed and calculated without thinking of nominal variables such as the price level" (2006: 227; boldface in the original).

16 Mishkin further argues that "we typically refer to models with slowly adjusting (sticky) prices as **Keynesian models**, because it was John Maynard Keynes who first developed macroeconomic models in which the classical dichotomy did not hold" (2015: 223; boldface in the original).

4 On interpreting a controversial passage in David Hume's "Of Money"

The impediment of Keynes's influence

Introduction[1]

To explain the short-term, possible stimulative effect of money on output and employment, David Hume (1752) discusses in a famous and controversial passage of his essay, "Of Money," the various stages through which an increased quantity of money affects production, employment, and prices, including wage rates. The major classical writers, aware that wage rates were settled by contracts and did not change concurrently with variations of commodity prices, interpreted Hume's explanation as one of lagging wage rates behind changes in commodity prices, besides changes in other contracted rates such as interest and rents. Richard Cantillon (1755: 267–9) gives a similar description of new money's impact on prices and production, explicitly acknowledging the role of contracts. The phenomenon is what the classical economists, including Henry Thornton (1802), T. R. Malthus (1811), Ricardo (*Works*, 1: 101–2, 160; 4: 36–7), and J. S. Mill (*Works*, 3: 511, 564–5), referred to as "forced saving" in periods of rising commodity prices (Ahiakpor 2009).[2] E. A. J. Johnson (1937), Eric Roll (1938), Michael Duke (1979), Thomas Humphrey (1982a), Istvan Hont (1983), and Geoffrey Wood (1995) are among the modern interpreters of Hume's "Of Money" to entail the lagging of wage rates behind commodity prices. The lagged-wage rates interpretation of Hume is also similar to explanations of monetary dynamics by some early neoclassical writers, including Marshall, Irving Fisher, Neville Keynes, and Frank Taussig, who did not refer to Hume's essay on money but rather to Ricardo's and J. S. Mill's. Mark Blaug (1995: 34; italics added) also makes the connection between Hume's monetary analysis and those of Knut Wicksell and Irving Fisher that include "forced saving, falling real rates of interest, [and] wages *lagging behind* prices," citing Don Patinkin (1987: 640–3) as reference.

However, John Maynard Keynes's (1936: 12, 307, 309) considerable influence in reviving the argument, severely criticized, for example, by J. S. Mill (*Works*, 3: 479–80, 691–3, 699–70), that prices are determined primarily by variations in wage rates or the "wage-unit" – a wage cost-push theory of inflation – has encouraged an alternative, lagging-prices interpretation of Hume's controversial passage. J. S. Mill declares, "General low wages do not cause low prices, nor high wages high prices, within the country itself. General prices are not raised by a rise of wages" (*Works*, 3: 692) and "increased wages, when common to all descriptions of productive labourers, and when really representing a greater Cost of Labour, are always and necessarily at the expense of profits" (*Works*, 3: 699–700). This after having acknowledged, "But that high wages make high prices, is a popular and wide-spread opinion. The whole amount of error involved in this proposition can only be seen thoroughly when we come to the theory of money" (*Works*, 3: 479).

Keynes occasionally slipped into arguing the lagging of wage rates behind rising or falling commodity prices, but it is the opposite sequence that dominates his analyses. For example, Keynes (1936: 301; italics added) argues:

> In addition to the final critical point of full employment at which money-wages have to rise, in response to an increasing effective demand in terms of money, fully in proportion to the rise in the prices of wage-goods, we have a succession of earlier semi-critical points at which an increasing effective demand tends to raise money-wages *though not fully in proportion to the rise in the price of wage goods*; and similarly in the case of a decreasing effective demand.

However, according to Keynes, classical theory "has taught us to believe that prices are governed by marginal prime cost in terms of money and that money-wages largely govern prime cost. Thus if money-wages change, one would have expected the classical school to argue that prices would change in almost the same proportion" (1936: 12). At best, Keynes here appears to be confusing microeconomic analysis with macroeconomic analysis. An increase in the cost of an input, including wages, may lead to a reduction in the supply of a product and cause its price to rise. But if more of the community's income were spent on that product, less would be spent on others. Thus, it is impossible for the average of all prices to rise because wages have risen in the production of one commodity or in an industry.

But, following Keynes's wage cost-push theory of inflation, Eugene Rotwein (1955) interprets Hume's (1752) controversial passage in "Of Money" to have been arguing that output and employment would rather decrease after prices fully have risen to reflect an increased quantity of money and wage rates. To make consistent meaning of the passage, which Morris Perlman (1987: 274) describes as "one of the most controversial passages in David Hume's economic essays," he substitutes the "price of manufactured goods" (280) in place of Hume's "price of labor." John Berdell (1995: 1210) credits Perlman's analysis with having done us "a notable service in clarifying Hume's archaic use of the term 'the price of labour' to indicate the price of final goods." David Laidler and Roger Sandilands (2010: 583) agree: "Morris Perlman (1987) has argued persuasively that the word 'labour' in the . . . quote from Hume should be read as meaning 'the output of labour'."[3]

Carl Wennerlind (2005, 2008) most closely follows Keynes's economic analysis in interpreting the controversial passage. He employs the wage cost-push theory of inflation, the consumption expenditure multiplier, and Keynes's conflation of bank credit (deposits) with currency sometimes in defining money, rather than Hume's limiting the term "money" to specie. Thus, according to Wennerlind, Hume argues that an increased inflow of money leads to increased production and employment, higher wage rates, then higher commodity prices, as the increased incomes of labor are spent. The higher wage rates and higher prices chase each other "until the multiplier process comes to an end" (2005: 229). The alternative Keynesian interpretation ignores Hume's arguing in "Of Interest" (1752: 51) that contracts had become prevalent in most market transactions, which must include contracts to pay wages, interest, and rents, after having noted the existence of contracts in "Of Money" (1752: 43). The alternative interpretation also contrasts with the monetary analyses of Hume's contemporaries, including Cantillon, Josiah Tucker (1776), and Smith (1776).

This chapter explains why the alternative lagged-prices interpretation of Hume's controversial passage is inconsistent with his argument regarding the temporary stimulative or depressing effect of variations in the quantity of money (and credit) on output and employment until commodity prices and wage rates fully have adjusted to the variation. Hume wrote "Of Money" and other economic essays to explain observed phenomena, not merely to engage in speculative explanations; he sought to "*reconcile reason to experience*" (1752: 41; italics original). In "Of the Balance of Trade," Hume also claims to be seeking a "general theory" (1752: 67) of money. This contrasts, for example, with Michael Duke's (1979: 586) interpreting Hume to have engaged in "historical empiricism." Wennerlind makes a similar claim, suggesting a lack of unified and consistent theorizing by Hume, especially regarding the Quantity Theory in "Of Money." Wennerlind argues: "the primary explanation [of Hume's essay on money] must focus on Hume's *methodological pragmatism* and the fact that he chose thematic essays, rather than a more systematic treatise, to express his ideas on political economy" (2005: 236; italics added).

A dissenting referee on my manuscript for the *History of Economic Ideas* also argued:

> Hume did not intend to build a dynamic model of the economy, but, rather, meant to draw attention to "two observations, which may, perhaps, serve to employ the thoughts of our speculative politicians" and which are at odds with the asserted irrelevance of the quantity of money for the prosperity of the Nation. . . . Thus Hume is not interested in explaining why and how all prices rise, this being consistent with his belief in the quantity theory of money, but how and why output and employment increase. And this conclusion is not challenged by whichever answer is given to the question raised by the author [Do prices rise before wage rates or the reverse?]

However, taking into account Hume's analyses in his other relevant writings, especially "Of Interest," his explicit acknowledgment of the difficulty for producers to shift high wage costs onto product prices in "Of Taxes" (1752: 87), and some of his correspondence, we can fill in the gap in his explanation of the adjustment of wage rates and prices to variations in money's inflow in the controversial passage consistently to fit a general theory. A consistent interpretation of Hume's passage also helps us to appreciate his monetary policy recommendation to the "magistrate" – increasing quantity of money, if possible, in a growing economy in order to keep the level of prices from falling, not promoting inflation.

The gap in Hume's confusing or controversial passage

Hume wanted to explain that the level of prices in an economy reflects the proportion of money (specie) to output in the long run, but that variations in the quantity of money and credit affect the rate of production and employment in the transition to the long-run proportionality. This is because money is merely a representation or a measure of the value of commodities; money is not a means of production such that its greater quantity in an economy assures a greater rate of production and employment growth. Rather, increased production, from the development of the arts and industry would itself attract more money into an economy as domestic prices fall relative to those abroad, generating increased exports. Thus, Hume opens his essay, "Of Money," with the observation that the absolute quantity of money in an economy is of little consequence in the long run:

> Money is not, properly speaking, one of the subjects of commerce; but only the instrument which men have agreed upon to facilitate the exchange of one commodity for another. It is none of the wheels of trade: It is the oil which renders the motion of the wheels more smooth and easy. If we consider any one kingdom by itself, it is evident, that the greater or less plenty of money is of no consequence; since the prices of commodities are always proportioned to the plenty of money.
>
> (1752: 33)

Hume repeats the point in the second part of his essay: "The absolute quantity of the precious metals is a matter of great indifference" (1752: 46). Money in Hume's analysis is specie, while paper money is a means of extending credit. Thus, Hume refers to banknotes as "paper credit" or "fictitious money" (1752: 35). There is therefore only one quantity theory of money relating the level of prices to the ratio of money to output or to money's supply relative to its demand in Hume's analysis. This contrasts with Wennerlind's (2005: 224–5, 227–31) claiming there are two theories: one in which money is endogenous and non-neutral, the other where money is exogenous and fully neutral.

Hume precedes the controversial passage with acknowledging the short-run positive effect of an increased rate of money's inflow: "in every kingdom, into which money begins to flow in greater abundance than formerly, every thing takes a new face: labour and industry gain life; the merchant becomes more enterprising, the manufacturer more diligent and skillful, and even the farmer follows his plough with greater alacrity and attention" (1752: 37). He relates such positive short-run effect to the experience of Europe: "Since the discovery of the mines in AMERICA, industry has increased in all nations of EUROPE, except in the possessors of those mines; and this may justly be ascribed, amongst other reasons, to the encrease of gold and silver" (ibid.).[4] He notes that such evidence contradicts the expected ultimate influence of a greater abundance of money in a kingdom, namely, "heightening the price of commodities, and obliging every one to pay a greater number of these little yellow or white pieces for every thing he purchases" as well as raising "the price of every kind of labour," both of these effects also being disadvantageous to a nation in its "foreign trade" (ibid.). The higher product prices reduce exports while the higher wage rates may reduce profits and productions as a result (see also Hume's "Of Commerce" 1752: 15–6).

Hume elaborates the short-run dynamics of money on an economy thus:

> To account, then, for this phenomenon, we must consider, that though the high price of commodities be a necessary consequence of the increase of gold and silver, yet it follows not immediately upon that increase; but some time is required before the money circulates through the whole state, and makes its effect be felt on all ranks of people. At first, no alteration is perceived; by degrees the price rises, first of one commodity, then of another; till the whole at last reaches a just proportion with the new quantity of specie which is in the kingdom. In my opinion, it is only in this interval or intermediate situation, between the acquisition of money and rise of prices that the encreasing quantity of gold and silver is favourable to industry.
>
> (1752: 37–8)

Hume repeats the argument in "Of Interest":

> All augmentation [of money] has no other effect than to heighten the price of labour and commodities . . . In the progress towards these changes, the augmentation may have some influence, by exciting industry; but after the prices are settled, suitably to the new abundance of gold and silver, it has no manner of influence.
>
> (1752: 48)

Thus, Hume clearly states the short-run, non-neutral effect of money, owing to the "just" proportion of money to commodities having been disturbed from its previous level.[5] Note also that Hume talks about commodity prices rising, first of one, and then another, not the prices of labor rising at the beginning. The last sentence in the quote above as well as Hume's repetition of the point in "Of Interest" is the basis for interpreting him to have argued money's non-neutrality in the short run and the neutrality of money on the growth of output and employment in the long run, but which Wennerlind (2005: 227–31) disputes. Margaret Schabas (2008: 136) also disputes our reading a short-run versus long-run analysis of money's influence in Hume's analysis. She insists there is no time dimension in Hume's analysis. I dispute her claim below.

Hume's argument above also contrasts with Humphrey's (1991: 6) view that Hume argues a long-run, non-neutral view of money in which the lagging of prices behind the inflow of money keeps output and employment growth continually increasing, thus yielding a downward-sloping, long-run Phillips curve. Indeed, Hume also argues the possibility of an increased quantity of money having a positive impact on the "manners and customs of the people" (1752: 46), resulting in an increased rate of production in the long run. But it is the changed manners and customs of a people that produce the long-term economic growth rather than the increased quantity of money itself, Hume insists: "we mistake, as is too usual, a collateral effect for a cause" (41), if we argued the opposite causation.

Significant in Hume's explanation of the short-run, non-neutrality of money are two elements: (1) the initial non-awareness of all market participants of the increasing quantity of money and its effect on prices, and (2) the non-instantaneous adjustment of all market prices, including the price of labor (wage rates). Hume earlier makes the point in his 1 November 1750 letter to Oswald:

> I agree with you, that the increase of money, if not too sudden, naturally increases people and industry, and by that means may retain itself; but if it do not produce such an increase, nothing will retain it except hoarding. Suppose twenty millions brought into Scotland; suppose that, by some fatality, we take no advantage of this to augment our industry or people, how much would remain in the quarter of a century? Not a shilling more than we have at present.
> (Quoted in Rotwein 1955: 197–8)

However, in the course of elaborating the short-run price adjustment process Hume describes the initial stages of money's effect on output and employment without the rise of prices, but ends the passage with the increased "price of labour" without explaining why or when product prices start to rise. Perlman (1987: 278) appropriately observes, "In the detailed description of the process . . . prices of commodities do not seem to be mentioned. It is as though we get a story with the promised denouement left out." Hume's controversial elaboration proceeds as follows:

> When any quantity of money is imported into a nation, it is not at first dispersed into many hands, but is confined to the coffers of a few persons, who immediately seek to employ it to advantage. Here are a set of manufacturers or merchants, we shall suppose, who have received returns of gold and silver for goods which they sent to CADIZ. They are thereby enabled to employ more workmen than formerly, who never dream of demanding higher wages, but are glad of employment from such good paymasters. If workmen become scarce, the manufacturer gives higher wages, but at first requires an encrease of labour; and this is willingly submitted to by the artisan, who can now eat and drink better, to compensate his additional toil and fatigue. He carries his money to market, but returns with greater quantity and of better kinds, for the use of his family. The farmer and gardener, finding, that all their commodities are taken off, apply themselves with alacrity to the raising more; and at the same time can afford to take better and more cloths from their tradesmen, whose price is the same as formerly, and their industry only whetted by so much new gain. It is easy to trace the money in its progress through the whole

commonwealth; where we shall find, that it must first quicken the diligence of every individual, before it increase the price of labour.

$$(1752: 38)^6$$

Interpreting Hume's passage above, Schabas (2008: 139–40) claims it is because the "workers are . . . paid in full-bodied coins [with which] they can pay off their debts with local shopkeepers, [and] leave with choicer cuts of meat and fresher ale" that they consider the recipients of specie from Cádiz good paymasters. Furthermore, she argues, "It is the weight and sound of jangling coins in the pocket that induces greater productivity" of the workers. Now previously unemployed people who find employment at the going wage rate may be inclined to regard their employers as "good paymasters" whether they are paid in coin or in paper money. Besides, in Hume's economy, coins were the principal means of payment. However, Hume also explains in "Of the Balance of Trade" that banknotes were "used in all payments for goods, manufactures, *tradesmen's labour of all kinds*; and these notes, from the established credit of the companies [banks], passed as money in all payments throughout" (1752: 71; italics added). Also, in a 10 July 1769 letter to Morellet, Hume acknowledges money's deriving its usefulness in the market exchange process not from its intrinsic value "but as something which another will take" readily from its possessor (Rotwein 1955: 214). Schabas makes the same point: "As long as the notes are legal tender and widely accepted, they have the same capacity [as specie] to stimulate production and trade" (2008: 140–1).

In attempting to connect Hume's narrative of money's initial effect on production at unchanged prices with his stated goal of accounting for the ultimate rise of prices, readers influenced by Keynes's wage cost-push theory of prices have interpreted the passage differently from the earlier (classical and early neoclassical) interpretation of lagging wage rates behind commodity prices. Hume, indeed, appears to provide little good guidance in the passage for bridging the gap. He argues that when workers become scarce and employers are obliged to offer higher wages, "an encrease of labour" is first required of them. If such increase of labor is in terms of the "additional toil and fatigue" or longer hours of work, it would not lead to an increase in the unit cost of output and depress the rate of profits.

Even if we interpreted "an encrease of labour" to mean higher labor productivity, a higher wage rate in compensation for it would not result in an increase in the unit cost of output, reducing the quantity produced and possibly the rise of product prices, a point Tucker (1776: 34) well makes with a question: "Is it not much cheaper to give 2s. 6d. a Day in the rich Country to the nimble and adroit Artist, than it is to give only 6d. in the poor one, to the tedious, aukward [sic] Bungler?" Tucker (1776: 35–9) also cites numerous examples in England and Scotland to refute the notion that the high wages cause high prices, noting: "the Fact itself is quite the Reverse of this seemingly just Conclusion" (36; see also Hont 1983: 286). But Tucker did not accuse Hume of having argued high wages causing high prices. In his 4 March 1758 letter to Lord Kames in response to Tucker's observations, Hume does not object to Tucker's point either (see Rotwein 1955: 199–202).

Smith (*WN*, 1: 84–5) pretty much repeats Tucker's arguments, but without reference to him.

Also, in the absence of worker scarcity that requires nominal wage increases, an increased production and employment could result from the new money (income to exporters) having enabled its recipients to hire more workers "who never dream of demanding higher wages." They were (a) previously unemployed and (b) unaware – yet to perceive – that the real wage rate would soon be declining since the new money had yet to make "its effect be felt on all ranks of people." In the very next paragraph, Hume argues that "the specie may encrease to a considerable pitch, before it have this latter effect" (39), namely, the increased "price of labour." So, what causes the rise of product prices Hume earlier describes in the passage?

Filling in the gap in Hume's controversial passage

In attempting to fill in the gap in Hume's controversial passage, it may be helpful first to account for the possible sources of increased exports that would have led to the manufacturers or merchants receiving the money (gold and silver) from Cádiz, but which Hume does not tell us. Consistent with Hume's price-specie-flow analysis – money flows after lower prices among trading nations (see also Smith *WN*, 1: 460: "money necessarily runs after goods, but goods do not always or necessarily run after money") – the relevant sources include (a) a rise in the price of exportable goods abroad, (b) a fall in the domestic price of exportable goods, owing to an increase in the productivity of domestic industry, and (c) a fall in domestic prices, following an increased rate of cash hoarding[7] (or a contraction of domestic credit). None of these sources is consistent with the rise of wage rates before the rise of product prices.

In the case of higher prices of exportable goods abroad, the increased inflow of money would enable domestic producers to hire more workers in order to increase production, with or without the offer of higher wages. The incentive to increase domestic production also would remain for as long as domestic prices are below foreign prices.[8] And when domestic prices rise, the increased profitability of production would remain for as long as wage rates are unchanged and real wages have decreased or the rate of nominal wage's increase has yet to catch up with the rate of price increase. The increased rate of production would come to an end when the rise of nominal wage rates has reduced the rate of profits and the level of domestic prices has caught up with foreign prices. At that point, the level of money, output, employment, prices, and wage rates would be higher than when the process began, but their growth rates would return to zero or to the rates before the increased rate of money's inflow. The end result appears to be what Hume (1752: 35) describes:

> That provisions and labour should become dear by the encrease of trade and money, is in many respects, an inconvenience; but an inconvenience that is unavoidable, and the effect of the public wealth and prosperity which are the end of all our wishes. It is compensated by the advantages, which we reap

from the possession of these precious metals, and the weight, which they give the nation in all foreign wars and negociations [sic].

It is the higher domestic prices that Hume considers an inconvenience. Although nominal wage rates would have increased, Hume does not consider that an inconvenience:

> It is true, the English feel some disadvantages in foreign trade by the high price of labour, which is in part the effect of the riches of the artisans, as well by the plenty of money: But as foreign trade is not the most material circumstance, it is not to be put in competition with the happiness of so many millions.
>
> ("Of Commerce" 1752: 15–16)[9]

Were the increased inflow of money to have arisen from an increased productivity of domestic manufacturers and lowered domestic prices (and raised real wages rates), there would not be the need to raise nominal wage rates before the rise of domestic prices. A rise of nominal wage rates would raise the real wage rate even further and thus depress profit rates (or create losses). Rather, the increased inflow of money would be acting to restore the domestic price level and sustain the profitability of the increased rate of production. This reasoning appears consistent with Hume's arguing, the "good policy of the magistrate consists only in keeping [money], if possible, still encreasing; because, by that means, he keeps alive a spirit of industry in the nation, and encreases the stock of labour, in which consists all real power and riches" (1752: 39–40). Similarly, were the increased exports to have arisen from a depressed domestic price level, following an increased rate of money hoarding or a contraction of domestic credit, the inflow of money would be restoring the domestic price level as well as profitability in production. There would be no need to hire additional workers beyond their level before the contraction of circulating money or credit, let alone their being hired at increased wage rates.

Hume's recommendation of money's increase to the magistrate in a growing economy, which is not the same thing as his having argued "in favour of creeping inflation" (Blaug 1995: 42), may appear to conflict with his concluding comments in "Of the Balance of Trade":

> In short, a government has great reason to preserve with care its people and its manufactures. Its money, it may safely trust to the course of human affairs, without fear or jealousy. Or if it ever give attention to this latter circumstance [money's adequacy], it ought only to be so far as it affects the former [its people and its manufactures].
>
> (1752: 77)[10]

Similarly, Hume (1752: 61) argues, "I should as soon dread, that all our springs and rivers should be exhausted, as that money should abandon a kingdom where there are people and industry. Let us carefully preserve these latter advantages [people and industry]; and we need never be apprehensive of losing the former [money]."

The apparent conflict may be resolved by noting that Hume's price-specie-flow mechanism takes time to adjust the quantity of money to the changing level of prices, as Hume (1752: 40) explains,

> The alterations in the quantity of money, either on one side or the other, are not immediately attended with proportionable alterations in the price of commodities. There is always an interval before matters be adjusted to their new situation; and this interval is as pernicious to industry, when gold and silver are diminishing, as it is advantageous when these metals are encreasing.

A government's ability to shorten the lag in money's response to falling domestic prices would thus be helpful.

In the case of money's decrease, Hume describes a depressed production and employment condition in the short run:

> The workman has not the same employment from the manufacturer and mer-chant; though he pays the same price for everything in the market. The farmer cannot dispose of his corn and cattle; though he must pay the same rent to his landlord. The poverty, and beggary, and sloth, which must ensue, are easily foreseen.
>
> (1752: 40)[11]

Here too, Hume does not explain the cause of money's outflow; neither does he describe the sequence of price and wage rate adjustments. However, three possible sources of money's decrease discernible from Hume's price-specie-flow analysis include (a) a fall in the prices of importable goods abroad, (b) a contraction in domestic production that has led to a rise of domestic prices, and (c) an inflation of domestic credit (paper money) that has caused a rise of domestic prices. Again, none of these causes is consistent with a lagged-prices adjustment process or wage rates falling ahead of product prices.

A fall in the price of importable goods abroad would divert demand from domestic goods to imports. Inventories would accumulate, losses would occur, and producers would react by cutting back production and laying off some workers while the contracted wage rates are still in place. Producers also would reduce their prices in accordance with the reduced product demand. Only after workers have accepted reduced nominal wage rates would the profitability of production be restored, leading possibly to some workers being re-hired. At the end of the adjustment process, the price level, output, and employment would be lower than before the money's outflow began. Were workers to bargain for or accept lower nominal wage rates at the onset of the reduced demand for domestic goods, producers' reducing commodity prices would not be accompanied with worker lay-offs. The poverty and sloth Hume describes could thus be avoided.[12]

In the case of a higher level of domestic prices, owing to a contraction of domestic production, Hume would consider money's outflow the natural and desirable process of restoring the appropriate balance between money and commodities, consistent with the quantity theory of money, and the elimination of an inconvenience. Similarly, were money's outflow to arise from an increased emission of paper money or "paper credit" inflation, Hume would consider the adjustment to a lower level of prices desirable. Thus in "Of Public Credit" Hume (1752: 95 n.–96 n.) argues:

> We may also remark, that [the] increase of prices, derived from paper credit, has a more durable and a more dangerous influence than when it arises from a great increase of gold and silver: where an accidental overflow of money raises the price of labor and commodities, the evil remedies itself in a little time: The money soon flows out into all the neighboring nations: The prices fall to a level: And industry may be continued as before; a relief, which cannot be expected, where the circulating specie consists chiefly of paper, and has no intrinsic value.

However, Hume also acknowledges in "Of the Balance of Trade" that the increase of paper credit initially increases output and employment, just as an increase of money does: "We observed in Essay III ["Of Money"] that money, when encreasing, gives encouragement to industry, during the interval between the encrease of money and the rise of prices. A good effect of this nature may follow too from paper-credit" (1752: 68 n.; see also 70–1). Hume's argument here contradicts Wennerlind's insistence that "for Hume, exogenous money is fully neutral" and "only endogenous increases in the money stock [are] favorable" to production (2005: 231, n. 14).

In "Of Interest," Hume also discusses the inflow of money following a "foreign conquest" that decreases interest rates in the short run (1752: 57–8) and excites "industry" (48). Such acquisition of money can hardly be described as "resulting from an underlying expansion of domestic industry" that has increased exports (Wennerlind 2005: 224). What Hume apparently feared, and therefore cautioned against, was the temptation to rely upon excessive paper credit creation as a means of promoting economic growth. Thus, he continues: "but it is dangerous to precipitate matters, at the risk of losing all by the failing of that credit, as must happen upon any violent shock in public affairs" (1752: 68 n). The safe and beneficial bank credit is one founded upon the prior money deposits of savers: "private bankers are enabled to give such credit by the credit they receive from the depositing of money in their shops" (70); contrast this with Keynes's (1930: 1, 25–6; 1936: 167, 372–3; 1937c: 668) insistence that savings do not supply banks with their loanable funds.

The emission of paper credit beyond the supply of savings may promote output and employment growth in the short run when the increased circulation of money that it creates causes the "price of labour and commodities" to rise, and the rise of commodity prices preceding the rise of wage rates – the forced-saving mechanism. Thus, reacting to Hume's short-run, positive impact of money on output and employment in "Of Money," which also may derive from the increase of credit (paper money), Thornton (1802: 239; italics added) argues,

> It must be also admitted, that, provided we assume an excessive issue of paper to lift up, as it may for a time, the cost of goods *though not the price of labour*, some augmentation of stock will be the consequence; for the labourer, according to this supposition, may *be forced* by his necessity to *consume fewer articles*, though he may exercise the same industry.

Other classicals who have explained the same lagged-wage rates adjustment process include Ricardo (*Works*, 3: 318–9), Jeremy Bentham (*Economic Writings*, 1: 270), Thomas Malthus (1811: 96–7), and J. S. Mill (*Works*, 3: 510–12, 562–5).[13]

These writers added to Hume's analysis the injustice to fixed-income earners (wages, interest, and rentals) caused by the diminution of their real incomes and consumption as prices rise. Also, note that the forced-saving doctrine (or mechanism) does not require the existence of full employment, as some analysts, including Keynes (1936: 80) and a dissenting referee on my manuscript for the *History of Political Economy*,[14] have claimed (see Ahiakpor 1997a, 2009; Dennis O'Brien 2004: 194–6). In fact, Keynes's preference for monetary policy to cause "a fall in the value of the existing money-wages in terms of wage-goods . . . [from] a rise in the price of [wage-goods]" (1936: 8) or "a gradual and automatic lowering of real wages as a result of rising prices" (264) to cure unemployment derives from the classical forced-saving mechanism he failed to recognize.

The role of contracts in holding back wage rates, interest rates, and rental rates when prices change is a well-known phenomenon. Profits increase when prices rise, and losses may occur when prices fall in the short run. Hume (1752) describes the prevalence of contracts in a "cultivated" or monetized society, such that even the landlord "demands his rent in gold and silver. . . . Great undertakers, and manufacturers, and merchants, arise in every commodity; and . . . the coin enters into many more contracts" (43). It must be such contracts that keep the farmer paying "the same rent to his landlord" although he "cannot dispose of his corn and cattle" (40), while the quantity of money is decreasing and prices are falling. Hume also notes in "Of Interest" contracts in business transactions, initially between artisans and peasants in "the infancy of society" (51) and then contracts attaining a greater "intricacy" as industry increases. Hume hardly could have failed to recognize that the wages of workers in manufacturing enterprises were specified in contracts. In his 6 April 1758 letter to Lord Elibank, Hume notes that "the Wages of a Tradesman, such as a Bricklayer, Mason, Tiler &c was *regulated* at ten pence a day" (Ernest Mossner 1962: 442; italics added). Yet, a dissenting referee for the *History of Economics Review* bases her/his rejection of my manuscript on the claim that Hume did not recognize contracts regarding wages, interest, and rents in his time (discussed below).

Smith (*WN*, 1: 74; italics added) also explains wage rate determination by contracts: "What are the common wages of labour depends every where upon the *contract* usually made between [masters and workmen], whose interests are by no

means the same." It also must be contracts that kept the wages of labor from varying with commodity prices, as Smith (*WN*, 1: 83) observes:

> The wages of labour do not in Great Britain fluctuate with the price of provi-
> sions. These [prices] vary every-where from year to year, frequently from
> month to month. But in many places the money price of labour [wage rate]
> remains uniformly the same sometimes for half a century together. . . . The
> high price of provisions during these ten years past has not in many parts of
> the kingdom been accompanied with any sensible rise in the money price of
> labour.

Similarly, Ricardo (*Works*, 1: 105) recognizes the contractual nature of wage rates:
"Like all other contracts, wages should be left to the fair and free competition of
the market, and should never be controlled by the interference of the legislature."
J. S. Mill (*Works*, 3: 926) argues the same for loans: "Loans are not the only kind
of contract, of which governments have thought themselves qualified to regulate
the conditions better than the persons interested."

Richard Cantillon (1755: 267–9) earlier notes the short-run fixity of rentals and
wage rates in his description of the adjustment process of prices and wages, following an increased quantity of money from the mines. His narrative appears to
explain better the monetary dynamics that Hume's controversial passage does not
make clear.[15] Cantillon explains:

> If the increase of actual money [specie] comes from Mines of gold or silver in
> the State the Owner of those Mines, the Adventurers, the Smelters, Refiners,
> and all the other workers will increase their expenses in proportion to their
> gains. They will consume in their households more Meat, Wine, or Beer than
> before, will accustom themselves to wear better cloaths, finer linen, to have
> better furnished Houses and other choicer commodities. . . . The altercations
> of the Market, or the demand for Meat, Wine, Wool, etc. being more intense
> than usual, will not fail to raise their prices. These higher prices will determine
> the Farmers to employ more land to produce them in another year: these same
> Farmers will profit by this rise of prices and will increase the expenditure of
> their Families like the others.
>
> (267)

Cantillon then refers to the forced saving incurred by fixed-income earners: "Those
then who will suffer from this dearness and increased consumption will be first of
all the Landowners, during the *term of their Leases*, then their Domestic Servants
and all the Workmen or *fixed Wage-earners* who support their families on their
wages" (269; italics added).

Hayek (1935) thus considers Hume's controversial passage in "Of Money" to be
the "Better known . . . somewhat shorter exposition" (9) of Cantillon's explanation
of "the actual chain of cause and effect between the amount of money and prices"
(8). Cantillon wrote his essay before his death in 1734, and the essay is known

to have circulated informally long before its formal publication in 1755. Hayek finds Hume's words so closely to resemble those of Cantillon's that "it is hard to believe that he had not seen one of those manuscripts of the *Essai* which are known to have been in private circulation at the time when the *Discourses* were written" (9). Hayek (1985: 238) repeats that observation after an extensive study of Cantillon and his work, noting, "From a comparison of Hume's monetary theory with that of Cantillon one gets the inescapable impression that Hume must in fact have known Cantillon." Hayek (1985) also traces Cantillon's influence on the monetary writings of Hume's contemporaries, including Montesquieu and Postlethwayt's Dictionary of 1751.[16]

On the other hand, the greater clarity of Cantillon's exposition raises the question of why Hume's version is so unclearly worded, if he had seen it.[17] It is also puzzling that the major classical writers on monetary dynamics, including Smith, Thornton, Ricardo, and J. S. Mill, do not mention Cantillon's 1755 *Essai*, but refer to Hume's. Marshall (1923: 41, n. 1; italics added) also refers to "the acute though *little known* Cantillon" who, along "Harris . . . together with others, led up to Hume and Adam Smith" to clarify the role of credit in extending the exchange function of money. Nevertheless, Hume's lack of clarity in the controversial passage need not invite the insertion of the lagged-prices after wage rates argument that those influenced by his monetary analysis have explained to be erroneous. That both Hume and Cantillon were describing a similar economy in which contracts held back wages and rents behind the rise of commodity prices, following the increased quantity of money, can hardly be in dispute.

Irving Fisher (1926: 787) is an excellent early neoclassical illustration of the role of contracts in producing the lagged-wages adjustment, besides interest and rentals, in the short run, following variations in the quantity of money or credit before Keynes popularized the alternative lagging of prices behind wage rates. Fisher's explanation follows Alfred and Mary Marshall's (1879: 156–7), repeated in Marshall (1920: esp. 493–4, 515). Frank Taussig (1921: 1, 298, 299) also makes the same point regarding wage rates:

> That wages go up more slowly than prices is one of the best-attested facts in economic history. It holds good of almost all sorts of hired persons. . . . It is due mainly to the force of custom, which is especially strong as to wages. . . . To the extent that prices of commodities advance faster than expenses for the labor [employers] buy, the payers of wages gain. . . . Conversely, the business class as a whole commonly loses in periods of falling prices. Then, since the same forces tend to keep wages stable, a fall in prices brings loss.

Robert Skidelsky (1983: 231; italics added) quotes John Neville Keynes's (J. M. Keynes's father) 1886 argument in evidence to the Royal Commission on the Depression of Trade and Industry, including "the ratio of profits to wages [falling] as a result of the fall in *money wages lagging behind* the fall of prices" and "the fall of prices [increasing] the burden of [business] debt" among reasons for the discouragement of industry during depressions (see also Skidelsky 1995: 80–1).

The modern Philips curve analysis employs the same lagged-wage rates adjustment process: when the actual inflation rate turns out to be higher than expected, the real wage rate falls and more workers are hired. But when nominal wage rates adjust to the actual inflation rate, the unemployment rate rises again to its "natural rate," and vice versa (Ahiakpor 2009). David Laidler (1991: 103) also observes that "The 'wage lag doctrine' is a time-honoured one which some commentators attribute to David Hume."

Thus, based upon extant monetary analysis and Hume's intent to employ principles to "reconcile *reason to experience*" (1752: 41; italics original), it appears more legitimate to employ the lagged-wage rates adjustment process to fill in the gap in the controversial passage. Were Hume deliberately to have changed his mind to argue the lagging of prices behind wage rates, as Perlman (1987: 274) claims, it would be a glaring self-contradiction in both the essay on money and several others of Hume's *Political Discourses*, as we further see below. Hume's contemporaries and subsequent classical writers on money, including Josiah Tucker, Smith, Thornton, Ricardo, Jeremy Bentham, and J. S. Mill, most likely also would have noted his error. However, Perlman does not reveal where Hume argues the earlier position or explain why Hume could have changed his mind in contradiction to arguments in the same and other essays.

The alternative lagged-prices interpretations of Hume's controversial passage

Eugene Rotwein (1955), like Hayek, considers the sequence of output, employment, prices, and wage movements that Hume sought to describe in the controversial passage to have been treated better in Cantillon's essay. However, he notes a significant difference in their accounts: "unlike Hume, Cantillon treats the effects of an increase in the quantity of money as largely inflationary from the outset and gives primary emphasis to its influence on the distribution of income" (lxiii, n. 2). But Cantillon's reference to increased production by farmers who "employ more land to produce in another year" (1755: 267) contradicts Rotwein's inference. Rotwein also considers it an "unresolved ambiguity" (1955: lxv) Hume's unclear explanation of the sequence of wage and price adjustments in the first part of the essay and his emphasis on the ability of money to influence the "spirit of industry" of a people and thus promote real economic growth in the second part of the essay. He reasons that the increased "price of labor" with which Hume concludes the controversial passage must lead to increased production costs and raise product prices.

Rotwein does not directly cite Keynes's wage cost-push theory as a basis for his interpretation of Hume's passage. But Keynes (1936: 12) argues that the wage cost-push theory of inflation should have been employed by the classical economists rather than their "preoccupation with the idea that prices depend on the quantity of money." Joan Robinson (1938) admits the "theoretical possibility" of an increased quantity of money causing the rise of prices. But she also insists on the rise of money wage rates being the real cause of inflation: "the essence of inflation is a rapid and continuous rise of money wages. Without rising money wages, inflation cannot occur, and whatever starts a violent rise in money wages starts inflation" (510–1).[18]

Rotwein thus appears to have followed the wage cost-push theory to conclude from Hume's essay that Hume meant instead to argue a contraction of output and employment in the long run: "Careful examination will show that, far from holding that rising prices were in any sense beneficial, Hume seemed to assume that – due to belated wage increases – they produced or were symptomatic of a *decline* in employment" (1955: lxv, n. 1; italics original).[19] Rotwein therefore declares previous interpretations of Hume's analysis, including those of E. A. J. Johnson and Jacob Viner, to be wrong. He also accuses Eric Roll of having "further compound[ed] the usual error by gratuitously reading a class bias into [Hume's] analysis," namely that "Hume was 'quite happy' that the price rise was 'at the expense of labour'" (ibid.). But the short-run adjustment process at the expense of labor – product prices rising ahead of wage rates – is precisely what the forced-saving doctrine explains.

In arguing that an increase in wage rates ahead of prices must be accompanied by a decline in employment (and output), Rotwein draws correctly on a well-established classical principle. That is, employers cannot easily pass higher wage rates onto product prices and also keep expanding output and employment. But Hume clearly argues in "Of Money" (1752: 37) that the increased inflow of money (specie) causes an increased *level* (not growth) of output and employment in the long run, besides having raised prices and wage rates. Douglas Vickers (1957) also disagrees with Rotwein's interpretation of Hume's analysis and points rather to the existence of a "methodological tension" (227) between Hume's employing the Quantity Theory in the first part of the essay and arguing money's possible positive effect on the "manners and customs of the people" (231) in the second part. However, Vickers does not address the sequencing of price and wage rate changes in Hume's essay.

Morris Perlman (1987) employs Keynes's wage cost-push theory of inflation to interpret Hume's controversial passage. He insists that the passage had been "misinterpreted and criticized by both the Mills, and it has been variously interpreted and criticized by a large number of historians of thought ever since" (274). He also considers the main problem with previous interpretations of Hume's narrative to be their having read the "price of labour" to mean the "wage rate" (276). Rather, he interprets "labour" to mean "manufactured goods" (278) and the price of labor to mean the "price of manufactured goods" (280). Perlman supports that interpretation with a reference to a 1933 edition of the *Oxford English Dictionary* that defines "labour" to include "the outcome, product, or result of toil" (278, n. 3). He also cites statements from some others, including Richard Cantillon, Sir James Steuart, and Arthur Young, that appear to affirm that usage of the term "labour." With such interpretation, Perlman explains the passage in three steps: (1) merchants and manufacturers receive more money, (2) they increase the demand for labor that "leads to a rise in the money wage" and therefore "a rise in real wages," and (3) "the rise in real wages leads to an increase in the supply of effort" (276). He then concludes:

> With this usage of the term labor, the story told by Hume of the way in which the increase in the quantity of money affects industry and the prices has its

promised denouement. The story starts with a rise in wages and finishes, as promised, with a rise in the prices of manufactured goods.

(280)

There are several problems with Perlman's interpretation. First, Hume's passage starts with the intent to account for rising commodity prices, not wages:

> Though the *high price of commodities* be a necessary consequence of the encrease of gold and silver, yet it follows not immediately upon that encrease; but some time is required before the money circulates through the whole state and makes its effect be felt on all ranks of people. At first, no alteration is perceived; by degrees *the price* rises, first of one commodity, then of another; till the whole at last reaches a just proportion with the new quantity of specie which is in the kingdom.
>
> (1752: 37–8; italics added)

Hume also here appears clearly to mean by "commodities" all produced goods rather than only "agricultural products," as Perlman (1987: 278) claims.

Second, there are numerous instances in Hume's writings where he refers to the wage rate as the "price of labour," for example, in "Of Interest" (1752: 59), "Of the Balance of Trade" (1752: 63, 68), "Of Taxes" (1752: 87–8), and "Of Public Credit" (1752: 96). Were we always to interpret Hume to mean by "the price of labour," the price of manufactured goods, we would find some of his arguments rather awkward, if not meaningless. An example is Hume's 1766 letter to A. R. J. Turgot:

> The Tradesmen who work in Cloath, that is exported, cannot raise the Price of their Labour; because in that Case the Price of the Cloath wou'd become too dear to be sold in foreign Markets: Neither can the Tradesmen who work in Cloath for home Consumption raise their Prices; since there cannot be two Prices for the same Species of Labour. This extends to all Commodities of which there is any part exported, that is, to almost every Commodity. Even were there some Commodities of which no part is exported, the Price of Labour employ'd in them, cou'd not rise; for the high Price wou'd tempt so many hands to go into that Species of Industry.
>
> (Quoted in Rotwein 1955: 208–9)

Hume's explanation reads more coherently with "the price of labour" understood as the wage rate. He could not have been arguing, "The price of labor's output employed in producing output" or "The price of manufactured goods employed in" producing goods exported. The same usage of "the price of labour" to mean the wage rate appears in Oswald of Dunnikier's 10 October 1749 letter to Hume (1955: esp. 191–6) as well as in Thornton (1802: 239). Smith (*WN*, 1: 40, 41, 88, 95, 96, 223), Ricardo (*Works*, 1: 94, 303; 2: 228, 268), and Malthus (1836: esp. 111–35, 217–23) also use "the money price of labour" to refer to the wage rate; Alfred and Mary Marshall (1879: 156) employ the same usage. It is indeed true that the term "labor" may be used in different senses in the English language, but Perlman's denial that Hume meant the wage rate in the context of the controversial passage appears incorrect.

Third, the version of Hume's "story" Perlman quotes also explains that the increased quantity of gold and silver enables the merchants and manufacturers "to employ more workmen than formerly, *who never dream of demanding higher wages*, but are glad of employment from such good paymasters" (italics added). Hume's explanation does not start with the rise of wages, as Perlman argues. And even when workmen become scarce, Hume insists that an "encrease of labour" is first required of them before they are paid higher wages.

Perlman evidently introduces the rise of wages before more workmen are hired because he employs a continuous flow supply and demand for labor model of wage rate determination with "upward-sloping supply curves of labor" (1987: 278). The model appears to follow Keynes's (1936: 257) incorrect attribution of "an assumed fluidity of money-wages" to classical analysis. In that model, no additional labor could be hired without an increase in the nominal wage rate. Thus, Perlman argues that the classicals, including J. S. Mill, who did not interpret Hume's passage as he does, may be excused for their having had difficulty with the modern, Keynesian, conception of the labor market. But it is rather the Keynesian labor-market model Perlman employs that fails to capture Hume's own analysis correctly.[20] Indeed, just as the increased demand for commodities in Hume's narrative does not immediately lead farmers, gardeners, and other tradesmen to raise their prices but rather to increase their rates of production, so can we appreciate that the presence of wage contracts delays the rise of nominal wage rates, following the increased demand for labor until later in Hume's analysis.[21]

Fourth, Perlman's interpreting Hume to have argued the rise of nominal wage rates before the rise of product prices conflicts with Hume's own recognition of the pressure of wage rates on profits per unit of output. In several instances, Hume argues that employers would not be inclined to raise their wage offers unless product prices first rose, particularly in the case of exportable goods. For example, "No labour in any commodities, that are exported, can be very considerably raised in the price, without losing the foreign market; and as some part of almost every manufactory is exported, this circumstance keeps the price of most species of labour nearly the same after the imposition of taxes" ("Of Taxes" 1752: 88 n). The same argument appears in Hume's letter to Turgot, quoted above. Also, were workers to ask for higher wages because of higher taxes on commodities they consumed, Hume explains the difficulty they would face in obtaining the increase: "By what contrivance can [an artisan] raise the price of his labour? The manufacturer who employs him will not give him more: Neither can he, because the merchant who exports the cloth, cannot raise its price, being limited by the price which it yields in foreign markets" (ibid.: 87).

The logic behind the argument is the inverse wage-profit relation, frequently associated in the literature with Ricardo: "a rise of wages, from the circumstance of the labourer being more liberally rewarded . . . does not, except in some instances, produce the effect of raising prices, but has a great effect in lowering profits"

(*Works*, 1: 48–9). The exception is the case of money's own prior depreciation in value. Thus, "the rise of wages will not raise the prices of commodities. . . . All commodities cannot rise at the same time without an addition to the quantity of money" (*Works*, 1: 105; see also Ricardo *Works*, 1: 126–7). J. S. Mill (*Works*, 3: 479–80) argues the same point: "There is no mode in which capitalists can compensate themselves for a high cost of labour, through any action on values or prices. It cannot be prevented from taking its effect on low profits" (479). J. S. Mill (*Works*, 3: 699; italics added) forcefully concludes:

> The doctrine, indeed, that a rise of wages causes an equivalent rise of prices, is . . . self-contradictory: for if it did so, it would not be a rise of wages; the labourer would get no more of any commodity than he had before, let his money wages rise ever so much; a rise of real wages would be an impossibility. This being equally contrary to reason and to *fact*, it is evident that a rise of money wages does not raise prices; that *high wages are not a cause of high prices*. A rise of general wages falls on profits. There is no possible alternative.

See also J. S. Mill (*Works*, 2: 413–4).

Also referring to Ricardo's statement above, J. E. Cairnes (1873: 60) argues that "An increased supply of money . . . tends, by one mode of its operation, to raise prices in advance of wages, and thus to stimulate production; by another, to raise wages in advance of prices, and thus to check it [production]."[22] Hume's essay on money argues the increase of output and employment from the increased inflow of money. That is why the Keynesian lagged-prices interpretation appears inconsistent with it.

Perlman (1987: 284) also interprets Hume to have employed a money-supply (rather than capital- or savings-supply) theory of output and employment in the second part of the essay, "Of Money," an interpretation Berdell (1995, 2002: esp. 69–84) endorses. But the interpretation conflicts with Hume's cautioning against mistaking "a collateral effect for a cause" (1752: 41). It is increased production which attracts money from other trading nations rather than an increased quantity of money reliably causing an increased rate of long-run production.

Carl Wennerlind (2005) employs both Keynes's wage cost-push theory of inflation and Keynes's consumption expenditure multiplier analysis to fill in the gap in Hume's controversial passage. He follows Rotwein's (1955: lxiii) use of Keynes's multiplier argument, as if it were the same as Hume's (1752) explaining the diffusion of economic activity among different sectors of an economy, along with declining prices: "The small profit of the merchant [owing to the increase of public credit] renders the commodity *cheaper*, causes a greater consumption, quickens the labour of the common people, and helps to spread arts and industry throughout the whole society" ("Of Public Credit," 93–4; italics added). But Hume's explanation is more in line with a "multiplying principle" (Ahiakpor 2001). It is not Keynes's multiplier argument in which consumer spending drives aggregate demand and raises prices, while savings are a withdrawal from the expenditure stream.

Wennerlind (2005) also considers only one source of money's increased inflow, namely, an "improvement in the arts and industry" that has led to a "greater output

(Y_1), [and] a falling price level (P_1)" (220). He does not dwell on Hume's reference to employers' initially hiring additional workers "who never dream of demanding higher wages." Rather, he quickly asserts, "In order to attract additional labor power, they [manufacturers] are soon forced to increase wages" (229). He adds that the rising wages cause employers to raise their prices in an escalating process, and yet also keep expanding output (and employment):

> The higher wages . . . force the manufacturers to increase their prices (P_2). However, since these workers now enjoy a higher real wage, they expand their consumption, spreading the process from sector to sector, gradually increasing wages (W_1) and prices (P_2),[23] eventually forcing the multiplier to a halt once the price level is brought back into equilibrium $(P_2 = P_0)$ . . . the end result is that output is greater $(Y_2 > Y_1 > Y_0)$, wages are higher $(W_1 > W_0)$ and the quantity of money has increased $(M_1 > M_0)$.

Wennerlind argues the above along with claiming that the higher wages do not raise "the labor cost per unit [of output] . . . because of the improvements in productivity" (2005: 230; see also Wennerlind 2008: 111, in which he repeats the point). But if the raised wages do not raise the unit cost of production, why would they "force the manufacturers to increase their prices"? Besides, Wennerlind's argument has no role for wage contracts holding back wage-rate increases in the short run while producers are able to raise their prices in concert with the relatively higher foreign prices. The forced-saving mechanism, an integral part of the Quantity Theory of money (Blaug 1995: 34), is simply missing in Wennerlind's analysis, just as in Keynes's.

Wennerlind's interpretation also entails two other problems. First, a fall in the domestic price level $(P_1 < P_0)$, because of the increase in the "arts and industry," already raises real wage rates (at existing nominal wage rates) and may reduce profit rates. The increased export demand would thus be restoring the domestic price level, through the price-specie-flow mechanism, as well as raising profits rates. If, upon the inflow of money, nominal wages were raised before prices, the profit-rate recovery would be frustrated. Secondly, the argument that domestic producers wait to be pushed by increases in nominal wage rates to raise their prices towards those abroad is inconsistent with firms' profit-maximizing behavior. Firms would rather take advantage of higher foreign prices to raise their own prices before the increased demand for labor causes them to raise nominal wage rates. Moreover, market prices are not dependent upon firms' historical costs of production as Keynes's mark-up pricing argument may suggest.

However, so prevalent is Keynes's influence with the wage cost-push theory of pricing that a referee rejecting my manuscript for the *Journal of the History of Economic Thought*, in a little over ten (10) single-spaced pages report, argues:

> The initial impact of the spending of new money is, **first, for the wages bill for new workers to increase** and then for there to be a rise in the hourly wage rate for existing workers, but only in return for increased output. And,

explicitly, for these money wage increases then to be spent on existing goods whose prices do not immediately rise (*because their costs have already been incurred*). . . . Only when, in the next stage, the increased wages of the next set of workers are spent on the increased output of the first set that now comes to market do these "first set" prices need to rise to reflect increased wage costs. First the goods are produced for whatever it costs; only thereafter are they sold, at a market price that will tend to reflect the *past costs*, so long as the increased circular flow of stage two workers' wage incomes will suffice to take these goods off the market at those higher prices."

(boldface in the original; italics added)

The referee must have had little acquaintance with firms' pricing behavior. Prices do not depend upon historical costs.

Wennerlind's lagged-prices interpretation of Hume's passage also appears to be inconsistent with Hume's description of the miserable state of "poverty, and beggary, and sloth" that afflicts an economy when money decreases and prices fall, and for the counter of which Hume recommends, if possible, an increasing quantity of money as the "good policy of the magistrate." If wage rates decreased before product prices, there would be no losses to producers and possibly no reduced employment either. But Hume's argument is rather consistent with the lagged adjustment of wage rates behind product prices, just as Thomas Malthus in his 16 July 1821 letter to Ricardo notes: "We know from repeated *experience* that the money price of labour never falls till many workers have been for some time out of work" (quoted in Ricardo *Works*, 9: 20; italics added).[24]

In his *Principles*, Malthus makes the point: "If a country loses its advantages in regard to exportable commodities, it will lose a portion of its precious metals by an adverse exchange, and the fall in prices will continue till the reduced money price of labour balances the disadvantages, and the trade of barter returns" (1836: 128). Hawtrey (1913: 40–3) gives a similar account of the adjustment process of falling prices and increased unemployment, before money wage rates decline:

> Wages will cling to their customary rate until the stress of unemployment begins to drive them down; they will follow the downward movement of money and prices at an interval; and at last, when the movement of prices stops, there will be an accumulated weight of unemployment only to be relieved by a continuance of the movement of wages.

(43)

Wennerlind (2005) also does not recognize the price-level stabilization intent (not a call for inflation, contra Blaug 1995: 42) of Hume's monetary policy prescription to "the magistrate." Instead, he argues that Hume's recommendation be interpreted, not as asking for "the state to expand the money supply" (2005: 224), but as Hume's "instructing the magistrate to implement and execute laws favorable to industry" (231). It was also, he adds, Hume's "call for the magistrate to improve conditions for industry and, in that way, generate an increase in the money stock through increased exports" (232; see also Wennerlind 2008: 113).

Now the English magistrate was not in the position of determining the conditions of industry or regulating the inflow of money, just as Wennerlind (2005: 232) acknowledges: "the eighteenth-century English magistrate had no influence over the money supply. The magistrate dealt with the implementation and execution of civil laws." The mercantilist policies of Hume's day also included subsidies and bounties for exporters and high tariffs on importable manufactured goods in order to promote increased net exports in return for increased specie inflows. Hume's critique of such policies was to explain their ineffectiveness in promoting economic growth since the resulting domestic price increases would reduce foreign demand for exports and their production. A magistrate at court had no means of undoing such laws. Moreover, Hume referred to "the magistrate," singular, not to magistrates, plural; there must have been numerous magistrates in the United Kingdom who adjudicated cases brought before them.

Wennerlind also employs Keynes's (1930, 1936) broad definition of money that includes bank deposits or bank credit, contrary to Hume's definition of money as specie only, to dispute the interpretation of Hume's policy recommendation to the magistrate as a reference to the quantity of money. He asserts, "Where Hume directly discusses the issuance of paper money, he refers to the *banks* or *public banks* (285); where he treats public securities, which had 'become a kind of money' (353), he refers to the issuing authority as the *public* or the *state*, never the magistrate" (2005: 232; italics original). Indeed, it was because Hume was not referring to paper money or credit, whose quantity easily can be varied, but rather to money (specie), whose supply mostly depends upon net exports, that he qualifies his recommendation with, "if possible." Other than debasing the currency, a government was unable readily to increase the quantity of money to counter a falling level of domestic prices. Only increased exports would achieve that, but with some lag.

However, interpreting "the magistrate" as an officer of the state in charge of the currency or the sovereign yields a more consistent meaning than Wennerlind's interpretation as an executor of trade laws. C. George Caffentzis (2008: 164) recognizes the magistrate in Hume's essay as a government official "in charge of debasing the currency." He explains, "Debasement, according to Hume, could be acceptable just so long as the operation is done 'to preserve the illusion, and make [the new coin] be taken for the same [as the old coin]'" (162). Wennerlind (2005: 234) also argues, "Hume suggests that a debasement of the coin had the capacity to generate a multiplier process similar to that of an inflow of gold from abroad." This after he claims that Hume "was adamant about the undesirability of increases in the money supply that do not originate from increased industry and expanded exports" (226), even though he also argues that Hume "believed that debasements of coin and the use of private paper money were not inherently detrimental, as long as certain restrictive conditions were met" (234). In self-contradiction, Wennerlind claims, "Neither debasement nor private credit money was available to the government to use as policy instrument to stimulate industry" (234), although he cities Hume's "antipathy towards repeated debasements . . . [and Hume's] calling Edward VI's Great Debasement (1542–50) a 'pernicious expedient' . . . while also scorning Elizabeth's monetary manipulations" (235).

Furthermore, Caffentzis's interpreting the magistrate as an overseer of money's debasement appears consistent with Hume's favorable opinion of "the frequent operations of the French king on the money; where it was always found, that the augmenting of the numerary value did not produce a proportional rise of the prices, at least for some time" (1752: 39). Hume's comment immediately follows his controversial passage in "Of Money." Interpreting Hume's "magistrate" as a euphemism for the sovereign also appears supported by the *Oxford English Dictionary*'s definition of the magistrate to include the sovereign: "first magistrate: *in a monarchy, the sovereign*: in a republic, usually the president" (1989: 189; italics added).[25] Hume also refers to the French king (Louis XIV) as having "raised [money] three-sevenths, but prices augmented only one."

Moreover, it was the king (queen) or parliament in England who could affect the flow of money through laws relating to trade, coinage, or the emission of paper money, not a magistrate who was an administrator of trade laws. Also noteworthy is the fact that subsequent classical writers did not assign the regulation of money to the "magistrate" as Hume did, even as several of them took their cues on monetary analysis from Hume's essays on money, interest, and the balance of trade. It thus appears that Wennerlind's interpretation of Hume's controversial passage is due to the strong influence of Keynes's macro-monetary analysis on him, including the wage cost-push theory of inflation, the consumption expenditure multiplier, and Keynes's broad definition of money to include bank credit (M1 or M2).

Also, contrary to Wennerlind's claim that Hume employed two kinds of the Quantity Theory, it is more accurate to recognize only one Quantity Theory. The increased use of paper money or credit in payments, which Wennerlind regards as "exogenous money," decreases money's demand (to hold), leading to a reduction in money's value or higher prices. As Blaug (1995: 38–9) appears to recognize, but does not resolve, the persistent, modern ambiguities regarding the validity of the Quantity Theory of money center mainly on the definition of "money," which Friedman and Schwartz's (1970: 93–103) treatment of money's definition has not helped to clarify (see also Ahiakpor 2003b: Ch. 3).

Margaret Schabas (2008) questions our reading of short-run versus long-run analysis in Hume's "Of Money," allegedly because Hume "never gives us a concise measure of [time] interval" (136). She claims such reading of Hume "is to succumb to an anachronism" since in Hume's "essay 'Of Money' his most prevalent temporal interval is *two to three centuries*" (136; italics added). A referee rejecting a 2008 version of my manuscript for the *History of Political Economy* makes a similar claim:

> [The paper's] argument rests on giving greater veracity to Hume's ascription of a short-term temporal lag between inflation and the increase in wages. The case is not convincing. For one, there is no concrete measure of time given by Hume. . . . The larger problem is that little to no attempt is made to situate

Hume in his historical context. Anachronisms abound. Not only did Hume never use the short run/long run distinction (Marshallian or other), he never used forced-saving mechanism as we know it, nor the Keynesian wage cost-push theory of inflation, not the Fisher equation. Hume was not Ricardo or Fisher, and to make him into one or more of them is to assume that there is a set of timeless truths about economic phenomena to which we are all groping with ever greater precision.

But as we have seen above, understanding Hume's definition of the short run to mean the interval of time before the full effect of a changed rate of money's inflow or outflow has made "its effect be felt on all ranks of people" (1752: 38) makes his arguments meaningful.

Schabas also appears to have reached her conclusion by comparing Marshall's (1920: 314–5; italics original) particular treatment of "normal prices" when the term "Normal is taken to relate to *short* periods of a few months up to a year" and "*long* periods of several years" to Hume's analysis. However, confronted with the possibility that an increase of imports would lower domestic prices, following the rise of prices due to a four-fold increase of money, for example, Hume explains to Oswald that "the lower prices . . . would [last] for *one year*, till the imported commodities be consumed" (quoted in Rotwein 1955: 197; italics added). Hume thereby distinguishes a short-run effect of increased imports from the long run. Similarly, Hume explains the interest-rate lowering effect of an increased accumulation of money in the short run until the increased money "has been digested and has circulated through the whole state," raised prices, and affairs "soon return to their former situation" (1752: 58).

Summary and conclusions

David Hume employed the Quantity Theory of money to argue that the long-run effect of variations in the quantity of money for an economy is mainly on its prices, including nominal wage rates. This is because money is not a factor of production but only facilitates the exchange of produced goods and services. However, in the process of explaining the short-run adjustment to the changed inflow of money, Hume did not clearly state the sequence of wage-rate and price-level changes. Richard Cantillon's (1755) monetary analysis that explicitly recognizes the short-term fixity of wage rates and rents better explains the price-wage dynamics in which wages lag behind prices. The major classical economists influenced by Hume's monetary analysis also employed the same sequence of price and wage-rate adjustment, some also criticizing the popular notion that higher wage rates cause higher prices. But Hume was not among those who argued the wage cost-push theory of price-level changes.

The lagged-wage rates adjustment process is also at the heart of the classical forced-saving mechanism. Similarly, some notable early neoclassical economists, including Marshall, Irving Fisher, Frank Taussig, A. C. Pigou, and R. G. Hawtrey, have employed the lagged-wages analysis, but without reference to Hume's essay on money; they referred instead to Ricardo's and J. S. Mill's arguments. There appears to be little good reason, therefore, for our employing the lagged-prices adjustment process to fill the gap in Hume's controversial passage in "Of Money," as if the passage were inconsistent with his other monetary analyses or the institutional realities of Hume's day.

The lagged-prices interpretation of Hume's passage appears consistent with Keynes's wage cost-push theory of inflation instead of the Quantity Theory and the application of the modern continuous flow supply and demand for labor model of wage rate determination. But that interpretation does not well fit Hume's own narrative in which, following the increased quantity of money, more workers are initially hired, "who never dream of demanding higher wages." It also does not accord well with the short-term economic misery of reduced output and employment Hume argues would result from an outflow or an insufficient quantity of money in the same essay. It rather appears more consistent with Hume's monetary analysis to argue that the increased rate of production and employment growth would cease once the change in wage rates has caught up with the change in product prices in the long run, but not that both output and employment would decrease to their original level, as Rotwein's (1955) interpretation concludes. That conclusion is relevant only to the case of domestic credit inflation that temporarily lowers interest rates, increases production and employment, but raises prices and wage rates subsequently. There is also considerable textual evidence to contradict Perlman's (1987) insistence that we interpret "the price of labour" in Hume's "Of Money" to mean the price of manufactured goods, and not the wage rate, in order to bridge the gap in the controversial passage.

Hume's monetary analysis includes recognizing that foreign competition restrains the ability of domestic producers to raise their prices as a means of accommodating higher wage costs. Consistency with that principle requires bridging the gap in the controversial passage with an interpretation in which, first, being able to charge higher prices, domestic producers would be willing to pay higher nominal wage rates until profit rates are restored to their level from before the increased inflow of money. Recognizing Hume's acquiescence with monetary debasement as a means of increasing the quantity of money in order to sustain the level of prices, we also may interpret his "magistrate" as the sovereign or a state officer in charge of monetary debasement rather than Wennerlind's enforcer of trade laws.

A referee for the *History of Economics Review*, not under the strong influence of Keynes's interpretation of classical monetary analysis, was persuaded by my argument in the 2014 version of the manuscript. The referee observes:

> As shown exhaustively in this long paper (37 pages, more than ten thousand words), [the] minority lagged-prices view is untenable. This minority reading depends on claiming that by "price of labour" in the disputed passage, Hume meant price of manufactured goods rather than wages, and that Hume had forgotten that in the preceding paragraph he had spoken of prices of goods changing. As the present paper gently puts it, "this interpretation yields some rather awkward readings of Hume's arguments" (p. 2), followed by the stronger remark that "it would be a rather glaring self-contradiction" (p. 14). The lagged-prices interpretation would mean that a monetary expansion would

cause short-run contraction of output, contrary to clearly-expressed views in Hume's "Of Interest" and "Of the Balance of Trade," published at the same time in the same volume as "Of Money" in 1752.

The referee then declares:

> I am entirely persuaded by the argument presented here that Hume meant [what] he wrote, that by price of labour he meant price of labour, and the lagged-wages adjustment process made explicit in others of his 1752 essays ("Of Interest" and "Of the Balance of Trade") was also what he meant in "On Money." Indeed, the case for the long-held, majority lagged-wages interpretation seems so conclusive, based on just a straightforward reading of Hume's 1752 essays rather than on new material or new interpretation, that I wondered why the case needed to be made again in print – until I saw in endnote 3 the quotations from Berdell (1995) and Laidler and Sandilands (2010) accepting and lauding Perlman's claim that by "price of labour" Hume meant price of final goods or output of labour, rather than price of labour. If such serious historians of thought are accepting such strained reading of Hume, the situation should be firmly corrected.

On the other hand, the dissenting referee (*History of Economics Review*) introduces her/his report (italics in the original) with:

> This paper offers some provocative considerations regarding a frequently discussed passage in Hume's theory of money. The paper highlights the ambiguity in Hume's elaboration and the fact that Hume does not provide all of the details required for an economist to situate him in a modern theoretical framework. The author of this paper therefore correctly points out that it is necessary to make some auxiliary assumptions in order to make sense of Hume's analysis – to fill in the *black box* connecting his premises to his conclusions. Add to this, the paper is well-written and clearly argued.

But the referee then declares:

> Unfortunately, I cannot recommend publication due to the fact that the intervention the author seeks to make is entirely incompatible with Hume's broader discussion. The notion that contracts make wage rates, interest rates, and rental rates sticky and therefore explain why an inflow of money has positive output effects is unsustainable.

Following my revision of the manuscript to emphasize the role of contracts to produce the forced-saving effect of monetary increase in Hume's analysis, besides in those of the classicals Hume influenced, the dissenting referee responds:

> I remain convinced that this paper does not merit publication – the revisions and comments do not get to the heart of the problem. The problem is that there

is no interest, rent, wage, and price stickiness in Hume's work that comes from contracts. In fact, part of why his theory is interesting is that he is one of the first to do away with stickiness. Indeed, in a correspondence with Lord Elibank, he talks about how prices and wages were fixed by contracts in medieval Europe, but that it is no longer the case.

The author certainly has not provided the requisite documentation.

My attempts since June 2014 to discover evidence of this referee's claim of Hume's arguing the absence of contracts in his time, including posting a request on the History of Economics Society's listserv and contacting directly Margaret Schabas and Carl Wennerlind, co-editors of *David Hume's Political Economy* (2008), never yielded that evidence. The journal's editor also could not secure the evidence from the referee. I can only conclude that the referee must have employed a dishonest device to prevent acceptance of my manuscript.

Keynes (1930, 1936) restored respectability to the wage cost-push theory of inflation that classical and early neoclassical monetary analysis argued to be erroneous in his efforts to turn the Quantity Theory of money from explaining the level of prices into a theory of interest rates, hence "output as a whole." In fact, Hume discusses the temporary interest rate reduction effect of an increased inflow of money but not in the long run in "Of Interest" (1752: 57–8). Keynes appears to have ignored that essay by Hume while arguing his liquidity-preference theory of interest rates. Thus, William Nordhaus and Paul Samuelson (1998: 588), for example, argue, "Cost-push inflation does not appear to have been present in the early stages of market economies. It first appeared during the 1930s and 1940s. . . . In looking for explanations of cost-push inflation, economists often start with wages, which are clearly an important part of businesses' costs" (see also David Colander and Edward Gamber 2002: 309–10; Peter Kennedy 2010: 301–2).

Keynes's linking wage rates to the determination of product prices served his interest to argue the rejection of nominal wage rate cuts as a means of reversing an increasing level of unemployment when prices are declining in a depression. Keynes (1936), rather, lauds trade unions' resistance to wage rate reductions as a cure for unemployment as their being more reasonable than economists who, recognizing the demand curve for labor being downward sloping and that a reduced demand must lead to a reduction in the market price of a product, argued otherwise. "It is fortunate," Keynes insists, "that the workers, though unconsciously, are instinctively more reasonable economists than the classical school, inasmuch as they resist reductions of money-wages, which are seldom or never of an all-round character, even though the existing real equivalent of these wages exceeds the marginal disutility of the existing employment" (1936: 14). Nominal wage rate reductions, Keynes claims, rather, would reduce product prices and further burden businesses in debt, "with severely adverse effects on investment" (264).

Keynes's arguments linking the level of prices to wage rates are inaccurate and have been misleading. The consensus interpretation of Hume's "Of Money," which entails (a) wage rates lagging behind the movement of prices (also argued in Keynes 1936: 301) and (b) the need for increasing the quantity of money to keep the level of prices from falling, is more consistent with Hume's intent. The lagging of prices after wage rates or a wage cost-push theory of inflation, the "price of labour" meaning the "price of manufactured goods," and the notion that magistrates were enforcing trade laws in order to promote the requisite quantity of money's inflow to an economy, are not.

Notes

1 I base this chapter on my unpublished paper, "On a Confusing Passage in David Hume's 'Of Money': Lagged-Wage Rates vs Lagged-Prices Interpretations," discussed at the Western Economic Association International Conference in San Francisco, June 29–July 3, 2012. That paper is a significantly revised version of my, "Hume on Money, the Price Level and Wage Rates: In Search of a Consistent Interpretation," discussed at the History of Economics Society Annual Meetings, York University, Toronto, Canada, June 27–30, 2008. My last attempt in 2014 to get it published was frustrated by a dissenting referee's incorrect insistence that contracts did not feature in Hume's monetary analysis. This version benefits from my incorporating suggestions and reactions to criticisms from journal referees both in agreement and in dissent with my analysis.
2 Among monetary analysts who do not recognize the lagged wage-rates adjustment being at the heart of the classical forced-saving doctrine are David Laidler and Roger Sandilands (2010: 581–6). They rather emphasize the Austrian version of forced saving that focuses on interest rate adjustments, following increased bank credit and the subsequent changes in the structure of production, as the only way properly to understand the forced-saving doctrine. This in spite of Hayek's (1933: 219n) own recognition of "J. Bentham, H. Thornton, T.R. Malthus and a number of other writers in the early 19th century, down to J. S. Mill" as having argued the concept of "forced saving" differently from his preferred "Austrian" version that "does not need to manifest itself in changes in the value of money" (219–20). Laidler (1999: 38, n. 13) also affirms Hayek's point.
3 I explain below the error of Perlman's claim.
4 Ricardo (*Works*, 4: 36) credits Hume with being the first to observe that "a rise of prices, has a magic effect on industry . . . one of the advantages, to counterbalance the many evils attendant on a depreciation of money, from a real fall in the value of the precious metals, from raising the denomination of the coin, or from the over-issue of paper money." Similarly, J. S. Mill (*Works*, 3: 563; italics added) argues, "The notion that an increase of the currency quickens industry . . . was *set afloat* by David Hume, in his Essay on Money."
5 Following Irving Fisher (1922: 159–60) or A. C. Pigou (1917), we may represent that proportion or the price level as $P = HV/Q$ or $P = H/kQ$, where P = the price level or the weighted average of prices, H = quantity of money (specie or currency), V = money's velocity, Q = index of commodities, and k = proportion of income a community holds in cash, the inverse of money's velocity. Hume emphasizes the role of money's velocity or circulation in determining the level of prices when he points out that

> prices do not so much depend on the absolute quantity of commodities and that of money, which are in a nation, as on that of the commodities, which come or may come to market, and of the money which *circulates*. If the coin be locked up in chests, it is the same thing with regard to prices, as if it were annihilated
>
> (1752: 42; italics added)

and "It is the proportion between the *circulating money*, and the commodities in the market, which determines the prices" (43; italics added). Contrast with Berdell's (1995: 1209) claim that velocity "does not figure in Hume's discussion" in "Of Money."

6   Fisher (1922: 62) argues a similarly delayed impact of an increased quantity of money on prices: "The surplus money is first expended at nearly the old price level, but its continued expenditure gradually raises prices. In the meantime, the volume of purchases will be somewhat greater than it would have been had prices risen more promptly. In fact, from the point of view of those who are selling goods, it is the possibility of a greater volume of sales at the old prices which gives encouragement to an increase of prices." See also Fisher (1926: 787–8, 792).

7   Hume explains in "Of Money" that it is the circulating money that affects prices. Thus, by reducing the proportion between circulating money and commodities, money's hoarding causes "every thing [to] become cheaper, and the prices gradually fall" (1752: 43). Hume also argues in "Of the Balance of Trade" that the act of hoarding has the capacity to attract large sums of money "from all the neighbouring Kingdoms" (1752: 72). Thus, Duke's (1979: 582 n) view that "Hume generally treated the supply of money as completely exogenous, and he never presented the demand for money in the sense of the Marshallian demand apparatus" appears incorrect.

8   Duke's (1979: 583) claim that Hume abstracted from the "implications of the specie-flow mechanism when the price level begins to rise" appears unwarranted. In Duke's view, "as soon as the price level begins to rise, specie will begin to flow out, disrupting the continuance of money increase."

9   Similarly, Smith (*WN*, 1: 90) does not consider high wages an inconvenience: "The liberal reward of labour . . . as it is the effect of increasing wealth, so it is the cause of increasing population. To complain of it, is to lament over the necessary effect and cause of the greatest public prosperity."

10 Wennerlind (2005: 233) incorrectly, I contend, interprets this passage as having "nothing to do with monetary policy, but rather with the government's trade policy." But a country's "people and its manufactures" are the former concerns to which Hume refers, "its money," the latter.

11 Hume is here evidently addressing the reader of his essay, not anyone in the marketplace who may not be aware of the relevant economic principles. Understood this way, Robert Lucas's (1996) puzzle at Hume's statement is resolved. Lucas, invoking the rational expectations proposition, asks: if "the real consequences of money changes are 'easy to trace' and 'easily foreseen' . . . why do these consequences occur at all?" (663–4). Also, the farmer pays "the same rent to his landlord" because of the contract and some workers lose their jobs because wage rates have yet to decrease.

12 Hawtrey (1913: 41) describes a similar adjustment process: "if the adjustment could be made entirely by a suitable diminution of wages and salaries, accompanied by a corresponding diminution of prices, the commercial community could be placed forthwith in a new position of equilibrium, in which the output would continue unchanged."

13 Jacob Viner (1937: 188) evidently relies on the gap in Hume's controversial passage to argue that Hume had a different type of "forced saving" in which "commodity prices do not rise immediately or do not rise in as great proportion as the increase in money, and the money left over is available for additional expenditures and consequently for the employment of additional labor." However, it is not clear who is thus forced to save, if product prices do not rise. If increased real income leads to increased saving, such saving is voluntary, not forced. Rather, as Viner himself notes, forced saving entails a reduction in "the amount of real consumption" (188) by fixed-income earners, due to the rise of product prices.

14 The referee sees no ambiguity in Hume's controversial passage, claiming, "The ambiguity comes when we try to fit Hume into a full-employment neoclassical model that was a later invention (forced saving allows us to do that) or into a neokeynesian [sic] Phillips Curve model that was yet a later invention." Here again is Keynes's (1936: 80–1) unhelpful influence regarding the meaning of forced saving, as occurring only with the full employment of labor, but which is incorrect.

15 Wennerlind (2005: 227) acknowledges Hume's controversial passage being "strikingly similar to Richard Cantillon's analysis of monetary dynamics."

16 However, Wennerlind (2008: 126, n. 33) considers Cantillon's influence on Hume's thought unlikely, arguing, "Since Cantillon's *Essai* . . . circulated in France prior to its publication, it is conceivable, though unlikely, that Hume encountered a copy during his travels."

17 William Grampp (1992) cautions against citing Cantillon's work as having influenced or contributed to the analyses of others, even where the subsequent work is of a superior quality. He cites the example of Cantillon's arguing that the accumulation of specie be a policy of government, which is an inferior position to Hume's reliance on the price-specie-flow mechanism to distribute money appropriately among trading nations, making "the balance of trade . . . non-agenda as a policy objective" (65). I thank a referee for the *History of Economics Review*, who was supportive of my manuscript, for bringing Grampp's warning to my attention.

18 Robinson (1975: 125) still insists, "The price level had nothing to do with banking policy, it depended on money-wage rates." Another post-Keynesian, wage cost-push theory interpretation of Hume's "Of Money" is Jan Kregel's (1989) claim that Hume was suggesting "we [should] have an incomes policy rule which implies that if wages could be kept from rising by more than the increase in the 'greater alacrity and attention', then money growth could be channeled completely into real output and employment growth, with stable wage costs per unit of output and prices" (73).

19 Remarkably, Perlman (1987: 277; italics original) cites incorrectly this argument by Rotwein to include him among those who have argued that "the wage increase *follows* the price increase and occurs at the end of the process." He cites James Angell (1925: 25) as the only analyst he knew to have interpreted Hume as having argued the rise of wages before the rise of prices. Angell, like the other modern interpreters of Hume as having argued the wage cost-push theory of inflation, shows no awareness of the forced-saving phenomenon. Angell (1925: 26) also misrepresents Hume as having denied "the existence of any connection between the quantity of money and interest rates," without qualifying Hume's argument as a long-run equilibrium proposition, as in Hume's "Of Interest."

20 Similarly, a referee for the *Journal of the History of Economic Thought*, under the Keynesian continuous flow labor market model, argues: "The paper's creative and persuasive case for the price movements in advance of wage movements deserves an accompanying and validating account of what we can say, and can't say, about Hume's conception of the labor market behavior in response to monetary shocks. . . . I urge the author to look the problem of explaining what could be going on in the labor and output market in the eye. . . . If there is a monetary expansion that increases output it must cause the real wage to rise because we *move along an (upwards sloping) labor supply curve*," assuming "there is "full employment" (italics added). The referee was not paying careful attention to Hume's own argument.

21 Duke (1979: 579) attempts to capture this aspect of Hume's analysis with a horizontal portion of the labor supply curve, although with respect to the real wage rate instead of the nominal wage rate. But the point is that the labor market does not operate quite along the same principles as the supply and demand for produced goods and services that are not sold on contracted prices.

22 For more discussion of this classical principle (but without reference to Hume), Marshall's adherence to it, and its contrast with the Keynesian wages-leading-prices argument, see Arthur W. Marget (1938–1942: 2, 584–90).

23 In spite of Wennerlind's narrative, a referee rejecting my manuscript for the *History of Political Economy* writes: "I've looked at that [Wennerlind's] article. The emphasis is entirely on the relationship between increases in output and increases in money, and not at all on whether wages rise before prices, or prices rise before wages." The referee also does not recognize the existence of the alternative interpretation of monetary dynamics,

claiming, "It is not however clear to me that the supposed two traditions actually exist, and the author risks attacking a position that no one defends."

24 Ricardo's (*Works*, 9: 25) disputing Malthus's argument seems to be more about the time duration before wage rates fall.

25 I thank George Caffentzis for alerting me to this definition of the magistrate in the *Oxford English Dictionary*.

5 Milton Friedman's misleading influence from interpreting the Great Depression with Keynes's broadly defined money

Introduction[1]

John Maynard Keynes (1936) cited the Great Depression during which the US Fed increased its quantity of money significantly but prices fell, production decreased, and unemployment rose by historic amounts (from about three to twenty-five percent) between 1930 and 1933 as proof of the irrelevance of classical monetary analysis, particularly the Quantity Theory of money, to an economy in depression. Keynes arrived at this conclusion from having given up on (a) treating the Quantity Theory as explaining the level of prices from money's (currency) supply and demand at all times and (b) savings being the source of funds for business investment; thus, the public's increased demand for cash amounted to dissaving, which should contract economic activity. These are among principles Keynes taught in his earlier lectures on money, based upon Marshall's testimonies before the 1888 Gold and Silver Commission and the 1899 Indian Currency Committee (Keynes 1983: 693–8) before he turned the Quantity Theory into a theory of "output as a whole."

Milton Friedman did not address these deficiencies in Keynes's treatment of classical monetary analysis while arguing that Keynes's interpretation of the Great Depression was "completely wrong" (Friedman 1970b: 11). However, Friedman undertook to counter views of monetary policy promoted by Keynes's interpretation as, "monetary policy is an ineffective instrument for stemming deflation" (1960: 20) or that "Monetary policy was a string. You could pull on it to stop inflation but you could not push on it to halt recession" (1968a: 1; see also Friedman and Schwartz 1963: 348). Friedman disregarded his teacher Henry Simons's (1936) interpretation of the Great Depression as reflecting mostly the effect of excessive cash hoarding by the public, the same view Keynes also argued. Rather, Friedman adopted Keynes's (1936: 167, n. 1) broad definition of money that commingles money (currency, according to the classical unit-of-account definition)[2] with the public's deposits (savings) with banking institutions to derive the now familiar "money stock," M1 and M2, to dispute Keynes's interpretation (see Friedman 1960, 1967, 1968a, 1970b; Friedman and Schwartz 1970: 103). But that definition obscures recognition of the public's dissaving that mostly generated the economy's contraction. The dissaving is buried under "monetary disturbance" (Friedman

1960: 23), or "declines in deposit-currency and deposit-reserves ratios" (Friedman and Schwartz 1963: 347), or a collapsing "money multiplier."

Building mostly upon Clark Warburton's earlier writings,[3] Friedman (1960, 1968a, 1970b) and Friedman and Schwartz (1963) argue that it was a one-third contraction in the "money stock" or "monetary total" between 1930 and 1933 that caused the catastrophe. In its most widely known form, Friedman's 1967 Presidential address, he claims,

> Keynes and most other economists of the time believed that the Great Contraction in the United States occurred despite aggressive expansionary policies by the monetary authorities – that they did their best but their best was not enough. Recent studies have demonstrated that the facts are precisely the reverse: the U.S. monetary authorities followed highly deflationary policies. The quantity of money in the United States fell by one-third in the course of the contraction . . . because the Federal Reserve System *forced* or permitted a sharp reduction in the *monetary base*, because it failed to exercise the responsibilities assigned to it in the Federal Reserve Act to provide liquidity to the banking system.
>
> (1968a: 3; italics added)

In fact, the monetary base or "high-powered" money (H) increased by 20.49 percent, from \$6.98 billion in January 1930 to \$8.41 billion by March 1933 when the US went off gold (Friedman and Schwartz 1963: 803–4; see also Irving Fisher 1935: 5–6). Friedman's reference to the monetary base is indeed puzzling since he and Anna Schwartz (Friedman and Schwartz 1963) document numerous instances of the Fed having increased the quantity (see below).

Friedman's indictment of the Fed conflicts with the following facts to be illustrated: (1) a central bank may influence but cannot control the "money stock," M1 or M2; (2) the Fed's increased quantity of money (H) had been overwhelmed by the public's dissaving, reflected in its increased cash demand; (3) the Fed's money increases stopped waves of banking crises in 1930, 1931 and 1932; and (4) the Fed's adherence to currency convertibility into gold until March 1933 undermined its ability to expand the quantity of money (H). The last point was acknowledged by several commentators in a 1932 Chicago conference on the gold standard, including Lionel Edie (1932), John Williams (1932), and Jacob Viner (1932).[4] Indeed, Friedman and Schwartz (1963: 361) also argue that the Fed did not follow gold-standard rules during the depression.[5] Thus, Friedman (1968a: 3) argues, "The Great Contraction is tragic testimony to the power of monetary policy – not, as Keynes and so many of his contemporaries believed, evidence of its impotence" (see also Friedman 1970b: 11–12). Friedman (1970b: 17) also declares,

> Monetary policy had not been tried and found wanting. It had not been tried. Or, alternatively, it had been tried perversely. It had been used to force an incredible deflation on the American economy and on the rest of the world . . .

if Keynes had known the facts about the Great Depression as we now know them, he could not have interpreted that episode as he did.

But Keynes was referring to the Fed's money (H), not M1 or M2. He also was a dealer in securities and participated in discussions of antidepression policies in the US during the early 1930s. Keynes's familiarity with US financial data underlies his view that "in the United States at certain dates in 1932 there was a crisis . . . a financial crisis or crisis of liquidation, when scarcely anyone could be induced to part with holdings of money [hoarding] on any reasonable terms" (1936: 207–8), and the monetary authorities had lost effective control over interest rates. This was an illustration of Keynes's liquidity-trap proposition (Ahiakpor 2018a). Friedman, thus, appears rather to have been misled by Keynes's broad definition of money to draw the wrong lessons from the Great Depression, and to have left a misleading influence on monetary policy.

Friedman's misleading influence is reflected in Ben Bernanke's (2002) full acceptance of his indictment of the Fed for the Great Depression.[6] Apparently, to avoid a similar charge at the onset of the financial crisis in fall 2008, Bernanke led the Fed, as its chairman, to undertake massive purchases of securities, under Quantitative Easing 1, 2, and 3, almost exactly as Friedman and Schwartz (1963) argue the Fed should have done during the Great Depression.[7] Friedman and Schwartz also cite the absence of a strong leader within the Federal Reserve System as a key explanation for the System's alleged failure to take quick and decisive action to prevent the depression: "It was a defect of the financial system that it was susceptible to crises resolvable only with [a strong individual] leadership. The existence of such a system is, of course, the ultimate explanation for the financial collapse" (418).[8] Explaining the Fed's actions under his leadership, Bernanke (2015) argues:

> The Federal Reserve, born of the now little-known Panic of 1907, failed its first major test in the 1930s. Its leaders and the leaders of other central banks around the world remained passive in the face of ruinous deflation and financial collapse. . . . The Federal Reserve – the institution that I have dedicated the better part of my adult life to studying and serving – confronted similar challenges in the crisis of 2007–2009 and its aftermath. This time, we acted.
>
> (vii)

Friedman's monetary studies, aimed at contradicting Keynes, would have been helpful had he (a) recognized that Keynes was referring to the Fed's money (H) creation, (b) acknowledged the greater significance of the public's savings or dissaving in determining the "money stock" and economic activity, (c) acknowledged the gold-exchange standard's impediment to expansionary domestic monetary policy, just as a fixed exchange-rate regime,[9] and (d) explained the consistency of the depression with the classical Quantity Theory of money (H), contrary to Keynes's interpretation. Remarkably, Anna Schwartz, in an October 2008 *Wall Street Journal* interview, disavows the appropriateness of the Fed's monetary expansion to deal with the so-called "massive credit crunch," arguing, "The Fed has gone about as if the problem is a shortage of liquidity. That is not the basic problem. The basic problem for the markets is that [uncertainty] that the balance sheets of financial firms are credible" (see Carney 2008).

Interpreting the Great Depression consistently with classical monetary analysis, rather than with Keynes's broad definition of money and Keynes's views on the Quantity Theory, saving,[10] and the theory of interest, informs a more appropriate conduct of monetary policy than Friedman's (1960, 1968a, 1984b) constant money-growth rule. Outside of a gold standard, such policy is to vary the quantity of central bank money (H) to meet its demand in order to sustain the level of prices, as David Hume (1752: 39) argues, not to manipulate interest rates. The gold standard frustrates a central bank's ability to implement an independent expansionary monetary policy (see also Keynes 1931 and Joseph Schumpeter [1954] 1994: 732); it amounts to a fixed exchange-rate regime, a point Friedman (1953: esp. 179–80) well makes. It also would help resolve the long-running debate over the Fed's culpability for the Great Depression (see, e.g., Wheelock 1992; Wicker 1996; Eichengreen and Temin 2000; Hsieh and Romer 2006; Timberlake 2007) to address Keynes's conflicting definitions of money – narrow, sometimes, broad, other times – and his view of saving being equivalent to cash hoarding. The rest of the chapter elaborates on this prospect.

A central bank's limited influence over the "money stock," M1 or M2

Milton Friedman's fundamental criticism of the Fed's actions during the Great Depression was in defense of his belief in the enduring potency of monetary policy. His criticism presumes the ability of a central bank to control the volume credit included in the "money stock" and to conduct open market purchases regardless of the external and internal drains of gold under a gold standard. Thus, Friedman and Schwartz (1963: 318) insist: "the gold drain and the subsequent rise in discount rates [should have] been accompanied by extensive open market purchases designed to offset the effect of the external gold drain on high-powered money and of the internal currency drain on bank reserves." However, the "money stock" had not been assigned to the Fed to manage (see also Warburton 1946c).[11] Neither did the Peel's Act of 1844 in England, a model for the Federal Reserve System, assign the Bank of England that responsibility. Nevertheless, Friedman (1960: 44) insists, "The Reserve System's role is to control the stock of money," even as he also acknowledges the possibility only of a central bank's *influence* (see also Friedman 1968a: 3, 15). He notes, "In practice, it is easier said than done. It is never possible to know what changes are going on [among the determinants of the 'stock of money'] until after the event" (68). Friedman (1960: 31; italics added) also recognizes that "the amount of high-powered money is affected by factors *outside the direct control* of the [Federal Reserve] System."[12]

Indeed, the Federal Reserve Act (1913) intended the Fed to be the lender of *last resort* (not an activist leader in lending) to banks, following the banking crisis of 1907. Until then no centralized currency-creating institution existed and nationally charted banks printed their own notes on the basis of their paid-up capitals (savings) and their receipt of gold or deposits of "ultimate money," including gold coins, gold certificates, and greenbacks (Treasury money). The national bank notes were legally redeemable into gold or greenbacks upon demand. Banks that failed to redeem them were subject to having their charters revoked, with their paid-up capitals used to redeem their liabilities. Recognizing the inability of banks fully to redeem their liabilities in a panic under a fractional-reserve banking system led to the advocacy of a 100 percent reserve banking (see, e.g., Fisher 1935), which Friedman (1960: 56) also endorses.[13]

The private clearinghouse arrangements before the Fed's establishment never proved to be adequate in preventing banking panics, which were dealt with by the suspension of deposit redemption into cash: "Restriction was . . . a therapeutic measure to prevent a cumulation [sic] of bank failures arising solely out of liquidity needs that the system as a whole *could not* possibly satisfy" (Friedman and Schwartz 1963: 329; italics added). The Federal Reserve System, whose notes were also redeemable into gold or gold certificates on demand, was supposed to be the ultimate instrument to prevent a repeat of banking panics by quickly meeting the liquidity (cash) needs of commercial banks, the so-called "currency elasticity." Technically, however, the principle relies more on hope than on possibility. A banking panic is more the result of a sudden demand to withdraw savings (dissaving), which cannot readily be met under a fractional-reserve banking system, rather than an insufficiency of "ultimate money." Also, under a gold standard, a central bank never has enough currency to meet all of a community's money demand. That is why the real cure for a banking panic is the restoration of depositors' confidence (see Ricardo's, Walter Bagehot's, and J. S. Mill's arguments below).

The Fed's operational procedure to abide by its constitutional mandate (Article 1, Section 8 – "To coin Money, regulate the Value thereof") was to base its currency creation forty percent upon gold acquisitions "and additional collateral of 60 per cent in either gold or eligible paper" (Friedman and Schwartz 1963: 400), rather than on just about any securities presented to it. Thus, in the absence of "eligible paper," a much greater proportion of Fed currency was backed by gold, limiting its "free gold" for redeeming both domestic and external liabilities. Eligible paper was backed by real production, so that, on the premise of the classical Quantity Theory, such lending would not be inflationary or impair the Fed's gold-redemption ability. Smith (*WN*, 1: 328–37) suggests this principle – lending on "real" rather than on "fictitious" bills of exchange – for the safety of commercial banks, and it became the basis of the Bank of England's banking division's operational guide.[14] The 27 February 1932 Glass-Steagall Act, permitting government bonds to be included among permissible collateral against Federal bank notes (Friedman and Schwartz 1963: 321), eased that limitation and enabled the Fed to undertake massive purchases until July 1932 in its efforts to mitigate the ongoing price deflation.[15]

Only a central bank's credit creation amounts to money (currency) creation. However, when the currency is also representative of gold, even fractionally, the central bank loses its ability fully to increase the quantity independently of variations in the quantity of gold. The bank may sterilize gold inflows and prevent domestic price inflation, but it is ultimately powerless to prevent price deflation, following external and internal gold drains. The latter appears to have been the case during the banking panics, particularly after Britain's departure from gold in September 1931. Several analysts, including Friedman and Schwartz (1963), Hsieh and Romer (2006), and Timberlake (2007), have disputed the impact of gold outflows on the Fed's "insufficient" money (currency) creation during the depression. But Friedman and Schwartz and Hsieh and Romer also cite several instances where gold outflows undermined the Fed's actions. Timberlake's claim also appears to be founded upon his misreading Lionel Edie's (1932) plea to free up the Fed's "free gold" by allowing government bonds to be used as collateral against Fed money.

The public's influence over the "money stock"

Friedman's "money stock" includes commercial bank credit (BC) – the facility to make purchases without using one's own income[16] – that derives principally from the publics' savings or deposits (D), whether checkable or time deposits, whose variations are capable of frustrating a central bank's influence. Indeed, commercial bank credit is similar to the loans extended by non-bank lenders in an economy. But these are not considered "creators and destroyers of money" (see, e.g., Friedman 1960: 70; Warburton 1946c: 517). The description is misleading. Even though banks create deposits for their borrowers, such deposits are founded mostly upon the savings of bank customers. And when borrowers act upon their loans, only the recorded deposits are left on the liabilities column of a bank's balance sheet. Furthermore, banks acquire deposits at interest; until its prohibition in March 1933, banks paid interest on demand deposits too. Banks do not destroy their liabilities incurred at interest in order to lend. Also, banks do not lend money, but the public's savings. As Friedman correctly warns, "We speak of a man borrowing money when we mean he is engaged in a credit transaction" (1972: 200).

To appreciate the public's ability to frustrate a central bank's influence on the "money stock," M1 or M2, consider the following. Banks hold excess reserves (R_e) in readiness to meet depositors' demand for money (cash). So that, from the banking sector's balance sheet, $M1 = C + DD = C + R_{dd} + R_e + BC = H(1-\alpha) + BC$, where C = currency in circulation (held by the non-bank public), DD = demand deposits, R_{dd} = required reserves against demand deposits, $\alpha = R_{dt}/H$, ratio of required reserves against time deposits (R_{dt}), and $C + R_{dd} + R_e = H(1-\alpha)$, while $M2 = C + DD + TD = C + R_{dd} + R_{dt} + R_e + BC = H + BC$. BC is typically a much larger magnitude than H, and its variations tend to dominate variations in H. For M1, its multiplier, $m_1 = (cu + 1)/(cu + r_d + r_e)$, supposedly enables a central bank's open market purchases $(\Delta H > 0)$ to generate multiple dollar amounts of the "money stock," given cu (the non-bank public's currency-deposit ratio or currency drain), r_d (the required reserves-deposit ratio), and r_e (banks' excess reserves-deposit ratio) (see, e.g., Friedman 1960: 105–6). The M2, whose multiplier, $m_2 = (cu + 1 + t)/(cu + r_d + r_t t + r_e)$, where t = ratio of time deposits to demand deposits (TD/D) and r_t = ratio of reserves against time deposits, merely expands the extent to which time deposits contribute to the "money stock." But variations in cu and r_e can frustrate variations in H arising from open market operations.

Friedman (1960) does not split the reserves into required (R_d) and excess reserves (R_e). However, the separation helps to illustrate the difficulty a central bank faces in attempting to control the "money stock." Friedman occasionally concedes the point, as, for instance, when he states "a change on the part of banks in the fraction of their assets they wish to hold in the form of high-powered money affects the number of dollars of deposit money per dollar of high-powered money and so alters the total stock of money" (1960: 67); "the currency-deposit ratio and the deposit-reserve ratio are always experiencing changes that tend to produce perturbations in the behavior of the stock of money" (68); "Under present circumstances, even the stock of money is not directly controlled by the [Federal Reserve] System" (88); and "the total money stock for any given total of high-powered money is affected by the ratio of high-powered money to deposits that banks choose to hold and the ratio of currency to deposits that the public chooses to hold" (89). Friedman (1968a: 15) yet includes "the quantity of a monetary total — currency plus adjusted demand deposits, or this total plus commercial bank time deposits, or a still broader total" among the variables a monetary authority can control.

Furthermore, the "money stock" supply formula assumes an automatic multiple deposit expansion process, which obscures an individual saver's role in determining the multiplier's value. Thus, suppose an individual makes a bank deposit (D_0) in cash (or claims to cash), and the bank extends credit (loans), net of reserves, $BC_0 = (1 - r_d)(1 - r_e)D_0$. The new income generated by the loan expenditure enables its recipient to make a new bank deposit (savings), net of cash withholding or currency drain (cu), $D_1 = (1 - cu)BC_0 = (1 - cu)(1 - r_d)(1 - r_e)D_0$. The next loan, $BC_1 = (1 - r_d)(1 - r_e)D_1$, generates new spending and income out of which a new deposit may be made, $D_2 = (1 - cu)B_1 = (1 - cu)^2(1 - r_d)^2(1 - r_e)^2D_0$, and so on. If all income earners from the loan expenditures acted according to the formula, $D_t = (1 - cu)^i(1 - r_d)^i(1 - r_e)^iD_0$, the geometric summation of their deposits becomes the D in the "money stock" formula, $M = C + D$. However, the summation falls short of its maximum once an income recipient fails to make a new deposit into the banking system.

Friedman's belief in a central bank's ability to control the "money stock" thus presumes the cumulative deposit process is always realized, but which is unlikely. As Friedman (1960: 67) well recognizes, an increase in the public's demand for money to hold (cash hoarding or dissaving),[17] reduces the "money stock" for any quantity of central bank money released. Similarly, banks' increasing their own excess reserve-deposit ratios (r_e) reduces the amounts they lend out of deposited savings, and thus reduces the "money stock." Friedman and Schwartz (1963: 343; italics added) acknowledge the same:

As after the first banking crisis, the decline in the stock of money was *entirely* a consequence of the fall in the [deposit-currency and deposit-reserves] ratios.

High-powered money rose, this time by 4 per cent from March to August [1931], and so offset nearly half the contractionary effect of the declining deposit ratios.

Thus Friedman's (1960: 90) mandate to the Fed, "that the stock of money be increased at a fixed rate year-in and year-out without any variation in the rate of increase to meet cyclical needs," is impossible to achieve (Friedman 1968a: 16 repeats the mandate).[18]

When the public's confidence in the security of their deposits is shaken by the failures of some banks, this causes an increased demand for cash and/or gold, under the gold standard. The affected banks would need to liquidate their loans and investments (BC) in order to meet such demands, as occurred during 1930–33. Banks' sale of securities or asset liquidation also amounts to their increased demand for credit, which should increase discount or interest rates, again as occurred in the US, following Britain's departure from gold in September 1931. A central bank's purchasing those securities and increasing the quantity of its money (H), even at a higher discount rate, is thus not "contractionary" policy, contrary to Friedman's (1960: 19, 1968a, and 1970b) and Friedman and Schwartz's (1963: 395–6) description, and which has become the typical interpretation of the Fed's action in 1931 (see, e.g., Wheelock 1992; Eichengreen and Temin 2000; Hsieh and Romer 2006; Gary Richardson 2007).

Protecting the monetary base from decline is not contractionary policy; any more than selling more goods at a higher price when demand has increased correctly could be described as a contraction of the product's quantity. As Friedman (1960: 19) observes, the "measure arrested the gold drain," and high-powered money actually increased from $7.5 billion at the end of September to $7.74 billion by the end of December 1931 (Friedman and Schwartz 1963: 803). Rather, a central bank's sale of securities is contractionary, as it reduces the quantity of money (H). Lowering the discount rate at a time of gold outflows would have contracted central bank money even further, with no assurance that the public's savings (deposits) with banks would have increased to reduce the currency-deposit and banks' reserve-deposit ratios. However, higher interest rates, resulting from the raised discount rate, could encourage savers to economize on cash hoarding, and thereby possibly increase the "money stock," if the problem were not the public's shaken confidence.

Also, contrary to Friedman and Schwartz (1963), banks do not destroy or reduce deposits (liabilities) in order to obtain the needed cash. They claim, "It was the necessity of reducing deposits by $14 in order to make $1 available for the public to hold as currency that made the loss of confidence in the banks so cumulative and so disastrous. Here was the famous multiple expansion process of the banking system in vicious reverse" (1963: 346); Warburton (1946c: 517) makes a similar, mistaken, claim. The description derives from summary data that obscure the role of dissaving in the contractionary process, and is misleading. Rather, when a saver demands redemption of deposit into cash (or gold),[19] the bank draws upon its excess reserves to make the payment. Subsequently, the bank sells some of its investments (securities) to replenish the excess reserves. If a bank is unable to meet its depositors' demands for cash, it declares bankruptcy. This is how thousands of banks, mostly rural, non-members of the Federal Reserve System (Friedman and Schwartz 1963: 358–9; Wheelock 1992: 25; Wicker 1996: 102), failed between 1930 and 1933. Most other banks survived during the banking crises because they could sell their securities or borrow from the Fed to meet their cash withdrawal demands.[20] Furthermore, contrary to Friedman and Schwartz (1963), when a borrower pays back their loan, the effect is on the assets (not liabilities) side of the bank's balance sheet: excess reserves increase while loans decrease, the credit (created deposit) of the borrower having long disappeared from the liabilities column when the borrower acted upon the loan.

Friedman's presumed ability of the Fed to control M1 or M2 through variations in the quantity of high-powered money is further undermined by the gold-exchange standard. As Friedman and Schwartz (1963) observe, variations in the US gold stock frequently went against the Fed's actions to increase the high-powered money, as, for instance, during "the period after Britain's departure from gold saw a *sharp outflow*, particularly in September and October 1931, large enough to offset the gold inflow during the earlier segments of the contraction," while the Fed's discount purchases had increased (345–6; italics added). They further explain: "The reason the bond purchases [in April 1932] had no effect . . . is that they were *offset in part by a renewed outflow of gold* and the rest was more than offset by continued declines in the [deposit-currency and deposit-reserves] ratios" (347; italics added), the "bank failures [having] tapered off in February and March 1932." Also, "In February and March 1933 . . . [there] was a sharp spurt in gold coin and certificates. . . . Fears of devaluation were widespread and the public's *preference for gold* was unmistakable" (350; italics added). Friedman and Schwartz (1963) further observe: "All told, from August 1931 to January 1932, the rise of $330 million in high-powered money was accounted for by a rise of $560 million in discounts, $80 million in government securities, $270 million in other assets of the monetary authorities, *offset* by a decline of $580 million in the *gold stock*" (346; italics added), and "From April to July 1932, when Reserve System holdings of government securities went up by roughly $1 billion, the *gold stock fell* about half that amount, most of the outflow going to France" (347; italics added). They conclude: "From August 1929 to March 1933 as a whole, the change in high-powered money alone would have produced a rise of 17 ½ percent in the stock of money," all else constant.

These observations hardly justify Friedman's (1960: 19) describing the Fed as having been "passive" or "deflationary"; Friedman and Schwartz's (1963: 411) describing Fed actions as "passive" and "inept"; Friedman's (1968a: 3) claiming, "the U.S. monetary authorities followed highly deflationary policies"; or Friedman and Schwartz (1986: 40) claiming that "the establishment of the Federal Reserve System, in practice, did more harm than good." The evidence also contradicts such claims as, "the Fed just sat by and did nothing, so bank after bank failed" (Anna Schwartz in her 2008 *Wall Street Journal* interview); the Fed adopted a "policy of inaction . . . the Fed did nothing and let the economy slide further into the depression" (Humphrey 2001: 310, 311); and the Fed failed "to respond to the banking panics" and "refused to act despite the overwhelming monetary and real decline" (Hsieh and Romer 2006: 140, 172).

Timberlake (2007: 348) pieces together Lionel Edie's (1932) comments to suggest that Edie had disputed the gold standard's hindrance of the Fed's ability to expand the quantity of money (currency) adequately. But Edie argued the reverse and called for "the Federal Reserve to utilize United States government bonds as collateral for Federal Reserve notes during emergency periods" (1932: 114). Edie also warned that the gold standard would not survive unless adherence to it was weakened:

> I submit that the real threat to the gold parity is not to be found in the events which excite the public imagination but in the unstable factors which permit such an excessive contraction of credit as has been witnessed in the United States during the past two years. The gold standard can endure a great deal of abuse, but there are limits to its powers of endurance. Unless the vicious shrinkage of credit, which has gone on with accelerated vigor in the last six months and which continues up to the present moment, can be unmistakably brought to a halt, the gold parity will have little chance of survival in the United States.
>
> (127)

Indeed, following Britain's departure from gold in September 1931, Governor Harrison of the New York Fed "considered the gold position of the System paramount at [the] time and because of that would not be inclined to purchase Government securities" to boost the bond market (Friedman and Schwartz 1963: 381, n. 115).

That there was a sharp contraction in the stock of savings (demand and time deposits) because of the public's increased demand for cash, there can be no doubt. The real question is whether the Federal Reserve System, with its fairly autonomous twelve regional Reserve Banks maintaining their own gold reserves – the New York Reserve Bank twice had to borrow gold from the Chicago Reserve Bank, and was refused the third time in 1933 (Wicker 1996: 130) – was capable of supplying as much gold to meet both foreign and domestic demands and to prevent the "money stock" from contracting. Wicker (1996: 130) explains,

> To bolster the New York Bank's [gold] position, the Chicago Fed loaned the New York Fed $105 million on March 1 and another $60 million on March 2 which together with increased discounts and advances reduced the reserve ratio of the Chicago Fed to 56 percent; it had been as high as 80 percent two weeks earlier. When confronted with an additional request for $150 million on March 3, the request was refused on the grounds that the Chicago Bank's position would be seriously weakened.

The New York Reserve Bank had to suspend its adherence to the legal gold-reserve requirement for thirty days in March 1933 after both external and internal gold drains had reduced its "reserve percentage below its legal limit" (Friedman and Schwartz 1963: 327). Hsieh and Romer (2006, 171) also report Governor George Harrison of the Federal Reserve Bank of New York arguing in June 1932 that, with their gold-reserve ratio at "50 percent and that of the Federal Reserve Bank of Chicago at 75 percent, 'it is difficult to see why we should pump funds into the market which will then be siphoned off to Chicago'." Such was the nature of individual Reserve Banks' authority over their gold reserves that judging the capability of the Federal Reserve System on the basis of the total stock of gold in the US is not meaningful. It thus appears incorrect to argue, "Looking closely at Fed history from its beginnings in 1914, one sees clearly that an operational gold standard . . . virtually never constrained Fed policies" (Timberlake 2007: 350).

Timberlake (2007: 350) also appears to have misinterpreted Bagehot's argument that the gold standard did not fetter the Bank of England's lending ability *after* the suspension of the Bank Act. Rather, he invokes Bagehot (1873: 100) to argue that "the alleged 'gold standard' constraint becomes even more imaginary" when one understands that the Fed Board could have completely abrogated the Fed's gold-reserve requirement "so that *all* Fed gold was on the table to be used" (italics original; Timberlake 2008: 309 repeats the argument). But, if abrogating the gold-reserve requirement would have permitted the needed Fed's money creation, then the requirement must have been a hindrance or "fetter" on the Fed's ability, as some others, such as Barry Eichengreen (1992), have argued. Besides, the Fed thereafter could not meet its gold-redemption liabilities if it exhausted its gold stock.

The strict adherence to a gold standard causes variations in the quantity of gold to regulate a central bank's currency creation, rendering domestic price-level stabilization moot. That is why, in times of financial crises, governments typically suspended adherence to it. As John Williams (1932), discussing Fed policy during the depression, observes, "There is . . . a fundamental conflict between the principles of central banking and the principles of the gold standard" (148). Jacob Viner (1932: 35) also notes,

> A country on the gold standard binds itself to all the vagaries of gold as a standard of value. . . . For over a century writers have pleaded for the abandonment of the gold standard and the substitution of a managed paper currency, stabilized in terms of wholesale commodity prices, or of wages of labor, or of the price of wheat, or of the cost of living, or of the volume of outstanding credit. They have conceded that external stability must be sacrificed if internal stability is to be gained, but they have insisted that the latter is for most, if not all, countries by far the most important.

It was no coincidence that countries that abandoned the gold standard either before (Australia and New Zealand) or soon after Britain did in September 1931 quickly recovered from their economic depression while countries that took longer, including the US, experienced a longer-lasting depression (Friedman 1960: 20; Bernanke 2000, Ch. 1 and pages 78–84). The former countries could easily inflate their currencies and reverse their domestic price deflation. Such is the hindrance of the gold standard to the pursuit of domestic monetary policy that Keynes (1931) observed, following Britain's departure from gold:

> There are few Englishmen who do not rejoice at the breaking of our *gold fetters*. We feel that we have at last a free hand to do what is sensible. The romantic phase is over, and we can begin to discuss realistically what policy is for the best. . . . the great advantages to British trade and industry for our ceasing artificial efforts to maintain our currency above its real value were quickly realized.
>
> (1972, *Collected Writings*, IX: 245; italics added)

Further evidence of US Fed actions, dissaving/saving, and the economy

Data on the Fed's currency creation and variations in commercial banks' checkable and time deposits illustrate the significance of the public's dissaving in generating the contraction of the "stock of money" (Table 5.1). High-powered money increased from $6.83 billion at the end of the third quarter of 1930 to $8.41 billion (by $1.58 billion or 23.1 percent) at the end of the first quarter of 1933 while currency held by the non-bank public – a measure of the public's dissaving or cash hoarding – increased from $3.70 billion to $5.42 billion ($1.72 or 46.5 percent). At the same time, checkable deposits decreased from $21.77 billion to $14.9 billion (by $6.87 billion or 31.6 percent) while time deposits decreased from $20.18 billion to $13.23 billion (by $6.95 billion or 34.4 percent) and the "money stock" decreased from $45.65 billion to $33.55 billion ($12.1 billion or 26.5 percent).

The contraction of the public's savings during the Great Depression in the US is also reflected in the significant increase in the currency-demand deposit ratio, from 17 percent at end of third quarter of 1930 to 36.4 percent at end of first quarter of 1933 (114 percent increase) and the rise in the currency-time deposit ratio, from 18.3 percent to 41 percent (a 124 percent increase), over the same period (Table 5.2). Increases in the ratios were due more to decreases in demand and time deposits rather than to a significant increase in the quantity of currency (H) actually held. Reserves (vault cash) to demand deposit ratio also increased from 3.7 percent at end of third quarter in 1930 and reached 4.8 percent or 29.7 percent only, by the end of second quarter of 1933 (value for first quarter not available) while vault cash-time deposit ratio increased from 3.9 percent to 6.0 percent or 53.8 percent over the same period. Again, this was not because vault cash had increased (it declined by 11.7 percent from $0.795 billion to $0.702 billion), but because demand and time deposits had decreased. But if one merely looked at the M1 formula, $[(cu + 1)/(cu + r_{dd} + r_e).H(1 - \alpha)]$ or the M2 formula, $[(cu + 1 + t)/(cu + r_{dd} + tr_{td} + r_e).H]$, it might appear that the Fed badly failed its expected duty, according to Friedman (1960, 1968a), in not having expanded H enough to counter movements in the cu and r_e ratios.

Table 5.1 US money and "money stock," 1929–35

Year and Quarter		Currency Held by the Public	High-Powered Money	Deposits Adjusted, Commercial Banks		Total	Money Stock, Consolidated
				Demand	Time		
1929	I	3.89	7.15	22.55	20.14	42.69	46.58
	II	3.92	7.10	22.50	19.87	42.37	46.29
	III	3.91	7.08	22.84	19.94	42.78	46.69
	IV	3.86	6.98	23.12	19.75	42.87	46.73
1930	I	3.77	6.96	22.48	19.79	42.27	46.04
	II	3.71	6.91	22.08	20.00	42.08	45.79
	III	3.70	6.83	21.77	20.18	41.95	45.65
	IV	3.73	7.13	21.58	19.55	41.43	45.16
1931	I	3.87	7.09	21.16	19.40	40.56	44.43
	II	3.96	7.30	20.42	19.28	39.70	43.66
	III	4.22	7.50	19.71	18.44	38.15	42.37
	IV	4.59	7.74	18.13	16.53	34.66	39.25
1932	I	4.87	7.54	16.86	15.39	32.25	37.12
	II	4.87	7.79	16.18	14.96	31.14	36.01
	III	5.05	7.90	15.57	14.59	30.16	35.21
	IV	4.90	8.03	15.91	14.57	30.48	35.38
1933	I	5.42	8.41	14.90	13.23	28.13	33.55
	II	5.12	7.94	14.54	11.69	26.23	31.35
	III	4.92	8.09	14.64	12.01	26.65	31.57
	IV	4.89	8.30	15.11	11.90	27.01	31.90
1934	I	4.58	9.00	16.16	12.14	28.30	32.88
	II	4.62	9.26	16.86	12.55	29.41	34.03
	III	4.67	9.40	17.74	12.71	30.45	35.12
	IV	4.66	9.51	18.65	12.78	31.43	36.09
1935	I	4.73	10.16	19.88	12.94	32.82	37.55
	II	4.76	10.69	20.61	13.23	33.84	38.60
	III	4.80	10.97	21.94	13.25	35.19	39.99
	IV	4.92	11.58	22.62	13.45	36.07	40.99

Source: Table 5.2 in Friedman and Schwartz 1970: 68. Values are in billions of dollars, seasonally adjusted. High-powered money figures from Friedman and Schwartz 1963: 803–4.

The 30.7 percent increase of the "money stock," from $31.35 billion to $40.99 billion (or $9.64 billion) from the second quarter of 1933 to the end of 1935 owes more to increases in the demand and time deposits than to the Fed's increased money creation. High-powered money increased from $7.94 billion from the second quarter of 1933 to $11.58 billion (by $3.64 billion or 45.8 percent) while currency held by the non-bank public decreased by 10.6 percent from $5.12 billion

Table 5.2 US circulating currency, vault cash, currency- and vault cash-deposit ratios, 1929–35

Year and Quarter		Currency Held by the Public	Vault Cash	Currency-Demand D. Ratio	Currency-Time D. Ratio	Vault Cash-Demand D. Ratio	Vault Cash-Time D. Ratio
1929	I	3.89	.896	0.173	0.193	0.040	0.044
	II	3.92	.869	0.174	0.197	0.039	0.044
	III	3.91	.916	0.171	0.196	0.040	0.046
	IV	3.86	.874	0.167	0.195	0.038	0.044
1930	I	3.77	.867	0.168	0.191	0.039	0.044
	II	3.71	.848	0.168	0.186	0.038	0.042
	III	3.70	.795	0.170	0.183	0.037	0.039
	IV	3.73	.883	0.173	0.191	0.041	0.045
1931	I	3.87	.788	0.183	0.199	0.037	0.041
	II	3.96	.846	0.194	0.205	0.041	0.044
	III	4.22	.863	0.214	0.229	0.044	0.047
	IV	4.59	.816	0.253	0.278	0.045	0.049
1932	I	4.87	N.A.	0.289	0.316	N.A.	N.A.
	II	4.87	.786	0.301	0.326	0.049	0.053
	III	5.05	.700	0.324	0.346	0.045	0.048
	IV	4.90	.712	0.308	0.336	0.045	0.049
1933	I	5.42	N.A.	0.364	0.410	N.A.	N.A.
	II	5.12	.702	0.352	0.438	0.048	0.060
	III	4.92	.677	0.336	0.410	0.046	0.056
	IV	4.89	.739	0.324	0.411	0.049	0.062
1934	I	4.58	.760	0.283	0.377	0.047	0.063
	II	4.62	.780	0.274	0.368	0.046	0.062
	III	4.67	.780	0.263	0.367	0.044	0.061
	IV	4.66	.823	0.250	0.365	0.044	0.064
1935	I	4.73	.816	0.238	0.366	0.041	0.063
	II	4.76	.862	0.231	0.360	0.042	0.065
	III	4.80	.844	0.219	0.362	0.038	0.064
	IV	4.92	.870	0.218	0.366	0.038	0.065

Notes: Deposit and vault cash ratios based on data taken from Tables 2 and 24 in Friedman and Schwartz 1970. Currency values are in billions of dollars, seasonally adjusted. D = deposit.

to its low of $4.58 at the end of the first quarter 1934 before rising almost steadily to $4.92 by the end of 1935. Demand deposits increased steadily from $14.54 billion to $22.62 billion (by $8.08 billion or 55.6 percent), more than the amount of high-powered money's increase, while time deposits increased from $11.69 billion to $13.45 billion (by $1.76 billion or 15 percent) over the same period.

There thus appears to be little consistent relation between the level of high-powered money and the economy's performance between 1930 and 1935. The consistent relation is rather between the levels of demand and time deposits and the economy's behavior: both deposits (savings) decreased along with the economy's contraction between 1930 and first quarter of 1933; both deposits started to increase from the second quarter of 1933 and rose consistently in 1934 and 1935, along with the economy's recovery. The deposits' increases may be explained mainly by (a) the US going off gold in March 1933, which led to a halting of gold exports and the internal gold drain, (b) the government's assuring the public that only financially sound banks would be allowed to re-open after the national banking holiday, and (c) President Roosevelt's signing the bill establishing the FDIC in June 1933,[21] helping to restore the public's confidence in the security of their deposits.

However, when one focuses on the "money stock," there appears to be the con-sistency between its behavior and the economy's performance that Friedman has argued: "money stock" declined by 26.5 percent between the third quarter of 1930 and the first quarter of 1933, while the economy sharply contracted. The "money stock" increased by 30.7 percent between the second quarter of 1933 and the end of 1935, along with the economy's recovery. But we thereby miss recognizing the real driver of the economy's movement, namely, dissaving (cash hoarding) earlier and increased saving subsequently, rather than the Fed's rate of currency creation.

In attempting to assess the Fed's culpability for the Depression, it also is worth recalling that the National Credit Corporation, created in October 1931 and later transformed into the Reconstruction Finance Corporation (RFC) in January 1932, was supposed to give financial assistance to "solvent but illiquid" non-member banks, whose numbers dominated the bank failures. Wicker (1996) also lists finan-cial malpractices and mismanagement among the causes of bank failures, besides many being rather small, unit banks – promoted by US banking regulations (the McFadden Act of 1927 also prohibited branch banking) – and thus were vulner-able to defaults by borrowers facing crop failures and real estate losses at the time. Richardson (2007: 604, Table 5.3) also documents the number of weeks in which banks' insolvency was the cause of their failure having exceeded those of banks' illiquidity being the cause (although he himself interprets the data in the reverse). Indeed, the Bank of the United States in New York "ultimately paid off [only] 83.5 per cent of its adjusted liabilities at its closing on December 11, 1930" (Friedman and Schwartz 1963: 311). Thus, Walter (2005) makes a good case that the many bank failures in the depression were a shaking-out of an "overbanked" banking system whose necessary pruning was stopped with the institution of the FDIC. It also is noteworthy that the banking panics were not one continuous event from fall 1930 through winter 1933. The Fed's actions stopped sporadic banking panics before 1933, as Friedman and Schwartz (1963) recount.

Consistency of the Great Depression with classical monetary analysis, contra Keynes

Friedman could have defended the relevance of the classical Quantity Theory of money to the Great Depression without blaming the Fed for having "followed highly deflationary policies" (1968a: 3) or having forced "an incredible deflation on the American economy and the rest of the world" (1970b: 17). However, the correct explanation employs the classical unit-of-account definition of money, which was specie in classical times and central bank currency (H) in modern times, as in Hume (1752: 37), Smith (*WN*, 1: 42), Ricardo (*Works*, 4: 55), J. S. Mill (*Works*, 3: 577), Fisher (1922: 11), Marshall (1923: 13, 15), and Keynes (1936: 174, Ch. 15). But Keynes (1936) adopts a broad definition of money, claiming:

> We can draw the line between "money" and "debts" at whatever point is convenient for handling a particular problem. . . . It is often convenient in practice to include in *money* time-deposits with banks and, occasionally, even such instruments as (e.g.) treasury bills. As a rule, I shall, as in my *Treatise on Money*, assume that money is co-extensive with bank deposits.
>
> (167, n. 1; italics original)

Friedman (1960: 91) prefers Keynes's broad definition of money because "it seems to be somewhat more closely related empirically to income and other economic magnitudes" (see also Friedman and Schwartz 1970: 103).[22] But that basis for selecting M1 or M2 as money is analytically spurious since demand and time deposits (savings) derive concurrently from the public's income (GDP).

The classical Quantity Theory explains the level of prices by the quantity of money (H) supplied relative to its demand ($P = H/ky$);[23] inflation and deflation by the growth of money's demand relative to the growth of money's supply ($\%\Delta P = \%\Delta H - \%\Delta k - \%\Delta y$), using the Cambridge equation. The public's increased demand for money (H) to hold ($\%\Delta k$), reflected in the contraction of demand and time deposits (about $13.8 billion), compared to the $1.7 billion increase in Fed money between fall 1930 and winter 1933 confirms the classical explanation for deflation: the quantity of money demanded overwhelmed the quantity supplied. With fiat money, a central bank determines its quantity exogenously. But, under a gold standard, the quantity supplied is influenced by variations in the quantity of gold acquired. Thus, Friedman and Schwartz (1963) explain increases in the quantity of Fed money (H) by the inflow of gold, for instance, "the rise of $340 million in high-powered money, seasonally adjusted, was produced partly by an *inflow of $84 million of gold* . . . partly by an increase of $117 million in Federal Reserve credit outstanding" (342), and high-powered money "rose in January 1931, only because of a *continued gold inflow* offset the decline in Federal Reserve credit" (343; italics added).[24]

Indeed, Keynes (1924: 82–8) follows restatements of the classical Quantity Theory by Marshall (1923) and Pigou (1917), but he abandons it in the *General Theory*. According to Keynes, writing the *General Theory* was his "final escape from the confusions of the Quantity Theory, which had entangled" him,[25] and he was "returning to the doctrine of the older, pre-nineteenth century economists" (1939 preface to the French edition, Keynes 1974: xxxiv). Rather, Keynes argues that the supply of money, relative to its demand, should explain the level of interest rates, an argument Friedman adopts.[26] Only after interest rates have influenced investment decisions and production would the level of prices be determined by the supply and demand for output as a whole, just as prices are determined in individual commodity markets by their supply and demand (Keynes 1936: 292–6). Furthermore, Keynes argues that the price-level explanation in the Quantity Theory would be relevant only in times of full employment (1936: 209) when increases in the quantity of money would not be accompanied by increases in real output.

Ricardo's explanation of the inability of gold-back money and a fractional-reserve banking system to escape the consequences of a banking panic also well illustrates the consistency of classical monetary analysis with the Great Depression experience:

> [O]n those extraordinary occasions, when a general panic seizes the country, and when every one is desirous of possessing the precious metals as the most convenient mode of realizing or concealing his property. . . . [central] Banks have no security, *on any system*; from their very nature they are subject to them, as at no time can there be in a Bank, or in a country, so much specie or bullion as the monied individuals of such country have a right to demand. . . . A panic of this kind was the cause of the crisis in 1797; and not, as has been supposed, the large advances which the Bank had then made to Government. Neither the Bank nor Government were at that time to blame; it was the contagion of the unfounded fears of the timid part of the community, which occasioned the run on the Bank [of England], and it would equally have taken place if they had not made any advances to Government, and had possessed twice their present capital.
>
> (*Works*, 1: 358–9; italics original)

J. S. Mill (*Works*, 3: 574) reiterates Ricardo's point, noting that the depressed level of prices and commercial activity would persist for the duration of the excess demand for money: "If extra currency were not forthcoming to make . . . payments . . . money . . . must be withdrawn from the market for commodities, and prices, consequently, must fall. An increase of the circulating medium, conformable in *extent and duration* to the temporary stress of business, does not raise prices, but merely prevents this fall" (*Works*, 3: 516; italics added).

Walter Bagehot (1873), whose writing on central banking Friedman and Schwartz (1963) cite in their criticism of Fed actions, draws upon Ricardo's argument to urge the Banking Department of the Bank of England to hold a larger reserve of currency in order to meet other banks' demands at the onset of a banking panic. Bagehot similarly urges the other banks to hold adequate reserves to meet their own depositors' redemption demands in order to stave off a panic resulting from shaken public confidence (see also Frank Taussig 1921: 1, Ch. 29). But Bagehot also recognizes the limits to the banks' capability: "The bank or banks which hold the [normally adequate] reserve may last a little longer than the others; but if apprehension pass a certain bound, they must perish too" (27); similarly, Taussig (1921: 1, 405) argues, "Deposit banking implies that the banks have a great volume of demand liabilities, and a comparatively small amount of cash with which to meet them. If there is a general and sustained run on all the banks, the cash almost inevitably proves insufficient." Thus, only measures to restore the public's confidence in the security of their deposits could halt the rush to redeem deposits and end the falling level of prices and increasing unemployment in a commercial crisis: "The best palliative to a panic is a confidence in the adequate amount of the Bank [of England] reserve, and in the efficient use of that reserve. And until we have on this point a clear understanding with the Bank of England, both our liability to crises and our terror at crises will always be greater than they would otherwise be" (Bagehot 1873: 101). Marshall (1920: 591–2) also describes the effect of shaken public confidence that results in the disorganization of industries, falling prices, and rising unemployment, which needs the *restoration of confidence* to stop the price deflation and promote economic recovery: "The chief cause of the evil is a want of confidence" (592).

Friedman and Schwartz (1963: 395) also cite Bagehot's recommendation of free lending by a lender of last resort to criticize the Fed's responses during the depression. But they leave out Bagehot's (second) recommendation to the Banking Department that its "advances should be made on all *good* banking securities ... or every sort on which money is *ordinarily* and *usually* lent" (1873: 97; italics added). Taussig (1921: 1, 404) repeats Bagehot's prescription, arguing: banks of "unquestionable insolvency – the agents or the victims of ill-judged and unsuccessful investments ... must succumb to the inevitable." Also, "the condition on which aid is granted usually is, and always ought to be, that the bank in straits be solvent; that its loans and other assets prove on examination to be sound, and sufficient in the ordinary course of events to meet its liabilities" (1921: 1, 405). This appears to have been the principle of lending to only solvent but illiquid banks that the Fed and the RFC pursued. Moreover, Bagehot did not demand that the Currency Department of the Bank of England print more money than its bullion reserves would permit (under the 1844 Bank Act) to supply the Banking Department money to lend freely. Rather, he observes, if "the reserve in the Banking Department will not be enough for all such loans ... the Banking Department must fail" (1873: 97).[27]

Friedman and Schwartz (1963) also do not cite Bagehot's first rule for the lender of last resort in a banking panic, namely, to lend at *high interest rates*. The rule is consistent with the Fed's having raised the discount rate on 9 October 1931, two weeks after Britain's departure from gold, but which Friedman and Schwartz criticize as contractionary policy.[28]Bagehot (1873: 97; italics added) argues:

> These loans *should only be made* at a *very high* rate of interest. This will operate as a heavy fine on unreasonable timidity, and will prevent the greatest number of applications by persons who do not require it. The rate should be *raised early in the panic*, so that the fine may be paid early; that no one may borrow out of the idle precaution without paying well for it; that the Banking reserve may be protected as far as possible.

Taussig (1921: 1, 403; italics added) repeats Bagehot's first rule: "The rate of discount is indeed advanced [raised] by the Bank [of England], perhaps *sharply*; and it is advanced by other banking institutions also."

Price deflation tends to reduce the rate of economic activity by imposing losses on businesses, to the benefit of fixed-income recipients, such as wage, interest, and rental earners (see, e.g., Alfred and Mary Marshall 1879: 156–7; Marshall 1920: 493–4, 515; and Fisher 1926; see also Fisher's [1933] "debt-deflation" argument). This is the opposite of increased business profits arising from unanticipated increases in inflation until contracts are revised – the classical forced-saving mechanism. Thus, even though the Fed expanded the quantity of its money, employment and production still declined between 1930 and 1933 because of the six percent annual average rate of price deflation, owing to the public's excessive demand for money or dissaving.

The classics also explained the positive role of savings in economic activity, which Keynes however denied. They noted that money is merely the instrument for conveying savers' capitals to borrowers. For example, Smith (*WN*, 1: 373–4) writes:

> Almost all loans at interest are made in money. . . . But what the borrower really wants, and what the lender provides him with, is not the money, but the money's worth [. . .] the money, is as it were, but the deed of assignment, which conveys from one hand to another those capitals [savings] which the owners do not care to employ themselves. Those capitals may be greater in almost any proportion, than the amount of the money which serves as the instrument of their conveyance; the same pieces of money successively serving for many different loans, as well as for many different purchases.

Friedman (1967: 3), in effect, repeats the classical "capital" supply and demand mechanism. He notes that the rate of interest coordinates the capital transfer between lenders and borrowers. But he does not carry that insight into most of his monetary analysis, following instead Keynes's liquidity-preference theory of interest rates.

In contrast with Keynes's emphasis on central bank's money creation rather than the public's savings determining economic activity, Smith (*WN*, 1: 313) explains:

> In order to put industry into motion, three things are requisite; materials to work upon, tools to work with, and the wages or recompense for the sake of which the work is done. Money is neither a material to work upon, tools to work with; and though the wages of the workman are commonly paid to him in money, his real revenue, like that of all other men, consists not in the money, but in the money's worth; not in the metal pieces, but in what can be got for them.

Ricardo (*Works*, 3: 92) affirms Smith's argument, noting that, if central bank money were the principal source of economic growth, "no nation, but by similar means [paper money printing], could enter into competition with us, we should engross the trade of the world. To what absurdities would not such a theory lead us!"

The misleading effect of Friedman's interpretation of the Great Depression

Friedman blamed the Fed for having undertaken contractionary monetary policy during the Great Depression by raising the discount rate and not having increased the quantity of its money enough to have prevented a one-third contraction of M1 and M2. Ben Bernanke pleaded guilty to the charge in 2002 on behalf of the Fed and promised never to repeat the alleged mistake. The onset of the US Great Financial Crisis thus gave Bernanke the opportunity to redeem the Fed. He promoted an aggressive expansion of (high-powered) money, aimed at reducing the level of interest rates. Bernanke (2009: 1) dates the Fed's intervention in the financial markets from September 2007, when they reduced the federal funds rate by fifty basis points and "by a cumulative 325 basis points by the spring of 2008." The first of three Quantitative Easing programs – large purchases of short-term and long-term financial assets – started in November 2008. The goal was to "push down interest rates and ease credit conditions in a range of markets, despite the fact that the federal funds rate is close to its lower bound," in order to stimulate "aggregate demand" (Bernanke 2009: 5). The Fed's actions included (a) "lending to financial institutions," (b) "providing liquidity directly to key credit markets," and (c) "buying longer-term securities" (ibid.: 4).

The Fed also engaged in currency swaps with foreign central banks to enable them to "acquire dollars from the Federal Reserve to lend in their jurisdictions" (Bernanke 2009: 3). Such aggressive expansion of the Fed's balance sheet well follows Friedman and Schwartz's (1963: 391–406) suggested "Alternative Policies" to address the banking crises between 1930 and 1933, although Anna Schwartz criticizes the Fed's actions in 2008 as inappropriate (*Wall Street Journal* interview with Brian Carney [2008]). Rather than rescuing failing financial institutions, Schwartz argues, "Firms that made wrong decisions should fail. . . . You shouldn't rescue them. . . . Everything works much better when wrong decisions are punished and good decisions make you rich." But Friedman's (1960) and Friedman and Schwartz's (1963) interpretations of the Great Depression had left an indelible influence on Bernanke's Fed.

Indeed, Schwartz's criticism of Fed actions following the Great Financial Crisis was appropriate, given the significant differences between the US monetary systems in 1930–33 and those in 2008–14. First is the absence of the FDIC until January 1934. As Friedman (1960: 21) observes, the institution of deposit insurance "renders banking panics all but impossible . . . by eliminating any reason for runs to begin . . . it has been the most important structural change in our monetary system in the direction of greater stability." There were hardly any runs on commercial banks in fall 2008 since most depositors did not have more than the $100,000 per insured deposits. Raising the deposit insurance limit to $250,000 in December 2008 further assured that few would feel the security of their deposits threatened.

Rather than the sharp decreases in demand and time deposits between 1930 and 1933, demand deposits decreased by only 2.6 percent between the first and fourth quarters of 2007. They rather increased by 18.4 percent between the end of the first

and third quarters of 2008, before the onset of the Fed's first Quantitative Easing –
Bernanke's preferred "credit easing" (Table 5.3).[29] Savings deposits, including
money market deposit accounts, increased almost steadily between the first quarter
of 2007 and third quarter of 2008, from \$3,771.8 billion to \$4,033.4 billion or by
6.9 percent. Similarly, small time deposits increased by 6.1 percent almost steadily
from \$1,183 billion to \$1,255.7 billion over the same period. Unlike in the 1930s,
M1 increased by 6.1 percent from \$1,369.7 billion in the first quarter of 2007 to
\$1,453.8 billion by the third quarter of 2008, while M2 increased by 8.4 percent
from \$7,164.4 billion to \$7,769.2 billion over the same period.

Second, whereas prices declined at an average annual rate of 6 percent between
1930 and 1933, the GDP deflator increased by 2.7 percent in 2007 and by 2.0 percent in 2008. There was no price deflation to cure with the massive currency
increases in subsequent years, much of which was held as bank reserves, the Fed
having started paying 0.25 percent interest on reserves from October 2008.[30] Until
December 2015, the Federal Funds rate hovered around 0.12 percent, after having
declined steadily from 3.94 percent in January 2008 (federalreserve.org).

Third, the bank runs during the Great Depression contracted the level of checkable deposits that served as a means of payment. But the 2008 financial crisis
affected mostly investment banks, including Bear Sterns and Lehman Brothers,

Table 5.3 Currency in circulation, savings and time deposits, M1 and M2, 2007–10

Year and Quarter		Currency in Circulation	Demand Deposits	Savings Deposits	Small Time Deposits	M1	M2
2007	I	751.2	302.8	3771.8	1183.0	1369.7	7164.4
	II	755.0	304.5	3832.3	1186.1	1366.8	7249.9
	III	760.1	295.7	3869.2	1195.4	1369.8	7370.9
	IV	758.7	294.8	3858.9	1218.9	1366.5	7404.3
2008	I	761.8	297.2	3979.8	1217.1	1375.3	7618.1
	II	769.0	294.0	4024.9	1204.0	1386.2	7638.7
	III	780.1	351.9	4033.4	1255.7	1453.8	7769.2
	IV	812.1	464.6	4102.2	1378.0	1595.2	8155.2
2009	I	845.1	390.1	4374.8	1341.7	1563.3	8325.4
	II	853.1	437.4	4470.9	1278.9	1647.8	8374.3
	III	862.2	427.2	4613.2	1271.9	1659.9	8333.1
	IV	862.2	445.7	4848.5	1172.9	1696.6	8542.8
2010	I	871.6	447.1	4935.7	1106.2	1712.0	8511.7
	II	883.1	459.2	5074.3	1051.5	1722.8	8591.1
	III	899.7	479.3	5219.2	992.2	1765.7	8700.3
	IV	915.7	504.3	5355.9	922.9	1828.3	8812.2

Notes: Data from federalreserve.org. Values are in billions of dollars, seasonally adjusted; Demand
deposits with commercial banks only; Savings deposits include money market deposits with commercial
banks and thrift institutions; Small time deposits include deposits at commercial banks and thrift
institutions.

which had suffered losses on their investments in mortgage-backed securities. The so-called "credit crunch" of 2008 was about the difficulties of those investment banks refinancing their repurchase agreements, rather than commercial banks being unable to lend because depositors were withdrawing their savings. Besides, the investment banks rely mostly upon the commercial banks (the commercial paper market) as their principal source of funds, the banks in turn lending the public's savings (deposits).

However, Bernanke promoted Quantitative Easing to enable bank lending:

> I explained that if we [the Fed] failed to stabilize financial markets and *restart the flow* of credit, someone like my father, who once borrowed to build a new and larger store a block away from the original one, would be out of luck. . . . the Fed was helping to bring down mortgage rates, strengthen banks so that they could *make loans again*, and stabilize money market funds.
>
> (2015: 415–6; italics added)

But, while banks may increase or decrease their rates of lending, they never stop lending. In fact, demand and time deposits constituted 73.3 percent US commercial banks' sources of funds by October 2012 while borrowings from the Fed were less than 9 percent; loans as a percentage of total bank assets amounted to 59.9 percent (Hubbard and O'Brien 2014: 281). Yet the series of Quantitative Easing purchases aimed at depressing interest rates (Bernanke 2015: 415–6) follow Keynes's logic of the necessity of increased central bank money supply, rather than the public's savings, to fund business investment and to promote increased economic activity.

The failure of the US economy to recover quickly from the severe recession from December 2007 to July 2009, in spite of the massive increases in Federal Reserve asset purchases and increases in both M1 and M2, has been attributed to a return of Keynes's liquidity trap (see, e.g., Krugman 2013). But such attribution derives from the claimants' having transformed Keynes's (1936: 207) own hypothesis about long-term interest rates being stuck at some low (undefined) level because of the demand for money (cash) having turned absolute, into arguing: "increases in the money supply seem to have no effect" (Krugman 1998: 180; Ahiakpor 2018a elaborates on this point). The failure simply may be an indication that the wrong remedies were applied.[31]

It could not have helped that fiscal policy included such resource misallocating activities as bailing out failing large corporations, including General Motors and American International Group (AIG); allocating $700 billion to the Treasury for a Troubled Asset Relief Program (TARP) that included purchasing stocks of banking firms; funding new vehicle purchases while destroying used, but functional ones; and extending the unemployment compensation period from twenty-six to ninety-nine weeks.[32] The most that the monetary increases appear to have achieved was to have imposed a high inflationary tax on savers through negative real interest rates. A nine-month bank certificate of deposit (CD) that earned more than four percent in fall 2008 barely earned 0.05 percent in fall 2016.

Summary and conclusions

John Maynard Keynes indeed was mistaken in citing the Great Depression, with its price deflation, decreased production, and increased unemployment, in spite of increases in Federal Reserve money (H), not M1 or M2, as evidence of the irrelevance of classical Quantity Theory in a depression. To restore confidence in that theory and the effectiveness of monetary policy, Milton Friedman, along with Anna Schwartz, drew mainly upon arguments by Clark Warburton to indict the Fed for having failed its presumed responsibility of preventing the contraction of the "money stock" and to have caused the depression. Friedman gave little explicit recognition of the public's dissaving, and downplayed the impediment of the gold-exchange standard on the Fed's inability to expand the quantity of its money "enough" until March 1933. Having pleaded guilty to Friedman's indictment of the Fed for "ineptitude," "passivity," and responsibility for the depression, Ben Bernanke, as Fed Chairman, championed massive increases of Fed money under three Quantitative Easing programs to depress interest rates, following the US financial crisis of 2008.

Contrary to Keynes's influence through Friedman's interpretation of the Great Depression, the correct lessons include recognizing (a) the impossibility of a central bank's control of the total volume of credit included in the "stock of money," or M1 and M2; (b) the classical Quantity Theory of money's explanation of the level of prices as well as inflation or deflation by the supply and demand for central bank money (H), not M1 or M2; (c) that interest rates are determined mostly by the flow of savings relative to their demand – variations in central bank money may affect interest rates in the short run but not permanently; (d) that the flow of savings is the most important source of funds for business investment and the behavior of GDP, not central bank money; and (e) that the gold standard is not conducive to a central bank's independent expansionary monetary policy, as with a fixed exchange-rate regime. We can explain the Great Depression consistently with classical monetary analysis, but not with Keynes's broad definition of money and his treatment of savings as not the principal source of loanable funds.

Notes

1 This chapter draws on my paper, "Wrong Lessons from the Great Depression: Milton Friedman, Ben Bernanke, and the US Fed," presented at the History of Economics Society Annual Meetings, University of Toronto, Toronto, Canada, June 22–25, 2017. I thank Patrick Deutscher and George Tavlas for helpful comments on that paper without implicating them in any remaining errors, which are mine.

2 As previously noted, classical money is a community's unit of account or standard of value, which Keynes (1930: 1, 3) calls the "money of account" (see, e.g., Smith *WN*, 1: 42; 1978: 353, 368; Thornton 1802: 81, 90; Ricardo *Works*, 1: 369; 3: 104; J. S. Mill *Works*, 3: 502, 577). Irving Fisher (1922: 8; italics original) appears to have popularized the definition of money as "*what is generally acceptable in exchange for goods.*" However, Fisher (1922: 11) also excludes "a bank deposit transferable by check" from money, the definition of money Keynes (1930) adopts after having followed Marshall's (1923: 13–15) limiting money to only "coin and notes issued by Government" (see, e.g., Keynes 1924). When discussing liquidity-preference, hoarding, or central bank

monetary policy, Keynes (1936: 174, Ch. 15) also treats money as cash only. Similarly for Frank Taussig (1921: 1, 432), "[money] does not include the great item of [bank] deposits." Instead, "It includes specie, of course. . . . It includes bank notes and government notes convertible into specie. It includes paper, even tho not convertible, so long as this in fact passes freely" (ibid.)

3 Prominent among them are Warburton's April 1945 *Econometrica* and October 1946 *Journal of Political Economy* articles that attribute the Great Depression to the Fed's failure to prevent "monetary contraction," in which he defines money broadly to include "currency, demand deposits, time and savings deposits, and deposits of the United States government in Federal Reserve banks, but excludes interbank deposits and currency held by banks themselves" (1946b: 436). With that definition, Warburton (1946c) concludes: "monetary deficiency is the chief factor originating business depressions or amplifying minor recessions into severe depressions" and "monetary deficiency [has preceded] each business depression since establishment of the Federal Reserve System" (533). Explicit recognition of the public's dissaving hardly appears in his explanations.

4 I discuss below the errors of some analysts, including Chang-Tai Hsieh and Christina Romer (2006) and Richard Timberlake (2007), who dispute the gold standard's hindrance to the Fed's monetary expansion capability.

5 Friedman and Schwartz (1936: 361) observe, "We did not permit the inflow of gold to expand the U.S. money stock. We not only sterilized it, we went much further. Our money stock moved inversely, going down as the gold stock went up." But the "money stock" was dominated by the public's demand and time deposits, elements outside of a central bank's control. Friedman and Schwartz (1963: 345–7) also document several instances of the Fed's money expansion, which are however undermined by gold outflows, which I discuss below.

6 At Friedman's ninetieth birthday celebration in November 2002, Bernanke, then a Governor of the Federal Reserve System, declared: "Let me end my talk by abusing slightly my status as an official representative of the Federal Reserve. I would like to say to Milton and Anna: Regarding the Great Depression. You're right, we did it. We're very sorry. But thanks to you, we won't do it again." This after having acknowledged the "many lessons" that "practical central bankers, among which [he] now count[ed himself]," had learned from Friedman and Schwartz's analysis of the causes of the Great Depression.

7 Friedman and Schwartz applaud the July 1932 Emergency Relief Act that permitted the Reserve Banks to "discount for individuals, partnerships, and corporations, with no other sources of funds, notes, drafts, and bills of exchange eligible for discount for member banks" (1963: 321, n. 26; see also Bernanke 2009). They argue, "a vigorous monetary push" of that kind in 1931 "might have converted the faint signs of recovery [then] into sustained revival" (1963: 393). They ignore the fact that until February 1932, government bonds were not permitted as collateral against Fed currency. That restriction had limited the Fed's expansive monetary policy, as Edie (1932) explains, urging that the law be changed.

8 Elmus Wicker (1996: 125, 145) repeats the lack-of-leadership argument, even as he mostly seeks to absolve the Fed of Friedman's indictment for its "ineptitude" and responsibility for the Great Depression. Wheelock (1992: 13–23) disputes the significance of Benjamin Strong's absence, concluding: "The general thrust of [Fed] policy, however, appears consistent with that of Benjamin Strong" (23).

9 A "pure" gold standard is one in which gold coins or specie is used, not a paper substitute partially backed by gold (see Timberlake 2007).

10 So influential has been Keynes's macro-monetary analysis that hardly any analyst of the depression, including Friedman (1960, 1968a, 1970b), Friedman and Schwartz (1963), Wicker (1996), Bernanke (2000), and John Walter (2005) interprets the public's increased cash demand as dissaving and derive the economy's contraction and price deflation therefrom.

11 Warburton observes, "The [Federal Reserve] Act contained no provision giving the Federal Reserve Board or the Federal Reserve banks, either specifically or by reasonably clear inference, responsibility for monetary control in the sense of making it the duty of any officials in the system to estimate the most suitable quantity of money [the circulating media] for the use of the nation and to maintain the quantity of money in accord with the estimate of such" (1946c: 507). Of course, the lack of an assigned responsibility does not preclude attempting such control. My contention is that control of the "money stock" is beyond the capability of a central bank. Wicker (1996: 23, 57–8, 65, 103–4, 158, 165), on the other hand, excuses the Fed's failure to control the "money stock" by arguing that the money stock's determination with variations in the publics' currency-deposit ratio was not known until the publications of James Angell and F.K. Ficek (1933) and James Meade (1934).

12 Friedman's other admissions of only a central bank's influence rather than control over M1 or M2 include: "the Reserve System could *influence* the stock of money . . . by changing the amount of high-powered money . . . by buying and selling securities" and "rediscounting is a means whereby the Reserve System can *influence* the total stock of money" (1960: 32, 38; italics added).

13 A 100 percent reserve banking may prevent bank runs and secure financial stability, but at a huge cost in foregone economic growth from reduced saving. The public would hoard more of their unspent income in cash rather than pay the custodial fees to banks for their savings. The 100 percent reserve advocates appear oblivious to Smith's (*WN*, 1: 322–3, 340–1) explanation of the economic growth advantage of fractional-reserve banking.

14 It has been dubbed the "real bills doctrine" (Lloyd Mints 1945: 9) and much criticized for its alleged failure to recognize that "real bills" could be rediscounted multiple times a year and thus the principle could not safeguard against inflation (Henry Thornton 1802: 85–7); see also Mark Blaug 1996: 195–6). Friedman (1960: 26) calls the principle a "ubiquitous fallacy" and Timberlake (2007: 349) calls it "an incurably flawed doctrine." Following Thomas Humphrey (1982b, 2001), Timberlake blames the Great Depression mostly on the Fed's having followed the doctrine, even though there was price deflation rather than inflation. Humphrey's (1982b) illustration of the doctrine's alleged inflationary bias stems from his failure to interpret an increased production that motivates an increased demand for credit (real bills) from a central bank as tending to reduce the level of prices. Thus, the central bank's lending on the principle would merely restore the level of prices rather than be the source of an interminable inflation.

15 Hsieh and Romer (2006) omit this background to the Fed's massive purchases of government bonds and, rather, use the program mistakenly as proof that the gold standard had not earlier impeded the Fed's money expansion capability.

16 Charles Persons (1930) well illustrates this meaning of credit and its role in economic expansion in the US between 1920 and 1929. Failure to interpret credit this way has frustrated some analysts who are not sure whether anything other than checkable bank deposits should be called credit (see, e.g., Currie 1933).

17 Keynes failed to treat cash hoarding as the opposite of saving, as evident, for example, in his claim that "if a man hoards his savings in cash, he earns no interest, though he saves just as much as before" (1936: 167).

18 The Fed's failure to meet its target rates of M1 and M2 growth finally led Friedman (1984b: 50) to prescribe its freezing the monetary base as his preferred policy because zero growth is a politically easier number to defend: "Zero has a special appeal on political grounds that is not shared by any other number." Such a policy would have been (and would be) disastrous for the US or any other economy. Friedman would have benefited from consulting David Hume (1752) on monetary policy.

19 "Because of lack of confidence, there was a considerable hoarding of both notes and gold" and "A single depositor in one reserve district in the South . . . obtained through his Federal Reserve Bank $50,000 in gold to be hoarded because of his lack of confidence"

in 1932 (J. Laurence Laughlin 1933: 238, n. 12). Friedman and Schwartz (1963: 316) also note the internal currency drains resulting from the public's shaken confidence in banks and the external drains of gold "by foreigners fearful for the [Fed's] maintenance of the gold standard." See also Hsieh and Romer's (2006) on the external gold drains in 1932.

20 Friedman and Schwartz (1963) provide evidence of increased Federal Reserve loans and discounting of bills that led to increases in high-powered money, as, for example, when they write "High-powered money rose because Federal Reserve credit outstanding rose . . . primarily because of the sharp rise in discounts as banks, having no other recourse open to them, were driven to borrowing from the Reserve System, despite the unprecedentedly sharp rise in discount rates in October 1931" (346).

21 Instituting deposit insurance was part of the original Federal Reserve Act (1913), but it was deleted before its passage (Friedman and Schwartz 1963: 321, n. 29).

22 Friedman (1960: 99, 1968a: 12) refers to J. S. Mill's view of money as only "a contrivance for sparing time and labour." However, J. S. Mill's reference is to specie, not bank credit or savings that constitute an economy's source of capital (see, e.g., J. S. Mill *Works*, 2: 70–2). Friedman and Schwartz (1970: 96, n. 4) also cite Charles Rist's employing the classical definition of money as his having treated "bank notes and deposits as 'instruments of circulation,' but [which] cannot be considered money, because they are not a standard of value." They furthermore ignore Allen Meltzer's mentioning to them that, by money, "Fisher really meant high-powered money" (Friedman and Schwartz 1970: 98, n. 6).

23 But in his 1956 restatement of the Quantity Theory, Friedman argues that the "quantity theory is in the first instance a theory of the demand for money [including cash, demand, and savings deposits]. It is not a theory of output, or of money income, or the price level" (4). Subsequent studies of money's transmission mechanism, such as Friedman (1970a) and Laidler (1993b), have followed that lead.

24 We have already noted above the contractionary effect of gold outflows on the Fed's money creation.

25 As noted in Chapter 2 above, Keynes taught the Quantity Theory of money (cash) as the determination of money's value by its supply and demand in his lectures on money before the First World War. He also declared the theory "*absolutely valid*" (1983: 695; italics original).

26 Keynes (1936: Ch. 14) arrives at this conclusion after having failed to interpret "capital" in the classical theory of interest as savings or loanable funds, but as capital goods. Yet, Friedman (1967: 4) considers Keynes's monetary theory "sophisticated and modern," and his having turned the classical Quantity Theory into a theory of interest rates, merely an extension rather than its rejection (1970a: 168).

27 Table 1 in Bernanke (2000: 14) shows that the US gold stock declined by about six percent from 6478.9 metric tons in 1930 to 6072.7 metric tons by 1933 while the Fed still increased the level of currency by about twenty percent over the period. The increase was made possible by relaxing the gold-backing requirement in the February 1932 Glass-Steagall Act.

28 Wicker (1996) uses this timing to absolve the Fed of having caused the banking panic of fall 1931.

29 The data exclude deposits with other financial institutions, but these are small compared with deposits in commercial banks.

30 High-powered money more than doubled, from $0.814 trillion in 2007 to $1.683 trillion in 2008, and continued rising to $1.942 trillion in 2009, $1.97 trillion in 2010, $2.2675 trillion in 2011, $2.68 trillion in 2012, and $3.714 trillion in 2013. But the percentage of currency in circulation sharply declined from 97.3 in 2007 to 50.5 percent in 2008 and to 45.8 percent in 2009. In subsequent years, the percentages were 47.9, 38.7, 42.0, and 32.2, respectively. It is thus not surprising that the inflation rates have been low: 0.8 percent in 2009, 1.2 percent in 2010, 2.0 percent in 2011, 1.7 percent in 2012, and

1.5 percent in 2013 (IMF, *International Financial Statistics Yearbook 2014*). As Hume (1752: 42) explains, only the circulating money affects prices, not the absolute quantity: "If the coin be locked up in chests, it is the same thing with regards to prices, as if it were annihilated."

31 Stephen Williamson (2017) could not find any positive effect of the Fed's Quantitative Easing, observing, "There appears to be no evidence that QE works . . . to increase real GDP, if we compare Canada [which did not adopt the program] with the U.S. . . . there are good reasons to be skeptical that it works as advertised, and some economists have made a good case that QE is actually detrimental" (14).

32 It is beyond this chapter's scope to discuss the economic inefficiencies deriving from these fiscal policy measures, several of which Bernanke (2015) defends.

6 The modern free-banking advocacy

A casualty of Keynes's broad definition of money

Introduction[1]

As farfetched as it might seem, the modern free-banking advocacy is a casualty of John Maynard Keynes's (1936: 167, n. 1) broad definition of money to include central bank currency and banks' demand and savings deposits. Milton Friedman (1960) and Anna Schwartz (Friedman and Schwartz 1963) adopted that definition of money to accuse the US Fed of responsibility for the Great Depression (see Chapter 5 above). Friedman therefore argued the possibility that private "money" creation would have prevented the catastrophe, although he still supported a central bank's monopoly over currency creation and the regulation of private banking firms, the latter because of the third-party effects of a banking firm's behavior.[2] Friedman's apparent inconsistency prompted criticisms of his defense of government monopoly in the creation of money. The criticisms culminated in F. A. Hayek's (1976, 1978) revival of earlier free-banking advocacy (Vera Smith 1936) to question the desirability of a government monopoly in the production of money in a free society and urging the abolition of central banks.[3] Hayek argues that allowing the production of "money" (competing banknotes, none of which is the economy's unit of account) by private banking firms would best protect a society from inflation, deflation, and the resultant bouts of unemployment. His argument is founded on the belief that private producers of banknotes would be more motivated to regulate their quantities in order to preserve their purchasing power than a government monopoly producer of money: "there can be no doubt that free enterprise would have been both able to provide a money securing stability and that striving for individual gain would have driven private financial institutions to do so if they had been permitted" (1978: 97–8).

Hayek (1978: 23) cites (with the wrong date, 1975) Benjamin Klein (1974) as having anticipated his argument in favor of competitive currencies. However, Klein's model of competitive paper currencies does not argue the displacement of money, the unit of account, by any one of them. Klein recognizes that "gold was the single dominant unit of account and all the private notes were convertible into gold at fixed exchange rates" (1974: 440; see also Klein 1976). Neither did Walter Bagehot (1873), whose criticism of the Bank of England's monopoly over note issue within a sixty-five-mile radius from the center of London, many free-banking advocates, including Hayek (1978: 88), White (1984a: 43–4, 57, 145), and Selgin

(1988: 121, 2012: 347–9), cite in favor of their advocacy.[4] Bagehot's concern was about the inadequacy of the specie reserve for the banking system as a whole being held by the Bank of England: "If any large fraction of money was demanded, our banking system and our industrial system would be in great danger" (8). Moreover, "the reserve in the Banking Department of the Bank of England [has become] the banking reserve not only of the Bank of England, but of all London – and not only of all London, but of all England, Ireland, and Scotland too" (16).[5]

Like Friedman, Hayek does not limit his definition of money to an economy's unit of account but employs only the medium-of-exchange definition, which he attributes to Carl Menger.[6] That definition of money, perhaps also through Irving Fisher (1922: 5, 8), has become the norm in modern monetary and macroeconomic analysis (see, e.g., Friedman 1960; Friedman and Schwartz 1963, 1970; Tobin 1963; Laidler 1969). It contrasts with the classical unit-of-account definition that avoids commingling money – modern high-powered or "outside" money – with instruments of credit and wealth (bank deposits) or "inside money." The commingling tends to generate some inaccurate conclusions, as cautioned by Smith (1776), Francis Walker (1878), Friedman (1972), and Robert Greenfield and Leland Yeager (1986). These inaccurate conclusions, we will see, afflict the modern free-banking advocacy. For example, it is easier to appreciate that a government's control over the production of money, the unit of account, does not violate the freedom of individual firms to supply alternative means of payment such as checkable deposits or traveler's checks when these are recognized as money substitutes rather than their being constituents of the economy's money supply.

Several scholars in the modern free-banking movement have elaborated on Hayek's argument for abolishing central banks and allowing competitive note issuing by commercial banks. Their main difference with Hayek seems to be their recognizing the need for money as the unit of account besides competing banknotes as means of payment (see, e.g., White 1984c). White (1984a) provides both an outline of a theory of free banking and a historical justification for its return. White and George Selgin (1987) recount the evolution of the banking industry and sketch an image of a banking system that would have evolved, had governments not intervened to create central banks, building mainly upon Vera Smith (1936). Selgin (1988), drawing upon White (1984a), argues "the" theory of free banking to claim the greater ability of that system to (a) maintain "monetary equilibrium," (b) respond more effectively to the domestic demand for money and credit, and (c) promote a more efficient economic growth than a central-banking system. Subsequent writers, including Kevin Dowd (1989, 1992, 1993a, 1993b), David Glasner (1989), Steven Horwitz (1992), Kurt Schuler (1992), and Larry Sechrest (1993),[7] have asserted the alleged benefits of competitive issuing of banknotes, with or without the reinstitution of a metallic money.

Previous critics of the modern free-banking advocacy, particularly Friedman (1984a) and Friedman and Schwartz (1986), have focused on the resource costliness of a return to a commodity-money system. They have not argued the irrelevance of free banking to addressing the problems of inflation and deflation or the alleged infringement on the public's liberty in the choice of alternative means of payment by the government's monopoly production of fiat money. Most other people's instinctive reaction against the free-banking advocacy tends to be the informational costs that a multiplicity of banknotes, none of which is the unit of account, would impose on the community. As J. S. Mill (*Works*, 3: 502) observes, money being a "common measure of the values of different sorts" is the "first and most obvious" among the "principal inconveniences" alleviated by its use as a circulating medium. In the absence of a unit of account, "there would be no current price, or regular expression of value" (502). Similarly, Klein (1974: 443) argues: "If there are many monies and many sets of prices, the unit of account and medium of exchange functions of money are hampered. . . . computational-conversion costs increase with the number of independent monies within a market." Hayek's (1978) suggested scheme of regulating the quantity of private banknotes according to the value of a basket of commodities becomes extremely difficult, if not impossible, without a unit of account (see also White 1984c). Most free-banking advocates have tended to counter the objection with references to historical periods in which competitive banknotes existed; but all of those notes were not money but redeemable into specie or some legal-tender notes (money).

Moreover, any problems with modern central banks do not necessitate a return to competitive banknote issuing as the requisite solution. Modern central-bank money is the equivalent of previous specie money (the unit of account), while modern checks, even though they may not pass from hand to hand, are the equivalent of previous competitive banknotes that served as alternative means of payment. The cure for inflation or deflation lies with the regulation of a central bank's money supply to meet the growth of its demand, a point Hayek (1978) also argues repeatedly, but only in respect to privately issued banknotes. The ineffective criticisms of the modern free-banking advocacy thus far appear to have led to such declarations as: "If the free bankers are not correct . . . then it is odd that no one has yet managed to refute the case for free banking and ensure that the errors of this potentially dangerous point of view are exposed for all to see" and "we also need critics who can look at the work of others and help sift out the good ideas from those that are different or just plain wrong" (Dowd 1993b: xii–xiii, xv).

This chapter explains the redundancy of the modern free-banking advocacy and its advocates' inaccurate interpretation of the historical experience with free banking. We first review the classical distinction between money and instruments of credit used as means of payment, and then explain the redundancy of free-banking advocacy. The chapter proceeds by discounting the alleged advantages of free banking over a banking system inclusive of a central bank, and then discussing Friedman's implicit or inadvertent promotion of the free-banking advocacy. The critique of free-banking advocacy focuses on Selgin's (1988) exposition of "the" theory of free banking in its "mature form," which Selgin (2012) mostly restates. Among the high praises for Selgin's 1988 work is Richard Timberlake's (1991: 274) observation that Selgin's arguments

are so convincing that any statist who reads it is likely to press for even more controls for fear that the jig will soon be up. No one who reads this convincing exegesis will be able any longer to dismiss "free banking" as simply the brainchild of radicals and dreamers. Intellectually, if not politically, free market money is at the cutting edge of monetary economics and a force to be reckoned with.[8]

The chapter's conclusion is similar to Klein's (1974: 441–2) observation: "Present U.S. domestic monetary arrangements can usefully be described in terms . . . of multiple monies convertible into a single dominant money at fixed exchange rates. There is one dominant money (currency supplied by a government monopoly) and many privately produced nondominant monies (deposits supplied by different commercial banks)." The main difference with Klein's view is that our analysis recognizes bank deposits not as "money" but as the public's savings, whose volume is not totally under the control of commercial banks. That distinction avoids confusing money, a non-interest paying asset, with bank deposits (wealth) that pay interest; in Klein's theoretical model, all competing monies pay interest.

Money vs instruments of credit

Fundamental to recognizing the redundancy of modern free-banking advocacy is to distinguish money, the unit of account, from instruments of credit used as means of payment. Yet, so prevalent is the view of money primarily as a medium of exchange that some referees found my emphasis on recognizing the unit of account characteristic unhelpful. One, for the *History of Political Economy*, claims my distinction turns "a purely semantic point into one of substance, and a misleading substance at that." Another referee for the same journal insists, "This could never make any sense, since both concepts of money, together with others, are found throughout the classical literature, and of course this proves to be the case in the [my] paper." However, the significance of that distinction is that money serves both as the unit of account and a means of payment (see, e.g., Smith *WN*, 1: 36, 42, 52; 1978: 353, 368), but the other means of payment do not perform the unit of account function: No one measures the value of bread or an automobile in units of checks, checkable deposits, or electronic transfers.

According to the classical definition,[9] money is the particular commodity that measures the exchangeable value of all other commodities, such that money's rate of exchange between units of other commodities is their prices: "money is nothing but the representation of labour and commodities, and serves only as a method of rating or estimating them. Where coin is in greater plenty . . . a greater quantity of it [will be] required to represent the same quantity of goods" (Hume 1752: 37). Smith (*WN*, 1: 42) also explains, "At the same time and place . . . money is the exact measure of the exchangeable value of all commodities."

Money is also the particular commodity that may serve directly "as the instrument of . . . conveyance" (Smith *WN*, 1: 374) of income between buyers and sellers, and between owners of "capital" (savers) and borrowers. Credit, on the other hand, is a facility to make a purchase without income. Thus, Smith explains, "Money, like wine, must always be scarce with those who have neither wherewithal to buy it, nor credit to borrow it" (*WN*, 1: 458).[10] A banknote is thus an instrument of credit that may be acquired in the form of a loan or through redeeming one's deposited wealth (savings) with a bank. Furthermore, a non-fiat banknote, like a check, is an order to pay money. Its acceptance by a seller does not directly transfer money, but only a promise to pay money in the future. Thus, J. S. Mill (*Works*, 3: 553) argues, "An instrument which would be deprived of all value by the insolvency of a corporation cannot be money in any sense in which money is opposed to credit."

Rather than being creators of "money," banks are institutions that provide safe-keeping services for their customers' wealth and assist their depositors to transfer wealth in making payments either through checks or (previous) banknotes. Banks subsequently developed into lending their customers' deposited savings at interest through issuing banknotes or crediting the borrowers' accounts.[11] Instead of charging savers custodial fees, banks share their profits from lending by paying depositors interest. To meet their depositors' money demands, banks maintain reserves of their depositors' wealth in money. The reserves also enable banks to settle inter-bank claims generated by their customers' payments to creditors.

This is the sense in which, rather than being creators of money, "banks are simply intermediaries of loanable funds" (Selgin 1988: 55). On their own, banks cannot lend more than they receive from their depositors plus their equity capital. Henry Thornton's distinction between money and banknotes and the nature of their emergence through fractional-reserve banking also helps to clarifying the point:

> When confidence rises to a certain height in a country, it occurs to some persons, that profit may be obtained by issuing notes, which purport to be exchangeable for money; and which, through the facility of thus exchanging them may *circulate in its stead*; a part only of the money, of which the notes *supply the place*, being kept in store as a provision for the current payments.
> (1802: 90; italics added)[12]

The modern equivalent is lenders issuing checks redeemable in central-bank money and commercial banks crediting borrowers' accounts. Other lenders that were not note issuers extended their loans in the form of money (specie) itself.

In earlier periods of free banking, all other means of payment besides money, such as banknotes and bills of exchange, were recognized as "money substitutes." Thus, Hume (1752: 35) refers to them as "counterfeit money" or "paper-credit," as does Thornton (1802: 90); Smith (*WN*, 1: 310–1, 318, 503) calls them "promissory notes" or "bank money." Banknotes had carrying advantages over specie where large sums were involved, hence their emergence in popularity as wealth increased in economies. Hume observes,

> There are, it is true, many people in every rich state, who having large sums of money, would prefer paper with good security; as being of more easy transport and more safe custody. If the public [state] provide not a bank, private bankers will take advantage of this circumstance; as the goldsmiths formerly did in London, or as the bankers do at present in Dublin: And therefore it is better, it

may be thought, that a public company should enjoy the benefit of that paper-
credit, which always will have place in every opulent kingdom

(1752: 35–6).

The same relative convenience applies to modern checks in place of fiat money when
large sums are being transferred. To emphasize the substitution of banknotes for money
itself in circulation, Smith explains that the "whole paper money of every kind which
can easily circulate in any country never can exceed the value of the gold and silver, of
which *it supplies the place*, or which (the commerce being supposed the same) would
circulate there, if there was no paper money" (*WN*, 1: 318; italics added).[13]

Banknotes issued by different banks and bearing the same denomination in
specie (money) might not be accepted at par in the marketplace, depending upon
the public's perception of their issuers' creditworthiness. Hayek (1978: 107–8)
implicitly makes the same point. Thus Robert West (1974: 16) notes, "By the
time of the [US] Civil War there were literally thousands of state banks, issuing notes in thousands of varieties. The notes varied in value from par to near
zero, depending on the financial strength and trustworthiness of the issuing bank.
Notes which were perfectly good in one area might pass at a discount in another."
See also Klein (1974: 439–40), Friedman and Schwartz (1986: 50), Selgin (1988:
24–6), and Selgin and White (1994: 1727) for similar accounts. Until the Federal
Reserve imposed equal treatment of checks in the US, checks drawn upon rural
banks were not accepted at par as were checks drawn upon large city banks. Also
in England, for some time, checks drawn upon country banks were treated differently than those of London banks (see Quinn and Roberts 2008: 14–17). Only after
banknotes had attained the status of general acceptability, out of the "confidence in
the fortune, probity, and prudence" of their issuers, did they also serve widely as a
medium of exchange or part of the circulating media, having acquired "the same
currency as gold and silver money" (Smith *WN*, 1: 310).

In their monetary analyses, the classical writers also recognized that the increased
use of banknotes and bills of exchange as means of payment raised prices by causing an increased circulation of money itself (see Hume 1752, "Of Money"; Smith
WN, 1: 345;[14] Thornton 1802: 194, 197; Ricardo *Works*, 3: 90; and J. S. Mill *Works*,
3: 512–3). This follows from the Quantity Theory of money in which a reduction in
the demand for money to hold increases money's velocity and reduces the value of
money (inverse of the price level). But the higher domestic prices would lead to an
increase of imports (and a reduction of exports) and the export of the "excess" money
in payment for the imports. It also would induce an increase in the redemption of
notes into specie from their respective issuing banks and thus reduce the quantity of
banknotes in circulation – the phenomenon often described as "the law of reflux."

An increase in savings, following the increase of income (production), may
increase lending with banknotes without the rise of prices. As Hume, in "Of the
Balance of Trade," explains,

It is well known of what advantage it is to a merchant to be able to discount
his bills upon occasion; and every thing that facilitates this species of traffic

is favourable to the general commerce of a state. But private bankers are enabled to give such credit by the credit they receive from the *depositing of money* in their shops.

(1752: 70; italics added)

The increased production, facilitated by such lending, also tends to attract money's inflow from abroad through Hume's (1752) price-specie-flow mechanism and reverse any downward pressure on prices.

Furthermore, the classical writers referred to the unit of account or standard of value as money's first identifying function, not the medium of exchange function. Thus, Smith, in his *Lectures in Jurisprudence* explains:

In treating of opulence I shall consider. . . . Money as 1st The measure by which we compute the value of commodities (as a measure of value), [and] 2^d The common instrument of commerce or exchange"; and "Money as I observed now serves two severall [sic] purposes. It is *first* the measure of value. Every one tells you that the goods he has to sell are worth so many pounds, shillings, etc., believing you know this as a measure. It is also the instrument of commerce, or medium of exchange and permutation."

(1978: 353, 368; italics added)

This contrasts with the modern reference to the medium of exchange as the principal function or identifier of money. Hayek (1978: 51, n. 1; italics added), for example, argues that "To serve as a widely accepted medium of exchange is the *only* function which an object must perform to qualify as money." However, Hayek (1978: 63) also considers "suitability as a unit of account" among the functions to be performed by a currency.

Friedman (1960: 6) cites money's "central function," as its passage "from hand to hand" or a means of payment. In their extensive review of the definitions of money, from the classical period to the twentieth century, Friedman and Schwartz (1970: 93–103) do not cite the unit of account as the first identifier of money. Neither do they note Smith's (*WN*, 1: 306–7) reference to the "ambiguity of language" that has led to the application of the term "money" to income and wealth, besides specie or cash; see also Fisher (1922: 5). Friedman's (1972) cautioning about such confusion is only in respect of the theory of interest.

To appreciate the potential confusion in focusing on the medium-of-exchange function as money's primary identifier is Francis Walker's (1878: 405; italics original) explanation:

Money is that which passes from hand to hand in final discharge of debts and full payment for goods. The bank-deposit system allows the mutual cancellation of vast bodies of indebtedness which would, without this agency, require the intervention of an actual medium of exchange; but deposits, like every other form of credit, save the use of money; they do not perform the functions of money. *Money is what money does.*

Non-legal tender banknotes, like modern checks, were not the final means of discharging debts; they were claims on money. Clearinghouses helped to settle the specie claims among the note-issuing banks just as central banks now settle inter-bank claims in fiat money. Walker's point on checkable deposits evidently influenced Fisher's (1922: 11; italics original) argument that "while a bank deposit transferable by check is included as circulating media, it is not money. A bank *note*, on the other hand, is both circulating medium and money. Between these two lies the final line of distinction between what is money and what is not."

Marshall (1923), also referring to Walker's point on money's identifier, defines money as the ultimate means of payment:

> There is . . . a general, though not universal agreement that, when nothing is implied to the contrary, "money" is taken to be convertible with "currency," and therefore to consist of all those things which are (at any time and place) generally "current," *without doubt or special inquiry*, as means of purchasing commodities and services, and of defraying commercial obligations. Thus, in an advanced modern society, it includes all the *coin* and *notes issued by Government*.
>
> (1923: 13; italics added.)

Marshall further explains that

> an ordinary bank-note may be refused if tendered by a debtor in payment of an obligation; and, even when accepted by the creditor, it does not discharge the obligation, if the bank by which it is issued fails before the creditor has had time, with reasonable diligence, to present it for payment.
>
> (1923: 13, n. 3)

Nevertheless, Marshall reverses the primacy of the unit-of-account, among the functions performed by money, contrary to Walker's warning.[15] He cites the medium-of-exchange as money's first function, "admirably discharged by gold and silver and paper based on them" (16), and acknowledges Carl Menger's influence. Ludwig von Mises (1934) also distinguishes money from its paper substitutes. He was willing to "give the name of money-substitutes and not that of money to those objects that are employed like money in commerce but consist in perfectly secure and immediately convertible claims to money" (52). However, "the notes of the Austro-Hungarian Bank were in fact nothing but money-substitutes. The *money* of the country, as of other European countries, *was gold*" (59; italics added).

The modern definition of money that includes the public's wealth deposited with banks (savings), even as such deposits are designated as "inside money" (see, e.g., Laidler 1969; Friedman and Schwartz 1986; Selgin 1988), tends to obscure recognition of money from credit instruments. It appears to have encouraged most free-banking advocates to argue that, by allowing commercial banks to print their own notes or "currencies," these banks become suppliers of "money" rather than just continuing to be credit intermediaries.[16] For example, White (1988a), following

Hayek's (1978: 52) preference for "currency" in place of "money," envisions a plan whereby "currency issued by private banks [would] displace government currency [money]" (464). The vision fails to recognize private banknotes as instruments of credit rather than being money. Similarly, White asserts, "Historical precedent and monetary theory together suggest that the common money emerging from [note-issuing] competition would be currency and checking accounts issued by commercial banks or banklike financial firms" (1988a, 467).

Thus, White (1988b: xii; italics added) claims Selgin (1988) has reconstructed and extended "the theory of the *money supply* under free banking conditions, that is, where competing private banks are legally unrestricted in creating currency and demand deposits (and are compelled by market forces to make their liabilities redeemable for an outside money)." White (1989: 7), nevertheless, recognizes the analytical usefulness of identifying money with only the unit of account, but he chooses not to employ that identification consistently: "I differ from [Dale] Osborne by not identifying money exclusively with outside money, even though from many analytical purposes that is indeed the type of money on which it is appropriate to focus."

Even as some free-banking advocates recognize and warn against the dangers of confusing money with credit, their analyses still reflect that confusion. Thus, Sechrest (1993: 21) argues that it is erroneous "to posit that money and credit are identical. This is very common, but nonetheless false." He quotes Friedman's (1969: 263) observation that "The confusion of money and credit has been a primary source of difficulty in monetary policy. And recent experience indicates this is still so" (Sechrest 1993: 22). Yet, Sechrest employs Selgin's (1988: 31) definition of money as "units of *inside money* (currency plus demand deposits) held by the public during any given time period" (1993: 21; italics added), and sketches a "money supply" curve that is a "positively sloped market supply schedule [and] reveals the *quantities of money* banks will offer for goods and services at various rates of exchange" (23; italics added). He also "makes interest rate signals redundant for free banks" (18), which cannot be meaningful. Banks extend credit in return for interest payments, rather than to be repaid in goods and services.

Thus, free-banking advocacy can be seen to be redundant when it is recognized that note-issuing private banks were not creators of money but were credit intermediaries, the same function banks continue to perform under central-banking. Their claims are also in contrast with Vera Smith's (1936: 107; italics added) observation that J. E. Horn, who gave "the best exposition of the free-banking case" in the nineteenth century, as well as "many of the less prominent writers on free banking, *denied* that bank-notes *were money*."

Expectations from a "mature" free-banking system

In Selgin's (1988) theorizing about a "mature" free-banking system, (a) there would be no circulating commodity or "outside" money; all purchases would be made with banknotes or checks, (b) inter-bank clearings would be conducted in commodity or "outside" money, (c) there would be no state regulation of banks beyond regulations that apply to any other private firms, and (d) private clear-inghouses would regulate the business of banking. As several other free-banking advocates, including Dowd (1992: 2), Schuler (1992: 8), and Sechrest (1993: 3) have acknowledged, Selgin's first condition has never existed.[17] He appears to rely on Knut Wicksell's imaginary pure credit system in which money, properly so called, does not exist, and any amount of "money" demanded is readily sup-plied by banks unconstrained by savings: "No matter what amount of money may be demanded from the banks, that is the amount which they are in a position to lend (so long as the security of the borrower is adequate)" (1898: 110). Further-more, Selgin's theory does not explain how a clearinghouse acquires the "outside" money to settle inter-bank claims.

In periods of free banking, banks received specie deposits (savings) from their customers or acquired specie with their own savings (equity capital). In lieu of lending such gold or silver money, banks issued their own notes that were pledged redeemable in specie. Banks kept a sufficient amount of specie on reserve or on deposit with clearinghouses. Otherwise, a bank had to borrow from the clearing-house other banks' specie deposits to redeem its notes. Until governments took over the minting of specie, private producers, not banks, supplied them. Modern central banks have replaced previous specie money with fiat paper money, the ultimate medium in which modern private banks (ultimately) receive their custom-ers' deposits. Commercial banks now may keep reserves against deposits with a central bank to settle inter-bank claims arising from their customers' issued checks. Otherwise, banks borrow the fiat money either from the central bank or from other banks – the Federal Funds market in the US.

Free-banking advocates recognize the need for a clearinghouse's regulation of member banks, but they typically see no need for a government's regulation of banks beyond the level of other firms in the marketplace. Their claim is that a bank-ing firm is like any other business trading in goods and services. Clearinghouses would "conduct independent audits of member banks to assure each member that the others are worthy clearing partners . . . set common reserve ratios, interest rates, exchange rates, and fee schedules for their members" (Selgin 1988: 28). Clearing-houses also would undertake "establishing and policing safety and soundness stan-dards for member banks" (181, n. 39; see also White 1988a: 467; Dowd 1989: 194).

But the free-banking argument, that note-issuing banks be treated like other business firms, fails to appreciate fully the special nature of such banking. Other than issuers of traveler's checks, banks are the only firms capable of issuing their own liabilities to be employed as means of payment. Because of the forgone inter-est incomes or profits for holding reserves and equity capital, there is consider-able temptation for banks to extend loans (issue banknotes) beyond the margin of safety to meet depositors' redemption claims (see also Bagehot 1873: 14–6, 30). It is almost the same temptation bank-account holders face in attempting to make purchases with checks without sufficient funds (savings) on deposit. But it is much easier for banks to escape early detection of such fraud than the rest of the public. And the longer a bank's notes circulate before redemption, the more profitable is the note-issuing business.

To secure the public's claims to their deposits as well as the transfer of money promised in banknotes, governments have specified settlement mechanisms that may appear more intrusive for banking firms than for most other enterprises. The requirement of bond collateral for note-issuing banks in the US during the nineteenth century was one of such mechanisms. Under US free banking,

> Designated government bonds had to be deposited with a state authority as security for all circulating notes issued by a bank. The bank, so long as it remained solvent, was entitled to the interest on the bonds. But should it fail to honor its notes, the state would sell the securities and reimburse note holders out of the proceeds.
>
> (Rockoff 1974: 141)[18]

The US experience of some bank customers losing their deposits or being unable to redeem banknotes fully into money attest to the possibility of fraud in note-issuing banking (see, e.g., Friedman 1960: 6; Rockoff 1974; West 1974: 17–18; Rolnick and Weber 1983).

While concluding that most of the negative views about the free-banking era are exaggerations, Rolnick and Weber (1983) yet find that "about half of the free banks in the states [they] investigated closed, but less than a third of the banks that closed did not redeem their notes at par" (1084); about 8 percent of banks (34 out of 445) in New York state and 56 percent (9 out of 16 banks) in Minnesota. Further examination of the Rolnick-Weber data led James Kahn (1985: 885) to conclude that "free banking legislation often resulted in very high failure rates in those states relative to failure rates in non-free-bank states." Moreover, "The high failure rates, combined with the frequent inability of failed banks to pay note holders the par value of their notes . . . meant that the holding of free bank notes was a moderately costly (and risky) activity."

The failure of the Ayr Bank of Scotland, bringing down "eight small private bankers in Edinburgh, thinning the industry's ranks from twenty-nine in 1772 to twenty in 1773" (White 1984a: 30), is another illustration of the problem. Smith (*WN*, 1: 333–8) provides an extensive discussion of the imprudence of the Ayr Bank's lending in contrast with the diligence of lenders that were not note issuers in Scotland. Smith (*WN*, 1: 335) observes, "In the long-run, therefore, the operations of this bank increased the real distress of the country which it meant to relieve; and effectually relieved from a very great distress those rivals whom it meant to supplant." Similarly, Ricardo (*Works*, 1: 356) argues against the unrestricted power of banks to issue notes:

> Experience . . . shews, that neither a State nor a Bank ever had had the unrestricted power of issuing paper money, without abusing that power: in all States, therefore, the issue of paper money ought to be under some check and controul [sic]; and none seems so proper for that purpose, as that of subjecting the issuers of paper money to the obligation of paying their notes, either in gold coin or bullion.

It was also the opportunity for fraud in note issuing that led Smith to support prohibiting small-denomination paper money:

> Where the issuing of bank notes for such very small sums [as sixpence] is allowed and commonly practiced, many mean people are both enabled and encouraged to become bankers. A person whose promissory note for five pounds, or even twenty shillings, would be rejected by every body, will get it to be received without scruple when it is issued for so small a sum as sixpence. But the frequent bankruptcies to which such beggarly bankers must be liable, may occasion a very considerable inconveniency, and sometimes even a great calamity, to many poor people who had received their notes in payment.
>
> (*WN*, 1: 343)

Smith freely admits the violation of "natural liberty" entailed in the prohibition of small-denomination notes. However, he explains his stance with the analogy of erecting party walls to prevent the spreading of fire between buildings. It is to prevent endangering the "security of the whole society" by allowing complete freedom of enterprise in banking. Thus, only in the absence of small-denomination notes and banks being "subjected to the obligation of an *immediate* and *unconditional payment* of [their] notes as soon as presented" for money (gold and silver), "may their trade, with *safety to the public*, be rendered in all other respects perfectly free" (*WN*, 1: 350; italics added).

Edwin West (1997) misses Smith's reasoning for opposing the issuing of small-denomination banknotes. He thus incorrectly accuses Smith of an uncharacteristic and undue paternalism in not trusting poor people to choose their bankers just as they do their doctors for medical services.[19] In fact, Smith argues the advantage to the public of free competition in the issuing of banknotes:

> This free competition . . . obliges all bankers to be more liberal in their dealings with their customers, lest their rivals should carry them away. In general, if any branch of trade, or any division of labour, be advantageous to the public, the freer and more general the competition, it will always be the more so.
>
> (*WN*, 1: 350)

Vera Smith (1936: 9n) also observes, "Under complete freedom good banking depends not only on the ability of the bankers, but also on the public's having sufficient knowledge and experience to detect the good from the bad, the genuine from the fraudulent." Similarly, Friedman (1960: 6) argues:

> In fraud as in other activities, opportunities for profit are not likely to go unexploited. A fiduciary currency ostensibly convertible into the monetary commodity is therefore likely to be overissued from time to time and convertibility is likely to become impossible. Historically, this is what happened under so-called "free banking" in the United States and under similar circumstances in other countries.

Even in the modern age of "instant communication and rapid means of transport. . . . The possibility – and reality – of fraud by financial institutions remains" (Friedman and Schwartz 1986: 51). Selgin (1988: 148) admits the possibility of fraud in note issuing by banks, but doubts "it will happen more regularly than in a system of deposit banks." Schuler (1992: 23) also admits the existence of fraud, arguing, "It occasionally caused individual banks, usually small ones, to fail." But he insists that it did not undermine the "stability of any free banking system" (ibid.).

Moreover, in the absence of possible fraud, the nature of fractional-reserve banking is such that banks never have enough cash reserves to redeem all their liabilities, should all savers demand deposit redemption. Thus, there is always room for bank runs and contagion in the banking industry, requiring ways to miti- gate their occurrence. Bagehot (1873: 27) cites Ricardo's discussion of this fact as a basis for his concern over the vulnerability of fractional-reserve banking; Fried- man and Schwartz (1986: 53–4) cite Bagehot's argument as one of their reasons for not leaving government completely out of the business of money's production. I have yet to encounter free-banking advocates acknowledging Bagehot's (1873: 10) view that "Money will not manage itself."[20]

A free-banking system is also incapable of dealing with bank runs and their contagion under the so-called "option clause." The "option clause" allowed a bank with insufficient money to redeem its notes to suspend redemption for up to six months while paying the existing market rate of interest to note holders. Its imple- mentation by some Scottish banks led to their notes being received (trading) at a discount, sometimes at four percent between London and Dumfries (Smith *WN*, 1: 346). Parliament subsequently abolished the issuing of such notes, which Smith supported. Smith (ibid.) describes as an "abuse" of the public the actions of some bank directors who threatened to invoke the "option clause" when note holders demanded redemption of considerable amounts of money (specie) between 1762 to 1764. Smith also points to the high uncertainty the clause's presence created for the public in receiving such notes.

Selgin (1988) admits the impossibility of the "option clause" to save a bank- ing system during a run: "Arrangements satisfactory for handling increases in currency [banknotes] demand may be worthless when it comes to handling increases in the demand for high-powered money" (133). He acknowledges, "A bank threatened with a redemption run cannot satisfy its panic-stricken clients by offering them its own notes" (159). Selgin and White (1994: 1725) also admit this problem with fractional-reserve banking. However, Selgin (1988: 134) minimizes the inadequacy of free banking to handle redemption runs, arguing that "arrangements for the emergency supply of high-powered money, while perhaps necessary to combat redemption runs, can also bring about infla- tion, and are therefore not desirable if all that is needed is some way to provide depositors with media for making hand-to-hand payments." But the demand for high-powered money is a demand for an asset to hold; the demand for banknotes is for an instrument of credit to spend. The increased demand to hoard money reduces spending on goods and services, and therefore depresses the level of prices.[21] Thus, the increased supply of high-powered money during bank runs does not cause inflation but rather stops the price deflation (see also J. S. Mill *Works*, 3: 516).

Dowd (1993a) attributes an "automatic stabilizing mechanism" to the implementation of the "option clause" but admits that its exact form is "difficult to predict beforehand" (32). He also believes the inconvenience the implementation of the clause would impose upon the community "would itself make the banking system considerably more stable by eliminating the possibility of a bank run starting because of the public's self-fulfilling expectations of a run" (33). This hardly recommends the scheme. Besides, Dowd's view of the "option clause" being a deterrent to a bank run is contrary to human nature. His assertion would be true if, in a conflict between self-interest (self-preservation) and communal interest, individuals typically did not choose self-interest. People may well be aware that a bank run would lead to the bank's failure. But, in the absence of deposit insurance, the first hint of a likely failure of a bank to redeem its liabilities would start most depositors running to redeem their savings before others do. Similarly, everyone knows that an orderly exit from a movie theater in the case of a fire outbreak would save more lives, but everyone rushes to the exit, nevertheless, to save themselves. As Smith (*WN*, 1: 346) also observes, the "optional clause" did not stop some depositors from demanding "gold and silver in exchange for a considerable number of [bank] notes," which then provoked the threat to invoke it.

Finally, the fact that clearinghouses set rules for member banks shows the need for not granting banks complete freedom of business conduct. However, a state regulation of banking firms is likely to be more effective than a clearinghouse's attempts to enforce banking rules. One has the authority of the state, the other, merely voluntary cooperation or the threat of exclusion from the "club." Thus Schuler (1992: 18) reports the futility of some clearinghouses' attempts to enforce common interest rates among their members, ill-advised though such an attempt was. Dowd (1994: 293–6) also recognizes the relative weakness of clearinghouses to enforce rules, but favors them over a central bank because their regulations would be at the pleasure of (club) members and be minimal. The rules of operation that central banks specify for commercial banks and other depository institutions are the replacement for those of the clearinghouses. Besides, as Charles Goodhart (1988: 8) has observed, the conflicts of interest that tended to impede the effective operations of competing clearinghouses are absent in a central banks' regulation of commercial banks. Specific criticisms of central bank regulations must therefore be seen as a different issue from whether banks deserve being regulated at all.

Some unfounded benefits claimed for free banking

The main advantages free-banking advocates claim for that system turn out to be unfounded. They include: (1) free banking better promotes "monetary system equilibrium"; (2) free banking better preserves a currency's value; and (3) free banking promotes a more efficient economic growth.[22] Selgin (1988) finds "monetary equilibrium" to exist "when there is neither an excess demand for money nor an excess supply of it at the existing level of prices" (54) or when "the nominal supply of inside money [adjusts] only in response to [changes] in spending associated with some real-balance effect" (102). But the demand for banknotes is a demand for an instrument of credit. Unless banks can draw upon their own equity capital or their customers' deposits, they cannot meet an increased demand for their notes, a point that Selgin (1988: 33) recognizes: "A free bank adds to its gross income by enlarging its holdings of interest-earning assets. But it can only do this by either attracting more depositors . . . or by losing some of its reserves" (see also White 1989: 4). As credit intermediaries, therefore, banks would have to increase their interest on deposits to attract more funds (savings) to lend at a higher rate of interest when loan demands increase. Thus, Selgin's "monetary equilibrium" should be analyzed in terms of interest rate adjustments rather than price level changes. And "monetary equilibrium" would exist whether interest rates rise or fall. Correctly understood then, free banking has no advantage over a central-banking system where commercial banks extend loans by crediting borrowers' accounts instead of printing banknotes.

Sechrest (1993: 40) also illustrates the failure of many free-banking advocates clearly to distinguish money from instruments of credit in their arguing the determination of monetary equilibrium. He represents equilibrium determination with two diagrams that show the supply and demand for "money" determining the purchasing power of money under both a central-banking system and a free-banking system. Furthermore, the money supply, defined to include the public's deposits with banks, should be a positive function of interest rates rather than being a vertical supply curve. Given $M1 = [(cu + 1)/(cu + r_d + r_e)].H(1 - \alpha)$, where H = High-powered money, α = fraction of high-powered money held against time deposits (R_{dt}/H), cu = currency-deposit ratio, r_d = required reserve-deposit ratio, and r_e = economic or excess reserve-deposit ratio, an increase in interest rates (owing to an increased demand for credit) would cause both cu and r_e to contract: the public economizing on cash holding and banks minimizing their reserves in order to expand loans.

Adopting Selgin's definition of "monetary equilibrium," Horwitz (1992) also argues some inconsistent claims, including (a) "If monetary equilibrium is maintained, the monetary authority would not be the cause of any change in relative prices or the price level," (b) "Under free banking, M is *endogenous* to changes in V (the inverse of money demand divided by income) if both M and V refer to bank-issued money and not base money," and (c) "An expanding economy (i.e., a rising Y), under free banking, will of necessity cause P to fall as the banking system holds MV constant" (134; italics original).[23] But it is impossible for the operations of banks to keep "money" multiplied by its velocity constant where the public is free to vary their savings rate (deposits) as well as their demand for (base) money, the unit of account.

Moreover, "monetary equilibrium" in Selgin's theory of free banking is not the same thing as the maintenance of the value (purchasing power) of money or zero inflation. Rather, Selgin objects to the goal of price-level stabilization on several grounds, including (a) that it interferes with a rise in the value of money, owing to increased productivity or cost reductions, (b) that it is difficult to construct an accurate or acceptable index of the price level, and (c) that there are lags between changes in the quantity of money, however defined, and changes in the level of prices. But variations in the supply of banknotes affect the value of money or the level of prices only indirectly, to the extent that they affect the demand for money to hold or money's velocity. In a central-banking system, the use of checks instead of cash (money) in payments affects money's velocity and thus, indirectly, the level of prices. Variations in the quantity of central-bank money, relative to its demand, directly determine variations in the level of prices (see Chapter 2 above).

Selgin's first objection to price-level stabilization apparently follows Hayek's (1933) long-standing preference for a secularly rising value of money, but which he reversed in 1976: "The convenience of [money's] use is decidedly in favour of a currency which can be expected to *retain* an approximately *stable value*" (20; italics added). Hayek's (1978) call for the denationalization of money also was aimed at promoting the stability of money's value, an argument he (1984a: 34) repeats: "the best we can hope for is a money of which the average purchasing power would remain constant"; and "I have . . . become convinced that a money of stable value is really the best we can hope for. . . . A stable measure of value would eliminate much of the uncertainty that everyone holding a contract stipulating future payments is now compelled to bear" (1984b: 326). The preference for a stable purchasing power of money in order to preserve the equity or sanctity of contracts goes well back to John Locke's 1692 objections to money's debasement by the sovereign (see Eltis 1995: 13–15).

Experience abundantly illustrates the point that variations in central bank money relative to its demand determine the value of money (inverse of the level of prices). The US Federal Reserve expanded the currency by about twenty-five percent (from $4 billion to $5 billion; Fisher 1935: 5–6) between 1930 and 1933 and yet the price level declined by an average annual rate of six percent during that period because of the about $16 billion contraction in both demand and time deposits, reflecting an excess demand for money (cash) (see Chapter 5 for details.) Similarly, Japan in the late 1990s and early 2000s experienced price deflation in spite of its central bank's high average rate of currency creation.[24] On the other hand, the US experienced price inflation during the mid-nineteenth century, a period of free banking, following the California gold discoveries. As Robert Whaples (2008: 3) reports, "Soaring gold output from the California and Australia gold rushes is linked with a thirty percent increase in wholesale prices between 1850 and 1855. Likewise, right at the end of the nineteenth century a surge in gold production reversed a decades-long deflationary trend." Friedman (1960: 13) also notes that from "1896 to 1913 wholesale prices in the United States rose by 50 per cent," following the increased supply of gold from the application of "the cyanide process to the extraction of gold from the low-grade ores of South Africa" and gold discoveries in Alaska and elsewhere.

The claim that free-banking promotes a more efficient economic growth is also unfounded. The claimants sometimes point to Smith's praising fractional-reserve banking in the *Wealth of Nations* in its defense (e.g., White 1984a: 24). Selgin (1988: 149–50) does not invoke Smith's view, but merely asserts the claim.

However, Smith's point was not about free banking *per se* – the freedom of banks to print their own notes – but rather the ability of banks to lend their depositors' savings to producers while reserving enough money (specie) to meet redemption demands: "It is not by augmenting the capital [savings] of the country, but by rendering a greater part of that capital active and productive than would otherwise be so, that the judicious operations of banking can increase the industry of the country" (*WN*, 1: 340). This is the process by which Smith (*WN*, 1: 341) compares the judicious operation of banking to the creation of a "wagon-way through the air." Commercial banks continue to perform the same credit intermediation function under a central-banking system by crediting borrowers' accounts with loan amounts instead of issuing banknotes.

Friedman's implicit contributions to the free-banking advocacy

The claims in defense of free banking are mostly responses to Friedman's (1960: 6–8) arguments outlining the appropriateness of a government's monopoly in the production of money and its regulation of banking, while also including banks among "issuers of money" (8). Klein's (1974) analysis of the feasibility of competitive banknotes or currencies, while recognizing the need for a unit of account, is also mainly in response to Friedman's (1960) doubts about the sustainability of the price level when fiduciary paper monies are permitted (see also Friedman and Schwartz 1986: 45). And the first among measures Friedman (1960) considers to promote financial stability in the US is "permitting banks to issue currency as well as deposits subject to the same fractional reserve requirements and to restrict what is presently high-powered money to use as bank reserves" (69). Thus, when some free-banking advocates wonder about the consistency of an adherent to free-market principles, who yet accepts a central bank's monopoly over money's production, it is typically to Friedman's argument they refer. Now if "money" includes the public's savings with banking firms, it appears legitimate for free-banking advocates to question the right of the state to infringe upon the forms in which individuals would hold their wealth (private property). Friedman's championing the medium-of-exchange definition and broad measure of money (M2), following Keynes's influence, therefore has provided an impetus to free-banking advocates to argue against a perceived wrong – a government's violation of individual liberty or private property rights.

In expressing his skeptical view of Hayek's (1984a) free-banking advocacy, Friedman (1984a) appears to distinguish money from its substitutes issued by banks: "I am all in favour of the changes in legislation [Hayek] proposes which would give private banks the greatest latitude in the way of offering *substitutes for money*" (43; italics added). But Friedman loses the distinction between money and its substitutes in the rest of his argument:

> There is every reason in the abstract to approve Professor Hayek's proposals for removing any legal obstacles to the development of private *competitive*

money. There is little basis in experience for expecting any widely used *private moneys* to emerge in major countries unless governmental monetary management becomes far worse than it has been in the post-World War II period.

(45–6; italics added)

None of the competitive banknotes that Hayek was advocating is an economy's unit of account, and properly to be considered money. Indeed, Hayek (1978: 107) concedes, "If only one kind of money is permitted, it is probably true that the monopoly of its use must be under the control of government."

A second impetus Friedman's work has provided the modern free-banking advocacy is his severe and frequent criticisms of the Federal Reserve's operations. Friedman (1960, 1968a, 1970b) and Friedman and Schwartz (1963) do not separate central-bank money from bank deposits in their claim that the Fed, out of its ineptitude – pursuing "a policy of drift and inaction" (1963: 415) – was responsible for the thirty-three-percent reduction of the US "money stock" between 1929 and 1933. But this was a period when the Fed had expanded the quantity of money (its liabilities) by more than twenty percent. It makes quite a difference to interpret the episode as the Fed not having expanded the quantity of money enough to meet its increased demand and to have prevented the price level from falling, than to claim that they were responsible for the "money stock" (M2) to have declined by one-third. The same result would have occurred had commercial banks issued banknotes redeemable in (base) money.

Thus, Friedman's (1960: 31; italics added) describing the 1929–33 episode as "the failure of the Federal Reserve to expand the amount of high-powered money *sufficiently* to prevent widespread bank failures arising out of initial attempts by the public to convert deposits into currency" appears more accurate. Besides, the US did not go off the gold standard until March 1933; each dollar had to be backed at least forty percent by gold until then, and the Federal Reserve System had been losing its gold reserves to foreign countries, mainly France. However, Friedman downplayed the role of the gold-exchange standard in frustrating the Fed's base money expansion efforts (see Chapter 5 above). Friedman's subsequent criticisms of the Fed's inability to control the growth of adjusted M2[25] in order to achieve "monetary stability" as well as to prevent deflation and inflation appear to have encouraged free-banking advocates', including Hayek's (1978), search for an alternative to central banking.

Friedman's persistent criticisms of the Federal Reserve system for its alleged failure to control the "money stock" are inconsistent with his own recognition that the Fed cannot control an important element of the money supply multiplier, namely, the currency-deposit ratio: "In the main . . . the Reserve System must regard the currency-deposit ratio as determined by forces *outside its control*" (1960: 31; italics added). Friedman also recognizes that there is "no fixed mechanical relation between reserve requirements and the actual reserve-deposit ratio" (ibid.; see also 67–8, 88–9). A central bank can change the currency (H) and the required reserve-deposit ratio (r_d) in the "money supply" formula,

$M1 = [(cu + 1)/(cu + r_d + r_e)]H(1 - \alpha)$, but the banks and non-bank public determine the excess reserve-deposit ratio (r_e) and currency-deposit ratio (cu). A central bank has even less influence over M2, which includes the savings (time)-deposits (TD) and its accompanying reserve ratio: $M2 = [(cu + 1 + t)/(cu + r_d + r_t t + r_e)]H$, where t = ratio of time deposits to demand deposits (TD/D) and r_t = ratio of reserves against time deposits (see Chapter 5). Yet, Sechrest (1993: 1–2), for example, cites Friedman's (1985) criticisms of the Fed to argue: "In short, free banking means the total deregulation of the banking industry. It is the thorough application of the principles of laissez-faire to the one realm of economic activity where most 'free market' economists have assumed such principles cannot be applied: money and banking" (3).

Friedman's (1984b) advocacy of freezing the monetary base (H) as his ultimate solution to the Fed's inability to regulate the "money stock" also has encouraged some free-banking advocates in their quest to abolish central banks. Selgin (1988: 167) and White (1988a: 464, 1989: 14) have endorsed Friedman's proposal. Indeed, Friedman's (1984b: 53) proposal that "the money-creating powers of the Federal Reserve" be abolished as "the best real cure" to monetary instability in the US well fits the free-banking advocacy. White (1984b: 132) argues, "We need not choose between rival plans for bureaucratic central bank regulation of money and credit; we may choose instead to abolish the central bank and let the competitive market for currency regulate itself" (see also White 1989: 3, 2012: 25). Glasner (1989) argues that "market forces alone, without any special role for the state, would suffice to provide the public with a stable medium of exchange," and "modern monetary theory is finally recognizing the possibility that the determination of the *supply of money* could be safely left to competitive forces" (xi, xii; italics added). Dowd (1989: 194; italics added) declares, "Free banking is simply the application of free trade to the business of *issuing money*, and it is desirable for much the same reasons that free trade in anything else is usually desirable, and for other good reasons besides."

Hayek, in effect, argues against that scheme: "A stable price level and a high and stable level of employment do not require or permit the total quantity of money to be kept constant or to change at a constant rate" (1978: 77). But his argument leaves unclear what "the total quantity of money" means. Had Friedman employed the classical (Hume-Smith) definition of money as the unit of account rather than Keynes's broad definition of money and argued the equivalence of modern checks to previous private banknotes as substitute means of payment, he might have persuaded Hayek of the nullity of his complaint: "What is so dangerous and ought to be done away with is not government's right to issue money but the exclusive right to do so and their power to force people to use it and to accept it at a particular price" (Hayek 1976: 11). The public is free to hold or use money (H) or not. Their demanding to hold money, relative to the quantity supplied by a central bank, determines the value of money (level of prices) in an economy. Traveler's checks, credit and debit cards, and other forms of electronic means of payment are all provided by private firms. But Pascal Salin (1984: 3; italics added) summarizes the mistaken views of central-bank-eliminating advocates, arguing,

"It seems . . . that there is no theoretical justification for opposing competition in the production of *money*. We therefore accept – as a general rule – the competitive production of money."

Had Friedman adopted the classical unit-of-account definition of money (H), over which production a central bank has complete control, he also could have avoided his 1984 base money-freezing proposal. He could have drawn upon Hume's (1752: 39–40) advice to the "magistrate" (meaning the sovereign in old English; see *Oxford English Dictionary* 1989: 189) to keep the quantity of money (specie), if possible, increasing "because, by that means, he keeps alive a spirit of industry in the nation, and encreases the stock of labour, in which consists all real power and riches." Instead, Friedman's rationale for freezing the base money is political expediency: "Zero has a special appeal on political grounds that is not shared by any other number. . . . It is hard, as it were, to go to the political barricades to defend 3 rather than 4, or 4 rather than 5. But zero is . . . qualitatively different" (1984b: 50). Friedman here applies his long-held constant money-growth rule to the monetary base instead of to the price level – zero inflation targeting – which is consistent with Hume's "good policy" recommendation.

Summary and conclusions

Adherents to free-market philosophy have long sought a framework for the conduct of monetary policy which would be conducive to individual liberty and economic prosperity. It was in that pursuit that Henry Simons (1948) argued in favor of rules over discretion in the conduct of monetary policy, a proposition Friedman (1960: 84–100, 1968b) subsequently advanced. They also argued for a 100 percent reserve backing of demand deposits as a means of dealing with the inherent instability of fractional-reserve banking. Friedman's repeated criticisms of the Fed's operations as having failed appropriately to manage the quantity of money, defined as M1 or M2, following Keynes's (1936) broad definition of money, influenced Hayek's (1978) alternative proposal for the issuing of currencies by commercial banks rather than adopting Friedman's favored constant money-growth rule.

Having adopted Keynes's broad definition of money rather than the classical unit-of-account definition, following Friedman, modern free-banking advocates tend to blur the private domain in the provision of alternative means of payment and that of a government's production or regulation of "money." Non-fiat banknotes were not "money," and modern commercial banks continue to perform the same credit intermediation function of the note-issuing banks of the past. A modern central-banking system also does not deny commercial banks their ability to provide other means of payments as supplements to money as banknotes did in the past. Thus, to frame free-banking advocacy as a challenge to an alleged view that "governments are more fit to provide media of exchange than private firms," (Selgin 1988: 3) overlooks the similarity between earlier banknotes and modern checks. Bagehot (1873), whose views on central banking are influential with free-banking advocates, rather worried about the capability of those banks, particularly the Bank of England, to produce enough money (specie or 100 percent bullion-backed notes) to meet its demand in a panic. But modern central banks are capable of printing as much of their own notes as demanded, if they are not on a gold or any other commodity standard.

A return to commercial banks' issuing of notes would not thereby deal with the problems of business fluctuations, inflation, or deflation. Commercial crises occurred in periods without central banks; they are not the natural outcome of a monopoly over fiat money creation. Bouts of optimism or pessimism may affect the flow of credit in an economy and cause business fluctuations. And the reckless inflation of credit that Marshall (1920: 591), for example, notes as "the chief cause of all economic malaise" may be initiated by a central bank or by commercial banks, a point Schuler (1992: 23) also makes well. The form of issuing credit, whether through banknotes or checkable deposits, is not the crucial determining factor.

Inflation also does not occur merely because of a central bank's monopoly over money creation. Rather, it results from the creation of money in excess of the growth of its demand. Deflation results from the opposite rate of money's creation, as the 1930–33 experience in the US and recent Japanese deflation show. Dowd's (1989: 194) claim that, unless a country adopts free banking, "there is no alternative route to monetary stability, and . . . we shall face more banking crises and eventual resurgence of inflation," thus attributes too much to the capability of a free-banking system. Central banks just need to heed Hume's (1752) insights in "Of Money" and "Of Interest" and focus on preserving the purchasing power of money. They should leave interest rates alone to their determination by the supply and demand for savings. Free-banking advocates thus argue a redundancy from having followed Friedman's broad definition of money that he, in turn, adopted from Keynes (1936: 167, n. 1).

Notes

1 This chapter draws upon my unpublished paper, "Money, Credit, and Banking: The Redundancy of Free-Banking Advocacy," discussed at the History of Economics Society Annual Meetings, Montreal, Quebec, Canada, June 20–22, 2014. The chapter benefits from some critical comments from journal referees. I very much appreciate the supportive comments from the paper's discussant at the conference, Don Mathews, as well as from Greg Christainsen and Steve Shmanske, without implicating them in any remaining errors in my argument. Those are mine. My attempts to get reactions from some of the leading free-banking advocates were met with silence. I gave up trying to publish the paper in a journal after having had conflicting reactions from referees. One for the *Journal of Money, Credit and Banking* felt my approach limited "the paper to being a history of economic thought paper rather than a general interest paper," while another for the *History of Political Economy* felt, "The paper's main topic is current or recent debates about the desirability of free banking. Its admittedly quite extensive deployment of historical material is ancillary to this purpose. Hence it belongs, if anywhere, in a journal devoted to modern monetary economics, or to surveys of contemporary economic issues, rather than in a journal devoted to the history of thought, particularly one like *HOPE* which already has many competing demands on its limited space."

2 Friedman and Schwartz (1986: 40) reaffirm their 1963 view that "the establishment of the Federal Reserve System, in practice did more harm than good." They conclude

that "leaving monetary and banking arrangements to the market would have produced a more satisfactory outcome than was actually achieved through government involvement" (59). This in spite of their continued belief that "the possibility that private issuers can . . . provide competing, efficient and safe fiduciary currencies with no role for governmental monetary authorities remains to be demonstrated" (58).

3 In his *The Constitution of Liberty*, Hayek (1960) wonders about the consistency of a government's monopoly over money's production with individual liberty in a free society but does not therein vigorously pursue free-banking advocacy. The worldwide price inflation of the 1970s appears to have been the catalyst to Hayek's promotion of free banking, having correctly attributed the inflation to the excessive money creation by central banks (see also Hayek 1984a, 1984b).

4 Note that free-banking advocates of the eighteenth and nineteenth centuries were seeking the freedom of all commercial banks to issue banknotes rather than the freedom to create money (specie), the unit of account.

5 A referee for the *History of Political Economy*, rejecting my manuscript, however misrepresents Bagehot as having "regarded free banking as the natural system that market forces would produce if left to themselves by government." Issuers of private banknotes were not creators of money (specie).

6 Hayek (1978: 51; italics original) explains, "Money is usually defined as *the* generally acceptable medium of exchange" and "This definition was established by Carl Menger" (51, n. 1). In Menger's 1892 *Economic Journal* article, his first name is spelled, "Karl."

7 Ron Paul (2009: 191n) cites Sechrest's work in his arguing the abolition of the US Federal Reserve System.

8 Roger Garrison (1990: 832) also argues, "Selgin does more than provide a fresh hearing for free banking. By framing monetary questions in the broadest context, he contributes importantly toward the integration of price theory and monetary theory." Reviews of White (1984a) by Zvi Eckstein (1985), Charles Goodhart (1987), and Boyd Hilton (1988) are not so glowing.

9 David Hume's (1752) "Of Money" and Smith's (1776) chapter on money and banking clearly distinguish money from its substitutes or "paper credit." Glasner (1989: ix; italics added) fails to recognize Smith's distinction between them and claims, the "ultimate figure in economics, Adam Smith, strongly supported free competition in the supply of *money*." Glasner should have argued that Smith supported competition in the issuing of money substitutes.

10 Smith here uses "credit" to mean creditworthiness.

11 Selgin and White (1987) thus mostly describe the evolution of fractional-reserve banking rather than the evolution of "free banking."

12 Somehow, Thornton's clear position on money being different from its substitutes appears to have been lost on some monetary analysts. Some referees have declared me wrong for pointing out the difference. See also Geoffrey Wood (1995) who claims, "Thornton . . . classified [money substitutes] with money, while Wicksell regarded them as influences on money's velocity" (113).

13 Ricardo (e.g., *Works*, 1: 352–72; 3: 90–9) closely follows Smith's treatment of paper money as a substitute for money (specie; see also J. S. Mill *Works*, 3: 354–5).

14 Thus Glasner (1989: 178, 204) misinterprets Smith as not having followed Hume's Quantity Theory of money. He fails to recognize the Quantity Theory as the supply and demand for money (specie or modern central bank money), rather than the supply and demand for banknotes (credit), determining the level of prices.

15 Walker (1878: 7) seeks to warn about the focus of money's medium-of-exchange function as its prime identifier. But he makes his argument rather unclearly: "There is to be observed . . . an unfortunate confusion of the functions of a common denominator and of a common measure of value. And I make bold to say that the failure of nearly all writers on this subject [money], to discriminate between the two offices, has caused no small part of the contradiction and confusion of the popular, and even of the scientific

discussion of the subject." It is hard to see the difference between "a common denominator" and "a common measure" of value.

16 Walker laments: "Certainly, the word Currency has proven a most disastrous substitute [for money or paper money], inducing infinite confusion and contradictions" (1878: 275–6).

17 Selgin (1988: 16) might shield his theorizing from this criticism with the observation that "history furnishes an inadequate basis for drawing theoretical conclusions about free banking."

18 In Canada, "bank-note issues were limited to the amount of the bank's paid-in capital, but for many years the ceiling was too high to have any effect" (Dowd 1992: 35). Also, "in 1908, Canada amended its banking law to allow note issue of up to 115 per cent of bank capital during the months of peak demand, and in 1913 loosened note-issue limits still further" (ibid: 36).

19 Selgin (2008: 35n) also fails to take into account Smith's reasoning for supporting the ban on small-denomination notes.

20 Unhelpfully, Bagehot (1873) uses "money," "cash," "loan-fund," "'borrowable' money," "floating money," "loans," "credit," and "capital" interchangeably in his discussion leading up to the declaration rather than the Hume-Smith specie definition of money.

21 Sechrest (1993: 41) makes almost the same analytical error with his claim that an increase in "k" in the Cambridge equation will not lead to a fall in the price level: "If the Cambridge cash balance k increases, then the money supply as well as the demand for money increases so that equilibrium money holdings increase (which is consistent with the rise in k), but neither the price level, nominal income, nor real income changes." But $P = H/ky$, and an increase in k must reduce P. Even when H (high-powered money) is replaced by $M = H + BC$ (since $M = C + D$, but $D = C + R$, where C = currency in circulation, R = bank reserves, and BC = bank credit), an increase in the demand for H cannot be met by note-issuing banks, and prices must fall.

22 Dowd (1989: 2) summarizes all these as dismantling the present "apparatus of state control [over money creation would] allow market forces to establish a sounder and more efficient monetary system."

23 Sechrest (1993: 29; italics added) repeats the impossible claim that "free banks [can] maintain *constant* the supply of inside money multiplied by its velocity of circulation." What can banks do when depositors demand withdrawal of their deposits?

24 The annual growth rates of Japan's monetary base between 1999 and 2008 were as follows: 44.5 percent, −19.9 percent, 19.4 percent, 11.8 percent, 12.0 percent, 3.8 percent, 0.9 percent, −18.7 percent, 1.3 percent, and 5.5 percent, amounting to a 6.1 percent annual average rate. But the annual inflation rates, measured by the consumer price index, were −0.3 percent, −0.7 percent, −0.8 percent, −0.9 percent, −0.2 percent, 0.0 percent, −0.3 percent, 0.2 percent, 0.1 percent, and 1.4 percent, an annual average rate of − 0.15 percent. Measured by the GDP deflator, there was price deflation each year between 1999 and 2008 at an annual average rate of −1.22 percent (see International Monetary Fund, *International Financial Statistics Yearbook 2009*).

25 Friedman's adjusted M2 includes "currency held by the public plus adjusted demand deposits plus time deposits in commercial banks but excludes time deposits in mutual savings banks, shares in savings and loans associations, and the like" (1960: 90–1).

7 Saving and capital

Roy Harrod's failure to recognize Keynes's misinterpretations in the classical theory of interest

Introduction[1]

The extent to which John Maynard Keynes's misinterpretation of the classical theory of interest has persisted in modern macroeconomics is remarkable. Much of that is due to Roy Harrod's failure to recognize Keynes's fundamental misunderstandings of the concepts of saving and "capital" employed in the classical theory of interest. Harrod's clarifying what Keynes had misunderstood might have made a significant difference to Keynes's attitude towards the classical theory. Keynes sought Harrod's opinion, as well as that of some of his other colleagues, on the validity of the classical theory, particularly as discussed in Marshall's *Principles of Economics*. Harrod (1951: 453) explains that he did not fault the classical theory as being "a nonsense theory" as Keynes had argued but rather "supplied him a diagram purporting to reconcile the classical theory with his theory, and he incorporated this in the [*General Theory*] – the only diagram in it." It turns out that Harrod's suggestion of how Keynes could derive equilibrium interest rates from the diagram conveys his own misrepresentation of classical interest rate analysis that requires a single savings-supply curve rather than a family of such curves.[2]

Keynes's failure to associate savings with the supply of loanable funds, coupled with Harrod's concessions that the classical theory is "invalid" or "incomplete," assured that his suggested diagram would rather help to crystallize Keynes's misinterpretation of the theory. The most Harrod's criticisms of Keynes appear to have achieved was for Keynes to bury the clearest clue to recognizing his misinterpretation of "capital" in the classical theory in an appendix to Chapter 14 of the *General Theory*, as Harrod explains in a 7 October 1935 letter to Dennis Robertson: "I share your feeling entirely about his attacks [on the classical theory of interest]. I have attacked him for them, but have only succeeded in getting the most offending chapter printed in smaller type as an appendix" (quoted in Besomi 2000: 370).

Of course, Harrod was not alone in missing Keynes's misinterpretation of "capital" in the classical theory of interest. Hicks ([1939] 1946: 153) alludes to the significance of the meaning of "capital" in the debate over the classical theory but he does not focus on Keynes's interpretation of the concept. Dennis Robertson (1937, 1940) was a most notable exception among Keynes's contemporaries in recognizing Keynes's confusion over "capital" in Marshall's restatement of the classical theory. But he chose to defend Marshall's restatement in the language of "loanable funds," which failed to impress Keynes (1937a: 210). Modern commentators on Keynes's dispute with the classical theory, including S. C. Tsiang (1956), Axel Leijonhufvud (1968, 1981), Don Patinkin (1965 [1956], 1976), Pascal Bridel (1987), David Laidler (1999), Jörg Bibow (2000), Michael Lawlor (1997, 2006), and Jérôme de Boyer (2010), all fail to pay attention to Keynes's misinterpretation of "capital."

Lawlor (1997) does a significant disservice to scholarship on Keynes's disputes with the classical theory of interest. He deletes altogether Keynes's appendix to Chapter 14 in his restatement of Keynes's, "The Classical Theory of the Rate of Interest," without explaining why Keynes felt the need to substitute "money" for "capital" and "prices of capital-goods" for "interest" in the Marshall restatement of the classical theory Keynes (1936: 186–7) cited for correction. Keynes's substitutions give the clue to his misunderstanding. But, failing to recognize the clue, Lawlor (2006: 162) declares to be valid, "Keynes's quip that 'Interest' really has no business to turn up at all in Marshall's *Principles of Economics* – it belongs to another branch of the subject" (this repeats Lawlor 1997: 360). Similarly, ignoring the problem with Keynes's misinterpretation of "capital," de Boyer (2010: 265, 279, 282) declares Keynes's criticisms of the classical theory of interest to have been "well founded."

This chapter explains Harrod's failure to recognize Keynes's fundamental misunderstanding of the classical theory of interest, besides his own incomplete representation of the theory to Keynes. The chapter also explains how Keynes could have resolved his difficulties with the classical theory with a savings or "capital" supply and demand diagram, had he interpreted "capital" correctly. The failure of Harrod's suggested diagram to clarify issues for Keynes also appears well to illustrate the point that formalism – use of mathematical equations and diagrams – without conceptual clarity hardly is conducive to settling analytical disputes in economics.[3] As Keynes (1936: 298) himself prophetically points out, "Too large a proportion of recent 'mathematical' economics are mere concoctions, as imprecise as the initial assumptions they rest on, which allow the author to lose sight of the complexities and interdependencies of the real world in a maze of pretentious and unhelpful symbols."

This chapter is not an attempt to re-open the so-called "Loanable Funds vs Liquidity-Preference" debate, as a referee for the *History of Political Economy*, recommending rejection of the manuscript upon which it is based, misunderstood me to have been attempting to explain. Indeed, S. C. Tsiang's (1956) reconciliation of Keynes's liquidity-preference theory and the loanable-fund theory claims "a victory of the loanable funds theory on practical issues" (552), but mostly repeats Robertson's drawing equivalency between the two theories. But, as Ahiakpor (1990, 2003b: 90–5) explains, that debate was an unfortunate distraction from understanding why Keynes failed to recognize a valid theory of interest in Marshall's *Principles*. The distraction took the form of Keynes's critics (a) conceding that some savings may be hoarded, contrary to the classical definition of saving which excludes cash hoarding (e.g., "No political economist of the present day can by saving mean mere hoarding"; Thomas Malthus, quoted in Mark Blaug 1996: 161), (b) their seeking unduly to find similarities between

Keynes's liquidity-preference theory and the loanable-funds theory of interest, and (c) their not focusing on Keynes's misinterpretation of "capital," as he reveals most clearly in the appendix to Chapter 14 of the *General Theory*. In fact, both Keynes's liquidity-preference theory and the Austrian time-preference theory of interest are subsumed under the classical theory of interest, correctly interpreted. Some of Keynes's critics also failed to note the error of his treating the demand for "finance" as "transaction demand for money"; we demand money to hold, credit to spend. Moreover, it is not money that is invested but savings, of which money may be "the instrument of their conveyance" (Smith *WN*, 1: 374).

The chapter continues with restating a summary of the classical "capital" supply and demand theory of interest as background for recognizing its misinterpretation by Keynes, followed by a clarification of Keynes's misreading the classical theory in Marshall's *Principles*, drawing partly on Ahiakpor (1990). Next, I explain the unhelpfulness of Harrod's concessions to Keynes on the validity of the classical theory and de Boyer's crystallizing Keynes's confusions in models.

Marshall's restatement of the classical theory of interest

The classical theory of interest is simply an application of the classical theory of value – the explanation of market prices by supply and demand – to capital or savings,[4] not capital goods. In restating the theory of interest, Marshall (1920: 60; italics added) follows "the language of the market-place [that] commonly regards a man's capital as that part of his wealth which he devotes to acquiring an income *in the form of money*," just as the classical economists, including Smith, Ricardo, and J. S. Mill, did. Marshall adds that "economists have no choice but to follow well-established customs as regards the use of the term capital in ordinary business, i.e. trade-capital" (1920, 647). That is, when a businessperson talks about looking for "capital" to start or expand an enterprise, they mean by "capital," loanable funds, not capital goods.[5] It is in the sense of "capital" as funds that Smith (*WN*, 1: 358) explains, "Capitals are increased by parsimony. . . . Whatever a person saves from his revenue [income] he adds to his capital, and either employs it himself in maintaining an additional number of productive hands, or enables some other person to do so, by lending it to him for an interest, that is, for a share of the profits."

Following Smith, Ricardo (*Works*, 2: 331) argues that "capital is not bought and sold, it is borrowed at interest, and a great interest is given when profits are high." Of course, capital goods may be bought or sold. Similarly, J. S. Mill (*Works*, 3: 655) affirms the funds meaning of "capital" when he explains, "Loanable capital is all of it in the form of money. Capital destined directly for production exists in many forms; but capital destined for lending exists normally in that form alone." And "What [a person] really lends is so much capital [savings]; the money is the mere instrument of transfer" (*Works*, 3: 508).

Marshall (1920: 61–2; italics added) also describes interest thus:

> The payment made by a borrower for the *use of a loan* for, say, a year is expressed as the ratio which that payment bears to the loan, and is called

interest. And this is also used more broadly to represent the money equivalent of the whole income which is derived from capital. It is commonly expressed as a certain percentage on the "capital" *sum of loan*. Whenever this is done the capital must not be regarded as a stock of things in general. It must be regarded as a stock of one particular thing, *money*, which is taken to represent them. Thus £100 may be lent at four per cent., that is for an interest of £4 yearly.[6]

Marshall's statement and some others cited below also show Lawlor's insufficient familiarity with Marshall's *Principles* when he (Lawlor 1997: 360, 2006: 162) agrees with Keynes that Marshall's restatement of the theory of interest rate was not in monetary terms.

Following the classical explanation of the meaning of "capital," it is easy to understand that savings supply the "capital" or loanable funds (besides new central bank money or credit) borrowed at interest in the capital or credit markets ($S = S_c$).[7] In the marketplace, savings are a positive function of the rate of interest offered savers, per unit of time, while all other factors that influence the amounts supplied by savers shift the savings function. As Marshall affirms, "if a person expects, not to use his wealth himself but to let it out on interest, the higher the rate of interest the higher the reward for saving" (1920: 195). Also,

> A rise in the rate of interest offered for capital, i.e. in the demand price for sav-ing, tends to increase the volume of saving. For in spite of the fact that a few people who have determined to secure an income of a certain fixed amount for themselves or their family will save less with a high rate of interest than with a low rate, it is a nearly universal rule that a rise in the rate increases the *desire* to save.
>
> (196; italics original)

However, failing to appreciate the above, Bibow (2000) applauds Keynes's denial that savings provide loanable funds. In Bibow's judgment, Keynes's criticism of the classical savings-supply and demand theory of interest, "more importantly, on a more practical level [spares us] from those popular, but misguided policy measures that stress, chronologically, saving before investing" (826). He appears unaware of the corrections to Keynes's view, including by Pigou (1936), Rob-ertson (1936), Viner (1936), and Knight (1937); Chapter 8 below elaborates my criticism of Bibow's endorsement of Keynes's argument.

Evidently, to save, one first must have income. That is why a correct statement of the savings-supply function must explain that, *given the level of income*, more savings would be forthcoming into the credit or capital market when interest rates rise, and vice versa – a movement along an upward-sloping savings-supply curve.[8] On the other hand, an increase in the level of income shifts the savings-supply curve to the right – savers offering more funds at the same rate of interest than before. The reverse is true when income decreases. Other factors that shift the savings-supply curve include a change in the rate of income taxes, a change in time preference or the degree of impatience to consume, a change in savers' expectation of inflation or deflation, a change in households' expectation of longevity, and a change in households' desire to hoard cash (Keynes's liquidity-preference, e.g. 1936: 174). Most of these factors may be represented by a savings equation, $S = Y(1 - t) - C - \Delta H_h$, where Y = nominal income, t = tax rate, C = consumption expenditure, and ΔH_h = change in households' desire for cash balances or hoarding.

Thus, rather than being a passive or negative act (Keynes 1930: 1, 172, 1936: 74, 210), saving constitutes an active demand for interest- and/or dividend-earning financial assets ($S = S_c = \Delta FA^d$), including bank deposits, mutual fund shares, bonds, and stocks.[9] Thus, the rate of interest is the inverse of the price of financial assets (P_{FA}), $i = \$X/P_{FA}$. Put differently, to save is to "invest" in "trade or on loan, so as to derive interest or profit from them" (Marshall 1920: 192), or to purchase financial assets, including "Government, or other familiar stock exchange securities" or "to commit [one's savings] to the charge of a bank" (Marshall 1923: 46). Alternatively, "an increased rate of saving . . . takes the form of an increased demand for securities" (Robertson 1936: 187).[10] Thus, the decision to save is one of *three* an individual considers regarding the use of disposable income, namely, consumption, investment in financial assets (saving), and acquiring cash balances (hoarding).[11]

The demand for "capital" or savings is to enable borrowers to purchase goods and services sooner than they could with their own incomes. Significant for understanding Keynes's confusion regarding the classical theory of interest requires keeping in mind that circulating capital includes the funds for paying wages before the inflow of revenues as well as cash-on-hand to meet the daily expenses of a business enterprise (see Smith *WN*, 1: 295–9; J. S. Mill *Works*, 2, Chapter 5, "Fundamental Propositions Respecting Capital," and Chapter 6, "On Circulating and Fixed Capital"; Marshall 1920: 63). That is, investment, which is the employment of borrowed "capital" or savings in the sphere of production is more than the purchase of producers' or capital goods, the meaning of investment Keynes employs: "we must mean by this [definition of investment] the current addition to the value of the *capital equipment* which has resulted from . . . productive activity" (1936: 62; italics added; see also Keynes 1930: 2, 207). Hawtrey (1950: 43), in the classical tradition, appropriately contrasts Keynes's definition of investment with its ordinary meaning as the "acquisition of income-yielding securities or property, not Keynes's sense of the accumulation of capital assets and unconsumed goods."

The savings- or investment-demand schedule is a negative function of the rate of interest: the higher the rate of interest the fewer funds are demanded, per unit of time. As Marshall (1920: 432) explains,

> The demand for a loan of capital is the aggregate of the demands of all individuals in all trades; and it obeys a law similar to that which holds for the sale of commodities; just as there is a certain amount of a commodity which can find purchasers at any given price. When the price rises the amount that can be sold diminishes, and so it is with regard to the use of capital.

Like the supply function, other factors besides the rate of interest influence the desired amount, the shifts factors. Thus, an increase in the expectation of profits by businesses – increased "marginal efficiency of capital" (Marshall 1920: 432–3) – shifts the savings-demand curve to the right, just as a decrease in business tax rates would. A decrease in the expectation of inflation decreases the demand for savings or "capital." And to obtain loans, a borrower supplies a loan note (an IOU). Thus, the demand for "capital" or savings constitutes the supply of financial assets in the loans market ($D_c = \Delta FA^s$).

The "capital"- or savings-supply function (S_c) interacting with the "capital"- or savings-demand function (D_c) in a credit or "capital" market thus determines an equilibrium interest rate. Furthermore, these two functions are independent of each another; a shift of one does not cause a shift of the other, but rather a movement along it.[12] Thus, beginning from an initial equilibrium, an increased demand for "capital" first creates an excess demand at the current rate of interest. The interest rate attains a new (higher) equilibrium level when the quantity of savings supplied increases – households having reduced their demand for cash holdings and/ or their rate of consumption in order to offer more savings – while the quantity of "capital" or savings demanded decreases until the excess demand is eliminated (see Figure 7.1a).

On the other hand, households' increased demand for cash (increased liquidity preference, $\Delta H_h > 0$) reduces the flow of savings at the current rate of interest – the

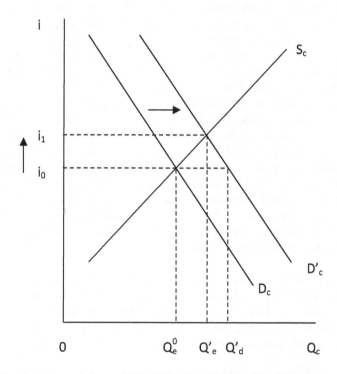

Figure 7.1a An increased demand for capital (D'_c) creates an excess demand at i_0 until interest rate rises to restore equilibrium at i_1 where $S_c = D'_c$.

saving- or "capital"-supply curve shifts to the left – causing the equilibrium rate of interest to rise and a movement along the "capital"-demand curve. Also, an increase in the community's time preference increases the level of consumption, C, and reduces the flow of savings, $S = Y(1 - t) - C - \Delta H_h = (\Delta FA^d < 0)$, causing the equilibrium interest rate to rise, all else equal. Thus, the classical theory of interest incorporates both Keynes's preferred liquidity-preference[13] and the Austrian time-preference theories of interest that tend to be cited as alternatives to the classical theory. Keynes (1936: 242) quotes Marshall's time-preference explanation in the *Principles*, but fails to appreciate its logic: "Everyone is aware that the accumulation of wealth, and the rate of interest so far sustained, by the preference which the great mass of humanity have for present over deferred gratifications, or, in other words, by their unwillingness to 'wait'." Remarkably, the promoters of both the time-preference and liquidity-preference alternative theories of interest were motivated by the same factor, namely, their confusion over the meaning of "capital" in the classical theory of interest. Eugen Böhm-Bawerk argued the former, and Keynes the latter; Ahiakpor (1997b or 2003b: Ch. 6) elaborates.

Indeed, the classical supply and demand for "capital" theory of interest may be stated in terms of the purchase and sale of financial assets. The increased demand for capital is effected through an increased supply of financial assets ($S'_{FA} = D'_c$), creating an excess supply at their current price (P^0_{FA}; see Figure 7.1b). The excess

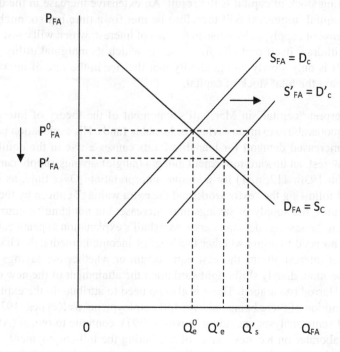

Figure 7.1b An increased supply of financial assets ($S'_{FA} = D'_c$) creates an excess supply at P^0_{FA} until the price of financial assets falls to restore equilibrium at P'_{FA} where $S'_{FA} = D_{FA}$.

supply is eliminated when the price of financial assets falls (P'_{FA} => interest rate rises), enticing the quantity demanded to increase – a movement along a down-ward-sloping financial-assets demand curve.

Marshall (1920: 443–4) employs the above theory of the rate of interest that Keynes (1936: 186–7; italics added) quotes from the *Principles* to illustrate his disagreement with the classical theory:

> Interest, being the price paid for the use of capital in any market, tends towards an equilibrium level such that the aggregate demand for capital in that market, at that rate of interest, is equal to the aggregate stock forthcoming there at that rate. If the market . . . is a small one – say a single town, or a single trade in a progressive country – an increased demand for capital in it will be promptly met by an increased supply drawn from surrounding districts or trades. But if we are considering the whole world, or even the whole of a large country, as one market for capital, we cannot regard the aggregate supply of it as altered quickly and to a considerable extent by a change in the rate of interest. For the general *fund of capital* is the product of *labour and waiting*; and the extra work, and the extra waiting, to which a rise in the rate of interest would act as an incentive, would not quickly amount to much, as compared with the work and waiting, of which the total existing stock of capital is the result. An extensive increase in the demand for capital in general will therefore be met for a time not so much by an increase of supply, as by a rise in the rate of interest; which will cause capital to withdraw itself partially from uses in which its marginal utility is low-est. It is only slowly and gradually that the rise in the rate of interest will increase the total stock of capital.

Now interpret "capital" in Marshall's statement of the theory of interest that Keynes quotes above to mean savings or loanable funds. His explanation becomes this: an increased demand for loanable funds causes a rise in the equilibrium rate of interest, an upward movement along a (single) savings-supply curve (see also Pigou 1936: 117, n. 1) for a similar interpretation. Over time, as income increases following the "extra work, and the extra waiting" enticed by the rise of interest rates, the supply of savings may increase, but not simultaneously with the shift of the savings-demand curve. Marshall's explanation appears complete. There is no need to argue whether the level of income immediately changes as the rate of interest attains the new equilibrium or whether the savings-supply curve also immediately shifts rightward upon the attainment of the new equilib-rium, as Harrod has argued. There is also no need to attribute to the explanation the assumption of there being "always full employment" as Keynes (1936: 191) does and some analysts, including Lawlor (1997), continue to repeat (Ahiakpor 1997a elaborates on Keynes's error of attributing the full-employment assump-tion). Furthermore, there is no need to invoke exogenous wage rates or Say's Law of markets, as de Boyer (2010) argues, in order to explain the attainment of a new equilibrium.

Dennis Robertson (1940: 12), who appears more clearly to have understood Marshall's explanation in the *Principles* than Harrod, affirms the above interpretation:

> The rate of interest [is] the market price of the hire of something which Marshall called "free or floating capital," which others have called "capital disposal" or "command over capital," which recent writers seem to have settled down to calling "loanable" or "investible funds." This price, like other market prices, can be conceived as emerging from the interaction of schedules of supply and demand, showing the amount of loanable funds which, at given hiring-prices, people are respectively willing to put on to, and to take off, the market during the slice of time selected for observation.

The above restatements of the classical theory of interest follow closely, for example, that of J. S. Mill's (*Works*, 3: 647) succinct explanation:

> The rate of interest will be such as to equalize the demand for loans with the supply of them. It will be such, that exactly as much as some people are desirous to borrow at that rate, others shall be willing to lend. If there is more offered than demanded, interest will fall; if more is demanded than offered, it will rise; and in both cases, to the point at which the equation of supply and demand is re-established.

Frank Taussig (1921: 2, 20–33) gives a similar explanation, "in simple form under the theory of value" (27), and illustrates it with single savings supply and demand curves (27, 29). Keynes (1936: 176) refers to Taussig's analysis but fails to be impressed by it: "Professor Taussig (*Principles*, vol. ii. p. 29) draws a supply curve for saving and a demand curve representing 'the diminishing productiveness of the several instalments of capital,' having previously stated (p. 20) that 'the rate of interest settles at a point where the marginal productivity of capital suffices to bring out the marginal instalment of saving'." In fact, Taussig devotes three chapters (38, 39, and 40) in Volume II of his *Principles*, to explaining interest rate determination by the supply and demand for savings. The explanation includes, "Interest, then, appears as the result of an act of exchange by which a quantity of money (or commodities) now in hand, is given for a greater quantity of money (or commodities) to be returned in the future" (1921: 2, 9): Taussig also relates the explanation in Chapter 39, p. 28, note 1, to his analysis of market price determination (the theory of value), employing the supply and demand diagram, in Chapter 13 of Volume I.

From the above explanations of the classical theory of interest, we can appreciate the error in claims such as, "there was no precise attempt in the classical literature to distinguish between savings and the supply of loans, on the one hand, and between investment and the demand for loans, on the other" (Patinkin 1965 [1956]: 367). We also can recognize Leijonhufvud's (1968: 214) error in asserting that "the pre-Keynesian guardians of the Neoclassical heritage," including Marshall, had left incomplete a resolution of the problem of "capital and interest – the major lacuna which must be filled before the capstone could be put on the grand structure of value theory on which all major theorists since Adam Smith had labored." It is also truly remarkable that Bibow's (2000) claiming the loanable-funds theory of interest is a fallacy could find acceptance for publication in the *History of Political Economy*; Chapter 8 below elaborates Bibow's errors of argument. I report in the conclusion below the equally remarkable excuses some referees gave for their defense of Keynes's misinterpretation of Marshall and for their rejection of my manuscript criticizing Bibow (2000) for publication. Next, we clarify further Keynes's confusion (similar to Ahiakpor 1990).

Recognizing Keynes's difficulties with the classical theory of interest

Keynes provides clear evidence of his misinterpretation of "capital" in Marshall's restatement of the classical theory of interest he quotes in the appendix to Chapter 14 of the *General Theory*. Reacting to the first sentence, Keynes writes: "It is to be noted that Marshall uses the word 'capital' not 'money' and the word 'stock' not 'loans'; yet interest is a payment for borrowing *money*, and 'demand for capital' in this context should mean 'demand for loans' of money for the purpose of buying a stock of capital-goods" (1936: 186 n.; italics original). Believing that Marshall was referring to capital goods and not loanable funds, Keynes continues with his criticism:

> But the equality between the stock of capital-goods offered and the stock demanded will be brought about by the *prices* of capital-goods, not by the rate of interest. It is equality between the demand and supply of loans of money, i.e. of debts, which is brought about by the rate of interest.
>
> (ibid.; italics original)

Keynes's misreading of "capital" in Marshall's restatement of the theory of interest to mean capital goods also appears in his retort to Marshall's explanation that "An extensive increase in the demand for capital in general will therefore be met for a time not so much by an increase of supply, as by a rise in the rate of interest." Keynes (1936) asks, "Why not by a rise in the supply price of capital-goods?" (187, n. 2). Sound economic analysis argues that a fall in interest rates, owing to an increase in the supply of savings or credit – say from an increase in central bank money (cash)[14] or cash dishoarding by banks or households ($\Delta H_h < 0$) – may increase the volume of funds borrowed to purchase capital goods, given the level of wage rates. The increased demand for capital goods would then increase their prices. That analysis appears to be Keynes's reasoning behind his continued criticism of Marshall's explanation:

> Suppose, for example, that the "extensive increase in the demand for capital in general" is due to a *fall* in the rate of interest. I would suggest that the

sentence should be rewritten: "In so far, therefore, as the extensive increase in the demand for capital-goods cannot be immediately met by an increase in the total stock, it will have to be held in check for the time being by a rise in the supply price of capital-goods sufficient to keep the marginal efficiency of capital in equilibrium with the rate of interest without there being any material change in the scale of investment; meanwhile (as always) the factors of production adapted for the output of capital-goods would be used in producing those capital-goods of which the marginal efficiency is greatest in the new conditions.

(Keynes ibid.; italics original)

And when Marshall points out, "It cannot be repeated too often that the phrase 'the rate of interest' is applicable to old investments of capital only in a very limited sense," Keynes (1936: 187, n. 3; italics original) retorts: "In fact we cannot speak of it at all. We can only properly speak of the rate of interest on *money* borrowed for the purpose of purchasing investments of capital new or old (or for any other purpose)."

In Keynes's understanding, interest rates are determined by the supply and demand for money (cash or liquidity; see, e.g., 1936: 169). In a 27 August 1935 letter to Harrod disavowing his originating the liquidity-preference theory of interest, Keynes points out that he was "not really being so great an innovator, except as against the classical school, but have important predecessors and [was] returning to an age-long tradition of common sense" (1973: 552) In his 1939 preface to the French edition of the *General Theory*, Keynes also explains that, in arguing the liquidity-preference theory of interest, he was "returning to the doctrine of the older, pre-nineteenth century economists" (1974: xxxiv). He must either have been unaware of, or had been unimpressed by, David Hume's (1752) correction of that mercantilist idea in his essay, "Of Interest," which influenced the classical writers, including Smith, Ricardo, and J. S. Mill. Lawlor's (2006) attempt to place Keynes's monetary thought in a historical context fails to recognize these sources.

Thus, Marshall's alleged explanation of interest rate determination by the supply and demand for capital goods, as Keynes misunderstood him to have been arguing, made no sense:

The perplexity which I find in Marshall's account of the matter is *fundamentally due*, I think, to the incursion of the concept "interest," which belongs to a monetary economy, into a treatise which takes no account of money. "Interest" has really no business to turn up at all in Marshall's *Principles of Economics*, – it belongs to another branch of the subject.

(1936: 189; italics added)[15]

All this, in spite of Marshall's (1920: 341; italics added) explanation:

The rate of interest is a ratio: and the two things which it connects are both *sums of money*. So long as capital is "free," and the *sum of money* or general purchasing power over which it gives command is known, the net money income, expected to be derived from it, can be represented at once as bearing a given ratio (four or five or ten per cent.) to that sum. But when the *free capital* has been invested in a particular thing, its money value cannot as a rule be ascertained except by capitalizing the net income which it will yield: and therefore the causes which govern it are likely to be akin in a greater or less degree to those which govern rents.

In his 1939 preface to the French edition of the *General Theory*, Keynes (1974: xxxiii–iv) repeats his misidentification of "capital" in the classical theory of interest with capital goods.

Besides his confusion over the meaning of "capital" in the classical theory of interest, Keynes also latches on to Marshall's explanation that the rise of interest would act as an incentive for "extra work" (1936: 187) to argue that "this assumes that income is *not* constant" (ibid.: 187, n. 1; italics original). This appears to be Keynes's basis for claiming that a shift in the demand for capital will also shift the capital-supply curve,[16] thus leaving no determinate equilibrium interest rate, or that the supply and demand curves for capital are not independent. But in the period of the equilibrium interest rate adjustment, following an increased demand for savings or "capital," income has yet to change. When later the level of income rises, the savings-supply curve also may shift to the right (increase).

Marshall makes the same point in the *Principles*, which Robertson (1936: 185) quotes in response to Keynes's criticism:

> And with the growth of openings for the investment of capital there is a constant increase in that surplus of production over the necessaries of life which gives the power to save. . . . Every increase in the arts of production, and in the capital accumulated to assist and support labor in future production, increased the surplus out of which more wealth could be accumulated.

Thus, Robertson concludes: "If, in the world of causation, today's saving is the great-grandchild of last year's rate of interest, surely that does not prevent it from being also a parent of today's rate" (1936: 186).

Harrod's unhelpful concessions to Keynes on Marshall's (classical) theory of interest

Keynes (1973: 13, 559) invites Harrod to "Look through . . . my various quotations from classical economists [including Marshall] and tell me which of them is not nonsense." Harrod replies:

> I don't find the long passage from Marshall (ch. 16) nonsense. I find it harder to understand some of your criticisms. . . . Subject to the ordinary difficulties of *expressing* any of these things in *language*, the M[arshall] passage seems to me crystal clear and your criticism in the text comparatively difficult to

follow. . . . What I don't like about the chapter is that implied allegation that Marshall's system of thought was fundamentally confused, whereas I believe the *confusion* to be due to *your failure* to think yourself back into the system of thought that you have abandoned.

(20 September 1935 letter in Keynes 1973: 13, 560–1; italics added)

Harrod here hints at the problem of "language" or definitions for Keynes but does not pursue it. Earlier, Harrod had described some of Keynes's criticisms of Marshall and others as constituting "a confusion . . . guerilla skirmishing . . . fussy, irrelevant, dubious, hair-splitting and hair-raising" (Keynes 1973: 13, 530, 534, 556), evidently because he understood the "capital" supply and demand theory of interest as saying the same thing as the loanable-funds supply and demand theory.

In a 30 August 1935 letter, Harrod tells Keynes that he had "no excuse for saying . . . that the classical economists who assumed that the supply [of savings] *schedule* could be treated as a constant, *were not making sense* when they said that the rate of interest was determined by supply and demand of saving" (Keynes 1973: 13, 554; italics original). He earlier had insisted to Keynes: "I hold there is sense in saying that interest equates the demand for investment to the supply of saving" (ibid.: 540). Harrod again is here consistent in restating the classical theory of interest, but it could not be meaningful to Keynes unless he also understood "investment" to mean employment of loanable funds in the sphere of production. However, Keynes's view of investment is only the acquisition or production of capital goods (Keynes 1930: 2, 207).

Harrod also had clarified Marshall's interest theory that Keynes restates in a 27 August 1935 reply to him:

I do not think that Marshall failed to appreciate the distinctiveness of the concepts of marginal efficiency of capital and the rate of interest. He knew that there was a schedule of marginal efficiencies and he thought that interest was determined by this and the schedule of propensity to save. Now you [Keynes] use both these schedules, but to determine the level of income, the relevance of whose variations in this nexus he [Marshall] did not appreciate.

(Keynes 1973: 13, 548–9)

Keynes rejects Harrod's claim that he was employing Marshall's schedules to determine the level of income: "I think this is overstating a great deal the clearness of Marshall's thought, since it overlooks the fact that my definition of marginal efficiency of capital is quite different from anything to be found in his work or in that of any other classical economist" (Keynes 1973: 13, 549).[17] Harrod's failure to recognize the differences between Marshall's and Keynes's definitions of the marginal efficiency of capital, saving, investment, coupled with his concession that the classical theory had neglected variations in the level of income, were to prove unhelpful to his attempts to persuade Keynes of his misinterpretation of the classical theory of interest.

Harrod's concession includes his claiming in the 30 August 1935 letter to Keynes that "they [classics] were wrong to take [income] as constant, but having made that mistake their argument was quite logical" (Keynes 1973: 13, 554). Earlier (12 August 1935), Harrod had written to Keynes, arguing, "The essence of your point I feel to be that the *cet. par.* clause of the supply and demand analysis, which in this case includes the level of income, is *invalid.* The classical theory [therefore] is invalid but not nonsense" (ibid.: 540; italics original). Perhaps most fatally, Harrod also concedes: "'The propensity to save and the schedule of marg[inal] efficiency are two curves which do not intersect anywhere because they are not in *pari materia.*' Agreed" (ibid.: 555). But, in fact, the two curves should refer to loanable funds; one, to the supply of savings and the other, to the demand for savings.

As Harrod (1951: 453) later explains, "It seemed to me then – and still seems so – that [Keynes] was himself in some confusion about what the classical position really was; that he had not fully thought it through." To help Keynes resolve his "confusion," Harrod instructed him to construct a family of savings-supply curves on the basis of different levels of income and to find that changes in the demand for "capital" would still bring about equilibrium interest rates at different levels of income. This supposedly was to take account of "the operation of multiplier affecting the level of income" (Keynes 1973: 13, 555). But the multiplier process, if it existed, could not be instantaneous in determining the level of income.[18]

Keynes responds to Harrod's suggestion by first crediting him with having understood his [Keynes's] own theory of interest, adding, "I think the construction in the note . . . is both correct and very useful as a help to exposition, and I shall like to appropriate it" (1973: 13, 557). Keynes adds: "You will see that I have, in a sense, shifted my ground in the [illustration of the classical theory of interest]. I have gained a great deal from your hard knocks, and I would like some more" (ibid.: 559 n.). However, Keynes did not think Harrod had represented the classical theory correctly:

> But what you say seems to me to fail either as a statement of what the classical theory says or as a justification of its subject to special assumptions. I make a great distinction between the classical theory of employment, which does make perfect sense and works all right on certain special assumptions, and the classical theory of the rate of interest *makes no sense* on any assumptions whatever.
>
> (ibid.: 557; italics added)

In a 27 August 1935 long letter to Harrod, Keynes firmly rejects the classical savings supply and demand theory of interest:

> My theory is that the rate of interest is the price which brings the demand for liquidity [cash] into equilibrium with the amount of liquidity available. It has *nothing whatever* to do with *saving.* . . . I am substituting demand and supply analysis for liquidity instead of that for savings. . . . Marshall you say "thought interest was determined by the schedule of marginal efficiencies and

the schedule of the propensity to save"; he forgot that incomes could change. I am saying something totally different from this when I say that *interest is determined by the demand and supply for liquidity*. . . . Without bringing in liquidity preference the position of equilibrium is entirely indeterminate, and any method, such as the classical one, which endeavours to arrive at the rate of interest without bringing in liquidity preference is bound to be circular in the worst possible sense of the word.

(Keynes 1973: 13, 550–1; italics added)

The difference between Keynes's (mercantilist) money supply and demand theory of interest and the classical savings supply and demand theory could not be any clearer. But as we have seen above, the classical theory incorporates savers' liquidity preference (ΔH_h).

Keynes's rejecting Harrod's representation of the classical theory of interest is understandable because Harrod had not persuaded him to recognize that the "classical supply curves" must refer to "capital" or loanable funds while the "marginal efficiency of capital" curves must refer to the "demand curves for loanable or investible funds." Thus, Keynes (1936: 179–84) subsequently maintains his view above as he employs Harrod's suggested diagram, noting that "the classical theory not merely neglects the influence of changes in the level of income [a concession to Harrod's claim], but involves formal error" (179). Keynes (1936: 180 n) also relates the diagram he derives from Harrod's suggestion to that of Robertson's 1934 *Economic Journal* article, but fails to recognize that Robertson's schedules refer to savings or investible funds.

Such was the state of miscommunication between Harrod and Keynes over the savings-supply curves and investment-demand schedule (curve) that, after shifting the "investment demand-schedule" in the suggested diagram, Keynes still could not find a new equilibrium interest rate on any savings-supply curve. I illustrate in Figure 7.2 how Keynes could have interpreted the effect of a decreased demand for "capital," if he had interpreted "capital" to mean savings or loanable funds rather than capital goods.

Keynes (1936: 180–1) defines an XX' curve as the "investment demand-schedule" and a Y curve as one that "relates the amounts saved out of an income . . . at various levels of the rate of interest" or the savings-supply curve, and "I" represents both investment and savings. Thus, a shift (decrease) of the investment demand-schedule from $X_1X'_1$ to $X_2X'_2$ at the rate of interest, r_1, if the interest rate is understood to be determined by the intersection of the savings and investment-demand functions, should first result in an excess supply of savings over the amounts demanded for investment, indicated by the distance, $I_1I'_1$. The equilibrium interest rate should then fall to r'_1 along the same savings-supply curve while the funds borrowed decrease to I_2. Keynes could not derive this conclusion because he understood the investment-demand schedule to refer directly to capital goods rather than to savings or loanable funds. We also here see no need for the multiple savings-supply curves that Harrod insisted were necessary. But in Keynes's reasoning, we would need to have the rate of interest determined by the supply and

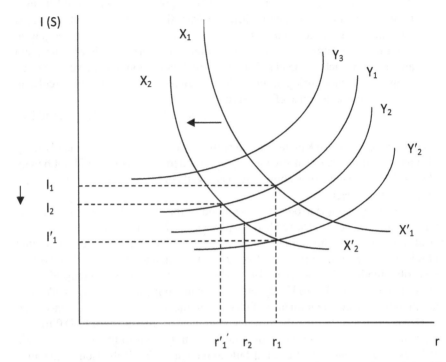

Figure 7.2 A reproduction of Keynes's diagram. A decrease in investment demand should
lead to an excess supply of savings $(I_1I'_1)$ and a reduction in equilibrium interest rate from r_1 to r'_1 if investment demand correctly refers to funds, not capital
goods. Keynes failed to derive r'_1.

demand for liquidity (cash) before we know whether the $X_2X'_2$ curve intersects
the Y_2 curve (if the interest rate declines to r_2) or the Y'_2 curve (if the interest rate
stayed at r_1).

Also, note that Keynes's diagram has the rate of interest on the horizontal axis
(the determining variable) and "the amount of investment (or saving)" (1936: 180)
on the vertical axis (the dependent variable). Thus, rather than an effort to explain
the determination of interest rates by the supply and demand for investment funds,
Keynes uses the diagram to illustrate the determination of investment – purchases
of capital goods – following changes in the level of interest rates. Keynes therefore concludes that "the X-curve and the Y-curves tell us nothing about the rate of
interest. They only tell us what income will be, if *from some other source* we can
say what the rate of interest is" (181; italics added). Had Keynes understood that
the investment-demand and savings-supply schedules determine interest rates, he
might have drawn Figure 7.3 instead. The illustrations of new equilibrium interest
rates in Figures 7.2 and 7.3 show the error of Lawlor's (1997, 2006) and de Boyer's
(2010) agreement with Keynes's criticisms of the classical theory of interest. They,

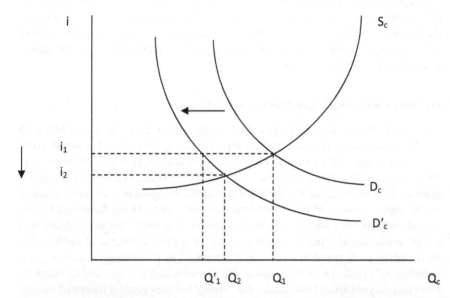

Figure 7.3 An alternative representation of Keynes's query: A reduction in investment demand, understood as a reduction in the demand for capital (funds), should create an excess supply of savings (Q'_1Q_1) and reduce the equilibrium rate of interest from i_1 to i_2.

like Keynes, appear not to understand the classical "capital" supply and demand theory of interest.

Furthermore, had Harrod convinced Keynes that the investment-demand schedule in the classical theory is a demand for funds, not directly a capital-goods demand function, Keynes (1936: 142–3) might have avoided claiming that an increase in the "marginal efficiency of capital" does not raise the rate of interest but only increases the quantity of capital goods purchased at the existing interest rate. Similarly, Keynes (1936: 177) might not have objected to the proposition that "each additional act of investment will necessarily raise the rate of interest, if it is not offset by a change in the readiness to save." The separation of savings from the provision of investment funds was such a fundamental position for Keynes, which he subsequently repeats: the "supply of [liquid resources] depends on the terms on which the banks are prepared to become more or less liquid . . . saving does not come into the picture at all" and "The investment market can become congested through the shortage of cash. It can never become congested through the shortage of saving. This is the most fundamental of my conclusions within this field" (1937c: 668, 669). Indeed, Keynes (1930: 1, 25–6) also denies that savings supply the funds loaned by banks.

Keynes's claim that an increased investment-demand does not raise the rate of interest is the "startling conclusion" Hicks (1937: 152) nevertheless was willing to accept, in apparent contradiction to Hick's own analysis that "a rise in the marginal-efficiency-of-capital schedule *must raise* the curve IS; and, therefore, although it will raise Income and employment, it will also *raise the rate of interest*" (154; italics added). Hicks (1937: 149) also earlier recognized in classical analysis the fact that "An increase in the inducement to invest (i.e., a rightward movement of the schedule of the marginal efficiency of capital) will tend to raise the rate of interest, and so affecting saving."

De Boyer's crystallizing Keynes's confusion

As shown above, Harrod struggled to clarify the meaning of terms Marshall employed in stating the classical theory of interest, also referring to the problem of language and Keynes's confusion, especially in Harrod's 20 September 1935 letter. In their reactions to the *General Theory* several of Keynes's contemporaries also pointed out his different meanings assigned to economic terms or his misunderstanding of the theories he was criticizing. Thus, Robertson (1936) considered Keynes's liquidity-preference theory of interest "not as a refutation of a common-sense account of events in terms of supply and demand for loanable funds, but as an alternative version of it" and that "its *terminology* seems to [him] unfortunate" (1936: 183; italics added). He also considered it "something of a mystery" that Keynes would not "admit the validity" of the classical theory of interest as explained in Marshall's *Principles* (1937: 431). He believed the Marshallian approach "accords with the ordinary *language* of the marketplace" and has other advantages over Keynes's besides (1940: 20).

Pigou (1936) was bewildered trying to understand Keynes's criticisms of Marshall and wondered how "an author [Keynes], whose powers of exposition enabled him to write on the philosophy of Probability in a way that amateurs could follow ... is barely intelligible to many ... of his own professional colleagues?" (119). He traced the problem first to Keynes's "loose and inconsistent use of *terms*" (119–20; italics added) and argued, "The lack of clarity in Mr. Keynes' explanation [of the process of investment] is *mainly* due ... to a lack of clarity in his thought" (122; italics original). Viner (1936: 158; italics added) notes that in Keynes's book,

> no old term for an old concept is used when a new one can be coined, and if old terms are used *new meanings* are generally assigned to them. The definitions provided, moreover, are sometimes of unbelievable complexity. The old-fashioned economist must, therefore, struggle not only with new ideas and new methods of manipulating them, but also with a *new language*."

Hicks (1936) recognizes Keynes's "*new definitions* of saving and investment" as reflecting a "very *important change* in point of view" (239; italics added). He favors Keynes's interest theory over the classical alternative, and declares: "It is a great strength of Mr. Keynes's theory of interest that it conceives the rate of interest, from the outset, as a money rate" (245). He adds that Keynes's method "is a perfectly legitimate method, but it does not prove other methods to be wrong. The choice between them is purely a method of convenience" (246). While Harrod (1951) never recovered from his mistaken concessions to Keynes, Hicks

(1989) subsequently admits the superiority of the classical theory of interest over Keynes's liquidity-preference alternative. He uses Marshall's savings supply and demand framework to explain the behavior of interest rates: "a fall in the demand for savings (much more plausibly than an increase in supply) could well have been responsible for a fall in interest . . . So I now think that Marshall, after all, does win that trick game" (78).[19]

Frank Knight (1937) finds that, in Keynes's treatment of saving and investment, "familiar terms and modes of expression seem to be shunned on principle in this book" (108). He also considers "the title of book IV [to be] hardly in strict accord with the author's *new-fangled definitions* of investment and saving" (111; italics added) and that Keynes's "theory of interest is the most difficult part of the whole construction to take seriously" (112). Hawtrey's (1937) "Alternative Theories of Interest" is concerned mainly to clarify "questions of *terminology*" (436), noting how Keynes had "*misunderstood* my own definitions" (438; italics added) such as capital, saving, and investment.

Yet de Boyer (2010) claims, "the leading neoclassic [sic] contemporaries of Keynes, such as Hawtrey, Harrod, Robertson, and Hicks, did not fault Keynes for misunderstanding the *neo-classical terminology*, [thus] it is highly likely that the problem does not lie at the level of understanding of language" (264 n.; italics added). He reaffirms Keynes's confusion over the comparative statics analysis of interest rate determination, invokes an unnecessary labor market condition for the validity of the classical theory of interest, and several times reasserts Keynes's claim that the classical theory of interest does not make sense:. "Keynes's criticism of classical theory is . . . well-founded" (2010: 279; see also 265 and 282). Also, although neither Harrod nor Keynes invoked exogenous money wages as relevant for explaining equilibrium determination of an economic system, de Boyer claims that to be requisite.

Several problems plague de Boyer's evaluation of the Harrod-Keynes exchanges. First, his own statement of the saving-supply function does not take into account the demand for money (cash), and thus cannot handle changes in Keynes's liquidity preference of savers. Second, he makes little use of the classical Quantity Theory of Money in determining the level of prices, but rather employs an equation that appears to determine the price level from the nominal wage rate divided by the marginal product of labor. That equation may be consistent with Keynes's aversion towards using the Quantity Theory of Money to explain the level of prices rather than the rate of interest – Keynes's wage cost-push theory of inflation. But the argument is inconsistent with economic theory. The money wage rate divided by the marginal product of labor rather defines the marginal cost of production. Third, de Boyer treats savings as a leakage from the expenditure stream, just as Keynes did: "The increase in income ceases once savings, representing a *leakage* from the mechanism whereby demand tracks income, are equal to investment" (2010: 267; italics added). This after explanations in Marshall's *Principles* and clarifications by Robertson, Hawtrey, Viner, and Knight, cited above, that savings constitute investment in financial assets.[20] De Boyer (2010: 268) himself also defines saving as "the demand for financial assets." Surely, sellers of financial assets spend their proceeds. Fourth, de Boyer thinks that considering individuals' deciding between consumption and holding financial assets is a "little-known characteristic of the Marshallian analysis of the rate of interest" (265), which is incorrect. That view belongs with Keynes (1936). As Knight (1937: 113) and Robertson (1937: 431, 1940: 16), among other analysts, long have pointed out in criticism of Keynes's two-margin analysis, income earners make their spending decisions on three margins in Marshall's analysis, namely, consumption, saving (buying financial assets), and holding money (cash).[21]

De Boyer also repeats several claims that already have been shown to be inaccurate. One is that "for Harrod, classical theory, as far as it *presupposed full employment* – therefore given income – remains coherent" (2010: 272; italics added). The classics did not assume full employment in their theory of interest (Ahiakpor 1997a and 2003b: Ch. 10 elaborate on this point). Another is that "Say's Law states that the markets for goods and financial assets can be in equilibrium *only if* the labor market is in equilibrium" (ibid.; italics added). Say's Law rather explains the interconnection between the markets for produced goods and services, such that the production of one commodity immediately opens a market or vent for other commodities (Say 1821a: 134–5). The law holds in conditions of disequilibrium (unemployment) in the labor market as well (see also Say 1821a: 86–8; Ahiakpor 2003a). Furthermore, de Boyer gives credence to Keynes's instantaneous multiplier-effect argument, by which an increase in investment spending immediately increases the level of income. De Boyer is apparently oblivious of the criticisms of Keynes's multiplier analysis by the likes of Pigou, Robertson, and Hawtrey (see Ahiakpor 2001 or 2003b: Ch. 12).

Finally, it is particularly baffling that de Boyer (2010: 276, 282) seeks to explain equilibrium determination in a monetary economy by invoking "exogenous money wages." Now the wage rate is the price of labor services, determined by their supply and demand in different employment centers, albeit entailed in contracts; Pigou (1933) makes the point very well.[22] Even though wage rates may change slowly behind variations in the level of commodity prices – the mechanism that produces forced saving when prices are rising (Ahiakpor 2009) – it appears inconsistent to rely upon exogenous money wages as the condition for "removing the [alleged] indeterminacy of equilibrium" (de Boyer 2010: 282). Who quotes or determines the exogenous (average) wage rate? How long does it last? Harrod and Keynes thus were wise not to have invoked exogenous money wages in order to derive equilibrium interest rates.

Summary and conclusions

Keynes revived the mercantilist money supply and demand theory of interest in the *General Theory*, which David Hume's (1752) "Of Interest" explains to be mistaken, because he could not recognize Marshall's restatement in the *Principles* or in any other "classical" sources to be valid. But one just has to read "capital" in the classical theory as referring to savings or loanable funds to recognize the theory's validity. Thus, Keynes was mistaken in his criticism of the classical theory of interest as "a nonsense theory" for having argued that interest rates are determined by the supply and demand for capital goods instead of by the supply and demand for money or liquidity. Harrod also erred in conceding to Keynes that the classics had an invalid theory of interest and that the classical theory was incomplete for not having taken account of the changing level of income when explaining equilibrium interest rate determination; Harrod (1951: 453) maintains the same erroneous view that the classics had "an incorrect theory of interest."

Harrod's suggested diagram unnecessarily includes a family of savings-supply curves instead of only one to interact with investment-demand schedules that Keynes clearly did not interpret as referring to the demand for investible funds, but rather to capital goods. Neither did Keynes interpret savings to mean the source of loanable or investible funds. Thus, Harrod's suggested diagram merely enabled Keynes to firm up and illustrate his mistaken belief that the classical theory of interest made "no sense on any assumptions whatever."

De Boyer's (2010) attempt to explain Harrod's failed efforts to dissuade Keynes from his erroneous criticisms of Marshall's restatement of the classical theory of interest employs arguments other than Harrod's failure to clarify for Keynes such classical concepts as "capital," savings, and investment. He ignores the broader literature regarding Keynes's misinterpretations of classical analysis. He also substitutes his own definitions of saving and investment-demand for Keynes's, thus missing a clear recognition of Keynes's problems of understanding. He engages in equation counting to explain equilibrium values, almost along the same lines as Hicks (1936). That approach at resolving the dispute between Keynes and the classicals resulted in Hicks's merely having papered over fundamental conceptual misunderstandings that are still embedded in the IS-LM model. De Boyer's efforts thus suffer the same fate: Apparent mathematical elegance with little illumination of the issues. By declaring Keynes's criticisms of the classical interest theory as "well-founded," on the basis of his own approach, de Boyer mostly crystallizes Keynes's confusions over the classical theory of interest.

Keynes's employing Harrod's suggested diagram was not "largely a peripheral aspect of [his] substantive discussion of the particular theory of interest he advances in the *General Theory*," as a referee (*Journal of the History of Economic Thought*), claims in rejecting my submission for publication. Rather, the diagram helps us clearly to recognize Keynes's confusion, besides his attempts to correct Marshall's statements in the appendix to Chapter 14. Instead, the referee argues, "The big question is the relationship, if any, between the Savings-Investment diagram and Keynes' analysis in Chapter 17 of the General Theory, which displays the influence of Sraffa, who oddly goes unmentioned in this paper. . . . It is Chapter 17 that establishes why Keynes treated interest as a monetary phenomenon rather than a real phenomenon." The referee also must not be aware of Keynes's (1939 preface to the French edition, 1974: xxxiii-iv) own explanation for not recognizing a valid theory of interest in classical economics: "it is the function of the rate of interest to preserve equilibrium, not between the *demand and supply of new capital goods*, but between the demand and supply of *money*" (italics added.)

Keynes here merely repeats what he says in the appendix to Chapter 14 of the *General Theory*.

Harrod's failure to dissuade Keynes from his mistaken criticisms of the classical theory of interest with the suggested diagram also illustrates the primacy of conceptual understanding if formalism, the use of equations and diagrams, is to assist in clarifying issues in economics. Indeed, Keynes (1937a) explains that he "occupied much space in the first half of [his] book by analyses and definitions of Income, Saving, Investment and other such terms [because of] the *widespread confusion* which has surrounded *these terms* in recent discussions, and the subtlety of the points involved" (249; italics added).

The clarifications Keynes needed include: (1) "capital" in the classical theory of interest refers to savings or loanable funds, (2) savers supply loanable funds through their acquisition of financial assets or deposits with banks, (3) investment in production is the employment of savings or loanable funds to purchase producer's goods as well as to hire the services of land and labor, what the classicals called fixed and circulating capital, and (4) "investment demand" refers to the demand for savings or loanable funds, not directly to capital goods. In the absence of such clarity of concepts, Harrod's employing algebraic equations and the suggested diagram got nowhere in having Keynes recognize the validity of the classical theory of interest. Keynes could have been spared the trouble of arguing "the various commodity-rates of interest," including those for wheat, copper, houses, and steel-plants in Chapter 17 of the *General Theory*, had Harrod clarified for him the meaning of saving or "capital" in the classical theory.

Modern macroeconomics continues to be dominated by the Keynes's liquidity-preference theory of interest, sometimes modified by the price-level and expectations effects. The modifications, in fact, belong in the classical tradition of the theory of interest (e.g., Hume 1752, "Of Interest"; Ricardo *Works*, 3: 91; J. S. Mill *Works*, 3: 656; Marshall 1923: 257). A careful attention to Keynes's conceptual problems with the meaning of "capital" and saving by Harrod, besides Harrod's own unnecessary requirement of a family of savings-supply curves in order to resolve a non-existent gap in the classical theory, might have fostered a greater appreciation of the logic of the classical theory of interest. Instead, as Leijonhufvud (1981, 131) has observed, "The theory of interest mechanism [has become] the center of the confusion in modern macroeconomics. Not all issues in contention originate there. But the inconclusive quarrels – the ill-focused, frustrating ones that drag on because the contending parties cannot agree what the issue is – do largely stem from this source."

However, Keynes's mistaken reading of the classical theory has so influenced another referee's (*History of Political Economy*) understanding of the classical literature that she or he asserted the following claims in rejecting my exposition of Harrod's and Keynes's misinterpretations of the classical theory for publication:

> Generations of specialists in the theory [of interest] have found the classical theory at best obscure and at worst wrong. Hawtrey may have been the first writer in the English literature to voice this sentiment. Any of the many

versions of his [Keynes's] own suggested improvements on this head to Marshall's theory offers his insight into this issue. For historical accounts Bridel (1987), Laidler (1991, 1999) and Lawlor (2006) are good sources. None of these sources confirms the opinion of the author [myself] that the classical theory of interest was clear or well-suited to a short-run setting. Moreover, as they all show, the mystical quantity of "free-capital" to which Alfred Marshall so often referred in this context, and on which a large part of the author reviewed depends upon, is at best a slippery and fictional concept. It seems that Keynes was correct in his opinion that Marshall's theory of interest was nowhere clearly stated.

The referee further believes, "The most classic and still valuable paper on [the] controversy is that by Tsiang (1956). Also worth reading on the theory and history of this issue [the 'loanable-funds' versus 'liquidity preference' theories of interest] is Leijonhufvud (1981), Laidler (1988) and Bibow (2000)." But Tsiang (1956: 547) judges that "Keynes was confused in adding after his concession as to the demand for 'finance,' almost a second thought, that this demand for 'finance' is 'quite distinct from the demand for active balances which will arise as a result of the investment activity while it is going on'."[23] Furthermore, Tsiang (1956: 552) awards victory to the loanable-funds theory over Keynes's alternative, while the references the referee cites do not.

Also, failing to note the possibility of deriving equilibrium interest rates from Keynes's diagram without his invoking the cash (money) supply and demand theory of interest, the referee furthermore claims,

> This reviewer has found the lone diagram in the *General Theory* to be a useful device for seeing what Keynes is getting at with his argument. Moreover, I have had many successes in using that diagram when teaching the General Theory to generation [sic] of un-initiated students. This, a priori, makes me suspect that the author [myself] of the paper is barking up the wrong tree. Careful reading of the paper confirms this opinion.

The referee's having taught Keynes's flawed argument with that diagram to many (a generation of) students could not bear to accept my correction of it. Such is the extent of the miseducation of many a student perpetuated by Keynes's insistence on interest rates being determined only by money's supply and demand rather than savings or loanable funds.

Another referee (*History of Political Economy*) shows no serious inclination to understand the point of my manuscript, namely, Harrod did a disservice to macro or monetary analysis by suggesting the diagram to Keynes, along with the concessions that the classical theory of interest is faulty and incomplete. The referee writes,

> I'm afraid I can't make much of this [paper's] argument. I would have thought that given the criticism of Veblen, Robinson and others concerning

the confusion of capital as a value sum and a team of machines it would require more evidence to convict Keynes of not having noticed this.[24] I don't much like Harrod's picture, but I have always the problem that Harrod did not understand what Keynes was trying to do. In particular, I find the presentation in the paper of liquidity preference incompatible with Keynes' discussion with Townsend pointing out that it was possible for the liquidity premium and thus the rate of interest to change without any change in the balance sheets of the central bank or financial institutions, and thus no change in any possible definition of "cash". Finally it is not helpful to describe as "classical" the determination of prices or interest rates by means of "supply and demand" post-Sraffa.

None of the restatements of the classical theory of interest above, including J. S. Mill's (*Works*, 3: 647), impresses this referee. Thus, the scholars heavily influenced by Keynes continue to ignore evidence of his misinterpretation of "capital" in the classical theory of interest.

Notes

1 This chapter is based upon my paper, "On Harrod's Unhelpful Suggested Diagram to Keynes on the Classical Theory of Interest," discussed at the History of Economics Society Annual Meetings, University of Notre Dame, South Bend, IN, June 17–20, 2011. I thank John Berdell for comments on that paper without implicating him in any errors of mine in the chapter. I gave up trying to publish the paper because of the strenuous resistance to it from referees for the *History of Political Economy* and the *Journal of the History of Economic Thought*. One referee acted for both journals, reproducing virtually the same comments and references. The resistance to expositions of Keynes's errors of analysis among Keynes adherents, I have found, is rather strong. The chapter incorporates my reactions to some of the referees' mistaken criticisms. I also draw upon my unpublished comment on de Boyer (2010) that was rejected for being too long and too focused only on his work.
2 Rod O'Donnell (1999) and Daniele Besomi (2000) have clarified that Harrod only suggested how Keynes could draw such a diagram. They do not address Keynes's fundamental misinterpretation of "capital" in the classical theory of interest or Harrod's error in suggesting multiple savings-supply curves instead of just one to determine equilibrium interest rates, following changes in investment demand.
3 Hicks's (1937) failed attempt with the IS-LM model to resolve dispute between Keynes and his critics over his theories also illustrates the point. So does de Boyer's (2010) employing equations and diagrams to evaluate Harrod's correspondence with Keynes on the classical theory of interest, only to reach his mistaken conclusion that Keynes was correct in his criticism.
4 See also Frank Taussig (1921: 2, Ch. 39, esp. 27–30). As Robertson (1940: 20) explains, the classical theory "accords with the general tendency of modern theory to emphasize the unity pervading economic phenomena; the rate of interest appears as a special case of the general theory of pricing."
5 Since the confusion in the language of economics from the 1930s (Ahiakpor 1998 elaborates on this) economists now qualify "capital" with "financial" in order to refer to loanable funds and identify capital firmly with capital goods. Some Austrian economists, frustrated with the different meanings associated with "capital," have suggested that "the term be banned entirely from scientific usage" (Hayek 1941: 9).

Eugene Böhm-Bawerk (1891: 23) earlier laments that economics "is struck, as it were, by a . . . confusion of tongues, and [has become] involved in an endless wrangle as to what kind of thing it is that properly is called capital!"

6 Marshall's statement is similar to Keynes's (1936: 222): "The money rate of interest . . . is nothing more than the percentage excess of a sum of money contracted for forward delivery, e.g. a year hence, over what we may call the 'spot' or cash price of the sum thus contracted for forward delivery."

7 In the absence of variations in central bank money, savings supply the "capital" offered on loan or credit ($S = S_c = S_{CR}$). Thus, Ricardo (*Works*, 5: 436–7) explains that credit "does not create Capital, it determines only by whom that Capital should be employed." However, a central bank's purchasing securities increases the volume of loanable funds or credit beyond the flow of savings ($S_{CR} = S_c + \Delta H$; H = currency or high-powered money).

8 In light of Harrod's criticism of the classical theory of interest for assuming income being fixed, it is noteworthy that Keynes himself, in effect, admits the point: "I . . . would not deny that the rate of interest may perhaps have an influence . . . on the amount saved *out of a given income*" (1936: 178; italics original). But a referee (*Journal of the History of Economic Thought*) defends Keynes's criticism of the classical interest theory and Harrod's supplying a family of savings-supply curves instead of one to help Keynes sort things out, arguing: "Keynes does not contest that 'the postulates of the classical theory are applicable' when income is fixed, but varying. It is the reason why the readers of the *General Theory*, except the author of the article [myself], think that the family of saving curves (Y_3, Y_1, Y2, and Y'_2) is helpful."

9 This understanding of saving helps one recognize the error of Keynes's paradox of thrift proposition (Ahiakpor 1995) or Keynes's liquidity-trap proposition (Ahiakpor 2018a).

10 Keynes (1930: 1, 172), however, defines saving merely as "the negative act of refraining from spending the whole of [one's] income on consumption."

11 Reacting to Keynes's treatment of saving and hoarding in the *General Theory*, Viner (1936: 159) correctly observes that savers "have investment habits, and abhor idle cash as nature abhors a vacuum."

12 Yet so influenced is de Boyer by Keynes that he employs Keynes's functions' dependency argument: "Assume the existence of an initial equilibrium and suppose a change in the marginal efficiency of capital. The *supply curve* [of financial assets] shifts, prompting a *shift* of the demand curve by an unknown amount" (2010: 271; italics added). But an increase in supply should cause a downward movement along the demand curve, according to price theory. Moreover, a change in the marginal efficiency of capital rather should shift the demand curve for savings, not the supply curve. And why would any curve shift by "an unknown amount" to arrive at some definite equilibrium interest rate?

13 Marshall (1920: 279–80) discusses the effect of changes in the "unwillingness to part with money," the equivalent of Keynes's liquidity-preference, on the demand and supply functions for goods and services in the marketplace. See also Marshall 1920: 190–2 and Robertson 1937: 431, 1940: 27.

14 A central bank's money creation increases the flow of loanable funds or credit from $S_{CR} = S_c$ to $S_{CR} = S_c + \Delta H^s$, shifting the credit-supply curve to the right and lowering the equilibrium rate of interest in the short run until the price level rises and interest rates recover. This is the "liquidity effect" of new money, followed by the "income or price-level" effect (see, e.g., Friedman 1972). Marshall (1923: 257) explains the same process. See also J. S. Mill *Works*, 3: 656 for a similar explanation, following those of Ricardo (*Works*, 3: 91) and Hume (1752, "Of Interest"). Indeed, Knut Wicksell (1935: 79–80) acknowledges Ricardo's influence on his own explanation of the same phenomenon now widely attributed to him by modern writers, including Leijonhufvud (1981) and Laidler (1999).

15 Indeed, Marshall's statement of the theory of interest in the *Principles* is consistent with what he explains in *Money, Credit and Commerce* (1923: esp. 73–6, 254–8), including references to "loanable capital."

166   *Saving and capital*

16 This reflects Harrod's influence on Keynes; I elaborate below.
17 Keynes (1936: 139–41) reverses himself on this point and claims similarity between his use of the term "marginal efficiency of capital" and that of Marshall's and Irving Fisher's "rate of return over cost."
18 Founded on the notion that savings are a withdrawal or a leakage from the expenditure stream rather than the source of investible or loanable funds, the Keynesian multiplier analysis turns out to be erroneous; Ahiakpor 2001 elaborates on this point, including criticisms of Keynes's multiplier argument by A. C. Pigou, R. G. Hawtrey, and Dennis Robertson.
19 For accounts of Hicks's fifty-three-year-long process of getting to recognize the superiority of Marshall's theory of interest over Keynes's liquidity-preference theory, see Hicks 1989: 72, n. 2 and Ahiakpor 2003b: Ch. 11.
20 For a summary of the meaning of saving as funds borrowed to be spent, from the likes of Smith, Ricardo, and J. S. Mill, see Ahiakpor 1990 or 2003b: Chs. 4 and 5.
21 Also, see Ahiakpor 2003b: 91–2, 2018a.
22 Note that Pigou in that book does not claim the existence of continuous full employment in labor markets, contrary to Keynes's (1936) misattribution of that assumption to him; Ahiakpor 1997a elaborates on this point.
23 Even here, Tsiang is being mistakenly generous in treating Keynes's demand for "finance" as the same thing as "current transaction demand for money" (1956: 549). It is not money businesses invest, but savings or credit. Money is demanded to be held.
24 The referee evidently never cared to read documentation of Keynes's confusion over the meaning of "capital" in Ahiakpor 1990.

8   Saving and the errors of Keynes's critique of the loanable funds theory of interest

Introduction[1]

Jörg Bibow (2000) traces Keynes's (1936) criticisms of the loanable funds theory of interest to his having effectively made them in the *Treatise* (1930). In Bibow's judgment, Keynes's "*Treatise* disequilibrium analysis already proves that what was to become loanable funds theory later on is, indeed, *logically* inconsistent" (789; italics original). Thus, he argues that Keynes's denial of the validity of the classical theory of interest in the *General Theory* was simply a re-affirmation of his earlier logically consistent critique of the loanable funds theory: "in the *Treatise* Keynes preemptively kills off what was to become loanable funds theory after *The General Theory*" (797). Indeed, Dennis Robertson's early treatment of interest rate determination did not closely follow Marshall's (1920, 1923), but whose lineage Robertson (1936, 1937, 1940) subsequently claims in his puzzlement at Keynes's (1936) rejection of the classical "capital" supply and demand theory of interest. Keynes (1937b: 241, n. 2) thus appears to have been correct in arguing, "I regard Mr. Hawtrey as my grandparent and Mr. Robertson as my parent in the paths of errancy, and I have been greatly influenced by them," in his disagreeing with the validity of the classical theory of interest. To Keynes, the flaw in the classical theory is its arguing that the supply and demand for capital goods determine interest rates, while the loanable funds theory advocates had their flaw in claiming that increased savings supply loanable funds that cause a reduction in equilibrium interest rates. But both of Keynes's charges fundamentally derive from his misinterpretation of saving. The classics meant by saving, the supply of loanable "capital," but which Keynes (1936: 186–90) misinterpreted as capital goods (Ahiakpor 1990).[2] However, Robertson, Keynes's undergraduate student, along with the other neoclassicals, including R. G. Hawtrey, J. R. Hicks, and Bertil Ohlin (A. C. Pigou, as well), allowed cash hoarding to be included in savings, contrary to the classical definition of saving.

When saving is correctly defined as the acquisition of interest- and/or dividend-earning financial assets (e.g., Smith *WN*, 1: 358–9; Marshall 1920: 192, 1923: 46), Keynes's claim to have found a flaw in the neoclassical loanable funds theory of interest turns out to be incorrect. As Smith explains, the reason we save is "the desire of bettering our condition" (*WN*, 1: 362); cash hoarding, which pays no interest or dividends, could not be what people do when they save. Besides, no one borrows in order to hoard cash; they could not pay back the principal and interest when the loan's term is up. Also, increased saving by the public does not create "cash flow shortfalls" for consumption goods producers so as to nullify the interest rate reduction effect of increased saving, as Keynes (1930: 1, 145–6) claims and Bibow (2000: 795, 2001: 595–601) reasserts.[3] Some borrowed savings are spent on consumption goods too (Smith *WN*, 1: 359; J. S. Mill *Works*, 2: 70).

This chapter explains why previous attempts to resolve the liquidity-preference versus loanable funds theory dispute between Keynes and his contemporaries have proved unsatisfactory and given Bibow (2000, 2001) the confidence to assert Keynes's victory in that dispute. Keynes's liquidity-preference theory of interest rates persists as a legitimate alternative to the classical or loanable funds theory of interest in many macroeconomics textbooks. It is the basis of the upward-sloping LM curve and underlies Keynes's incorrect liquidity-trap proposition (Ahiakpor 2018a). Its persistence mostly reflects the failure of historians of economic thought to have fully clarified the classical meaning of money, saving, and "capital" that Keynes's work has obscured, besides the determination of most Keynes adherents not to reexamine Keynes's claims.[4]

There is need to pay careful attention to the definitions of these concepts by David Hume, Smith, Ricardo, and J. S. Mill, whose works Marshall (1920, 1923) drew upon to restate the classical theory of interest and the Quantity Theory of money. Even Robertson, Keynes's persistent critic over the theory of interest, paid hardly any attention to the classical literature. Rather than drawing upon that literature to address Keynes's conceptual problems in the *Treatise*, Robertson regarded the issues Keynes was grappling with as remaining "a field of appalling intellectual difficulty" and Keynes's ideas, "fertile and penetrating" (1931: 395). Bibow's (2000, 2001) bibliographies also show that he has paid scant attention to the classical definitions.

Keynes's unhelpful definitions of saving and investment

In the *Treatise*, Keynes defines saving simply as an individual's unspent income on consumption, $S = Y(1 - t) - C$: "Thus 'saving' relates to units of money and is the sum of the difference between money-incomes of individuals and their money-expenditures on current consumption" (1930: 1, 172). Keynes even considers savings deposited with banks as "hoarding" (1930: 1, 141, 144, n. 1). This follows his having defined "hoards" as the "stocks of liquid consumption-goods, and 'investing' (1930: 1, 125) to mean, *not the purchase of securities* by members of the public, but the act of the entrepreneur when he makes an addition to the capital of the community" (1: 141, n. 1; italics added). Keynes (1936: 74) similarly treats saving merely as the "excess of income over what is spent on consumption," which is therefore a withdrawal from expenditure stream. Thus, Keynes argues:

> An act of individual saving means – so to speak – a decision not to have dinner today. But it does *not* necessitate a decision to have dinner or to buy a pair

of boots a week hence or a year hence or to consume any specified thing at any specified date. Thus it depresses the business of preparing to-day's dinner without stimulating the business of making ready for some future act of consumption. It is not a substitution of future consumption demand for present consumption-demand, – it is a net diminution of such demand.

(1936: 210; italics original)

Keynes (1930) reasons that saving inflicts a deficit of cash flow upon producers of consumption goods, leading immediately to the reduction of their prices. Thus, while "savers are individually richer by the amount of their savings . . . the producers of consumption-goods, who have sold their current output at a lower price than they would have got if the savings had not taken place, are poorer by an equal amount" (1930: 1, 174). Consequently, Keynes argues,

Saving, instead of resulting in an increase of aggregate wealth, has merely involved a double transference – a transference of consumption *from* the savers to the general body of *consumers* [because of the fallen price of consumer goods], and a transfer of wealth *to* the savers from the general body of *producers*, both total consumption and total wealth remaining unchanged.

(1: 174; italics original)

Keynes's argument would be correct only if saving meant the hoarding of cash. Otherwise, increased saving, by transferring more non-consumed income to issuers of financial assets, would increase the price of those assets or securities, lower interest rates, and enable the funds acquired thereby to be spent on both non-consumption and consumption goods. The "general body of producers" therefore does not lose from increased saving; that is, increased saving does not change total spending.[5]

Keynes also sets up a source of confusion by defining investment not as the acquisition of interest- and/or dividend-earning assets by households or the employment of borrowed savings in the sphere of production, as the classics explain, but as only the acquisition of produced goods not purchased for consumption: "'investment' relates to units of goods" rather than to "units of money" (1930: 1, 172).[6] And while saving is a negative act in Keynes's view, "Investment . . . is the act of the entrepreneur whose function it is to make the decisions which determine the amount of the non-available output, and consists in the positive act of starting or maintaining some process of production or of withholding liquid goods" (1: 172; see also 1930: 2, 207). In the *General Theory*, Keynes similarly defines investment as "the current addition to the value of the capital equipment which has resulted from the productive activity of the period" (1936: 62).

Furthermore, according to Keynes, entrepreneurs are not constrained in their ability to invest by savings. Rather, "the proportion of the total output which shall be available [for consumption] has been determined *unequivocally* by the amount of investment which the entrepreneurs have decided to make" (1930: 1,

173; italics added).[7] Keynes's divorcing investment from savings is complete in his declaring,

> Thus when positive investment is taking place, consumption falls short of output quite *irrespective of the volume of saving*; and when investment is negative, consumption exceeds output also quite *irrespective* of the volume of saving. In short, the increase or decrease of capital depends on the amount of investment and *not on the amount of saving*.
>
> (1930: 1, 173; italics added)

Note that "capital" in Keynes's declaration refers to capital or producer's goods while saving refers to money-income not spent on consumption.

However, ignoring that savings are not cash hoarding, Keynes further reasons that an *individual's* act of saving, unless accompanied by "an additional act of investment by an entrepreneur" (1930: 1, 173) would depress the price of consumption goods:

> There is now in the market one purchaser less for consumption-goods, with the result that their prices fall. This fall of prices increases the purchasing power of the money-incomes of the rest of the community and they are able, therefore, to increase their consumption by the amount which the saver has foregone, whilst spending the same amount of money as before.
>
> (ibid.)

In fact, product prices do not immediately fall because of a reduction in their demand by one buyer. At worst, that may lead to a seller's income falling. It must take an accumulation of buyers' reduction of demand before product prices would fall. Rather, sellers initially may increase their inventories or producers reduce their rate of production before reducing their prices, following a reduced demand. But in Keynes's reasoning, one individual's saving leads to an escalating fall of consumption goods' prices: "If, however, these others then proceed to reduce correspondingly their money-expenditure on consumption and, consequently, to increase their savings, this only has the effect of still further increasing the purchasing power of the balance of their income which they do spend" (1: 173).

Keynes's argument may appear similar to Pigou's in *The Economics of Welfare* (1920: 812) quoted by Robertson (1931: 410, n. 1). However, contrary to Robertson's employment of Pigou's argument in support of Keynes's view of increased saving causing an accumulation of unpurchased goods, Pigou's point was to explain why such reasoning is "incorrect." Pigou (1920: 812–4) explains that businesses do not keep accumulating unsold goods in the face of reduced demand. He draws upon Professor Wesley Mitchell's argument in *Business Cycles* to make the point that, as depression proceeds,

> The accumulated stocks of goods carried over from the preceding period of prosperity are gradually disposed of. Even when current consumption is small,

manufactories and merchants can reduce their stocks of raw materials and finished wares by filling orders chiefly from what is on hand and confining purchases to the small quantities needed to keep full assortments.

(813)

Yet, Robertson (1931: 409–10) praises Keynes's argument as being

> right in laying stress on 'hoarding' as a dominant feature of trade depression. In this respect I feel sure his work [*Treatise*] is of high significance; for nine out of ten people, including many bankers, are still quite unable to see how, under a modern banking system, deposits which are 'in' the banks can fail to be 'used' by the banks in some way or other.

But as shown in Chapter 5 above, banks are not so much hoarders of money (cash) as are the public when confidence in banks is shaken, resulting in trade depression and possible price deflation.

Keynes also separates savings from investment even as he recognizes that savings may be used to purchase financial or real assets:

> That saving can occur without any corresponding investment is obvious, if we consider what happens when *an individual* refrains from spending his money-income on consumption. It does not matter what he does with the surplus – whether he deposits it at his bank, pays off a loan or buys a house or a security – provided it is not accompanied by an additional act of investment by an entrepreneur.

(1930: 1, 173; italics added)

In this view of saving, Keynes evidently does not distinguish "investment-demand" from "investment," the former being the acquisition of funds through issuing IOUs or debt instruments. Keynes thus appears not to appreciate that banks do not simply store up the public's deposits, but lend most of them (net of reserves) to borrowers, including "investors" or producers, who spend them. Keynes further ignores what the lenders do when repaid principal and interest, what the sellers of houses do with the proceeds of their sales, or what sellers of securities do with the funds they acquire.

All these recipients of savings spend them: those repaid their loans may make new loans to be spent or they themselves spend on consumption. The banks lend most of the savings to earn interest income. Similarly, the sellers of securities (investment demand) employ their funds productively in order to earn profits, out of which they pay interest on bonds or equity holders' dividends. Thus, if the prices of consumption goods fell, those of non-consumption goods would rise, leaving the general level of prices unchanged.

Keynes does not reach the above conclusions because he employs a set of unwarranted assumptions:

> a fall in the price of consumption goods due to an excess of saving over investment does not in itself – if it is unaccompanied by any change in the

bearishness or bullishness of the public or in the volume of savings-deposits, or if there are compensating changes in these two factors – require any opposite change in the price of new investment goods.

(1930: 1, 145)[8]

However, interpreting saving as the public's acquisition of financial assets supplied by investment-funds demanders or acquiring bank deposits that are loaned out, nullifies Keynes's enabling assumptions. Furthermore, Keynes does not accept the necessity of savings to fund borrowers' spending because he was convinced that banks' loans do not depend upon the public's deposited savings. Thus, without accounting for a bank's ability to redeem its liabilities in the form of loans to borrowers, Keynes insists,

> "a bank may create a claim against itself. It may itself purchase assets, i.e. add to its *investment*,[9] and pay for them, in the first instance at least, by establishing a claim in favour of a borrower, in return for his promise of subsequent reimbursement; i.e. it may make loans or advances".
>
> (1930: 1, 24; italics added)[10]

This even though Keynes well recognizes that borrowers quickly spend their loans rather than leave them on deposit, in contrast with savers for whom he claims banks passively open deposit accounts: "borrowing customers generally borrow with the intention of paying away *at once* the deposits . . . created in their favour" (1930: 1, 25; italics added). Ignoring that fact, Keynes argues,

> Practical bankers, like Dr. Walter Leaf, have [concluded] that for the banking system as a whole the [loan-creation] initiative lies with the depositors, and that the banks can lend no more than their depositors have previously entrusted to them. But economists cannot accept this as being the commonsense which it pretends to be.
>
> (1: 25)[11]

Keynes's firm belief in the autonomy of bank loans from deposited savings leads to his insistence that "Each Bank Chairman . . . may regard himself as the passive instrument of outside forces over which he has no control; yet the 'outside forces' may be nothing but himself and his fellow-chairmen, and *certainly not his depositors*" (1930: 1, 27; italics added). It is from such conviction that Keynes declares he has shown,

> [t]he familiar controversy as to how and by whom bank-deposits are "created" is a somewhat unreal one. There can be no doubt that, in the most convenient use of language, all deposits are "created" by the bank holding them. It is certainly not the case that the banks are limited to that kind of deposit, for the creation of which it is necessary that depositors should come on their own initiative bringing cash or cheques.
>
> (1930: 1, 30)[12]

Keynes does not mention banks having to make loans out of their equity capital (savings of banks' owners), borrowing from other banks, or borrowing from a central bank. He carries his view of bank loans being independent of savings also into the *General Theory*. He subsequently argues that "banks . . . control . . . the supply of money" (1937b: 248) and "the investment market can become congested through the shortage of cash. It can never become congested through the shortage of saving. This is the most fundamental of my conclusions within this field" (1937c: 669).

But the financial intermediation process Dr. Walter Leaf explains, and which Keynes rejects, is the familiar (savings) deposit expansion process explained in Chapter 5 above: A saver makes a deposit (in cash or claim to cash) with a bank, which the bank holds initially as reserves, $D_0 = R_0$. The bank extends credit (loan) on the basis of the deposit, holding back required reserves (R_d/D) and excess reserves (R_e/D) to meet the depositor's (saver's) expected future cash withdrawal, $BC_0 = (1 - r_d)(1 - r_e)D_0$, where r_d = required reserves-deposit ratio, r_e = excess reserves-deposit ratio. The savings generated out of the loan expenditure, net of cash hoarding (C/D = cu), equals $D_1 = (1 - cu)(1 - r_d)(1 - r_e)D_0$, where cu = households' or income-earners' currency-deposit ratio or currency drain. The next round of bank credit becomes, $BC_t = (1 - r_d)(1 - r_e)D_1 = (1 - cu)(1 - r_d)^2(1 - r_e)^2D_0$, and so on. Thus, bank loans, net of their own equity capital, are always some fraction of the community's deposits: $BC_t = (1 - cu)^t(1 - r_d)^{t+1}(1 - r_e)^{t+1}D_0$, t = 1, n. while deposits are, $D_t = (1 - cu)^t(1 - r_d)^t(1 - r_e)^tD_0$, t = 0, n. Banks' variations of their excess reserve-deposit ratios may change the volume of their loans, but the loans could not exceed the flow of depositors' savings unless banks also drew upon their own equity capital or borrowed from a central bank or from elsewhere.

Robertson ([1922] 1957) mostly follows the above logic of the deposit expansion and bank lending process when he observes that "the making of a bank loan is seen as the act not . . . of a fraudulent magician, but of a faithful steward, administering to the best of its ability a fund of *congealed saving* which has been *built up in the past*" (74; italics added). But Robertson leaves open a misperception by also claiming for an imaginary (Wicksellian) single-banking system, its ability to make loans without the receipt of savings: "Supposing [a bank] receives somehow (we need not for the moment enquire how) an accession to its reserves, we can be pretty sure that it will expand its loans by an amount several times as great as the increase in its reserves," since the bank "makes a profit on its loans" (75).[13] He does not say what would keep a bank from lending before it felt "a continuous pressure . . . to expand its loans," profitable as lending mostly is.[14] Even when Robertson addresses the case of a multi-banking system, he delays acknowledging that banks "may not, in the first instance, [make loans] much larger than the new [reserves themselves]" (76). This after arguing, "For with such a system, *as every banker knows*, it is *not open* to a bank which receives an accession of £1000 to its reserves *immediately to expand* its loans *by eight or nine times* that amount" (76; italics added). Indeed, the first loan can only be a fraction of the deposit ("accession"), $BC_0 = (1 - r_d)(1 - r_e)D_0 < D_0 = R_0$.

It is from the above mistaken belief that savings do not supply banks' loanable funds that are spent on investment or consumption goods, such that "the rate of interest is fixed at the level where the supply of credit, in the shape of saving, is equal to the demand for credit, in the shape of investment[-demand]" (Keynes 1937b: 245) that Keynes derives his mistaken conclusion that increased saving does not reduce the rate of interest. And this is a proposition Bibow (2000, 2001) cites as having exposed the fallacy of the loanable funds theory of interest.

Saving and the demand for financial assets

It helps to avoid one of Keynes's errors in his criticizing the loanable funds theory of interest to recognize savings as the acquisition of interest- and/or dividend-earning assets: "Whatever a person *saves* from his revenue [income] he *adds to his capital*, and either employs it himself in maintaining an additional number of productive hands, or enables some other person to do so, by lending it to him for an *interest*, that is, for a *share of the profits*" (Smith *WN*, 1: 358; italics added). Similarly, Ricardo explains:

> There are two ways in which capital [funds] may be accumulated: it may be saved either in consequence of increased revenue, or of *diminished consumption*. If my profits are raised from 1000*l*. to 1200*l*. while my expenditure continues the same, I accumulate annually 200*l*. more than I did before. If I save 200*l*. out of my expenditure, while my profits continue the same, the same effect will be produced; 200*l*. per annum will be added to my capital.
>
> (*Works*, 1: 131; italics added)

Marshall (1920: 191–6, 443–4, 482–4) makes the same point elaborately, citing the contributions of Smith and Ricardo, in particular, in restating the theory of "capital" (savings) and interest, and explaining interest as the reward for "waiting" to consume one's income. Thus, Marshall reacts to the confusions in Professor Eugen v. Böhm-Bawerk's disputing the validity of the classical "capital" supply and demand theory of interest by noting, the "scientific doctrine of capital has had a long history of continuous growth and improvement . . . during the last three centuries. Smith appears to have seen indistinctly, and Ricardo to have seen distinctly, almost everything of primary importance in the theory, very much as it is known now" (1920: 484). Marshall (1923) also directly links savings with the acquisition of interest- and/or dividend-earning financial assets rather than focusing on the difference between disposable income and consumption, as in Keynes's definition of saving, $S = Y(1 - t) - C = (\Delta FA^d + \Delta H_h)$. Marshall also explains: "in 'western' countries even peasants, if well to do, incline to *invest* the greater part of their savings in Government, and other familiar *stock exchange securities*, or to *commit* them to the charge of *a bank*" (1923: 46; italics added).

Understanding saving in the classical tradition – which is what savers actually do – also helps to link saving with consumption by productive laborers in the classical literature. Smith explains,

> By what a frugal man saves, he not only affords maintenance to an additional number of productive hands, but like the founder of a public workhouse, he

establishes as it were a *perpetual fund* for the maintenance of an equal number in all times to come. . . . No part of it can ever afterwards be employed to maintain any but *productive hands*, without an evident loss to the person who thus perverts it from its proper destination.

(*WN*, 1: 359–60; italics added)

Smith also links savings with *consumption* by those employed with the borrowed funds:

What is annually saved is as regularly consumed as what is annually spent, and nearly in the same time too; but it is consumed by a different set of people. That portion of his revenue which a rich man annually spends, is in most cases consumed by idle guests, and menial servants, who leave nothing behind them in return for their consumption. That portion which he annually saves, as for the sake of the profit it is immediately employed as a capital, is *consumed in the same manner*, and nearly in the same time too, but by a different set of people, by *labourers*, *manufacturers*, and *artificers*, who reproduce with a profit the value of their annual consumption.

(*WN*, 1: 359; italics added)

J.-B. Say's (1803) rendition of Smith's argument is that "the values which the wealthy save out of outlays on their personal pleasures in order to add to their capitals . . . are consumed; they furnish markets for many producers; but they are *consumed reproductively* and furnish markets for the useful goods that are capable of engendering still others, instead of being evaporated in frivolous consumption" (quoted in Baumol 1977: 150; italics added). Lautzenheiser and Yasar (2016: 104–5), in their defense of Keynes's failure to appreciate savings being spent reproductively, cite savings being employed to purchase "more machines" and thus impairing the business of bread production. But some or most of those employed in making machines purchase the bread that the savers may have abstained from consuming. Besides, with increased incomes from production employing more machinery, the demand for bread also will increase.

It was from understanding Smith's explanation of saving that Ricardo countered Thomas Malthus's reservations about too much saving inhibiting economic growth. Malthus first concedes: "It is not, of course, meant to be stated that parsimony [saving], or even a temporary diminution of consumption, is not often in the highest degree useful, and sometimes absolutely necessary to the progress of wealth" (quoted in Ricardo *Works*, 2: 325–6). Malthus's reservation is,

that no nation can *possibly* grow rich by an accumulation of capital, arising from a permanent diminution of consumption; because, such accumulation being greatly beyond what is wanted, in order to supply the effective demand for produce, a part of it would very soon lose both its use and its value, and cease to possess the character of wealth.

(Ricardo *Works*, 2: 326; italics original)

Ricardo's effective rebuttal of Malthus's argument is: "By accumulation of capital from revenue is meant an increase of *consumption* by *productive labourers* instead of unproductive labourers. Consumption is as certain in one case as in the other, the difference is only in the quantity of *productions returned*" (*Works*, 2: 326–7 n.; italics added). Ricardo further notes, "Mr. Malthus never appears to remember that to save is to spend [on income-earning assets], as surely, as what he exclusively calls spending" (*Works*, 2: 449).

Indeed, saving does not entail "a permanent diminution of consumption" as Malthus feared. Rather, increased saving is the path to raising the level of consumption in the future, as incomes increase. J. S. Mill makes the same point, arguing: "Whatever increases the productive powers of labour, creates an *additional fund* to make savings from, and enables capital to be *enlarged* not only *without additional privation*, but concurrently with an *increase of personal consumption*" (*Works*, 2: 70; italics added; see also J. S. Mill *Works*, 2: 83–4).

Ricardo also has in mind the fact that increased savings decrease equilibrium interest rates, and possibly alter savers' allocation of income between saving, consumption, and cash hoarding, if necessary: the three-margin analysis that Keynes (1930, 1936) fails to employ. Malthus recalls the same analysis by Ricardo:

> Whenever capital increases too fast, the motive to accumulation diminishes, and there will be a natural tendency to spend [on consumption] and save less. When profits rise, the motive to accumulation will increase, and there will be a tendency to spend a smaller proportion of the gains, and to save a greater. These tendencies, operating on individuals, direct them towards the just mean, which they would more frequently attain if they were not interrupted by bad laws or unwise exhortations.
>
> (Ricardo *Works*, 2: 449)

As Smith already explained, the reason we save is to better ourselves. Few would maintain the same rate of saving if it meant diminishing their own well-being.

J. S. Mill incorporates the Smith-Ricardo explanations in his second and third fundamental theorems respecting "capital," namely, (1) "capital" is "the result of saving" (*Works*, 2: 68) and (2)

> The word saving does not imply that what is saved in not consumed, nor even necessarily that its consumption is deferred; but only that, if consumed immediately, it is not consumed by the person who saves it. If merely laid by for future use, it is said to be hoarded; and while hoarded, it is not consumed at all. But if employed as capital, it is all consumed; though not by the capitalist. Part is exchanged for tools or machinery, which are worn out by use; part for seed or materials, which are destroyed as such by being sown or wrought up, and destroyed altogether by the consumption of the ultimate product. The remainder is paid in wages to productive labourers, who consume it for their daily wants; or if they in their turn save any part, this also is not, generally

speaking, hoarded, but (through savings banks, benefit clubs, or some channel) re-employed as capital, and consumed.

(Works, 2: 70)

J. S. Mill thus emphasizes the fact that "Saving, in short, enriches, and spending impoverishes, the community along with the individual; which is but saying
in other words, that society at large is richer by what it expends in maintaining
and aiding productive labour, but poorer by what it consumes in its enjoyments"
(Works, 2: 72).

The significance of the classical definition of saving, which Marshall also
employs, leads us readily to recognize that saving does not entail cash hoarding.
Marshall's version of the classical view, which Keynes (1936: 19; italics added)
quotes but fails to interpret correctly, states:

> The whole of a man's income is expended in the purchase of services and of
> commodities. It is indeed commonly said that a man spends some portion of
> his income and saves another. But it is a familiar economic axiom that a man
> *purchases labour and commodities* with that portion of his income which he
> *saves* just as much as he does with that he is said to spend. He is said to spend
> when he seeks to obtain present enjoyment from the services and commodi-
> ties which he purchases. He is said to save when he causes the labour and the
> commodities which he purchases to be devoted to the production of wealth
> from which he expects to derive the *means of enjoyment* [i.e., profits or inter-
> est income] in the *future*.

Contrast with Keynes's (1936: 210) insistence that saving "is not a substitution of
future consumption-demand for present consumption-demand, – it is a net diminution of such demand." Indeed, Keynes (1936: 20) misinterprets Marshall to
have been arguing that "if people do not spend their money in one way they will
spend it in another." Keynes (1937a: 223) repeats the misinterpretation, claiming there is "the tacit assumption that every individual spends the whole of his
income either on consumption or on buying, directly or indirectly, newly produced
capital goods." But Marshall was talking about people spending their (disposable)
incomes in three ways, on consumption, savings, and holding money (hoarding).

Robertson unhelpfully follows Keynes's lumping saving with cash hoarding in
his focusing on the non-consumption of one's income as the meaning of saving
rather than separating the two, for instance, "A man is said to be *saving* if he spends
on consumption less than his disposable income" (*Economic Journal* 1933, quoted
in Robertson 1940: 77; italics original). Robertson thus does not explicitly address
the three separate returns to (a) saving, (b) cash hoarding, and (c) consumption to
income earners. He adopts various meanings of saving as the extent to which an
income earner "lacks" consumption or is "Lacking" – voluntarily or induced. By
induced or forced "lacking," Robertson means the reduction in real consumption of
fixed-income earners (wages, interest, and rents) that results from the rise of prices
or the classical forced saving, such as "the imposition of Lacking does not hit all

classes equally, but bears with special weight on those whose money-incomes do not respond readily to price-changes" (Robertson 1949: 75). Worse yet, Robertson includes saving in bank deposits in his definition of "hoarding," just as Keynes (1930: 1, 141) does, for instance, in the statement that "an increased desire of somebody to 'hoard,' that is, to keep resources idle in the form of bank deposits" (Robertson 1931: 401); Robertson (*Economic Journal* 1933, reproduced in 1940: 80) repeats the same treatment of saving as "hoarding."

In his *Money* ([1922] 1957: 178–9) Robertson repeats that misleading definition of saving as hoarding:

> a person . . . may be said to hoard in any period if he takes steps to increase the proportion existing at the beginning of that period between his money stock and his money income. A simple case of hoarding occurs if a man saves part of his income and leaves it on current account at a bank.

This was an unhelpful concession to Keynes, given Robertson's awareness that the "stream of money . . . is normally spent, *on the part of some one*" (1931: 400; italics original).

Bibow (2000: 800) cites Robertson's 1931 erroneous inclusion of saving in "hoarding" to argue his presumed fallacy of the loanable funds theory of interest rates (see also Bibow 2000: 822). Bibow (2001: 604, n. 3) also cites Keynes's 1938 criticism of Robertson for not having separated hoarding from saving in support of his own mistaken view of the loanable funds theory of interest being a fallacy: "It is Robertson's incorrigible confusion between the revolving fund of money in circulation and the flow of new saving which causes all his difficulties." But the confusion is Keynes's: money is demanded to hold whereas savings are a means to spend, as in "circulating capital."

Robertson also explains that his analysis in *Banking Policy and the Price Level*, which treats saving with banks as "hoarding," was very much influenced by his discussions with Keynes: "I have had so many discussions with Mr. J. M. Keynes on the subject matter . . . and have re-written [the relevant chapters] so drastically at his suggestion, that I think neither of us now knows how much of the ideas herein contained is his and how much is mine" (1949: 5). He notes, for example, "Induced Lacking belongs to Mr. Keynes" (1949: 50, n.). But Keynes's (1930, 1936) grouping saving with cash hoarding follows his having adopted a two-margin analysis of an income earner's spending decision rather than three margins concurrently.

The three-margin analysis is employed in the work of Pigou (1912: 425, 1924: 179–81), Lavington (1921: 30), and Robertson (1936: 189–90, 1940: 27; see also Patinkin (1965 [1956]: 94, 378–9). Marshall's (1920: 191–2; italics added) equalization of utilities at more than two margins is as follows:

> Anyone, who has a stock of a commodity which is applicable to *several uses*, endeavours to distribute it *between them all* in such a way as to give him the greatest satisfaction. If he thinks he could obtain more satisfaction by

transferring some of it from one use to another he will do so. If, therefore, he makes his distribution rightly, he stops in applying it to each several use at such a point that he gets an equal amount of good out of the application he is just induced to make of it to each separate use; (in other words, he distributes it between the *different uses* in such a way that it has the *same marginal utility* in each).

Instead, Keynes's two-margin approach fuses together the reward to saving (purchasing financial assets) and the utility services of cash hoarding as the alternative to the satisfaction from consumption:

> When a man is deciding what proportion of his money-income to save, he is choosing between present consumption and the ownership of wealth. . . ., in so far as he decides in favour of saving, there still remains a further decision for him to make. For he can own wealth by holding it either in the form of money (or the liquid equivalent of money) or in other forms of loan or real capital. The second decision [non-consumption] might be conveniently described as the choice between "hoarding" and "investing", or, alternatively, as the choice between "bank-deposits" and "securities".
>
> (1930: 1, 140–1)

But bank deposits are not cash hoarding; they earn interest income, just as securities, even if at a lower rate.

Keynes (1936: 166) repeats the above erroneous claim, which prompts Frank Knight's (1937) criticism of his liquidity-preference theory of interest as "the most difficult part of the whole [of Keynes's] construction to take seriously" (112).[15] Knight explains,

> It is self-evident that at any time (and at the margin) the rate of interest equates *both* the desirability of holding cash with the desirability of holding non-monetary wealth *and* the desirability of consuming with that of lending and so with both the other two desirabilities. For, to any person who has either money or wealth in any form, or to anyone who holds salable service-capacity, all three of these alternatives are continuously open.
>
> (ibid.: 112–3; italics original)

Mostly after the publication of Keynes's *General Theory* did Robertson start clearly to invoke Marshall's parentage for the loanable funds theory of interest he defended against Keynes's criticisms. Robertson (1940: 12) argues:

> The rate of interest [is] the market price of the hire of something which Marshall called "free or floating capital", which others have called "capital disposal" or "command over capital", and which recent writers seem to have settled down to calling "loanable" or "investible funds". This price, like other market prices, can be conceived as emerging from the interaction of schedules

of supply and demand, showing the amount of loanable funds which, at given hiring-prices, people are respectively willing to put on to, and to take off, the market during the slice of time selected for observation.

Robertson's argument follows Marshall's (1920: 443) explanation that "interest, being the price paid for the use of capital in any market, tends towards an equilibrium level such that the aggregate demand for capital in that market, at that rate of interest, is equal to the aggregate stock forthcoming there at that rate." Keynes (1936: 186–7) quotes an extended version of Marshall's explanation and misinterprets "capital" in the statement as capital goods. This in spite of Marshall's explanation, including, "the general *fund of capital*" (1920, 443; italics added) and the extensive explanation of interest being earned on loans of "capital" or savings (1920: 191–6; see Chapter 7).

But hardly does any Keynes scholar, including Patinkin (1976), Leijonhufvud (1968, 1981, 2006), Laidler (1999, 2006), Skidelsky (1983, 1995, 2016), Blaug (1995, 1996), Michael Lawlor (1997, 2006), Roger Backhouse (1999, 2006), and Bibow (2000, 2001) appear to have recognized Keynes's misinterpretation of "capital" as fundamental to his rejecting the classical theory of interest. Hume's (1752) essay, "Of Interest," negating any permanent role of money in determining the level of interest rates, also appears not to have made any impression on their interpretation of Keynes.[16]

Indeed, Keynes (1937b: 245) recognizes proponents of the loanable funds theory of interest as defending "the classical doctrine" regarding interest rate determination in Marshall. Marshall's statement of the classical theory of interest, which Robertson (1940) restates, can be seen as a close rendition of J. S. Mill's (*Works*, 3: 647; italics added), as noted earlier (e.g., in Chapters 5 above):

> The rate of interest will be such as to equalize the *demand for loans* with the *supply of them*. It will be such, that exactly as much as some people are desirous to borrow at that rate, others shall be willing to lend. If there is more offered than demanded, interest will fall; if more is demanded than offered, it will rise; and in both cases, to the point at which the equation of supply and demand is re-established.

Keynes's failure to separate saving from cash hoarding also underlies his insistence,

> It should be obvious that the rate of interest cannot be a return to saving or waiting as such. For if a man hoards his savings in cash, he earns no interest, though he saves just as much as before. On the contrary, the mere definition of the rate of interest tells us in so many words that the rate of interest is the reward for parting with liquidity [cash] for a specified period.
>
> (1936: 167)

Keynes (1936: 182) repeats the argument: "The mistake [in classical interest theory] originates from regarding interest as the reward for waiting as such, instead of as the reward for not-hoarding" (see also 1936: 174). But income not hoarded in cash could be used to purchase consumption goods which would not earn interest; only purchasing a financial asset does, as the classics explain.

Thus, attempts to sort out Keynes's dispute with the loanable funds theory of interest but without first separating saving from cash hoarding (e.g., Pigou 1936: 125; Viner 1936: 157; Hawtrey 1937: 441; Ohlin 1937: 425; S. C. Tsiang 1956), could not have been completely successful (Ahiakpor 2003b: 92–4). Bibow's (2000, 2001) revival of Keynes's side of the dispute shows this, indicating his little understanding of the classical theory of interest the neoclassicals were attempting to defend.[17] He believes,

> Keynes's vision of capital accumulation is diametrically opposed to the loanable fund one. Starting from an older vision of capital accumulation in corn economies, with a *real* saving fund as the classical source of investment 'finance,' loanable funds theorists merely annex hoarding and banks, i.e., *monetary* factors, to the usual corn economic picture.
>
> (2001: 609; italics original)

The classics described "corn economies"?

But read the classical literature in which savings may be transferred to borrowers through banks in the form of cash (money), banknotes, or discounted bills to be employed as "fixed" and/or "circulating" capital, inclusive of cash-on-hand, rather than savings disappearing "in the banking system" (Bibow 2001: 594, 606). Bibow's claims to have proven the fallacy of the loanable funds theory of interest become meaningless. Also, were Bibow fully conversant with the classical literature, he would not have attempted to defend Keynes's liquidity-preference theory against the loanable funds alternative with, "All money in this economy is of the 'inside' type" (2001: 595)! He also would not, in the same article, talk about banks supplying the "cash" needed by investors (ibid.: 610); "inside money" are bank deposits, not "cash."

The chronology of saving and investment

Keynes's apparently winning argument against the classical savings theory of interest and economic growth for his followers derives from his having included saving with cash hoarding while banks are able to finance investment spending without relying on savings. But the classical definition of saving as the purchasing of interest- and/or dividend-earning assets readily helps us to underscore the logical precedence of savings over investment spending, a point Bibow (2000) misses. Cash may be a means through which the public's savings are borrowed. Checks and electronic transfers also may be used. This is a point the classical economists labored to explain, for example, Smith (*WN*, 1: 373) comments: "Almost all loans are made in money, either of paper, or of gold and silver. But what the borrower really wants, and what the lender really supplies him with, is not the money, but the money's worth, or the goods which it can purchase."

Furthermore, the flow of investment spending over, say, one year, is typically greater than the quantity of money (cash) savers may employ in transferring savings to borrowers, as Smith (*WN*, 1: 374; italics added) well explains:

> Money, is as it were, but the deed of assignment, which conveys from one hand to another those capitals [savings] which the owners do not care to employ themselves. Those capitals may be greater in almost any proportion, than the amount of the money which serves as the *instrument of their convey-ance*, the same pieces of money successively serving for many different loans, as well as for many different purchases.

J. S. Mill (*Works*, 3: 508) reiterates the explanation:

> When one person lends to another . . . what he transfers is not the mere money, but a right to a certain value of the produce of the country, to be selected at pleasure; the lender having first bought this right, by giving for it a portion of his capital. What he really lends is so much capital; the money is the mere instrument of transfer.

That is why Ricardo (*Works*, 3: 92) warns of the "absurdity" of presuming that, by printing paper money to lend, a central bank can permanently lower interest rates and promote economic prosperity rather than diminish the value of banknotes themselves, which equals raising prices.

But Keynes claims that businesses' demand for "finance" is their demand for "money." He insists: "'finance' constitutes . . . an additional demand for *liquid cash* in exchange for a deferred claim. It is, in the *literal sense*, a *demand for money*" (1937b: 248; italics added). And to Keynes, only the banks supply money; savers play no role in the process of bank lending; Bibow (2000: 792–3) repeats Keynes's misunderstanding. He also argues, "Investment spending decisions – the firms' desire to accumulate – which set the pace of the system, are made by entrepreneurial investors. Their realization has nothing to do with the 'saving decisions' of households, whatever that may be" (2000: 816). Further failing to appreciate the savings-deposit expansion process outlined above, Bibow (2000: 820) reiterates Keynes's mistaken claim: "Finance necessarily precedes investment and saving. Saving, by contrast, can never be a source of finance for investment."

So impressed is Bibow by Keynes's mistaken declarations of the irrelevance of savings as the source of investible funds that he claims, because of Keynes's critique of the loanable-funds theory, "we [are] spared from those popular, but misguided, policy measures that stress, chronologically, saving before investing" (2000: 826). Also, Bibow (2001: 610; italics original) argues,

> In short, in monetary production economies, the classical saving fund is to be written out of the play. At any time, the investors' need for cash can only be satisfied out of two alternative sources, either by attracting already exist-ing deposits [by savers?], or by the banks' new creation of them [out of thin

air?]. . . . By contrast, additional saving, i.e., a rise in thrift, cannot possibly alleviate the investors' need for *money* (not saving!)

Were Bibow familiar with the classical literature explained above, he would have recognized the error in Keynes's claim that businesses seek money to invest rather than savings or loanable funds. Also, only central banks create money (cash), not banks (Keynes 1936: 174)!

Empirical evidence regularly has confirmed that where central banks have printed money (cash) excessively, they have not kept interest rates low or promoted increased investment and economic growth, but rather have caused higher rates of inflation and higher interest rates, just as Ricardo (*Works*, 3: 92) warns (see also Ricardo *Works*, 1: 363–4; Ahiakpor 2004: 604, n. 9). J. S. Mill (*Works*, 3: 656) similarly explains, "Suppose money to be in process of depreciation by means of an inconvertible currency . . . [the] increase of currency really affects the rate of interest, but in the contrary way to that which is generally supposed; by raising, not lowering it." Marshall (1923: 73) repeats the point: "a fall in the purchasing power of money tends, after a while, to raise the rate of interest on investments, whether for long periods, or short." This is the phenomenon Keynes (1930: 2, 198) calls the "Gibson Paradox"; but it is no paradox. It is a real tragedy for modern monetary and macroeconomic analysis and policy formulation that there continue to be significant adherents to Keynes's liquidity-preference theory of interest rates, in opposition to the classical "capital" or savings supply and demand theory.

Summary and conclusions

Keynes explains that he reached his liquidity-preference theory of interest rates *after* having failed to recognize a valid theory of interest in extant classical analysis, mostly in Marshall's *Principles*. Keynes argues that, in his critique of the classical theory of interest,

> The initial novelty lies in my maintaining that it is not the rate of interest, but the level of incomes which ensures equality between saving and investment. The arguments which lead up to this initial conclusion are independent of my subsequent [liquidity-preference] theory of the rate of interest, and in fact I reached it before I had reached the latter theory. But the result of it was to leave the rate of interest in the air.
>
> (1937b: 250)

Thus, when one understands the classical "capital" supply and demand theory of interest that the neoclassical writers were restating as the loanable funds theory, one readily can understand the significance of Keynes's misinterpreting "capital" to mean capital goods in that theory. It also helps to recognize his treating saving, not as purchasing interest- and/or dividend-earning assets by income earners, but merely as the non-consumption of income, to have aided his difficulties. Most Keynes scholars have ignored this aspect of Keynes's scholarship. They instead have been inclined only to tell the story of how Keynes developed a new macroeconomics – actually a revival of mercantilist monetary analysis that the classical writers, especially from Hume's (1752) essays, "Of Money" and "Of Interest," explained to be erroneous.

Dennis Robertson aided in sustaining Keynes's confusions over the loanable funds theory of interest by including saving with banks in "hoarding" and asserting that such savings may remain unspent. He praised Keynes's arguments in the *Treatise* that blame trade depression on "hoarding," and by implication, increased savings. Robertson also earlier thought it was legitimate to claim, "Saving is the one thing that cannot be saved" (1931: 400), again linking saving with "not spending money" (410, n. 1). Though banks always must keep cash reserves against savers' deposits, they always lend most of the saved funds to borrowers in order to earn interest income to cover their operating expenses and earn profits. If bank deposits could all be hoarded, then Keynes and his followers have a valid point in arguing that savings do not supply loanable funds. But Robertson's concession was a mistake; he easily could have learned otherwise from Smith's (*WN*) chapters on money and banking, and on "stock lent at interest."

It is testimony to the enduring influence of Keynes's work on some modern analysts that a referee (*History of Political Economy*), rejecting my shorter comment on Bibow (2000), argues, "Theorists and Historians rightly have grown tired of this inconclusive" loanable fund versus liquidity-preference debate. The referee mistakenly claims my paper

> Falters on the lack of recognition of the distinction between long-run and short run views. Loanable fund theory is really a long-run view of the factors that are important is [sic] determining the interest rate over long periods. JMK, and liquidity preference theory, for obvious reasons having to do with the state of the economies of the west in the 1930s, were focused on the short run determinants of interest (as well as the short run determinants of output, income, employment, etc. . . .

But the loanable funds theory of interest is not just about long-run determinants of interest rates; anyone who understands Hume's (1752) "Of Interest," that underlies restatements of the theory of interest by Smith, Ricardo, J. S. Mill, and Marshall, knows this. Besides, we must move from the short run to get to the long run.

The referee also considers it a demerit of my comment that I did not refer to Irving Fisher's writing on the theory of interest since Keynes claimed to have been influenced by him: "The lack of reference to Irving Fisher in defining the loanable funds view (in favor of Marshall and Ricardo) seems curious. JMK cited Fisher's work as influential in his own work and explicitly cites Marshall and Ricardo as writers that he is opposing his views to." But, as Ahiakpor (1990) explains, Fisher's treatment of the theory of interest was of little help to Keynes's recognizing his misinterpretation of the classical theory. Fisher had subscribed to the Austrian time-preference theory of interest and wrote, the "student should . . . try to forget all former notions concerning the so-called supply and demand of capital as the causes of interest. Since capital is merely the translation of future expected income into present cash value, whatever supply and demand we have to deal with are rather the supply and demand of future income" (1930: 32; see also Ahiakpor 2003b: 135). The referee's ignorance of the literature rather contributed a basis for her/his rejecting my comment on Bibow (2000).

Furthermore, the referee did not like my lack of "sympathy for JMK's position" against proponents of the loanable funds theory of interest. Strangely, to me, the referee believes, "Such sympathy seems called for if one is to objectively, and historically, evaluate how JMK pursued his chosen goals in 1936." But I was explaining the errors of Keynes's critique of the loanable funds theory of interest. My lack of sympathy for Keynes's position should be irrelevant to whether the case I made against Keynes was valid or not.

A second referee (*History of Political Economy*) also accepts as correct Keynes's (1930) claims of a cash-flow shortfall for producers of consumption goods, following increased savings, thereby causing producers to increase their borrowing and to nullify a downward pressure on interest rates. The referee does not recognize that businesses losing demand for their products do not increase their borrowing to maintain their rates of production but rather cut back on production instead. The referee also may not be conversant with the classical (Smith, Ricardo, J. S. Mill, Marshall) explanation that savings are spent by borrowers, including those hired in production, who spend some of the funds on consumption goods. Thus, the referee restates, incorrectly, Bibow's (2000) rendition of Keynes's *Treatise* argument:

> Keynes argues that the increase in thrift on the part of households cannot reduce the rate of interest analyzed in terms of the LF doctrine, because the increased supply [demand][18] of financial assets on the part of households trying to save will be exactly offset by the increased demand [supply] of financial assets on the part of producers seeking to cover the resulting shortfall of revenue from the sale of consumer goods from which they have to defray their costs of production.

And, rather than recognizing Keynes's path to his erroneous criticisms of the classical theory of interest being restated as the loanable funds theory, as I argued in my note, the referee believes my "marshalling of classical authorities against Keynes" to be "both tiresome and fruitless." This because my strategy "supposes that there is a logical error in the Keynesian position, and that the error can be exposed merely by citing authorities that Keynes and Bibow have already rejected."

But as I have explained above, Bibow might not have sided with Keynes's erroneous claims about interest rates not being determined by the supply and demand for savings or "capital" and that investment spending does not depend upon the availability of savings, had he understood the classical concepts of "capital," saving, and money. The principal errors in Keynes's critique of the loanable funds (classical) theory of interest derive from his (1) treating saving as only the nonspending of income on consumption, (2) failure to link savings directly with the supply of loanable funds, (3) belief in the ability of banks to create loans out of "thin air," and (4) treating investment demand as demand for money (cash) rather than as demand for credit or loans.

Such is the prevalence of Keynes's errors in modern macroeconomics in need of being corrected, at least for the Keynes adherents. To treat the loanable funds theory of interest as a fallacy is rather the fallacy. An increased demand for money (to hold) at the expense of purchasing financial assets (saving) reduces the flow of savings and raises interest rates, given the demand for savings, in the short run. But a decreased demand for money (to hold), concurrently with an increased demand for financial assets, increases the flow of savings and reduces interest rates in the short run, given the demand for savings (see also Chapter 7). Only by confusing saving with the demand for money (hoarding) does such a clear and correct conclusion escape an analyst, including Keynes and Bibow.

Notes

1 This chapter elaborates a comment I unsuccessfully tried to publish in the *History of Political Economy*, reacting to Jörg Bibow's (2000) article. A referee for the journal had cited it as a source from which I better could understand the confusion between Roy Harrod and Keynes over the classical theory of interest, contrary to the argument I was making in my submitted manuscript (see Chapter 7). I discuss two referees' reasons for rejecting my comment in the conclusion to this chapter. Given the prevalence of Keynes's liquidity-preference theory of interest in the macroeconomics literature, including its underlying his liquidity-trap proposition, it is worth explaining the flaws in Keynes's critique of the loanable funds theory of interest that Bibow (2000, 2001) and many Keynesians do not appear to have recognized. I also draw upon my unpublished comment on de Boyer (2010) that was rejected for being too long and too narrowly focused on his article.
2 Hardly does any Keynes scholar, including Bibow (2000, 2001), address this aspect of Keynes's dispute with the classical or loanable funds theory of interest.
3 A "cash flow shortfall" connotes businesses continuing to produce at an unchanged rate, following a decreased demand for their products, but not finding payments to cover their unchanged costs. Rather, businesses adjust their rates of production in order to eliminate inventories. Also, businesses facing a reduced demand do not increase their borrowing. But, failing to appreciate the point, Lautzenheiser and Yasar (2016: 105) repeat Keynes's employing the cash-flow-shortfall argument to credit him with having successfully attacked the classical "citadel," also citing Bibow (2000, 2001).
4 In private communication with Bibow (26 February 2018), I posed the following question: "Now, if one recognizes that banks lend most of the public's deposits (rather than hoard them); consumption goods producers do not necessarily continue at their original rates of production in the face of reduced demand; and that borrowed savings are always spent, some on 'productive workers' who spend them on consumption goods (Smith *WN*,1: 359, 'What is annually saved is as regularly consumed as what is annually spent, and nearly in the same time too; but it is consumed by a different set of people,' does your conviction in the fallacy of the loanable funds theory still stand? If so, how?" His response was, "Of course it stands." I pressed further, "How so?" His reply: "Because the argument is clearly right." No room for a reconsideration. See also Roy Grieve (2018), who insists on claiming that the classics presumed "income saved is automatically put into the production of capital goods" (275), after my pointing out his failure to interpret classical saving and investment correctly (2018b).

5 Robertson (1931: 399) makes the same point, which Bibow (2000) ignores. Robertson argues that a reduction in the price of consumption goods as a result of increased saving should increase the price level of investment goods. Robertson also notes Keynes's self-contradiction of denying that on page 136 of the *Treatise* but accepting it on page 143, adding, "we need not take the statement on p. 136 too much to heart" (1931: 398). However, Robertson undermines his own criticism of Keynes on this point by accepting the validity of Keynes's argument that "the additional savings of the public [may] remain unspent," that is, "hoarded" (399). Saving and hoarding are not the same thing, as previously explained.

6 Robertson (1931: 399–400) notes the "fog" that Keynes (1930) creates for understanding through his uses of "investment," "new investment goods," and "investments" at different places rather than in the ordinary sense of "stock exchange securities."

7 Ahiakpor (1995) explains why it is unhelpful to designate some products strictly as consumption goods and others as investment goods. Flour or fish bought for home cooking are consumption goods while they are a part of circulating capital if bought for further processing into bread or canned food. The same goes for lumber bought for home furniture repair being a consumption good while it is part of a furniture manufacturing company's circulating capital.

8 Bibow (2000, 2001) leaves out Keynes's qualifying conditions in reaching the conclusion that savings cause the price of consumption goods to fall without the price of non-consumption goods rising. Lautzenheiser and Yasar (2016: 106) appear to recognize the necessity of this condition for the conclusion, identifying Keynes's "bearishness" with increased hoarding. But they do not question Keynes's identification of increased saving with increased cash hoarding by banks.

9 Note that Keynes here uses "investment" in the financial sense, contrary to his insistence elsewhere only on its meaning acquiring "capital goods"!

10 Bibow (2001: 595, 610) repeats the erroneous claim. Irving Fisher (1935: 17) makes a similar claim about banks being capable of "manufacturing money out of thin air"! If banks could lend without depending upon someone else's savings, why would they pay interest to savers, dividends to equity holders, or borrow from a central bank at interest to lend?

11 Robertson's ([1922] 1957: 42) claiming that "Bank money [deposit] . . . is created not by the public but by the bankers, when they accord to the holders of cheque-books the right to draw cheques" is similar to Keynes's mistakenly denying the dependence of bank loans on the public's savings.

12 In reality, depositors do go "on their own initiatives bringing cash or cheques" to entrust their savings with banks.

13 For an explanation of the misleading nature of Wicksell's argument, see Ahiakpor 1999 or Ahiakpor 2003b: Ch. 7.

14 Like his teacher, Keynes (1930: 1, 25), Robertson also appears to doubt bankers' explanation that "They can only lend what the public has entrusted to them" ([1922] 1957: 76).

15 This appears to conflict with Knight's 16 September 1936 comment in his Business Cycle class as recorded by Perham C. Nahl (Cristiano and Fiorito 2016: 85): "Keynes's analysis of 'liquidity preference' seems to be the best part of his book. The term is all right when applied to frightened individuals, but poor as descriptive of business psychology." Knight (1937) appropriately does not endorse Keynes's employing liquidity preference to determine the level of interest rates as the Cristiano and Fiorito (2016: 76–7) reference to Knight's comment might suggest.

16 Hume explains that low interest rates arise from low demand to borrow, great riches to supply the demand or low profits arising from commerce rather than from the abundance of money, whereas high interest rates arise from a high demand to borrow, little riches to supply the demand, and high profits in commerce rather than from the scarcity of money (1752: 49).

17 This is truly remarkable since Bibow's (2000, 2001) analysis draws upon his 1995 Ph.D. thesis, and he presented his papers at several academic conferences in Europe and North America before their publication. Did no participants at these conferences or journals' referees alert him to the serious gap in his understanding of the relevant classical literature?
18 Savers demand financial assets; borrowers supply them.

9   The IS-MP model

A worse alternative to the IS-LM model

Introduction[1]

Macroeconomists continue to struggle with trying to develop models that accurately represent the workings of a monetary economy other than adopting the classical macroeconomic analysis Keynes's *General Theory* (1936) sought to displace. This because the "neoclassical synthesis" embodied in Hick's (1937) rendition of Keynes's (1936, 1937a) arguments in the IS-LM (originally IS-LL) model, supposedly superior to extant "classical" macroeconomic analysis in the works of Marshall[2] and A. C. Pigou, has been found to be unsatisfactory.[3] Thus, David Romer (2000) proposes his IS-MP model as an easier alternative to teaching the IS-LM model to undergraduate economics students and for "use as a starting point for policy analysis" (150). More importantly, Romer claims the model better represents central banks' focus since the early 1980s on controlling *real* interest rates rather than the level or growth rate of the "money stock," such as M1 or M2. Indeed, Milton Friedman (1984b) prescribes freezing a central bank's monetary base or zero growth of central banks' money, having found that his 1967 prescription (Friedman 1968a) of a constant M1 or M2 growth rule was not being followed. However, Friedman did not base the prescription on the desirability of a central bank's controlling interest rates, but rather on the unhelpful ground that zero is a more politically defensible number than any positive or negative growth rate for the quantity of money.[4]

The IS-MP model has failed to gain popularity with many macroeconomics textbook writers who rather focus on central banks' attempting since the 1990s to target inflation rates, using variations in short-term interest rates they can most influence as the means (Bernanke and Mishkin 1997). Among the macroeconomics textbook writers, I have found only R. Glenn Hubbard, Anthony O'Brien, and Matthew Rafferty (2014) to have taken the IS-MP model seriously. Hubbard and O'Brien's (2018) money and banking text also discusses the model extensively. This although Romer (2013: vi) cites N. Gregory Mankiw's intermediate macroeconomics text as a foundational companion to his exposition: "I have designed the [teaching] document to work most closely with N. Gregory Mankiw's textbook." Rather, Mankiw (2013: 533–4) discusses inflation targeting, just as most other macro texts, including those by Andrew Abel, Ben Bernanke, and Dean Croushore

(2014, 574–6), Robert Barro (2008: 386–7, 403–4), Olivier Blanchard and David Johnson (2013: 517, 526, 528–9), and Richard Froyen (2013: 334–8), none of which mentions the IS-MP model. Hubbard, O'Brien, and Rafferty (2014: 535–6) also discuss inflation targeting but emphasize skeptics' views on its usefulness than most other texts.

The IS-MP model is still at odds with economic reality for its retaining three fundamental problems of the IS-LM model, namely, (a) treating saving as a withdrawal from the expenditure stream to derive the IS curve, (b) treating some expenditures as "autonomous" of current income, and (c) treating interest rates as being determined by only a central bank's money (H) supply and demand in constructing the LM curve – Keynes's (1936) liquidity-preference theory of interest. Furthermore, the IS-MP model specifies no theory of inflation[5] other than claiming (incorrectly) there being inflation when an economy is operating beyond its natural output rate, but providing no specification of how the economy's natural rate is determined.

Among the advantages Romer claims for the IS-MP model is its simplicity of learning. But accordance with economic reality should matter a lot more than the simplicity of a model's being learned. A simple, teachable model may yet leave students with a poor understanding of the workings of the economy.[6] Other advantages Romer claims for the IS-MP model include: (1) "The assumption that the central bank follows an interest rate rule is more realistic than the assumption that it targets the money supply" (2000: 155); (2) "The new approach [describing] monetary policy in terms of the real interest rate" (ibid.: 156); (3) "The real interest rate rule [being] simpler than the LM curve" (ibid.); and (4) "With the new approach, the correct concept of money to consider [being] unambiguous" (ibid.: 162), that is, "high-powered money," not M1 or M2.

However, as John Maynard Keynes (1936) argues, "the object of our analysis is, not to provide a machine, or method of blind manipulation," but that we "know all the time what we are doing and what the words [we use] mean" (297).[7] But Hicks (1937) did not take Keynes's advice to examine the meaning of words in his modeling the IS-LM. Similarly, Romer's IS-MP model provides a "machine" supposedly to imitate a central bank's behavior, but attributes to that bank a capability it cannot have, namely, controlling real interest rates. The Keynesian IS-MP model thus appears to be worse than the IS-LM model.

Romer (2000: 166, 2013) also suggests an alternative, upward-sloping MP curve, arguing that to be "more realistic" because "central banks are likely to make the real [interest] rate depend on output [besides inflation]. Cutting the real rate when output falls and raising it when output rises directly dampens output fluctuations. Further, because high output tends to increase inflation and low output to decrease it, such a policy also dampens inflation fluctuations" (166).[8] However, Romer derives the upward-sloping MP curve merely by assertion: "it is natural to consider the possibility that the central bank's choice of the real interest rate depends on output as well as inflation. Formally, this assumption is $r = r(Y, \pi)$, with the function increasing in both arguments" (2000: 166); and "*When output rises, the central bank raises the real interest rate. When output falls, the central bank lowers the real interest rate*. . . . Thus r(Y) is an increasing function" (2013: 1, 2; italics original). The LM curve, on the other hand, is derived as nominal interest rates rising as the demand for money (H) increases, following an increase in real income, while the quantity of money is fixed. Moreover, an upward-sloping MP curve dilutes the presumption of a specific real interest rate target that a central bank allegedly controls since variations in the IS curve become determinants of the real interest rate as well.

Ultimately, Romer's model does not address the fundamental problems with Keynes's macroeconomic analysis. Interest rates are determined by the supply and demand for credit, of which a central bank's money creation is but a minor part, especially for industrialized economies. The level of prices is best explained by the level of a central bank's quantity of money relative to its demand, and inflation by the growth rate of central bank money relative to the growth rate of its demand – the classical Quantity Theory of money. Romer's neglecting the Quantity Theory, following Keynes's (1936, 1937a, 1939) claiming to explain the price level by aggregate output supply and demand instead, appears to have encouraged his mistaken declaration that "high output tends to increase inflation and low output to decrease it" (2000, 166). From an equation of the price level, $P = H/ky$, where H = high-powered money, k = proportion of the community's income desired to be held in cash, and y = real output or GDP, it should be clear that a high output rather keeps prices low, given the level of H, and vice versa. It is the supply of money (H) relative to its demand that determines the level of prices:

> If everything else remains the same, then there is this direct relation between the volume of currency and the level of prices, that, if one is increased by ten per cent., the other also will be increased by ten per cent. Of course, the less the proportion of their resources which people care to keep in the form of currency [k], the lower will be the aggregate value of the currency, that is, the higher will prices be with a given volume of currency.
>
> (Marshall 1923: 45)

Variations in relative commodity prices coordinate production decisions of producers and consumers, while variations in interest rates coordinate the decisions of savers and borrowers. A modern central bank replaces the automatic specie money's supply response to changes in its demand as reflected in variations in the value of money – David Hume's (1752) price-specie-flow mechanism in "Of the Balance of Trade" – if it targets a zero rate of inflation. Say's law of markets, requiring merely the application of the principles of supply and demand to commodities, services, credit, and money (currency) to understand, explains these insights (see Say 1821a: esp. Bk 1, Ch. 15). But because of the law's misrepresentation by Keynes (1936: 18–22, 25–6, 1937a), modern macroeconomics tends to have little use for it (Ahiakpor 2003a, 2018b).

Importantly, it should be recognized that Say's law does not assume that (a) full employment of labor always exists, (b) output supply creates its own demand, (c) product prices adjust instantaneously, (d) money (cash) hoarding does not exist, or (e) entrepreneurs form expectations about the future with certainty. Say's fundamental proposition is that "the mere circumstance of the creation of one product immediately opens a vent [or market] for other products [produced goods and services]" and "production alone furnishes [the] means" for consumption (Say 1821a: 134–5, 139); also Say (1821b: 13, 23, 24). The classics, particularly Smith, Jean-Baptiste Say, Ricardo, and J. S. Mill, also argued that producers base their productions on anticipated demand. Furthermore, producers adjust their productions as quickly as they can on the basis of actual market or effective demand (e.g., Smith *WN*, 1: 63–6; Say 1821a: 133–7; Ricardo *Works*, 1: 290–2; J. S. Mill *Works*, 3: 572). J. S. Mill also declares, "The future presents nothing which can be with certainty either foreseen or governed" (*Works*, 2: 165) and "the calculations of producers and traders being of necessity imperfect, there are always some commodities which are more or less in excess, as there are always some which are in deficiency" (1874: 67). The law of markets is also not about the market for labor or for land, which are inputs for production. There could be increased production along with increased unemployment of labor (Say 1821a: 86, 1821b: 65–6). Frank Knight correctly explained this in a 21 October 1936 lecture: "Say's law refers only to products exchanged on the market – it does not refer necessarily to labor. Does it have anything to do with productive factors? It says that a market tends to clear itself at a price. Keynes does not treat Say's law as the classical economist did" (quoted in Cristiano and Fiorito 2016: 95).

Some unresolved problems with the IS-MP model

The first unresolved problem with the IS-MP model is its deriving a downward-sloping IS curve with variations in nominal interest rates and real output to represent equilibrium in the goods market. Fundamental to the IS-LM model is Keynes's having turned the classical Quantity Theory of money from determining the level of prices to determining the level of interest rates, and thereby to derive a theory of "output as a whole" (1937a, 1939). Rather than interest rates being determined by the supply and demand for savings or credit (loanable funds) as savers purchase interest-earning financial assets, Keynes argued that savings are a withdrawal from the expenditure stream. But, as Marshall (1920: 192) explains, people invest their "earnings [savings] in trade or on loan, so as to derive interest or profits from them"; also Marshall (1923: 46) comments: "in 'Western' countries even peasant, if well to do, incline to invest the greater part of their savings in Government, or other familiar stock exchange securities, or to commit them to the charge of a bank." That is why, in Keynes's view, increased consumption spending or decreased saving is associated with increased business investment and production in the goods market. Keynes's (1936: 167) assumed lack of a positive connection between savings and the supply of loanable funds underlies Hicks's derivation of the IS curve such that high levels of nominal interest rates reduce business investment and consumption spending at a low level of real output. Lower nominal interest rates are argued to be necessary for both increased investment and consumption spending, leading to equilibrium at a higher level of real output along the IS curve.

Romer (2000: 150) restates the argument: "a higher interest rate reduces demand, it lowers the level of output at which the quantity demanded equals the quantity produced. There is thus a negative relationship between output and the interest rate." Romer (2000: 153) also argues: "the real interest rate is relevant to the demand for goods and thus to the IS curve," and his 2013 version of the IS-MP model employs the real interest rate throughout (see also Blinder 1997: 240). However, Hick's original IS curve is not depicted with respect to the real interest rate, although some might claim that it is because his model abstracts from inflation in the short run. It may well be that borrowers (and spenders) take into account the expected rates of inflation relative to nominal interest rates when taking loans. But such guesses would be rather imperfect and varied. Employing the nominal interest rate to derive the IS curve appears more reliable, assuming the IS curve is legitimate in the first place.

However, an increased rate of interest may result from an increased demand for loanable funds because of an improved expectation of business profits and technological innovations or discoveries. That would then be associated with an increased rate of investment, production, real output, and employment as well as increased consumption. On the other hand, a low level of interest rates, resulting from decreased business investment demand would be associated with a decreased level of production, employment, and consumption. Thus, a negatively sloped investment-demand curve is defensible, but not the negative association between the level of interest rates and production and spending equilibrium necessarily in the goods market as depicted by the IS curve. We correctly may envision shifts of a downward-sloping investment-demand function (for funds or credit) that interact with an upward-sloping savings-supply function to determine equilibrium interest rates. From such interest rate determination would derive levels of investment spending, output, employment, and consumption in an economy without invoking a central bank's money or credit creation. But Keynes (1936, 1937a) did not appreciate that conclusion.

Furthermore, the funds supplied by savers are a greater magnitude than only "the value of capital equipment" Keynes recognizes as "*current investment*" (1936: 62; italics original; see also Keynes 1930: 2, 207). The rest of the funds (savings) are spent to acquire raw materials, hire the services of labor (wages fund), rent land, and to keep as cash-on-hand – the classical "circulating capital" (see Smith *WN*, 1: 294–301; Ricardo *Works*, 1: 31, 52; J. S. Mill *Works*, 2: 91–9; Marshall 1920: 63, 677–82).[9] Thus, Hick's equating savings with investment to derive the IS curve does not accurately represent classical analysis or reality.

Also, the aggregate consumption function $[C = \alpha_0 + \beta Y(1 - t)]$ from which the IS curve is derived is inconsistent with the behavior of aggregate consumption spending for a closed economy. An individual may consume without production or income, if some others are willing to extend a loan or a gift to them out of their own incomes $(C_i = \alpha_i)$. However, the community as a whole cannot consume without anyone having produced anything.[10] Thus, correctly conceived, there is no positive intercept (autonomous consumption) to a closed economy's aggregate consumption function: at a zero level of output or income, consumption must be zero also: $C = \beta Y(1 - t)$. The autonomous aggregate consumption is an example of the fallacy of composition: what is true at the individual level need not be true at the aggregate level.

Similarly, in the absence of a central bank's money or credit creation, there cannot be any investment spending – expenditure of funds in the sphere of production – without firms either having borrowed the funds (sold financial assets, FAs, to savers) or having employed their own savings: $I = \Delta FA^s = \Delta FA^d = Y(1 - t) - \beta Y(1 - t) - \Delta H_h = \theta Y(1 - t)$, where ΔH_h = cash hoarding by households. Also, government spending depends upon taxes and/or borrowed funds (bond proceeds): $G = tY + \Delta B_g$, and $\Delta B_g = \gamma Y(1 - t)$.

Thus, the aggregate expenditure function employed to derive the IS curve, $AE = C + I + G$, where $C = \alpha_0 + \beta Y(1 - t)$, $I = I_0 - iI$, and $G = G_0$, following changes in the level of interest rates, inaccurately describes the workings of a (closed) monetary economy (Ahiakpor 2013). In the absence of variations in a central bank's money creation to affect interest rates in the short run, variations in consumption, investment, and government spending must leave total expenditures or "aggregate demand" unchanged. Decreased (private) consumption spending, because of increased taxation, merely transfers more income to the government to spend. Increased savings or increased purchases of financial assets by households (ΔFA^d) also transfer funds to businesses and/or the government (bonds or securities purchases, ΔFA^s) to spend. The IS curve therefore derives a misleading conclusion that "changes in aggregated demand, such as changes in government purchases, have real [expansionary or contractionary] effects" (Romer 2000: 152).[11]

Moreover, the upward shift of the aggregate expenditure curve, following a decrease in interest rates, employed to derive the IS curve, really reflects an increased spending made possible by an increased quantity of central bank money (ΔH). Otherwise, a decrease in the interest rate could have resulted from increased savings – increased purchase of financial assets rather than cash hoarding – which would increase investment spending in place of the reduced consumption. If interest rates declined from a decrease in investment demand, interest sensitive consumption spending could increase to sustain total spending. Another implication of recognizing the dependence of all expenditures on income is that the estimated multiplier may be infinite but the government's expenditure effect on income or output would be zero, at best (see Ahiakpor 2001).[12] If we took into account the typical lower efficiency of spending by bureaucrats, as compared with private individuals, the effect of increased government spending (beyond its legitimate functions)[13] on the economy's growth path would be negative.

The IS curve, by construction, also ignores variations in the public's demand for money ($\Delta H^d = k\Delta Y + \Delta kY$, where k = proportion of income the public wishes to hold in cash) as an important determinant of spending on produced goods and services. But incomes are also spent on acquiring money (cash) to hold for money's liquidity services. Thus, instead of deriving equilibrium in the goods market from equating only income (Y) with aggregate expenditure, $AE = C + I + G$, the equalization must be between the means for spending, including the additional money created by a central bank, that is, $Y + \Delta H^s$, with expenditure on goods and services, plus the amount of cash demanded to hold (hoarding), that is, $AE = C + I + G + \Delta H^d$. That formulation yields, $Y + \Delta(H^s - H^d) = C + I + G$. Thus, a positive excess supply of central bank money increases spending on produced goods and services and raises their prices while a negative excess supply of money decreases such spending and causes prices to fall.

A positive excess supply of money may yield increased production and employment in the short run, as in the classical forced-saving mechanism (Ahiakpor 2009), while a negative excess supply of money may yield the opposite (e.g., J. S. Mill *Works*, 3: 516, 574). The experience of the Great Depression (1930–33) well illustrates the latter outcome when there was a more than $18 billion contraction in both demand and savings deposits in commercial banks. This was the result of the public's seeking to redeem their deposits into money (cash), but their redemption demands could not be met by the little more than $1 billion increase in Federal Reserve money (Milton Friedman and Anna Schwartz 1963: 335–62, 803–4; see also Friedman and Schwartz 1970: 24–8, 68). That mostly explains the six percent annual price deflation, accompanied by the severe economic contraction and increased rate of unemployment during the depression.

Hicks's (1937) IS-LL model also replaces the classical "capital" supply and demand theory of interest rates with Keynes's (1936: 174, 1937a: 210–11) liquidity-preference theory, whereby the demand for central bank money (cash) to hold relative to its available quantity (not modern M1 or M2) determines the equilibrium rate of interest.[14] As Keynes (1936: 186–90) clearly indicates, the basis for his rejecting the classical theory is his having read it to be arguing that interest rates are determined by the supply and demand for "capital goods." But his reading of the classical theory was mistaken. "Capital" in the classical theory of interest refers to savings or loanable funds, as the term is used in the language of the marketplace (Marshall 1920: 60–2, 1923: 73; see also Smith *WN*: 1; 358, 372–4; Ricardo *Works*, 1: 126–7, 363, 2: 331, 3: 89–94; J. S. Mill *Works*, 3: 508, 647).

Besides, variations in a central bank's money creation typically form a minor proportion of the total volume of loans (credit) borrowed in an economy: $S_{CR} = S_c +/- \Delta H$, where S_c = supply of capital or savings. The principal sources of such funds are checkable deposits and various forms of saving deposits with financial institutions, including regular savings, small and large time deposits (CDs), money market deposit accounts, and money market mutual fund shares. The variations in a central bank's money creation may affect the level of interest rates in the short run (the "liquidity effect"), but their effect vanishes after the level of prices has reacted to the changed quantity of money (Hume 1752, "Of Interest"; Ricardo *Works*, 3: 91; J. S. Mill *Works*, 3: 656–7; and Marshall 1923: 257; see also Friedman 1972). The price-level (or income) and expectations effects of variations in the quantity of central bank money counter the initial liquidity effect on interest rates. Thus, interest rates may rise or fall, regardless of changes in a central bank's rate of credit creation.

Recognizing that interest rates are determined by the supply and demand for credit that is far greater than a central bank's volume of credit creation (ΔH) also alerts us to appreciating that changes in the public's savings behavior do change the equilibrium level of interest rates. The public's expectation of increased inflation or shaken confidence in the security of their deposits with financial intermediaries could contract the volume of savings (credit) and raise the level of nominal interest rates, given a central bank's rate of money creation. On the other hand, the public's expectation of living longer or expectation of a lower rate of inflation (or deflation), or a reduction in transactions costs associated with saving with financial intermediaries would increase the flow of savings and reduce the equilibrium level of nominal interest rates, given a central bank's rate of credit (money) creation. Furthermore, the expectation of increased business profits would increase the demand for credit and raise the equilibrium level of nominal interest rates, given the rate of central bank money creation. A loss of business confidence about the profitability of investment would decrease the demand for credit and decrease the equilibrium level of nominal interest rates. Thus, attributing to a central bank the ability to control the equilibrium nominal rate of interest ignores numerous others factors that determine the level of nominal interest rates, let alone the real rate, and is mistaken. Hubbard, O'Brien, and Rafferty (2014: 346–53), for example, well concede the point, even as they adopt the IS-MP model (analysis) with a horizontal MP curve defined over real interest rates.

Keynes (1924: 81–8) adopts the classical Quantity Theory as an explanation of the level of prices ($P = H/ky$, using the Cambridge equation), and from which we may derive a theory of inflation ($\%\Delta P = \%\Delta H - \%\Delta k - \%\Delta y$). Keynes acknowledges his indebtedness to Marshall (1923) and A. C. Pigou (1917) for the analysis. But Marshall drew much from Ricardo's monetary analysis; Ricardo in turn reflects the views of David Hume (1752) and Smith (1776) on the Quantity Theory of money.[15] That is, inflation results from the growth of central bank's money in excess of the growth of its demand to hold by the public (see also Marshall 1923: 45). Keynes (1936: Chs. 15 and 23, [1939] 1974: xxxiii–v), however, turns the classical Quantity Theory into a theory of interest rates – his liquidity-preference theory (Romer 2000: 150–1) – a reversion to the mercantilist argument[16] that Hume's (1752) essay, "Of Interest," explains to be incorrect.

Hume (1752: 49; italics original) explains:

> High interest arises from *three* circumstances: A great demand for borrowing; little riches to supply that demand; and great profits arising from commerce: And these circumstances are a clear proof of the small advance of commerce and industry, not of the scarcity of gold and silver [money]. Low interest, on the other hand, proceeds from the three opposite circumstances: A small demand for borrowing; great riches to supply that demand; and small profits arising from commerce: And these circumstances are all connected together, and proceed from the encrease of industry and commerce, not of gold and silver.

Subsequent classical writers, including Smith, Ricardo, and J. S. Mill, have also affirmed Hume's correction of the mercantilist view. Keynes appears to have been unaware of Hume's explanation.

Hicks (1937) offers no criticisms of Keynes's liquidity-preference theory of interest because he himself was not clear about the meaning of "capital" in the classical theory (Hicks 1936: 246, 1946: 153). Hicks also explains that he found Keynes's liquidity-preference theory agreeable because it accorded with his own earlier thinking about interest rate determination before Keynes's publication: "I recognized immediately, as soon as I read *The General Theory*, that my model and Keynes's had some things in common" (Hicks 1980/81: 140). He made little effort to recognize the meaning of "capital" in the theory of interest that his con-temporaries, particularly Hawtrey, Pigou, and Robertson, were defending against Keynes's criticisms: "it makes a great deal of difference which interpretation" we put on "capital": "the 'real capital' in the sense of concrete goods . . . or 'money capital.' This division of opinion is serious; it is a real dispute, in which one side must be right and the other wrong" (Hicks 1946: 153). It was Keynes who was wrong.

But Hicks (1980/81) subsequently disavows the usefulness of the IS-LM model: "I have myself become dissatisfied with [it] . . . that diagram is now less popular with me than I think with many other people" (139). Hicks (1989: 78) also gives up his defense of Keynes's interest theory against Marshall's restatement of the classical theory: "I now think that Marshall, after all, does win that trick game"; see further Hicks in Rima (1988: 5), noting: "Marshall, who was surely . . . the 'classi-cal' theorist whom Keynes had most in mind, was right in his day." Thus, Hicks's derivation of the LM curve employs a misleading theory of interest rates. Romer (2000, 2013), like most other macroeconomists, shows hardly any appreciation of Hick's change of mind regarding the usefulness Keynes's analysis.

It may be argued that Keynes (1936: 205) qualifies his liquidity-preference theory of interest and a central bank's ability to control interest rates with the argu-ment, "Corresponding to the quantity of money created by the monetary authority, there will, therefore, be *cet. par.* a determinate complex of rates or, more strictly, a determinate complex of rates of interest for debts of different maturities." But his proposition of a liquidity trap that would frustrate the ability of a central bank to decrease (long-term) interest rates (1936: 207), and his rejection of the classical Quantity Theory as an explanation of the level of prices, unless under full employ-ment of labor (1936: 209), may yet be cited as weakening his qualifying argument.

Other problems with Romer's IS-MP model

The first other major problem with Romer's IS-MP model is its lacking a theory of inflation, following his having discarded the Quantity Theory of money to explain the level of prices. The IS-MP model merely "assumes that inflation at any point in time *is given*, and that in the absence of inflation shocks,[17] inflation rises when output is above its natural rate and falls when output is below its natural rate" or "Inflation is *inherited* from the economy's *past*" (2000: 158; italics added). Simi-larly, "inflation equals its core level if output equals its natural rate, rises above the core level if output is above its natural rate, and falls below the core level if output is below its natural rate" and the "core inflation is given by last period's actual inflation" (167). But there is hardly any explanation of what determines the natural output rate or the core inflation rate.

Romer's assumption of inflation occurring only when the level of real output exceeds its "natural rate" is clearly contradicted by numerous experiences in which high rates of inflation have been associated with high rates of unemployment and economic contraction. The examples include the stagflation experience of the 1970s in the US and in several less developed countries during the 1980s and 1990s, such as Argentina, Brazil, Venezuela, Peru, and Chile (Ahiakpor 2003b: 77). Zimbabwe is an excellent recent illustration of the point. Zimbabwe's annual inflation rate "was 1,017% in 2006, 10,453% in 2007, and soared to 55.6 billion percent in 2008, before dropping to 6.5% in 2009" (Abel, Bernanke, and Croushore 2014: 470), while real production in the country collapsed.

According to the classical Quantity Theory of money, prices should be rising when the rate of goods production declines relative to the rate of money's creation by a central bank, and vice versa. In the presence of wage contracts, an unanticipated high rate of money creation by a central bank may cause an increased rate of inflation but entice an increased rate of production and increased hiring of labor in the short run (see, e.g., Fisher 1926). But even wage contracts are frequently revised to take into account the high rates of inflation, which generates the vertical long-run Phillips curve (Ahiakpor 2009). The quantity theory's explanation thus connects the phenomenon of inflation with a central bank's money creation relative to the growth of its demand rather than Romer's assertion of inflation occurring when production exceeds the natural rate.

The second other major (and perhaps crippling) problem with the IS-MP model is its fundamental assumption that "the central bank follows a *real* interest rate rule: that is, it acts to make the real interest rate *behave* in a certain way as a function of macroeconomic variables such as inflation and output" (Romer 2000: 154; italics added). The claim conflicts with Alan Blinder's observation as Vice-Chairman of the Board of Governors of the Federal Reserve System in the early 1990s. Blinder notes that "the *LM* curve no longer plays any role in serious policy analysis, having been supplanted by the assumption that the central bank controls the short-term *nominal* interest rate" (1997: 240; italics added). This because "there is now a strong professional consensus that the once-reliable *LM* curve fell prey years ago to ferocious instabilities in both money demand and money supply, themselves the product of rapid and ongoing financial innovation" (ibid.).

However, the alleged instabilities of the LM curve rather derive from the assignment of control over the growth of M1 or M2 to central banks (Friedman 1968a) when their multipliers, consisting of the banks' excess reserve-deposit ratio and the public's currency-deposit ratio are not constant through time.[18] Romer's MP curve avoids the alleged instability problem by adopting only high-powered money as the appropriate definition of money. N. Gregory Mankiw and Ricardo Reis (2018) also observe that "Modern macroeconomics . . . focuses more on the *nominal* interest rate" (90; italics added) and they report Gali and Gertler's (2007) "insights of modern macroeconomic models for monetary policy" to include "the importance for the central bank of *tracking* the flexible price equilibrium values of the natural levels of output and the real interest rate" (91; italics added), not that the central bank controls the real interest rate. Nevertheless, a central bank hardly can control the equilibrium nominal short-term interest rates, let alone the real interest rate.

On the US federal funds market, the Fed's securities purchases may put a downward pressure on nominal interest rates, while its sale of securities may cause the rates to rise. But in the absence of the Fed's purchases or sales of securities, the federal funds rate may rise or fall depending upon banks' net demand or supply of credit (demand for overnight repurchase agreements). Furthermore, the Fed does not fix the federal funds rate but rather attempts to achieve a target range; and there are variations in the rates paid in different percentiles among borrowers. The ninety-ninth percentile's borrowing rates frequently exceed the upper limit of the Fed's target range (federalreserve.gov). Moreover, the bursting of the Fed's upper limit of the range frequently has preceded the range's elevation by the Fed.

For example, between March and 15 December 2016, while the Fed's target range was between 0.25 and 0.50 percent, the Effective Federal Funds Rate (EFFR), a weighted average of borrowers' interest rates, trended upwards from 0.37 to 0.41 percent while the rate for the ninety-ninth percentile frequently exceeded the upper bound, ranging between 0.55 and 0.75 percent. Following the target range increase on 15 December 2016 to 0.50–0.75 percent, the rate for the ninety-ninth percentile varied between 0.75 and 0.82 percent while the EFFR varied between 0.55 and 0.66 percent. After the 16 March 2017 target range increase to 0.75–1.00 percent, the rate in the ninety-ninth percentile varied between 1.00 and 1.06 percent, while the EFFR varied between 0.83 and 0.91 percent. Between 15 June 2017 and 13 December 2017, when the target range was increased to 1.00 and 1.25 percent, the EFFR varied between 1.07 and 1.17 percent while the rate for the ninety-ninth percentile varied between 1.22 and 1.30 percent. Following the target range increase to between 1.25 and 1.50 percent on 14 December 2017, the EFFR varied between 1.33 and 1.44 percent while the rate for the ninety-ninth percentile varied between 1.50 and 1.62 percent, again much exceeding the upper target limit. The next target range increase was to between 1.50 and 1.75 percent on 22 March 2018. On 22 and 23 March 2018, the rate for the ninety-ninth percentile again exceeded the upper level of the Fed's target, being 1.81 percent.

Romer is thus overoptimistic in his view of the Fed's ability to control short-term interest rates. He believes,

> for the very short run, a nominal rate rule provides a better description of central bank's behavior than a real rate rule. Once we consider horizons beyond the very short run, a real interest rate rule is more realistic than a nominal rate rule [because] central banks reexamine their choice of the nominal rate frequently.
>
> (2000: 155)

The classical Quantity Theory of money also explains that, besides the growth rate of money's quantity, variations in the public's demand for money (currency) to hold affect the level of prices and the rate of inflation both in the short run and in the long run. Inflation rises when the demand for money decreases, and it falls as the demand for money increases ($\%\Delta P = \%\Delta H - \%\Delta k - \%\Delta y$). Keynes's (1924: 88–95) discussion of factors other than the quantity of money (currency) that affect the level of prices well recognizes the point. Thus, a central bank cannot precisely control the rate of inflation, whose value is needed to determine the real rate of interest, $r = i - \%\Delta P$. That is, the real rate at any point in time is not under the control or sole influence of a central bank; variations in the public's demand for money to hold have their impact. The failure of many central banks, including the US Federal Reserve System since January 2012, successfully to hit a specific inflation target, other than meeting a target range (Bernanke and Mishkin 1997; Blanchard and Johnson 2013: 526–8),[19] well attests to this fact.

Furthermore, the real interest rate may rise because the rate of inflation has declined, following an earlier reduction in the central bank's rate of money creation (the expectations effect), or from current sales of securities (monetary contraction) by the central bank, raising the nominal interest rate (the liquidity effect). Similarly, the real interest rate may fall because of the rise in the rate of inflation, following previous central bank purchases of securities (the expectations effect), or from current securities purchases (monetary expansion), lowering the nominal interest rate (the liquidity effect). Romer's MP curve (horizontal or upward-sloping) does not appear to take into account the above complications in the determination of real interest rates. Rather, he argues, with little reference to the inflationary or deflationary consequences of variations in the supply or demand for money (H), the

> central bank would like to have low inflation and high output. When inflation is high, its concern about inflation predominates, and so it chooses a high real rate to contract output and dampen inflation. When inflation is low, it is no longer as concerned about inflation, and so it chooses a lower real rate to increase output.
>
> (2000: 156)

But without a theory of inflation, other than inflation being inherited from the past or there being inflation when the output rate exceeds the natural rate, it is unclear how the central bank's high real interest policy is achieved when inflation is high or how the low real interest policy is achieved when inflation is low. Romer would have been better served to take seriously his arguing "the central bank's *influence* over the real rate" or "the central banks' ability *to influence* the real rate" (2000: 162, 163; italics added) rather than claiming a central bank's ability to control the real interest rate.

It is much clearer to urge a central bank's monetary contraction to curb inflation and monetary expansion to curb price deflation, which follows the classical Quantity Theory of money. The assumption that the central bank follows a real rate rule may well be "important for the [IS-MP] model's simplicity" (Romer 2000: 155), but implementing the rule entails complexities, if not defying the feasibility of what a central bank can do.[20] A central bank's focusing on maintaining the purchasing power of its currency – zero inflation rate – by matching the growth of money to the growth of its demand and letting nominal and real interest rates find their own market equilibrium levels is a more feasible and an efficient policy too. As David Hume (1752: 39–40) argues:

> The good policy of the magistrate [the sovereign][21] consists only in keeping [money], if possible, still encreasing; because, by that means, he keeps alive a spirit of industry in the nation, and encreases the stock of labour, in which consists all real power and riches. A nation, whose money decreases, is actually, at that time, weaker and more miserable than another nation, which possesses no more money, but is on the encreasing hand.

Hume's policy recommendation follows his explanation that, among trading nations that use specie in payment for exports and imports, they "preserve money nearly proportionable to the art and industry of each nation. All water, wherever it communicates, remains always at a level" (1752: 63, "Of the Balance of Trade"). However, the price-specie-adjustment mechanism takes some time to distribute money appropriately to the rates of production among trading nations:

> the alterations in the quantity of money, either on one side or the other, are not immediately attended with proportionable alterations in the price of commodities. There is always an interval before matters be adjusted to their new situation; and this interval is as pernicious to industry, when gold and silver are diminishing, as it is advantageous when these metals are encreasing.
>
> (1752: 40, "Of Money")

It was because, other than debasing the currency, a government could not increase the quantity of money that Hume qualified his recommendation of money's increasing quantity (in a growing economy) to the "magistrate" with "if possible."

A fiat (paper) money system has the advantage over a metallic money system in being able to increase the quantity of money quickly to sustain the level of prices from falling when the rate of output production causes a positive excess demand for money. In the presence of wage, interest, and rental contracts, such falling prices cause business losses and economic contraction that Hume describes as "poverty and beggary, and sloth" (1752: 40). Similarly, Alfred and Mary Marshall (1879) explain, "a fall in prices lowers profits and impoverishes the manufacturer: while it increases the purchasing power of those who have fixed incomes ... it impoverishes those who have to make, as most business men have, considerable fixed payments for rents, salaries, and other matters" (157). Preserving the level of prices is thus the requisite monetary policy of a modern central bank that has replaced the automatic monetary transmission through net exports.

Zero inflation rate targeting follows Hume's logic, not a positive inflation rate, be it one percent, two percent, or three percent or a range of between one and three percent, as several modern central banks have adopted. The zero inflation targeting also assures that nominal (and real) interest rates will find their own equilibrium levels, reflecting the excess demands for savings or credit, and to coordinate the savings and investment decisions in an economy.

Summary and conclusions

There are irremediable problems with the IS-LM model. Keynes (1973: 14, 79–81) did not fully endorse it as representing his views; neither did Keynes's contemporaries accept the model as correctly representing classical macroeconomic analysis. Hicks himself subsequently disavowed the model's analytical usefulness. The model's depiction of equilibrium determination in the goods market is inaccurate, by its treating savings as a withdrawal from the expenditure stream and aggregate consumption, investment, and government spending as having autonomous components. The model's determining interest rates solely by a central bank's money creation relative to money's demand is also misleading. David Romer's (2000, 2013) attempts to create a more relevant Keynesian model with the IS-MP alternative, but without addressing the above fundamental deficiencies of the IS and LM curves, thus could not have been successful.

The IS-MP model's attributing a real interest rate control policy to central banks is most problematic. Nominal interest rates are determined by the supply and demand for credit, of which a central bank's money creation typically forms a minor part, particularly in industrialized countries, such as the US. The rate of inflation is also determined by the growth rate of a central bank's money creation in excess of the growth of the public's demand for money – deflation by the reverse. A central bank thus does not fully control the rate of inflation, even though its rate of money creation may have the dominant influence. Controlling the real interest rate is thus extremely difficult for a central bank to achieve. The IS-MP model therefore turns out not to be a better alternative to the IS-LM model, flawed though is the latter.

The real path to deriving a meaningful macroeconomic model is to recognize the fundamental flaws in Keynes's (1936, 1937a) criticisms of classical macro-monetary analysis and resolve them. The resolution entails restoring (1) the Quantity Theory of money to its explaining the level of prices, and from which to derive a reliable theory of inflation, (2) interest rates to being determined by the supply and demand for savings or credit, and (3) savings to being the demand for interest- and/or dividend-earning assets, not the same thing as cash hoarding. But none of these is consistent with Keynes's or the Keynesian economics that Romer (2000, 2013) attempts to salvage. Romer (2000: 168–9) argues, "Keynes and Hicks appear to have made the right fundamental choices about how to develop a simple baseline model of short-run fluctuations" and he (Romer) has provided "more realistic and powerful" modifications to their efforts – "Keynesian Macroeconomics without the LM Curve."

Rather, the resolution entails applying the supply and demand framework, with money's demand curve being a rectangular hyperbola (Taussig 1921: 1, 234; Marshall 1923: 39–43, 282; Pigou 1912, 423, 1917). The resolution also requires correctly interpreting Say's law of markets as explaining the creation of demand for produced goods and services from the production of any (useful) commodity,[22] and thus the coordination of markets for produced goods and services and for money – implying nothing about the state of unemployment[23] – and recognizing modern central banks as having replaced specie money's automatic variations to sustain the level of prices in an economy or to meet money's excess demand. Modern central banks' pursuit of positive inflation targeting misses the latter classical insight.

Neither price inflation nor deflation is conducive to an economy's long-term growth. In the short run, the rate of inflation in excess of or below its anticipated value produces business fluctuations: a temporary increase in output and employment when the rate exceeds expectations and a temporary contraction when the rate is below expectations. Variations in business or public confidence also may produce economic fluctuations that need not require changes in the quantity of money as the cure. The appropriate remedy for an economic recession is first to understand its cause before attempting to deal with it. The US Great Depression (1930–33) entailed shaken public confidence in the banking system resulting in massive demands for money (cash) that the Federal Reserve System could not meet, partly due to its adherence to the gold standard. The Great Contraction (2007–9) was caused by the housing bubble's bursting but did not require massive increases in central bank money – so-called Quantitative Easing – to resolve (see Anna J. Schwartz in Brian Carney 2008 and Williamson 2017).

Notes

1 This chapter is based upon my paper, "Is the IS-MP Model a Better Alternative to the IS-MP Model?" presented at the History of Economics Society Annual Meetings, Loyola University, Chicago, IL, June 14–17, 2018.
2 Marshall's analysis builds mostly on the works of Smith, Ricardo and J. S. Mill. Ahiakpor (2003b: Ch. 11) explains Hick's failure to represent correctly classical macroeconomics.
3 Some textbook writers appear to believe that trying to understand the evolution of modern macroeconomic theories is a wasteful "detour into history of thought" (Frank and Bernanke 2002: xii) or that all the relevant or important confusions since Keynes's (1936) work have been settled (see, e.g., DeLong 2002: vii). But understanding the evolution of economic principles affords a better perspective for dealing with their problems while manipulations of functional forms alone often do not. Keynes (1936: 298) himself argues that much of such exercise results in modelers losing "sight of the complexities and interdependencies of the real world in a maze of pretentious and unhelpful symbols."
4 Friedman would have been helpful in fully recognizing that, because M1 or M2 is composed of the public's deposits with banking institutions, neither of them is subject to any precise control by a central bank, as illustrated in Chapter 5 above.
5 Romer envisions the possibility that "some prices may be completely flexible, and may therefore jump when the money stock increases" (2000: 163) or "Prices that are completely flexible jump immediately at the time of the increase in the money supply" (2013: 17). He specifies no process for such occurrence.
6 Robert Barro (1993: vi) observes, the IS-LM model "leaves students with a poor understanding of how the economy works."

7 Most of Keynes's disagreements with classical macroeconomics can be traced to his having assigned different meanings to such terms as saving, capital, investment, and money than the classics meant.

8 Romer's associating high output with high inflation and low output with low inflation is incorrect, as I explain below.

9 Keynes's (1930: 2, 207, 1936: 62) having limited "investment" to only the purchase of capital goods explains why he could not make a direct connection between the supply of savings and investment spending. Hawtrey (1950: 43) appropriately contrasts Keynes's definition of investment with its ordinary meaning as the "acquisition of income-yielding securities or property, not Keynes's sense of the accumulation of capital assets and unconsumed goods."

10 An anonymous reader of an early version of the paper upon which I base this chapter claims that the autonomous intercept applies to previous stocks of unconsumed output. But the IS-LM model is defined over currently produced goods and services (output) or income. Keynes (1939: xxxiii) declares: "the actual level of output depends, not on the capacity to produce, or on the pre-existing level of incomes, but on the current decisions to produce which depend in turn on current decisions to invest and on present expectations of current and prospective consumption."

11 Employing such reasoning, Romer (2013: 5) also claims, "The increase in government purchases raises planned expenditure at a given level of income. Thus . . . it shifts the planned expenditure up" in the Keynesian cross diagram. Furthermore, "government purchases are an *exogenous* variable of our model" (9; italics added).

12 Let $Y = C + I + G = \beta Y(1-t) + \theta Y(1-t) + tY + \gamma Y(1-t)$. Then $Y[1 - \beta(1-t) - \theta(1-t) - t - \gamma(1-t)] = 0$, even as the multiplier, $\eta = 1/[1 - \beta(1-t) - \theta(1-t) - t - \gamma(1-t)] = \infty$.

13 The government's legitimate functions, according to Smith (*WN*, 2: 208–9), include national defense, a tolerable administration of justice, and the maintenance of "certain public works."

14 A problem with Keynes's analysis is his shifting definition of money or "liquidity" between strictly cash, as on page 174 of the *General Theory*, and money to include bank deposits, and "occasionally even such instruments as (e.g.) treasury bills" (1936: 167, n. 1).

15 From Fisher's exchange equation, inflation is: $\%\Delta P = \%\Delta H + \%\Delta V - \%\Delta y$, where $V =$ is money's velocity in transactions, the inverse of the proportion of income the public desires to hold in cash, $k = 1/V$.

16 Keynes (1939) argues, "I am here returning to the doctrine of the older, pre-nineteenth century economists" (xxxiv), who argued that interest rates are determined by the supply and demand for money.

17 Convenient though "shocks" may have become in modern macroeconomic analysis, they are quite empty as descriptors of determining economic variables. "Shocks" provide a fog for analysts to derive their conclusions without clear explanations of the determining variables.

18 The M1 multiplier, $m_1 = (cu + 1)/(cu + r_d + r_e)$, while the M2 multiplier, $m_2 = (cu + 1 + t)/(cu + r_d + r_t t + r_e)$. A central bank thus cannot control M1 and M2 by varying the high-powered money (H) or the required-reserve ratio, r_d (see also Chapter 5 above).

19 Bernanke and Mishkin (1997: 111) recognize inflation to be "finely uncontrollable" because "inflation is very difficult to predict accurately." Blanchard and Johnson (2013: 526–8) seem to recognize the central bank's inability to control the rate of inflation as pertaining to the short run only, mainly because of its difficulty of controlling M1 and M2. But the difficulty of controlling inflation precisely lies in a central bank's inability to predict accurately variations in the public's demand for currency (H).

20 Even as they employ a horizontal MP curve to move the real interest rates as monetary policy, Hubbard, O'Brien, and Rafferty (2014: 353) admit, "Fed policy is not the only factor that affects the real interest rate."

21 As explained in Chapter 4 above, interpreting Hume's "magistrate" to mean the "sovereign" is more meaningful and also consistent with the *Oxford English Dictionary's*

defining the magistrate to include the "first magistrate: in a monarchy, the sovereign: in a republic, usually the president" (1989: 189).

22 A commodity that satisfies no one's needs would find no others with which to exchange.

23 Keynes (1936: 26) incorrectly imputes the assumption of full employment to Say's Law. Say (1821a: 86) explains the occurrence of technological unemployment. He also argues, the "blunders of the nation or its government" may curb production and cause the "labouring classes [to] experience a want of work" (1821a: 140; see also Ahiakpor 2003a).

Bibliography

Abel, Andrew B., Bernanke, Ben S., and Croushore, Dean (2014) *Macroeconomics*. 8th ed. New York: Pearson, Addison-Wesley.

Ahiakpor, James C.W. (1985) "Ricardo on Money: The Operational Significance of the Non-neutrality of Money in the Short Run." *History of Political Economy* 17 (Spring): 17–30.

_____ (1990) "On Keynes's Misinterpretation of 'Capital' in the Classical Theory of Interest." *History of Political Economy* 22 (Fall): 507–28.

_____ (1995) "A Paradox of Thrift or Keynes's Misrepresentation of Saving in the Classical Theory of Growth?" *Southern Economic Journal* 62 (July): 16–33.

_____ (1997a) "Full Employment: A Classical Assumption or Keynes's Rhetorical Device?" *Southern Economic Journal* 64 (July): 56–74.

_____ (1997b) "Austrian Capital Theory: Help or Hindrance?" *Journal of the History of Economic Thought* 19 (Fall): 261–85.

_____, ed. (1998a) *Keynes and the Classics Reconsidered*. Boston: Kluwer Academic Publishers.

_____ (1998b) "Keynes on the Classics: A Revolution Mainly in Definitions?" In *Keynes and the Classics Reconsidered*, edited by James C.W. Ahiakpor. Boston, Dordrecht, and London: Kluwer Academic Publishers: 13–32.

_____ (1999) "Wicksell on the Classical Theories of Money, Credit, Interest and the Price Level: Progress or Retrogression?" *American Journal of Economics and Sociology* 58, No. 3 (July): 435–57.

_____ (2001) "On the Mythology of the Keynesian Multiplier." *American Journal of Economics and Sociology* 60 (October): 745–73.

_____ (2003a) "Say's Law: Keynes's Success With It Misrepresentation." In *Two Hundred Years of Say's Law: Essays on Economic Theory's Most Controversial Principle*, edited by Steven Kates. Cheltenham, UK; Northampton, MA: Edward Elgar: 107–32.

_____ (2003b) *Classical Macroeconomics: Some Modern Variations and Distortions*. New York and London: Routledge.

_____ (2004) "The Future of Keynesian Economics: Struggling to Sustain a Dimming Light." *American Journal of Economics and Sociology* 63, No. 3 (July): 583–608.

_____ (2009) "The Phillips Curve Analysis: An Illustration of the Classical Forced-Saving Doctrine." *Journal of the History of Economic Thought* 31, No. 2 (June): 143–60.

_____ (2010) "On the Similarities Between the 1932 Harvard Memorandum and the Chicago Antidepression Recommendations." *History of Political Economy* 42, No. 3 (Fall): 547–71.

_____ (2013) "The Modern Ricardian Equivalence Theorem: Drawing the Wrong Conclusions From David Ricardo's Analysis." *Journal of the History of Economic Thought* 35, No. 1 (March): 77–92.

_____ (2018a) "On the Impossibility of Keynes's Liquidity Trap: Classical Monetary Analysis Helps to Explain." *History of Economic Ideas* 26, No. 1: 31–58.

_____ (2018b) "Keynes, Mill, and Say's Law: A Comment on Roy Grieve's Mistaken Criticisms of Mill." *Journal of the History of Economic Thought* 40, No. 2 (June): 267–73.

Angell, James W. (1925) *The Theory of International Prices*. New York: Augustus M. Kelley, 1965.

Angell, James W. and Ficek, Karel F. (1933) "The Expansion of Bank Credit." *Journal of Political Economy* 41 (February): 1–32.

Arnold, Roger A. (2008) *Macroeconomics*. 8th ed. Mason, OH: Thomson South-Western.

Backhouse, Roger E. (1985) *A History of Modern Economic Analysis*. Oxford and New York: Basil Blackwell.

_____ (1999) "Introduction." In *Keynes: Contemporary Responses to the General Theory*, edited by Roger Backhouse. South Bend, IN: St Augustine's Press.

_____ (2006) "The Keynesian Revolution." In *The Cambridge Companion to Keynes*, edited by Roger E. Backhouse and Bradley W. Bateman. Cambridge: Cambridge University Press.

Backhouse, Roger E. and Bateman, Bradley W. (2006) "A Cunning Purchase: The Life and Work of Maynard Keynes." In *The Cambridge Companion to Keynes*, edited by Roger E. Backhouse and Bradley W. Bateman. New York: Cambridge University Press: 1–18.

_____ (2011) *Capitalist Revolutionary: John Maynard Keynes*. Cambridge, MA: Harvard University Press.

Bagehot, Walter (1873) *Lombard Street: A Description of the Money Market*. Homewood, IL: Richard D. Irwin, 1962.

Barro, Robert J. (1976) "Perceived Wealth in Bonds and Social Security and the Ricardian Equivalence Theorem: Reply to Feldstein and Buchanan." *Journal of Political Economy* 84, No. 2 (April): 343–50.

_____ (1989) "The Ricardian Approach to Budget Deficits." *Journal of Economic Perspectives* 3 No. 2 (Spring): 37–54.

_____ (1993) *Macroeconomics*. 4th ed. New York: Wiley.

_____ (2008) *Macroeconomics: A Modern Approach*. Mason, OH: Thomson Higher Education.

_____ (2010) *Intermediate Macro*. Mason, OH: South-Western Cengage Learning.

Baumol, William J. (1952) "The Transactions Demand for Cash: An Inventory-Theoretic Approach." *Quarterly Journal of Economics* 66 (November): 545–56.

_____ (1977) "Say's (at least) Eight Laws, or What Say and James Mill May Really Have Meant." *Economica* 44 (May): 145–61.

Baumol, William J. and Blinder, Alan S. (2008) *Macroeconomics: Principles and Policy*, 10th ed. Mason, OH: Thomson/South-Western.

Bentham, Jeremy (1951, 1954) *Jeremy Bentham's Economic Writings*. Edited by W. Stark. 3 vols. London: Allen & Unwin.

Berdell, John F. (1995) "The Present Relevance of Hume's Open-Economy Monetary Dynamics." *Economic Journal* 105, No. 432 (September): 1205–17.

_____ (2002) *International Trade and Economic Growth in Open Economies*. Cheltenham: Edward Elgar.

Bernanke, Ben S. (2000) *Essays on the Great Depression*. Princeton, NJ: Princeton University Press.

_____ (2002) "Remarks by Governor Ben S. Bernanke at the Conference to Honor Milton Friedman." University of Chicago, Chicago, IL, November 8, 2002. www.federalreserve.gov/boarddocs/Speeches/2002/20021108/default.htm

_____ (2009) "The Stamp Lecture," London School of Economics, London, England, January 13, 2009. www.federalreserve.gov/newsevents/speech/bernanke2009113a.htm

_____ (2015) *The Courage to Act: A Memoir of a Crisis and Its Aftermath*. New York: W.W. Norton.

Bernanke, Ben S. and Mishkin, Frederic S. (1997) "Inflation Targeting: A New Framework for Monetary Policy?" *Journal of Economic Perspectives* 11, No. 2 (Spring): 97–116.

Besomi, Daniele (2000) "Keynes and Harrod on the Classical Theory of Interest: More on the Origin of the only Diagram in the General Theory." *Journal of the History of Economic Thought* 22 (September): 367–76.

Bibow, Jörg (2000) "The Loanble Funds Fallacy in Retrospect." *History of Political Economy* 32, No. 4 (Winter): 789–831.

_____ (2001) "The Loanable Funds Fallacy: Exercises in the Analysis of Disequilibrium." *Cambridge Journal of Economics* 25 (5): 591–616.

Blanchard, Olivier and Johnson, David R. (2013) *Macroeconomics*. 6th ed. New York: Pearson.

Blaug, Mark (1995) "Why Is the Quantity Theory the Oldest Surviving Theory in Economics?" In *The Quantity Theory of Money: From Locke to Keynes and Friedman*, edited by Mark Blaug. Aldershot and Brookfield, VT: Edward Elgar.

_____ (1996) *Economic Theory in Retrospect*. 5th ed. Cambridge: Cambridge University Press.

Blinder, Alan S. (1997) "Is There a Core of Practical Macroeconomics That We Should All Believe?" *American Economic Review* 87, No. 2 (May): 240–3.

Böhm-Bawerk, Eugen V. (1891) *The Positive Theory of Capital*. Translated by William Smart. Reprinted. Freeport, NY: Books for Libraries Press, 1971.

Branson, William H. (1972) *Macroeconomic Theory and Policy*. New York: Harper & Row.

Bridel, Pascal (1987) *Cambridge Monetary Thought: Development of Saving-Investment Analysis From Marshall to Keynes*. New York: St. Martin's Press.

Buchanan, James M. (1976) "Barro on the Ricardian Equivalence Theorem." *Journal of Political Economy* 84, No. 2 (April): 337–2.

Caffentzis, C. George (2008) "Fiction or Counterfeit? David Hume's Interpretations of Paper and Metallic Money." In *David Hume's Political Economy*, edited by Carl Wennerlind and Margaret Schabas. London and New York: Routledge: 146–67.

Cairnes, J.E. (1873) *Essays in Political Economy*. New York: Augustus M. Kelley, 1965.

Cantillon, Richard (1755) *Essay on the Nature of Trade in General*. Edited with an English translation and other material by Henry Higgs. London: Frank Cass, 1959.

Carney, Brian M. (2008) "Bernanke Is Fighting the Last War." *Wall Street Journal*, October 18, www.djreprints.com.

Chick, Victoria (1983) *Macroeconomics After Keynes*. Cambridge, MA: The MIT Press.

Clower, Robert W. (1965) "The Keynesian Counter-Revolution: A Theoretical Appraisal." Reprinted in *Monetary Theory*, edited by Robert W. Clower. Baltimore, MD: Penguin Books, 1969: 298–310.

_____ (1994) "The Effective Demand Fraud." *Eastern Economic Journal* 20, No. 4 (Fall): 377–85.

Clower, Robert W. and Howitt, Peter (1998) "Keynes and the Classics: An End of Century View." In *Keynes and the Classics Reconsidered*, edited by James C.W. Ahiakpor. Boston, MA: Kluwer Academic Publishers.

Colander, David (1995) "The Stories We Tell: A Reconsideration of AS/AD Analysis." *Journal of Economic Perspectives* 9, No. 3: 169–88.

Colander, David and Gamber, Edward N. (2002) *Macroeconomics*. Upper Saddle River, NJ: Pearson Education.

Colander, David C. and Landreth, Harry, eds. (1996) *The Coming of Keynesianism to America: Conversations With the Founders of Keynesian Economics*. Cheltenham and Brookfield: Edward Elgar.

Coppock, Lee and Mateer, Dirk (2014) *Principles of Macroeconomics*. New York: W.W. Norton.

Cory, B.A. (1962) *Money, Saving and Investment in English Economics 1800–1850*. London: Palgrave Macmillan.

Cristiano, Carlo and Fiorito, Luca (2016) "Two Minds That Never Met: Frank H. Knight on John M. Keynes Once Again -A Documentary Note." *Journal of Keynesian Economics* 4, No. 1 (Spring): 67–98.

Currie, Lauchlin (1933) "Treatment of Credit in Contemporary Monetary Theory." *Journal of Political Economy* 41, No. 1 (February): 58–79.

_____ (1934a) "The Failure of Monetary Policy to Prevent the Depression of 1929–1932." *Journal of Political Economy* 42, No. 2 (April): 145–77.

_____ (1934b) *The Supply and Control of Money in the United States*. Cambridge, MA: Harvard University Press.

Darity, William, Jr., and Goldsmith, Arthur G. (1995) "Mr. Keynes, the New Keynesians, and the Concept of Full Employment." In *Post-Keynesian Economic Thoery*, edited by Paul Wells. New York: Kluwer: 73–94.

Davidson, Paul (1991) *Controversies in Post Keynesian Economics*. Aldershot: Edward Elgar.

Davis, J. Ronnie (1968) "Chicago Economists, Deficit Budgets, and the Early 1930s." *American Economic Review* 58, No. 3 (June): 476–81.

_____ (1971) *The New Economics and the Old Economics*. Ames, IA: Iowa State University Press.

De Boyer, Jérôme (2010) "The Keynes-Harrod Controversy on the Classical Theory of the Rate of Interest and the Interdependence of Markets." *Journal of the History of Economic Thought* 32, No. 2 (June): 263–84.

DeLong, Bradford J. (2002) *Macroeconomics*. New York: McGraw-Hill Irwin.

DeLong, Bradford J. and Olney, Martha L. (2006) *Macroeconomics*. 2nd ed. New York: McGraw-Hill Irwin.

De Vroey, Michel (2016) *A History of Macroeconomics From Keynes to Lucas and Beyond*. Cambridge: Cambridge University Press.

Dornbusch, Rudiger, Fischer, Stanley, and Startz, Richard (2008) *Macroeconomics*. 10th ed. New York: McGraw-Hill Irwin.

Dow, Sheila C. (1985) *Macroeconomic Thought*. New York: Basil Blackwell.

_____ (2017) "Keynes and Gesell: Political and Social Philosophy, Epistemology and Monetary Reform." *Annals of the Fondazione Luigi Einaudi* 1, No. 1: 77–92.

Dowd, Kevin (1989) *The State and the Monetary System*. New York: St. Martin's Press.

_____ (1992) *The Experience of Free Banking*. London: Routledge.

_____ (1993a) *Laissez-faire Banking*. London and New York: Routledge.

_____ (1993b) "Forward." In *Free Banking: Theory, History, and a Laissez-Faire Model*, edited by Larry J. Sechrest. Westport, CT: Quorum Books.

_____ (1994) "Competitive Banking, Bankers' Clubs, and Bank Regulation." *Journal of Money, Credit and Banking* 26, No. 2 (May): 289–308.

Duke, Michael I. (1979) "David Hume and Monetary Adjustment." *History of Political Economy* 11, No. 4: 572–87.

Dutt, Amitava Krishna (2002) "Aggregate Demand-Aggregate Supply Analysis: A History." *History of Political Economy* 34, No. 2 (Summer): 321–63.

Eckstein, Zvi (1985) Review of "Free Banking: Theory, Experience, and Debate, 1800–1845." *Journal of Money, Credit, and Banking* 17, No. 3 (August): 412–14.

Edie, Lionel D. (1932) "The Future of the Gold Standard." In *Gold and Monetary Stabilization*, edited by Quincy Wright. Chicago: University of Chicago Press.

Edwards, James Rolph (1991) *Macroeconomics: Equilibrium and Disequilibrium Analysis*. New York: Palgrave Macmillan.

Eichengreen, Barry (1992) *Golden Fetters: The Gold Standard and the Great Depression, 1919–1939*. New York: Oxford University Press.

Eichengreen, Barry and Temin, Peter (2000) "The Gold Standard and the Great Depression." *Contemporary European History* 9, No. 2 (July): 183–207.

Ekelund, Jr., Robert B. and Hébert, Robert F. (2014) *A History of Economic Method and Method*. 6th ed. Long Grove, IL: Waveland Press.

Ekelund, Jr., Robert B. and Tollison, Robert D. (2000) *Macroeconomics: Private Markets and Public Choice*. 6th ed. New York: Addison-Wesley.

Eltis, Walter (1995) "John Locke, the Quantity Theory of Money and the Establishment of a Sound Currency." In *The Quantity Theory of Money: From Locke to Keynes and Friedman*, edited by Mark Blaug. Aldershot and Brookfield: Edward Elgar.

Fisher, Irving (1913) *Elementary Principles of Economics*. New York: Palgrave Macmillan.

―――― (1922) *The Purchasing Power of Money*. New and Revised ed. New York: Augustus M. Kelley, 1971.

―――― (1926) "A Statistical Relation Between Unemployment and Price Changes." *International Labour Review* 13 (June): 785–92, reprinted in *Journal of Political Economy* 81, No. 2, Part 1 (March–April) 1973: 496–502.

―――― (1930) *The Theory of Interest*. New York: Palgrave Macmillan.

―――― (1933) "The Debt-Deflation Theory of the Great Depressions." *Econometrica*, No. 4: 337–57.

―――― (1935) *100% Money*. New York: Adelphi.

Fontana, Giuseppe (2001) "Keynes on the 'Nature of Economic Thinking'." *American Journal of Economics and Sociology* 60 (October): 711–43.

Frank, Robert H. and Bernanke, Ben S. (2002) *Principles of Economics: Macro*. New York: McGraw-Hill Irwin.

―――― (2011) *Principles of Macroeconomics*. 2nd ed. New York: McGraw-Hill.

Friedman, Milton (1953) *Essays in Positive Economics*. Chicago: University of Chicago Press.

―――― (1956) "The Quantity Theory of Money: A Restatement." In *Studies in the Quantity Theory of Money*. Chicago: University of Chicago Press.

―――― (1960) *A Program for Monetary Stability*. New York: Fordham University Press.

―――― (1967) "The Monetary Theory and Policy of Henry Simons." *Journal of Law and Economics* 10 (October): 1–13.

―――― (1968a) "The Role of Monetary Policy." *American Economic Review* 58 (March): 1–17.

―――― (1968b) *Dollars and Deficits*. Englewood Cliffs, NJ: Prentice-Hall.

―――― (1969) *The Optimum Quantity of Money and Other Essays*. Chicago: Aldine Publishing.

_____ (1970a) "A Theoretical Framework for Monetary Analysis." In *Milton Friedman's Monetary Framework*, edited by Robert J. Gordon. Chicago, IL. University of Chicago Press: 1–62.

_____ (1970b) *The Counter-Revolution in Monetary Theory*. London: The Institute of Economic Affairs.

_____ (1972) "Factors Affecting the Level of Interest Rates." In *Money Supply, Money Demand, and Macroeconomic Models*, edited by John T. Boorman and Thomas M. Havrilesky. Boston: Allyn and Bacon: 200–18.

_____ (1974) "Comments on the Critics." In *Milton Friedman's Monetary Framework*, edited by Robert J. Gordon. Chicago: University of Chicago Press.

_____ (1977) "Nobel Lecture: Inflation and Unemployment." *Journal of Political Economy* 85, No. 3 (June): 451–72.

_____ (1984a) "Currency Competition: A Sceptical View." In *Currency Competition and Monetary Union*, edited by Pascal Salin, 42–6. Boston, MA: Martinus Nijhoff Publishers.

_____ (1984b) "Monetary Policy for the 1980s." In *To Promote Prosperity – U.S. Domestic Policy in the Mid – 1980*, edited John H. Moore. Stanford, CA: Hoover Institution Press: 23–60.

_____ (1985) "The Case for Overhauling the Federal Reserve." *Challenge* (July–August): 4–12.

_____ (1987) "Quantity Theory of Money." In *The New Palgrave*, edited by John Eastwell, Murray Milgate, and Peter Newman. Vol. 4. London and Basingstoke: Palgrave Macmillan: 3–20.

_____ (2008) "The Quantity Theory of Money." In *The New Palgrave Dictionary of Economics*. 2nd ed., edited by Steven N. Durlauf and Lawrence E. Blume. Vol. 6. New York: Palgrave Macmillan: 792–815.

Friedman, Milton and Schwartz, Anna J. (1963) *A Monetary History of the United States, 1867–1960*. Princeton, NJ: Princeton University Press.

_____ (1970) *Monetary Statistics of the United States*. New York: National Bureau of Economic Research.

_____ (1986) "Has Government Any Role in Money?" *Journal of Monetary Economics* 17: 37–62.

Froyen, Richard T. (2013) *Macroeconomics: Theories and Policies*. 10th ed. Upper Saddle River, NJ: Pearson Education.

Galbraith, James K. and Darity, William Jr. (1994) *Macroeconomics*. Boston, MA. Houghton Mifflin.

Gali, Jordi and Gertler, Mark (2007) "Macroeconomic Modeling for Monetary Policy Evaluation." *Journal of Economic Perspectives* 21, No. 4: 25–46.

Garrison, Roger W. (1990) Review of "The Theory of Free Banking: Money Supply Under Competitive Note Issue." *Southern Economic Journal* 46, No. 3 (January): 832–4.

Gibson, William E. (1970) "Interest Rates and Monetary Policy." *Journal of Political Economy* 78, No. 3 (May/June): 431–55.

Glasner, David (1989) *Free Banking and Monetary Reform*. Cambridge: Cambridge University Press.

Goodhart, Charles A.E. (1987) Review of "Free Banking: Theory, Experience, and Debate, 1800–1845." *Economica*, New Series 54, No. 213 (February): 129–31.

_____ (1988) *The Evolution of Central Banks*. Cambridge, MA: The MIT Press.

Gordon, Robert J. (2000) *Macroeconomics*. 8th ed. New York: Addison-Wesley.

_____ (2012) *Macroeconomics*. 12th ed. New York: Pearson, Addison-Wesley.

Grampp, William D. (1992) "Cantillon Reconsidered." In *Perspectives on the History of Economic Thought*. Vol. 7, edited by S. Todd Lowry. Aldershot: Edward Elgar: 64–75.

Greenfield, Robert L. and Yeager, Leland B. (1986) "Money and Credit Confused: An Appraisal of Economic Doctrine and Federal Reserve Procedure." *Southern Economic Journal* 53 (October): 364–73.

Grieve, Roy H. (2018) "Off Target: Professor Ahiakpor on Keynes, Mill, and Say's Law." *Journal of the History of Economic Thought* 40, No. 2 (June): 275–8.

Gwartney, James D., Stroup, Richard L., Sobel, Russell S., and Macpherson, David A. (2018) *Macroeconomics: Private and Public Choice*. 16th ed. Boston, MA: Cengage.

Haberler, Gottfried (1932) "Gold and the Business Cycle." In *Gold and Monetary Stabilization*, edited by Quincy Wright. Chicago: University of Chicago Press.

Hall, Robert E. and Lieberman, Marc (2008) *Macroeconomics: Principles and Applications*. 4th ed. Mason, OH: Thomson South-Western.

Hansson, Björn (1987) "Forced Saving." In *The New Palgrave*, edited by John Eastwell, Murray Milgate, and Peter Newman. Vol. 2. London and Basingstoke: Palgrave Macmillan: 398–9.

Harcourt, G.C. and Riach, P.A., eds. (1997) *A 'Second Edition' of the General Theory*. Vols. 1–2. London and New York: Routledge.

Harrod, Roy F. (1937) "Mr. Keynes and Traditional Theory." *Econometrica* 5 (January): 74–86.

———— (1951) *The Life of John Maynard Keynes*. London: Palgrave Macmillan.

Hartfield, H.R. 1934. "The Early Use of 'Capital'." *Quarterly Journal of Economics* 49 (November): 162–3.

Hawtrey, R.G. (1913) *Good and Bad Trade: An Inquiry Into the Causes of Trade Fluctuations*. Reprinted. New York: Augustus M. Kelley, 1970.

———— (1919) *Currency and Credit*. 4th ed. London: Longmans, Green, 1950.

———— (1933) *Trade Depression and the Way Out*. 2nd ed. London: Longmans, Green.

———— (1937) "Alternative Theories of Interest." *Economic Journal* 47 (September): 436–43.

———— (1939) "Interest and Bank Rate." *The Manchester School of Economics and Social Studies* 10, No. 2 (December): 144–52.

———— (1950) *Currency and Credit*. 4th ed. London: Longmans, Green.

Hayek, Friedrich A. ([1931] 1935) *Prices and Production*. 2nd revised and enlarged ed. London: Routledge.

———— (1932) "A Note on the Development of the Doctrine of 'Forced Saving'." *Quarterly Journal of Economics* 47 (November): 123–33.

———— (1933) *Monetary Theory and the Trade Cycle*. New York: Augustus M. Kelley, 1966.

———— (1939) *Profits, Interest and Investment*. Reprinted. New York: Augustus M. Kelley, 1969.

———— (1941) *The Pure Theory of Capital*. London: Routledge & Kegan Paul.

———— (1960) *The Constitution of Liberty*. Chicago: University of Chicago Press.

———— (1976) *Choice of Currency: A Way to Stop Inflation*. London: Institute for Economic Affairs.

———— (1978) *Denationalization of Money*. 2nd (Extended) ed. London: Institute for Economic Affairs.

———— (1984a) "The Theory of Currency Competition." In *Currency Competition and Monetary Union*, edited by Pascal Salin. Boston, MA: Martinus Nijhoff Publishers: 29–42.

———— (1984b) "The Future Monetary Unit of Value." In *Money in Crisis: The Federal Reserve, the Economy, and Monetary Reform*, edited by Barry N. Siegel. San Francisco: Pacific Institute for Public Policy Research.

_____ (1984c) *Money, Capital, and Fluctuations: Early Essays*. Chicago: University of Chicago Press.

_____ (1985) "Richard Cantillon: Introduction and Textual Comments Written for Hella Hayek's 1931 German Translation of Richard Cantillon's *Essai*." *Journal of Libertarian Studies* 7, No. 2 (Fall): 217–47.

Hicks, John R. (1936) "Mr. Keynes' Theory of Employment." *Economic Journal* 46 (June): 238–53.

_____ (1937) "Mr. Keynes and the 'Classics': A Suggested Interpretation." *Econometrica* 5 (April): 147–59.

_____ (1946) *Value and Capital*. 2nd ed. Oxford: Clarendon Press.

_____ (1977) *Economic Perspectives*. Oxford: Clarendon Press.

_____ (1980/81) "IS-LM: An Explanation." *Journal of Post Keynesian Economics* 3: 139–54.

_____ (1982) *Money, Interest and Wages*. Cambridge, MA: Harvard University Press.

_____ (1983) *Classics and Moderns*. Cambridge, MA: Harvard University Press.

_____ (1989) *A Market Theory of Money*. Oxford: Clarendon Press.

Hilton, Boyd (1988) Review of "Free Banking: Theory, Experience, and Debate, 1800–1845." *The English Historical Review* 103, No. 406 (January): 228.

Hollander, Samuel (1987) *Classical Economics*. New York: Basil Blackwell.

Hont, Istvan (1983) "The 'Rich Country-Poor Country' Debate in Scottish Classical Political Economy." In *Wealth and Virtue*, edited by Istvan Hont and Michael Ignatief. Cambridge: Cambridge University Press: 271–315.

_____ (2008) "The 'Rich Country-Poor Country' Debate Revisited: The Irish Origins and French Reception of the Hume Paradox." In *David Hume's Political Economy*, edited by Carl Wennerlind and Margaret Schabas. London and New York: Routledge.

Hoover, Kevin (2006) "Doctor Keynes: Economic Theory in a Diagnostic Science." In *The Cambridge Companion to Keynes*, edited by Roger E. Backhouse and Bradley W. Bateman. Cambridge: Cambridge University Press.

Horwitz, Steven (1992) *Monetary Evolution, Free Banking and Economic Order*. Boulder, CO: Westview.

Hsieh, Chang-Tai and Romer, Christian (2006) "Was the Federal Reserve Constrained by the Gold Standard During the Great Depression? Evidence From the 1932 Open Market Purchase Program." *Journal of Economic History* 66, No. 1 (March): 140–76.

Hubbard, R. Glenn (2000) *Money, the Financial System, and the Economy*. 3rd ed. Reading, MA: Addison-Wesley.

Hubbard, R. Glenn and O'Brien, Anthony Patrick (2014) *Money, Banking, and the Financial System*. 3rd ed. New York: Pearson.

Hubbard, R. Glenn and O'Brien, Anthony P. (2014) *Money, Banking and the Financial System*. 2nd ed. New York: Pearson.

Hubbard, R. Glenn, O'Brien, Anthony P., and Rafferty, Matthew (2014) *Macroeconomics*. 2nd ed. New York: Pearson.

_____ (2018) *Macroeconomics*. 3rd ed. New York: Pearson.

Hume, David (1752) *Hume's Writings on Economics*. Edited by Eugene Rotwein, 1955. Reprinted. Madison: University of Wisconsin Press, 1970.

Humphrey, Thomas M. (1982a) "Of Hume, Thornton, the Quantity Theory, and the Phillips Curve." *Federal Reserve Bank of Richmond Economic Review* (November/December): 13–18. Reprinted in *Money, Banking and Inflation: Essays in the History of Monetary Thought*. Aldershot: Edward Elgar, 1993: 242–7.

_____ (1982b) "The Real Bills Doctrine." *Economic Review* (Federal Reserve Bank of Richmond) 68, No. 5: 3–33.

_____ (1985) "From Trade-Offs to Policy Ineffectiveness: A History of the Phillips Curve." *Federal Reserve Bank of Richmond Economic Review*: 5–12. Reprinted in *Money, Banking and Inflation: Essays in the History of Monetary Thought*, pp. 234–41.

_____ (1991) "Nonneutrality of Money in Classical Monetary Thought." *Federal Reserve Bank of Richmond Economic Review* (April/March): 3–15. Reprinted in *Money, Banking and Inflation: Essays in the History of Monetary Thought*, pp. 251–63.

_____ (2001) "The Choice of a Monetary Policy Framework: Lessons From the 1920s." *Cato Journal* 21, No. 2: 285–313.

Hutchison, Terrence W. (1977) *Keynes v. the 'Keynesians' . . .?* Hobart Paperback 11. London: The Institute of Economic Affairs.

_____ (1981) *The Politics and Philosophy of Economic: Marxians, Keynesians and Austrians*. Oxford: Basil Blackwell.

International Monetary Fund (2001) *International Financial Statistics Yearbook, 2001*. Washington, DC: International Monetary Fund.

_____ (2009) *International Financial Statistics Yearbook 2009*. Washington, DC: International Monetary Fund.

_____ (2014) *International Financial Statistics Yearbook 2014*, Washington, DC: International Monetary Fund.

Jansen, Dennis W., Delorme, Charles D., and Ekelund, Jr., Robert B. (1994) *Intermediate Macroeconomics*. New York: West.

Johnson, Edgar A.J. (1937) *Predecessors of Adam Smith: The Growth of British Economic Thought*. Englewood Cliffs, NJ: Prentice-Hall; New York: Augustus M. Kelley, 1965.

Kahn, Richard (1931) "The Relation of Home Investment to Unemployment." *Economic Journal* 41 (June): 173–98.

Kennedy, Peter (2010) *Macroeconomic Essentials*. Cambridge, MA: The MIT Press.

Keynes, John Maynard (1911) Review of "The Purchasing Power of Money by Irving Fisher." *Economic Journal* 21 (September): 393–8.

_____ (1919) *The Economic Consequences of the Peace*. Reprinted in the *Collected Writings of John Maynard Keynes*. Vol. 2. London and Basingstoke: Palgrave Macmillan, for the Royal Economic Society, 1971.

_____ (1924) *Monetary Reform*. New York: Harcourt Brace.

_____ (1930) *A Treatise on Money*. Vols. 1–2. London: Palgrave Macmillan.

_____ (1931) "The End of the Gold Standard." In *Collected Writings of John Maynard Keynes, IX: Essays in Persuasion*, edited by Donald Moggridge. London and Basingstoke: Palgrave Macmillan, 1972.

_____ ([1932] 1982) "Broadcast on State Planning." *The Collected Writings of John Maynard Keynes*, XI, 14 March, in Activities 1931–1939, edited by Donald Moggridge. London and Basingstoke: Palgrave Macmillan.

_____ (1933) *Essays in Biography*. London: Palgrave Macmillan.

_____ (1936) *The General Theory of Employment, Interest and Money*. Paperbound ed. London and Basingstoke: Palgrave Macmillan, 1974.

_____ (1937a) "The General Theory of Employment." *Quarterly Journal of Economics* 51 (February): 209–23.

_____ (1937b) "Alternative Theories of the Rate of Interest." *Economic Journal* 47 (June): 241–52.

_____ (1937c) "The 'Ex-ante' Theory of the Rate of Interest." *Economic Journal* 47 (December): 663–9.

_____ (1938) "Mr. Keynes and 'Finance': Comment." *Economic Journal* 48 (June): 318–22.

_____ (1939) "Preface to the French Edition." In *The General Theory of Employment, Interest and Money*, edited by Paperbound. London and Basingstoke: Palgrave Macmillan, 1974.

_____ (1946) "The Balance of Payments of the United States." *Economic Journal* 56, No. 222 (June): 172–87.

_____ (1972) *The Collected Writings of John Maynard Keynes*. Vol. IX. Edited by Don E. Moggridge. London: Palgrave Macmillan.

_____ (1973) *The Collected Writings of John Maynard Keynes*. Vol. XIII. Edited by Don E. Moggridge. London: Palgrave Macmillan.

_____ (1983) *The Collected Writings of John Maynard Keynes. Volume XII: Economic Articles and Correspondence*. Edited by Donald Moggridge. London and Basingstoke: Palgrave Macmillan.

King, Robert G. (1993) "Will the New Keynesian Macroeconomics Resurrect the IS-LM Model?" *Journal of Economic Perspectives* 7 (Winter): 67–82.

Klein, Benjamin (1974) "The Competitive Supply of Money." *Journal of Money, Credit and Banking* 6, No. 4 (November): 423–53.

_____ (1976) "Competing Monies: Comment." *Journal of Money, Credit and Banking* 8, No. 4 (November): 513–19.

Knight, Frank (1937) "Unemployment: And Mr. Keynes's Revolution in Economic Theory." *Canadian Journal of Economics and Political Science* 3 (February): 100–23.

Kohn, Meir (1993) *Money, Banking, and Financial Markets*. 2nd ed. Fort Worth: The Dryden Press.

Kregel, Jan.A. (1989) *Inflation and Income Distribution in Capitalist Crisis*. New York: New York University Press.

Krugman, Paul (1998) "It's Baaack: Japan's Slump and the Return of the Liquidity Trap." *Brookings Papers on Economic Activity*, No. 2: 137–87, 204–5.

_____ (2013) "Monetary Policy In A Liquidity Trap." *The New York Times* at http://krugman.blogs.nytimes.com/2013/04/11

Krugman, Paul and Wells, Robin (2009) *Macroeconomics*. 2nd ed. New York: Worth Publishers.

Kydland, Finn E. and Prescott, Edward C. (1982) "Time to Build and Aggregate Fluctuations." *Econometrica* 50 (November): 1345–70.

Laidler, David (1969) "The Definition of Money: Theoretical and Empirical Problems." *Journal of Money, Credit and Banking* 1 (August): 508–25.

_____ (1991) *The Golden Age of the Quantity Theory*. Princeton, NJ: Princeton University Press.

_____ (1993a) "Hawtrey, Harvard, and the Origins of the Chicago Tradition." *Journal of Political Economy* 101, No. 6 (December): 1068–104.

_____ (1993b) *The Demand for Money: Theories, Evidence, and Problems*. 4th ed. New York: Harper Collins.

_____ (1999) *Fabricating the Keynesian Revolution: Studies of the Inter-war Literature on Money, the Cycle, and Unemployment*. New York: Cambridge University Press.

_____ (2004) "Monetary Policy After Bubbles Burst: The Zero Lower Bound, the Liquidity Trap and the Credit Deadlock." *Canadian Public Policy/Analyse de Politiques* 30, No. 3 (September): 333–40.

_____ (2006) "Keynes and the Birth of Modern Macroeconomics." In *The Cambridge Companion to Keynes*, edited by Roger E. Backhouse and Bradley W. Bateman. Cambridge: Cambridge University Press.

Laidler, David and Sandilands, Roger (2010) "Harvard, the Chicago Tradition, and the Quantity Theory: A Reply to James Ahiakpor." *History of Political Economy* 42, No. 3 (Fall): 573–92.

Landreth, Harry and Colander, David C. (2002) *History of Economic Thought.* 4th ed. Boston, MA: Houghton Mifflin.

Laughlin, J. Laurence (1933) *The Federal Reserve Act: Its Origin and Problems.* New York: Palgrave Macmillan.

Lautzenheiser, Mark and Yasar, Yavuz (2016) "Keynes's Attack on the Citadel: Proportionality, the Two-Price Theory, and Monetary Circulation." *Journal of Keynesian Economics* 4, No. 1 (Spring): 99–113.

Lavington, Frederick (1921) *English Capital Market.* Reprinted. New York: Augustus M. Kelley, 1968.

Lawlor, Michael S. (1997) "The Classical Theory of the Rate of Interest." In *A 'Second Edition' of the General Theory.* Chapter 20, edited by G.C. Harcourt and P.A. Riach. London and New York: Routledge.

—— (2006) *The Economics of Keynes in Historical Context: An Intellectual History of the General Theory.* New York: Palgrave Macmillan.

Leijonhufvud, Axel (1968) *On Keynesian Economics and the Economics of Keynes.* New York: Oxford University Press.

—— (1981) *Information and Coordination.* New York: Oxford University Press.

—— (2006) "Keynes as a Marshallian." In *The Cambridge Companion to Keynes,* edited by Roger E. Backhouse and Bradley W. Bateman. Cambridge: Cambridge University Press: 58–77.

Leontief, Wassily (1934) "Helping the Farmer." In *The Economics of the Recovery Program,* edited by Quincy Wright. New York: McGraw-Hill.

—— (1936) "The Fundamental Assumption of Mr. Keynes' Monetary Theory of Employment." *Quarterly Journal of Economics* 51 (November): 192–7.

Lesson, Robert (1997) "The Trade-Off Interpretation of Phillips's Dynamic Stabilization Exercise." *Economica,* New Series 64, No. 253 (February): 155–71.

—— (1998) "The Consequences of the 'Klassical' Caricature for Economics." In *Keynes and the Classics Reconsidered,* edited by James C.W. Ahiakpor. Boston, MA: Kluwer Academic Publishers: 125–40.

Lucas, Jr., Robert E. (1996) "Nobel Lecture: Monetary Neutrality." *Journal of Political Economy* 104, No. 4 (August): 661–82.

Lucas, Jr., Robert E. and Sargent, Thomas J. (1978) "After Keynesian Macroeconomics." Reprinted in Robert E. Lucas, Jr. and Thomas J. Sargent, eds. *Rational Expectations and Econometric Practice.* London: George Allen and Unwin, 1984.

Malthus, Thomas R. (1811) "The Question Concerning the Depreciation of Our Currency Stated and Examined." In *Occasional Papers of T.R. Malthus,* edited by Bernard Semmel. New York: Burt Franklin, 1963.

—— (1836) *Principles of Political Economy.* 2nd ed. New York: Augustus M. Kelley, 1964.

Mankiw, N. Gregory (1992) "The Reincarnation of Keynesian Economics." *European Economic Review* 36 (April): 559–65, excerpted in *A Macroeconomics Reader,* edited by Brian Snowdon and Howard R. Vane. London and New York: Routledge, 1997b.

—— (1993) "Symposium on Keynesian Economics Today." *Journal of Economic Perspectives* 7 (Winter): 3–4.

—— (1997) *Macroeconomics.* 3rd ed. New York: Worth Publishers.

—— (2010) *Macroeconomics.* 7th ed. New York: Worth Publishers.

_____ (2013) *Macroeconomics*. 8th ed. New York: Worth Publishers.

_____ (2015) *Principles of Macroeconomics*. 7th ed. Stamford, CT: Cengage.

Mankiw, N. Gregory and Reis, Ricardo (2018) "Friedman's Presidential Address in the Evolution of Macroeconomic Thought." *Journal of Economic Perspectives* 32, No. 1 (Winter): 81–96.

Marget, Arthur W. (1938–1942) *The Theory of Prices: A Re-Examination of the Central Problems of Monetary Theory*. 2 vols. Reprinted. New York: Augustus M. Kelley, 1966.

Marshall, Alfred (1887) "Memoranda and Evidence Before the Gold and Silver Commission." In *Official Papers by Alfred Marshall*, edited by J.M. Keynes. London: Palgrave Macmillan, 1926.

_____ (1920) *Principles of Economics*. 8th ed. Philadelphia, PA: Porcupine Press, 1990.

_____ (1923) *Money, Credit and Commerce*. New York: Augustus M. Kelley, 1960.

_____ (1926) *Official Papers*. London: Palgrave Macmillan.

Marshall, Alfred and Marshall, Mary Paley (1879) *The Economics of Industry*. London: Palgrave Macmillan.

McConnell, Campbell R., Brue, Stanley L., and Flynn, Sean M. (2018) *Macroeconomics: Principles, Problems, and Policies*. 21st ed. New York: McGraw-Hill Irwin.

Meade, James (1934) "The Amount of Money and the Banking System." *Economic Journal* 44 (March): 77–83.

Menger, Carl (1892) "On the Origin of Money." (Translated by Caroline A. Foley.) *Economic Journal* 2, No. 6 (June): 239–55. Note that the article cites Carl as Karl.

Mill, John S. (1965) *Collected Works*. Edited by J.M. Robson. London: University of Toronto Press.

_____ (1844) "On the influence of consumption upon production," in *Essays on Unsettled Questions in Political Economy* (2nd ed., 1874). London: Longmans, Green, Reader and Dyer. Reprinted. New York: Augustus M. Kelley, 1968.

_____ (1874) *Essays on Some Unsettled Questions of Political Economy*. 2nd ed. Reprinted. New York: Augustus M. Kelley, 1968.

Miller, Roger LeRoy (2012) *Economics Today, The Macro View*. 16th ed. New York: Addison-Wesley.

Minsky, H.P. (1985) "The Financial Instability Hypothesis: A Restatement." In *Post Keynesian Economic Theory*, edited by Philip Arestis and Thanos Skouras. Sussex: Wheatsheaf Books.

Mints, Lloyd W. (1945) *A History of Banking Theory in Great Britain and the United States*. Chicago, IL: University of Chicago Press.

Mises, Ludwig von (1934) *The Theory of Money and Credit*. Translated by H.E. Batson. London: Jonathan Cape.

_____ (1963) *Human Action*. New revised ed. New Haven, CT: Yale University Press.

Mishkin, Frederic S. (2015) *Macroeconomics*. 2nd ed. New York: Pearson.

Modigliani, Franco (1944) "Liquidity Preference and the Theory of Interest and Money." *Econometrica* 12 (January): 45–88.

Mossner, Ernest Campbell (1962) "New Hume Letters to Lord Elibank, 1748–1776." *Texas Studies in Literature and Language* 4, No. 3 (Autumn): 431–60.

Nelson, Charles R. and Plosser, Charles (1982) "Trends and Random Walks in Macroeconomic Time Series: Some Evidence and Implications." *Journal of Monetary Economics* 10, No. 2 (September): 139–62.

O'Brien, D.P. (1975) *The Classical Economists*. Oxford: Clarendon Press.

_____ (2004) *The Classical Economists Revisited*. Princeton and Oxford: Princeton University Press.

O'Donnell, Rod (1999) "The Genesis of the Only Diagram in the General Theory." *Journal of the History of Economic Thought* 21 (March): 27–37.

Ohlin, Bertil (1937) "Alternative Theories of the Rate of Interest." *Economic Journal* 47 (September): 423–7.

Oxford English Dictionary (1989) Prepared by J.A. Simpson and E.S.C. Weiner. Oxford: Clarendon Press.

Parkin, Michael (2000) "The Principles of Macroeconomics at the Millennium." *American Economic Review* 90, No. 2 (May): 85–9.

———— (2010) *Economics*. 9th ed. New York: Addison-Wesley.

Patinkin, Don (1965 [1956]) *Money, Interest and Prices: An Integration of Monetary and Value Theory*, 1st ed. (2nd ed.). New York: Harper & Row.

———— (1969) "The Chicago Tradition, the Quantity Theory, and Friedman." *Journal of Money, Credit, and Banking* 1 (February): 46–70.

———— (1976) *Keynes' Monetary Thought: A Study of Its Development*. Durham, NC: Duke University Press.

———— (1987) "Neutrality of Money." In *The New Palgrave: A Dictionary of Economics*. Vol. 3, edited by John Eatwell, Murray Milgate, and Peter Newman. London: Palgrave Macmillan.

———— (1990) "In Defense of IS-LM." *Banca Nazionale Del Lavoro Quarterly Review* 172 (March): 119–34.

Paul, Ron (2009) *End the Fed*. New York: Grand Central Publishing.

Perlman, Morris (1987) "Of a Controversial Passage in Hume." *Journal of Political Economy* 95, No. 2 (April): 274–89.

Persons, Charles E. (1930) "Credit Expansion, 1920 to 1929, and Its Lessons." *Quarterly Journal of Economics* 45, No. 1 (November): 94–130.

Persons, Warren M. (1931) *Forecasting Business Cycles*. New York: John Wiley.

Pigou, Arthur C. (1912) *Wealth and Welfare*. London: Palgrave Macmillan.

———— (1913) *Unemployment*. London: William & Norgate.

———— (1917) "The Value of Money." *Quarterly Journal of Economics* 37 (November): 38–65.

———— (1920) *The Economics of Welfare*. London: Palgrave Macmillan.

———— (1924) "The Exchange-value of Legal-tender Money," in *Essays in Applied Economics*, 2nd ed. Reprinted. New York: Augustus M. Kelley, 1965.

———— (1927) *Industrial Fluctuations*. London: Palgrave Macmillan.

———— (1933) *The Theory of Unemployment*. Reprinted. New York: Augustus M. Kelley, 1968.

———— (1936) "Mr. J.M. Keynes's General Theory of Employment, Interest and Money." *Economica* 3 (May): 115–32.

———— (1941) *Employment and Equilibrium*. Reprinted. Westport, CT: Greenwood Press, 1979.

Quinn, Stephen and Roberts, William (2008) "The Evolution of the Check as a Means of Payment: A Historical Survey." *Federal Reserve Bank of Atlanta Economic Review* 93, No. 4: 1–28.

Ricardo, David (1951, 1957) *Works and Correspondence*. Edited by Piero Sraffa. Cambridge: Cambridge University Press.

Richardson, Gary (2007) "Categories and Causes of Bank Distress During the Great Depression, 1929–33: The Illiquidity Versus Insolvency Debate Revisited." *Explorations in Economic History* 44: 588–607.

Rima, Ingrid (1988) "A Conversation With Sir John Hicks About 'Value and Capital'." *Eastern Economic Journal* 14 (January–March): 1–6.

Robbins, Lionel (1934) *The Great Depression*. New York: Palgrave Macmillan.

Robertson, Dennis H. (1922) *Money*. 4th ed. Chicago: University of Chicago Press, 1957.

——— (1926) *Banking Policy and the Price Level*. Reprinted. New York: Augustus M. Kelley, 1949.

——— (1931) "Mr. Keynes' theory of money. It should be refJournal." *Economic Journal* 41, No. 4 (September): 395–411.

——— (1934) "Industrial Fluctuations and the Natural Rate of Interest." *Economic Journal* 44, No. 176 (December): 650–6.

——— (1936) "Some Notes on Mr. Keynes' General Theory of Employment." *Quarterly Journal of Economics* 51, No. 1 (November): 168–91.

——— (1937) "Alternative Theories of Interest." *Economic Journal* 47 (September): 428–36.

——— (1940) *Essays in Monetary Theory*. London: Staples.

Robinson, Joan (1938) "Review of the Economics of Inflation." *Economic Journal* 48, No. 191 (September): 507–13.

——— (1975) "What Has Become of the Keynesian Revolution?" In *Essays on John Maynard Keynes*, edited by Milo Keynes. London and New York: Cambridge University Press.

Rockoff, Hugh (1974) "The Free Banking Era: A Re-examination." *Journal of Money, Credit and Banking* 6, No. 2 (May): 141–67.

Roll, Eric (1938) *A History of Economic Thought*. 5th revised ed. London and Boston: Faber and Faber, 1992.

Rolnick, Arthur J. and Weber, Warren E. (1983) "New Evidence on the Free Banking Era." *American Economic Review* 73, No. 5 (December): 1080–91.

Romer, David (1993) "The New Keynesian Synthesis." *Journal of Economic Perspectives* 7 (Winter): 5–22.

——— (2000) "Keynesian Macroeconomics Without the LM Curve." *Journal of Economic Perspectives* 14, No. 2 (Spring): 149–69.

——— (2013) "Short-Run Fluctuations." January. http://elsa.berkeley.edu/"dromer/index.html

Rotwein, Eugene (1955) "Editor's Introduction." In *David Hume: Writings on Economics*. Reprinted. Madison: University of Wisconsin Press, 1970.

Salin, Pascal (1984) "General Introduction." In *Currency Competition and Monetary Union*, edited by Pascal Salin. Boston, MA: Martinus Nijhoff Publishers: 1–26.

Samuelson, Paul A. (1948) *Economics*. New York: McGraw-Hill.

——— (1985) "Succumbing to Keynesianism." *Challenge* 27, No. 6 (January/February): 4–11.

Samuelson, Paul A. and Nordhaus, William D. (1998) *Economics*. 16th ed. New York: Irwin McGraw-Hill.

Say, Jean-Baptiste. ([1803] 1821a) A *Treatise on Political Economy*. 4th ed. New York: Augustus M. Kelley, 1964.

——— (1821b) *Letters to Mr. Malthus*. New York: Augustus M. Kelley, 1967.

Schabas, Margaret (2008) "Temporal Dimensions in Hume's Monetary Theory." In *David Hume's Political Economy*, edited by Carl Wennerlind and Margaret Schabas. London and New York: Routledge: 127–45.

Schiller, Bradley R. (2000) *The Macroeconomy Today*. 8th ed. New York: Irwin-McGraw-Hill.

Schuler, Kurt (1992) "The World History of Free Banking: An Overview." In *The Experience of Free Banking*, edited by Kevin Dowd. London and New York: Routledge.

Schumpeter, Joseph A. (1951) *Ten Great Economists: From Marx to Keynes*. New York: Oxford University Press.

_____ (1936) "The General Theory of Employment, Interest and Money by John Maynard Keynes." *Journal of the American Statistical Association* 31, No. 196 (December): 791–5.

_____ (1946) "John Maynard Keynes 1883–1946." *American Economic Review* 36, No. 4 (September): 495–518.

_____ (1954) *History of Economic Analysis*. New York: Oxford University Press, 1994.

Schwarzer, Johannes A. (2018) "Cost-Push and Demand-Pull Inflation: Milton Friedman and the 'Cruel Dilemma'." *Journal of Economic Perspectives* 32, No. 1 (Winter): 195–210.

Sechrest, Larry J. (1993) *Free Banking: Theory, History, and a Laissez-Faire Model*. Westport, CT: Quorum Books.

Selgin, George (1988) *The Theory of Free Banking: Money Supply Under Competitive Note Issue*. Totowa, NJ: Rowman & Littlefield.

_____ (2008) *Good Money: Birmingham Button Makers, the Royal Mint, and the Beginnings of Modern Coinage, 1775–1821*. Oakland, CA: The Independent Institute.

_____ (2012) "Central Banks as Sources of Financial Instability." In *Boom and Bust Banking: Causes and Cures of the Great Recession*, edited by David Beckworth. Oakland, CA: The Independent Institute.

Selgin, George and White, Larry H. (1987) "The Evolution of a Free Banking System." *Economic Inquiry* 25: 439–57.

_____ (1994) "How Would the Invisible Hand Handle Money?" *Journal of Economic Literature* 32, No. 4 (December): 1718–49.

Senior, Nassau W. (1836) *An Outline of the Science of Political Economy*. Reprinted. New York: Augustus M. Kelley, 1965.

Simons, Henry C. (1936) "Keynes Comments on Money." *Christian Century* 53 (July): 1016–7.

_____ (1948) "Rules versus Authorities in Monetary Policy." In *Economic Policy for a Free Society*. Chicago, IL: University of Chicago Press.

Skidelsky, Robert (1983) *John Maynard Keynes: Hopes Betrayed 1883–1920*. London: Palgrave Macmillan.

_____ (1995) "J.M. Keynes and the Quantity Theory of Money." In *The Quantity Theory of Money: From Locke to Keynes and Friedman*, edited by Mark Blaug. Aldershot and Brookfield, VT: Edward Elgar.

_____ (2016) "How Keynes Came to Britain." *Review of Keynesian Economics* 4, No. 1 (Spring): 4–19.

Smith, Adam (1776) *The Wealth of Nations*. Edited by E. Cannan. Vols. 1 and 2. Chicago: University of Chicago Press, 1976.

_____ (1978) *Lectures in Jurisprudence*. Edited by R.L. Meek, D.D. Raphael, and P.G. Stein. Oxford: Clarendon Press.

Smith, Vera C. (1936) *The Rationale of Central Banking and the Free Banking Alternative*. Indianapolis, IN: Liberty Press, 1990.

Snowdon, Brian and Vane, Howard R. (1997a) "Modern Macroeconomics and Its Evolution From a Monetarist Perspective: An Interview With Professor Milton Friedman." *Journal of Economic Studies* 24, No. 4: 191–221.

_____ (1997b) *A Macroeconomics Reader*. London and New York: Routledge.

Solow, Robert M. (1956) "A Contribution to the Theory of Economic Growth." *Quarterly Journal of Economics* 70 (February): 65–94.

_____ (2002) "'Analytical Aspects of Anti-Inflation Policy' After 40 Years." In *Paul Samuelson & The Foundations of Modern Economics*, edited by K. Puttaswamaiah. New Brunswick, NJ: Transaction Publishers: 71–7.

Steuart, James (1767) *An Inquiry Into the Principles of Political Economy*. Reprinted. Chicago: University of Chicago Press, 1966.

Taussig, Frank W. (1921) *Principles of Economics*. 3rd ed. Vols. 1–2. New York: Palgrave Macmillan.

Taylor, Fred M. ([1921] 1925) *Principles of Economics*. 9th ed. New York: Ronal Press.

Taylor, John B. (2000) "Teaching Modern Macroeconomics at the Principles Level." *American Economic Review* 90 (May): 90–4.

Taylor, Timothy (2008) *Macroeconomics: Economics and the Economy*. St. Paul, MN: Freeload Press.

Temin, Peter (2008) "Real Business Cycle Views of the Great Depression and Recent Events: A Review of Timothy J. Kehoe and Edward C. Prescott's Great Depression of the Twentieth Century." *Journal of Economic Literature* 46, No. 3 (September): 669–84.

Thornton, Henry (1802) *Paper Credit in Great Britain*. Edited by F.A. Hayek. Reprinted. New York: Augustus M. Kelley, 1965.

Timberlake, Jr., Richard (1991) "Review of the Theory of Free Banking: Money Supply Under Competitive Note Issue." *Journal of Money, Credit and Banking* 23, No. 2 (May): 272–4.

_____ (2007) "Gold Standards and the Real Bills Doctrine in U.S. Monetary Policy." *Independent Review* 11, No. 3 (Winter): 325–54.

_____ (2008) "The Federal Reserve's Role in the Great Contraction and the Subprime Crisis." *Cato Journal* 28, No. 2 (Spring/Summer): 303–12.

Tobin, James (1963) "Commercial Banks as Creators of 'Money'." In *Banking and Monetary Studies*, edited by Dean Carson. Homewood, IL: Richard D. Irwin: 408–19.

Tsiang, S.C. (1956) "Liquidity Preference and Loanable Funds Theories, Multiplier and Velocity Analyses: A Synthesis." *American Economic Review* 46 (September): 539–64.

Tucker, Josiah (1776) *Tracts on Political and Commercial Subjects*. 3rd ed. Clifton: Augustus M. Kelley, 1974.

Vickers, Douglas (1957) "Method and Analysis in David Hume's Economic Essays." *Economica* NS. 24, No. 95 (August): 225–34.

Viner, Jacob (1932) "International Aspects of the Gold Standard." In *Gold and Monetary Stabilization*, edited by Quincy Wright. Chicago: University of Chicago Press.

_____ (1936) "Mr. Keynes on the Causes of Unemployment." *Quarterly Journal of Economics* 51 (November): 147–67.

_____ (1937) *Studies in the Theory of International Trade*. New York: Harper.

Walker, Francis A. (1878) *Money*. Reprinted. New York: Augustus M. Kelley, 1968.

Walter, John R. (2005) "Depression-Era Bank Failures: The Great Contagion or the Great Shakeout?" *Federal Reserve Bank of Richmond Economic Quarterly* 91, No. 1 (Winter): 39–54.

Warburton, Clark (1946a) "Monetary Theory, Full Production, and the Great Depression." *Econometrica* 13, No. 2 (April): 114–28.

_____ (1946b) "Quantity and Frequency of the Use of Money in the United States, 1919–45." *Journal of Political Economy* 54, No. 5 (October): 436–50.

_____ (1946c) "Monetary Control Under the Federal Reserve Act." *Political Science Quarterly* 61, No. 4 (December): 505–34.

Wennerlind, Carl (2005) "David Hume's Monetary Theory Revisited: Was He Really a Quantity Theorist and an Inflationist?" *Journal of Political Economy* 113, No. 1 (February): 223–37.

———— (2008) "An Artificial Virtue and the Oil of Commerce: A Synthetic View of Hume's Theory of Money." In *David Hume's Political Economy*, edited by Carl Wennerlind and Margaret Schabas. London and New York: Routledge: 105–26.

West, Edwin G. (1997) "Adam Smith's Support for Money and Banking Regulation: A Case of Inconsistency." *Journal of Money, Credit and Banking* 29, No. 1 (February): 127–34.

West, Robert Craig (1974) *Banking Reform and the Federal Reserve 1863–1923*. Ithaca and London: Cornell University Press, 1977.

Whaples, Robert (2008) "California Gold Rush." In *EH.Net Encyclopedia*, edited by Robert Whaples, March 16, 2008. https://eh.net/encyclopedia/california-gold-rush/

Wheelock, David C. (1992) "Monetary Policy in the Great Depression: What the Fed Did, and Why." *Federal Reserve Bank of St. Louis Review* 74, No. 2: 3–28.

White, Lawrence H. (1984a) *Free Banking in Britain: Theory, Experience and Debate, 1800–45*. Cambridge: Cambridge University Press.

———— (1984b) "Free Banking and Currency Competition: A Bibliographical Note." In *Currency Competition and Monetary Union*, edited by Pascal Salin. Boston, MA: Martinus Nijhoff Publishers: 42–46.

———— (1984c) "Competitive Payments Systems and the Unit of Account." *American Economic Review* 74, No. 4 (September): 699–712.

———— (1988a) "Depoliticizing the Supply of Money." In *Political Business Cycles: The Political Economy of Money, Inflation, and Unemployment*, edited by Thomas D. Willet. Durham, NC: Duke University Press: 460–78.

———— (1988b) "Preface." In *The Theory of Free Banking. Money Supply Under Competitive Note Issue*. Totowa, NJ: Rowman & Littlefield.

———— (1989) *Competition and Currency: Essays on Free Banking and Money*. New York: New York University Press.

———— (2012) "Monetary Policy and the Financial Crisis." In *Boom and Bust Banking: Causes and Cures of the Great Recession*, edited by David Beckworth. Oakland, CA: The Independent Institute.

Wicker, Elmus (1996) *The Banking Panics of the Great Depression*. New York: Cambridge University Press.

Wicksell, Knut (1898) *Interest and Prices*. Translated by R.F. Kahn. Reprinted. New York: Augustus M. Kelley, 1965.

———— (1935) *Selected Papers on Economic Theory*. Edited with an Introduction by Erik Lindhal. Cambridge, MA: Harvard University Press, 1958.

Williams, John H. (1932) "Monetary Stability and the Gold Standard." In *Gold and Monetary Stabilization*, edited by Quincy Wright. Chicago: University of Chicago Press.

Williamson, Stephen D. (2014) *Macroeconomics*. 5th ed. New York: Pearson.

———— (2017) "Quantitative Easing: How Well Does This Tool Work?" *The Regional Economist*, The Federal Reserve Bank of St. Louis 25, No. 3 (Third Quarter): 8–14.

Wood, Geoffrey E. (1995) "The Quantity Theory in the 1980s: Hume, Thornton, Friedman and the Relation Between Money and Inflation." In *The Quantity Theory of Money: From Locke to Keynes and Friedman*, edited by Mark Blaug. Aldershot and Brookfield, VT: Edward Elgar.

Index

Note: Page numbers in *italics* indicate figures and in **bold** indicate tables on the corresponding pages.